Studies in Musical Genesis and Structure

General Editor: Lewis Lockwood, Harvard University

Studies in Musical Genesis and Structure
General Editor: Lewis Lockwood, Harvard University

Anna Bolena and the Artistic Maturity of Gaetano Donizetti
Philip Gossett

Beethoven's Diabelli Variations
William Kinderman

Robert Schumann and the Study of Orchestral Composition
The Genesis of the First Symphony, Op. 38
Jon W. Finson

Euryanthe

and Carl Maria von Weber's Dramaturgy of German Opera

MICHAEL C. TUSA

CLARENDON PRESS · OXFORD
1991

Oxford University Press, Walton Street, Oxford OX2 6DP
Oxford New York Toronto
Delhi Bombay Calcutta Madras Karachi
Petaling Jaya Singapore Hong Kong Tokyo
Nairobi Dar es Salaam Cape Town
Melbourne Auckland
and associated companies in
Berlin Ibadan

Oxford is a trade mark of Oxford University Press

Published in the United States
by Oxford University Press, New York

British Library Cataloguing in Publication Data
Tusa, Michael C.
  Euryanthe and Carl Maria von Weber's dramaturgy of German
  opera. – (Studies in musical genesis and structure).
  1. German music. Weber, Carl Maria von, 1786–1826
  I. Title II. Series
  780.92

    ISBN 0–19–315325–4

Library of Congress Cataloging in Publication Data
Tusa, Michael Charles.
  Euryanthe and Carl Maria von Weber's dramaturgy of German opera/
Michael C. Tusa.
—(Studies in musical genesis and structure)
  Includes index.
  1. Weber, Carl Maria von, 1786–1826. Euryanthe. I. Title.
II. Series.
ML410.W3T9 1991
782.1–dc20   90–43678

ISBN 0–19–315325–4

Typeset by BP Integraphics Ltd, Bath, Avon

Printed in Great Britain by
Bookcraft (Bath) Ltd, Midsomer Norton, Avon

to
Joseph C. and Ella Dawn Tusa

Contents

Editor's Preface

Historical musicology has recently witnessed vigorous efforts to deepen understanding of the means by which composers of various periods and traditions brought their works to realization. In part this trend has resulted from renewed and intensive study of the manuscript sources of works by many of the major figures in Western music history, especially those for whom new and authoritative complete editions are being undertaken. In part it has arisen from the desire to establish more cogent and precise claims about the formative background of individual works than could be accomplished by more general stylistic study. In many cases, the fortunate survival of much of the composer's working materials—sketches, drafts, composing scores, corrected copies, and the like—has stimulated this approach on a scale that no one could have imagined a century ago, when Gustav Nottebohm's pioneering studies of Beethoven's sketches and drafts first appeared.

This series provides a number of short monographs, each dealing with a single work by an important composer. The main focus will be on the genesis of the work from its known antecedent stages, so far as these can be determined from the sources. In each case the genesis of the work will be connected to an analytical overview of the final version. Every monograph will be written by a specialist, and, apart from the general theme of the series, no artificial uniformity will be imposed. The individual character of both work and evidence, as well as the author's special viewpoint, will dictate differences in emphasis and treatment. Thus some of these studies may stress the combination of sketch evidence and analysis, while others may shift the emphasis to the position of the work within its genre and context. Although no such series could possibly aim at being comprehensive, it will deal with a representative body of important works by composers of stature across the centuries.

In this book, Michael Tusa brilliantly solves the difficult task of discussing a celebrated work by a major composer that is practically inaccessible to modern audiences. Weber's *Euryanthe* was meant to be the crowning work in the career of this seminal figure in the German operatic tradition of the early nineteenth century. Weber himself designated it as a 'grand romantic opera' that blended hitherto separated genres; despite the complexities of its plot and music, he once called it 'a simple and serious work that seeks nothing other than truth of expression, passion, and characterization'. But because its defective libretto is apparently responsible for its virtual disappearance from the modern repertoire, few modern observers have been able to gain serious insight into the reasons why *Euryanthe* was regarded by numerous later commentators as containing Weber's 'most beautiful, richest, and most masterful music'. This last quotation is from none other than Richard Wagner, whose relationship to this work was traced by Tusa in a significant article in *19th-Century Music* (9, Spring 1986). In this book Tusa provides the first full-length study of *Euryanthe* ever made and firmly stakes out the claim that it is 'arguably the key work for understanding Weber's operatic aims'. Along with close scrutiny of its dramatic aims and compositional planning, Tusa provides insight into its genre and reception history. The result is a book that not only deepens our understanding of a major neglected work but may help to restore it to its true place in the history of romantic opera.

Harvard University   Lewis Lockwood

Author's Preface

The idea of devoting a study to Carl Maria von Weber's *Euryanthe* first occurred to me as I attended Robert Bailey's lectures on opera at Yale University in the early 1970s. *Euryanthe* had been a prominent and influential work on the German operatic horizon in which Richard Wagner matured, and yet, apart from John Warrack's excellent biography of Weber, little serious attention had been paid to the opera by twentieth-century musical scholarship. Accordingly, my 1983 Ph.D. dissertation at Princeton University was an investigation of the extant sources for the opera. The present monograph was prompted by Lewis Lockwood, who encouraged me to reshape my work on *Euryanthe* for inclusion in the series of studies on the compositional process that he was editing for Oxford University Press. I am indebted to Professor Lockwood in too many ways to enumerate here. His teaching and scholarship have been an inspiration and model for my own efforts, and the opportunity that he afforded me to return to *Euryanthe* has, I hope, resulted in a study that does more justice to Weber the music-dramatist than I was able to achieve at an earlier stage in my career.

The unfamiliarity and inaccessibility of *Euryanthe* admittedly poses certain problems for the potential reader of the present study. A recording is currently not available, nor is there in print a reliable score of the entire opera; perhaps the appearance of this monograph will stimulate interest both in the reissue of the fine EMI recording of the early 1970s and in the publication of a critical edition of the opera. Until such time as a new edition appears, I encourage the reader to consult Ernst Rudorff's 1866 edition of the full score, which was reissued in 1969 in a facsimile reprint by Gregg International Publishers Limited. In the anticipation that a critical edition will some day appear, I have included measure numbers in my discussions of passages from the opera, but these are of little help in conjunction with the older editions, which supply no measure numbers. To facilitate the location of the passages in question I additionally refer to the relevant lines of text or changes in tempo. The reader who does take the trouble to supply measure numbers to his own copy of the score should be alerted to the fact that in two instances I have followed Weber's autograph, rather than Rudorff's edition, for determining where a piece begins. In the Duetto No. 13, measure 1 marks the cadence to C major at the Allegro animato, and in the Duetto No. 15 measure 1 is placed at the start of the A-major Moderato.

A note on certain editorial policies is in order before we begin our investigation of the opera. Typical for their era, Weber and his librettist Helmina von Chezy were inconsistent in matters of spelling and in the way they designated passages in the opera. In the present study I have decided to standardize references to pieces in the opera according to the outline given in Chapter II, wherein I follow the designations in the most authoritative sources, Weber's autograph score and the first edition of the piano-vocal score, which the composer himself prepared. The resulting designations yield a mixture of Italian (Scena ed aria), French (Ouverture) and archaic German ('Scene' instead of 'Szene', 'Jaegerchor' instead of Jägerchor') that might be annoying to the purist. For my own taste, however, the archaic spellings give a sense of the period, and more importantly, the polyglot designations underscore the cosmopolitan nature of early nineteenth-century German opera. In general, I have retained the spellings encountered in the text documents that I transcribe. On the other hand, the musical examples taken from Weber's autograph draft make no attempt to be 'diplomatic' transcriptions, but instead try to present the musical evidence for alternative versions and cancellations in as logical and readable a manner as possible. Editorial additions in these examples are enclosed in square brackets. Unless otherwise noted, all translations are my own.

Over the years during which I have worked on this project I have incurred a number of debts that I can scarcely ever repay. I am especially grateful to Dr Wolfgang Goldhan, Frau Eveline Bartlitz and the staff of the Music Division of the Deutsche Staatsbibliothek in Berlin for facilitating my work with the great collection of Weber manuscripts housed in that famed library. Hans-Jürgen Freiherr von Weber graciously granted me access to a number of documents in his family's possession. My research also benefited greatly from the assistance of the following scholar-librarians and institutions: Dr Günter Brosche and the Österreichische Nationalbibliothek, Vienna; Dr Marian Zwiercan and the Biblioteka Jagiellońska, Kraków; Dr Franz Patzer, Dr Otto Brusatti and the Wiener Stadt- und Landesbibliothek, Vienna; Dr Wolfgang Reich and the Sächsische Landesbibliothek, Dresden; and Ms Olga Buth and the Fine Arts Library of the University of Texas at Austin. Financial support from the International Research and Exchanges Board (IREX) and the Mrs Giles Whiting Foundation facilitated my initial study of Weber's manscripts in Berlin in 1979–1980, and a grant from the University Research Institute of the University of Texas at Austin allowed further research in German and Austrian libraries in the summer of 1985.

In its earliest stages my work profited immensely from suggestions made by Professors J. Merrill Knapp and Harold S. Powers of Princeton University. More recently my colleague at the University of Texas at Austin, Patrick McCreless, offered insightful comments on Chapter VII of the present study. I owe an especially great debt to my former student Ms Hon Lun Yang for her tireless assistance with the musical examples. Lastly, I am grateful to Bruce Phillips, David Blackwell, and Edwin F. Pritchard of Oxford University Press for their encouragement, assistance, and patience in seeing this study through the various stages of publication.

M.C.T.

Austin, Texas
April 1990

Note: While this study was going through the press EMI did in fact reissue its complete recording of *Euryanthe*, thereby affording a new generation of opera lovers a splendid opportunity to acquaint themselves with this remarkable work.

Tables

Figure

Abbreviations

AmZ	*Allgemeine musikalische Zeitung* (Leipzig)
AmZ (Vienna)	*Allgemeine musikalische Zeitung mit besonderer Rücksicht auf den oesterreichischen Kaiserstaat* (Vienna)
BamZ	*Berliner allgemeine musikalische Zeitung*
BJ	Biblioteka Jagiellońska, Kraków
Brühl-Briefe	Weber, *Briefe an den Grafen Karl von Brühl*, ed. Kaiser
Chezy 1823A	Helmina von Chezy, 'Auch ein Wort über die "Euryanthe" von der Dichterinn'
Chezy 1823B	Helmina von Chezy, 'Erster Entwurf eines Scenariums der Euryanthe, Operndichtung für Carl Maria von Weber'
Chezy 1840	Helmina von Chezy, 'Carl Maria von Webers *Euryanthe*. Ein Beitrag zur Geschichte der deutschen Oper'
DTO	Denkmäler der Tonkunst in Österreich
GSD	Wagner, *Gesammelte Schriften und Dichtungen*
G. Weber-Briefe	'Carl Maria von Webers Briefe an Gottfried Weber', ed. Bollert and Lemke
JAMS	*Journal of the American Musicological Society*
JRMA	*Journal of the Royal Musical Association*
Lichtenstein-Briefe	*Briefe von Carl Maria von Weber an Hinrich Lichtenstein*, ed. Rudorff
MGG	*Die Musik in Geschichte und Gegenwart*, ed. F. Blume
ML	*Music & Letters*
MMW	Max Maria von Weber, *Carl Maria von Weber. Ein Lebensbild*
MQ	*Musical Quarterly*
MT	*Musical Times*
NZfM	*Neue Zeitschrift für Musik* (Leipzig)
ONB	Österreichische Nationalbibliothek, Vienna
PRMA	*Proceedings of the Royal Musical Association*
Reisebriefe	*Reisebriefe von Carl Maria von Weber an seine Gattin Caroline*, ed. Carl von Weber
Sämtliche Schriften	*Sämtliche Schriften von Carl Maria von Weber*, ed. Kaiser

SiMG	*Sammelbände der internationalen Musik-Gesellschaft*
WaMZ	*Wiener allgemeine Musik Zeitung*
Web.	Deutsche Staatsbibliothek, Berlin, *Weberiana* collection
ZfMw	*Zeitschrift für Musikwissenschaft*

Introduction

From its première in Vienna on 25 October 1823 to the present day, Carl Maria von Weber's *Euryanthe* has always been one of the most problematic works in the annals of opera. Eagerly awaited as the successor to his phenomenally popular *Der Freischütz*, the opera disappointed its early audiences, and although it eventually established itself as a staple on German stages in the mid-nineteenth century, it never achieved the widespread and enthusiastic public support necessary to guarantee a permanent place in the repertory; for all practical purposes, *Euryanthe* disappeared from the active repertory by the end of the nineteenth century. By no means has the opera's critical reception been consistently favourable throughout its history. From the start critics have poured an unrelenting and merciless stream of invective on Helmina von Chezy's libretto, whose cast of puppets, illogical and improbable situations, and artificial language have earned it a reputation as one the worst texts ever attached to a major opera. The noted Weber biographer John Warrack thus sums up one principal strain in *Euryanthe*'s reception, the thesis that the libretto was the tragic cause of the opera's ultimate failure to gain popular acceptance, when he describes the text as 'the rock upon which a potential masterpiece became wrecked'.[1] This view has in fact encouraged a number of Weber's admirers since the second half of the nineteenth century to attempt to rescue *Euryanthe* for the stage by revising or even altogether replacing the original text.[2] Nor have critics ever really reached a consensus of opinion about the merits of the opera's music. On the one hand, the likes of Robert Schumann, Franz Liszt, and Donald Francis Tovey lavished it with glowing praise, but knowledgeable figures like Franz Grillparzer, Franz Schubert, Louis Spohr, F. J. Fétis, and Edward J. Dent have found its music barely tolerable and in no way equal to that of *Der Freischütz*. Richard Wagner,

---

[1] John Warrack, *Carl Maria von Weber*, 2nd edn. (Cambridge, 1976), p. 287.
[2] For a summary of these uniformly unsuccessful experiments, which have attracted distinguished figures like Gustav Mahler, Hans Joachim Moser, and Donald Francis Tovey, see Robert Haas, *Aufführungspraxis der Musik* (Potsdam, 1934), and Warrack, op. cit., pp. 299–301.

Weber's most important critic and throughout his life an ardent admirer of Weber, vacillated in his own estimation of the opera's music, for early in his career he criticized it in no uncertain terms but in old age came to the point of view that *Euryanthe* contained Weber's 'most beautiful, richest, and most masterful music'.[3]

The problematic nature of the work, the ambivalence with which the opera has been received from Weber's day to the present, and the fact of its complete disappearance from the modern repertory will doubtless cause the potential reader to ask what justifies a book-length study of *Euryanthe*. It seems to me that three fundamental reasons command our attention and warrant such an extended study. First, *Euryanthe* distinguished itself from the vast majority of German operas of its day as an aggressively experimental work, both with respect to its large-scale structure and also with respect to its compositional approach. *Euryanthe* was Weber's first and only opera to forego the traditional dramaturgy of German opera, according to which musical pieces alternate with spoken dialogue, in favour of a continuous musical accompaniment for all sections of the opera; although not without precedent, this approach nevertheless conspicuously distanced the opera from the vast majority of its contemporaries on the German operatic scene. Beyond this, however, *Euryanthe* literally represented an attempt to establish a new genre, 'grand romantic opera,' predicated on the fusion of two operatic types previously kept apart. Second, as historians of opera have frequently noted, *Euryanthe* was an influential work that left its mark on operatic developments in the mid-nineteenth century. The great music historian August W. Ambros, whose first-hand knowledge of early nineteenth-century repertory made him more sensitive to such issues than we can possibly ever be, had no doubt about the opera's importance: '*Euryanthe* is a truly epochal work; Wagner is rooted in this score, no less so Marschner, who is totally different from him, and no less so Meyerbeer, who is fundamentally different from both, inasmuch as he did not [also] assimilate Italian and French elements'.[4] Although the present study is not devoted to the question of elucidating *Euryanthe* as one important

---

[3] 'Über das Opern-Dichten und -Komponieren im besonderen', in Richard Wagner, *Gesammelte Schriften und Dichtungen*, 2nd edn. (Leipzig, 1887–8), x. 167; hereafter cited as *GSD*. Compare this appreciation from 1879 with the nearly diametrically opposed view presented in 'Die deutsche Oper' (1834) quoted below in Chapter III, section 2.3.

[4] August W. Ambros, 'Carl Maria von Weber in seinen Beziehungen zu den Roman tikern der deutschen Literatur', *Culturhistorische Bilder aus dem Musikleben der Gegenwart*, 2nd edn. (Leipzig, 1865), p. 45.

stepping stone along the path to Wagner,[5] a point of view that has dominated the historiography of early nineteenth-century German opera in general,[6] a thorough understanding of this opera on more or less its own terms is necessary if one is to comprehend the works and issues on the German operatic landscape in which Wagner matured.

Third, and most pertinent to the present study, the flawed *Euryanthe*, rather than the more perfect *Freischütz*, is arguably the key work for understanding Weber's operatic aims as well as the difficult moment in history that he occupied as a composer of German opera. This thesis of course flies in the face of the traditional picture of Weber that places the beloved *Freischütz* at the centre of his entire *œuvre*, a view most succinctly summed up in Hans Pfitzner's assessment that 'Weber came into the world in order to compose the *Freischütz*.'[7] To be sure, this conventional image arose quite legitimately in that the *Freischütz* began to overshadow all of his other compositions even within Weber's lifetime, much to the composer's own chagrin, and its impact on the course of German opera for the two decades following its première cannot be underestimated. Yet, in a number of ways *Euryanthe*, which Weber himself seems to have valued as the greater opera, is the more fascinating and instructive work. Emboldened by the staggering success of the *Freischütz* and the flattering commission to compose a new opera for Vienna, the most prestigious and tradition-rich musical centre in the German-speaking world, Weber sought in *Euryanthe* to apply and extend certain principles that he had implemented in the *Freischütz* to a larger and more ambitious canvas; thus even if, as Hermann Abert concluded, *Euryanthe* reveals all too acutely Weber's limitations as a composer,[8] it also embodies more thoroughly and uncompromisingly his agenda for opera. Weber's active involvement in the forging of the libretto also guaranteed that the final version of the libretto, deficient though it may be in certain respects, nevertheless represents a direct manifestation of

[5] An interpretation already present by around 1850 and doubtless fostered by Wagner himself. See the comments on *Euryanthe* by Wagner's friend Theodor Uhlig in 'Richard Wagners Opern', *Deutsche Monatsschrift für Politik, Wissenschaft, Kunst und Leben*, 1/4 (1850): 297, reprinted in Helmut Kirchmeyer, ed., *Situationsgeschichte der Musikkritik und des musikalischen Pressewerdens in Deutschland. IV. Teil. Das zeitgenössische Wagner-Bild*, vol. iii (Regensburg, 1968), p. 762. On Wagner's relationship to *Euryanthe* see Michael C. Tusa, 'Richard Wagner and Weber's *Euryanthe*', *19th-Century Music* 9/3 (Spring 1986): 206–21.

[6] The standard reference work on German opera in the period 1813–1848, Siegfried Goslich's *Die deutsche romantische Oper* (Tutzing, 1975), clearly exemplifies this tendency.

[7] Hans Pfitzner, 'Was ist uns Weber?' in his *Gesammelte Schriften* (Augsburg, 1926), i.90.

[8] Hermann Abert, 'Carl Maria von Weber und sein *Freischütz*', in his *Gesammelte Schriften und Vorträge*, ed. Friedrich Blume (Halle, 1929), p. 450: 'Der "Freischütz" entfaltet Webers reinstes Wesen, die "Euryanthe" zeigt nur seine Grenzen.'

his dramaturgical ideals. And last but not least, the genesis of *Euryanthe* is more completely documented than any other of Weber's operas, as the preserved correspondence, libretto drafts, and composition drafts allow us to trace in great detail the birth pangs of both its text and music and thereby gain a unique glimpse into Weber's creative world.

What follows is thus an attempt to illuminate one very prominent and exceptional work from the relatively unfamiliar world of early nineteenth-century German opera through a close consideration of the surviving documentary sources for its genesis, and in so doing come to a better appreciation of Weber as a composer of dramatic music. To a certain extent the goal will be to understand the author through the work rather than to understand the work solely as an autonomous structure, an approach warranted by a few circumstances that should be recognized at the outset. In the first place, although widely recognized as a leading figure in the emergence of a decidedly Romantic school of composition in Germany in the first quarter of the nineteenth century and in the foundation of a German Romantic opera, Weber has nevertheless been largely neglected by twentieth-century scholarship; to this date there is no complete critical edition of Weber's music, correspondence, or diaries, an updated thematic catalogue and list of sources is sorely needed, and critical re-examinations of his life and works in the light of documentary evidence are few and far between.

A second reason for placing the composer alongside his work at the centre of the present study lies in the nature of the extant sources. Put bluntly, the preserved sources for *Euryanthe* hold no magical key for a new critical-analytical approach to the opera or to Weber's style in general, but instead provide information akin to the type that in anthropological studies is supplied by an informant from within an exotic culture. That is, the primary sources for the genesis of this opera speak less to issues commonly raised in modern musical analysis and criticism than to the circumstances of creation and certain fundamental questions about the composer's relationship to his work: how he approached and defined the task; what sorts of problems he encountered in shaping the most ambitious work of his career; how his artistic principles conditioned his compositional decisions; what priorities and criteria were important to him; what he intended to convey to audiences; and by what standards he assumed the work would be judged. This is not to plead that the only correct way to approach a work of art is to attune oneself entirely to the author's message to the exclusion of any other modes of reception; however, a certain sympathy for the composer's standpoint is especially necessary in the case of a problematic work like *Euryanthe*, which suffers in modern perceptions both from the present age's post-Wagnerian insistence on realistic drama as the basis for the opera libretto and from the hegemony of analytic and interpretive models that a priori are not sympathetic to its music. And in point of fact, a direct confrontation with the sources for the genesis of the opera ultimately does encourage one to raise critical questions that otherwise might not be asked and that thereby lead to new insights into the work and new critical approaches.

The following study is divided into three major parts. Part I orientates the reader to the unfamiliar opera and a number of contextual issues in a rather dark corner of recent Western music history in order to lay the groundwork for the subsequent documentary studies and analyses. Part II offers a close examination of the genesis of the much maligned libretto, an endeavour justified primarily by the fact that Weber himself exerted nearly total control over the numerous revisions of the libretto; as we shall see, much of the large-scale musical structure of the work was prefigured in the shaping of the libretto. In Part III we turn to the composition draft of *Euryanthe* as a springboard for a number of analytical and aesthetic issues, including tonal planning, the musical implementation of Weber's call for dramatic truth and characterization, form, and the compositional process.

At the end of an extended and insightful discussion of *Euryanthe* in *Oper und Drama*, Richard Wagner wrote that 'criticism has not given *Euryanthe* the degree of attention that it deserves on account of its uncommonly instructive content'.[9] That a close examination of *Euryanthe* may prove to be as 'instructive' for the modern student of opera as it was for Wagner in 1850 is the premiss of the following study.

---

[9] *GSD* iii. p. 292.

PART I: ORIENTATIONS

I. Biographical Overview

With the triumphant première of *Der Freischütz* in Berlin on 18 June 1821, Carl Maria von Weber (1786–1826), at the age of 34 already widely respected as composer, critic, pianist, and *Kapellmeister* of the German Opera in Dresden, overnight became the most celebrated German opera composer since Mozart. Weber's new-found fame led directly to the composition of *Euryanthe*. Following its première, *Der Freischütz* was next taken up at the Kärntnerthortheater in Vienna on 3 November of the same year.[1] Despite numerous alterations imposed by the local censor, including the complete suppression of Samiel and the Hermit and the conversion of the magic bullets into magic darts (*Freibolzen*),[2] the opera proved so successful in the Austrian capital that the newly designated chief of the Viennese opera, the Neapolitan impresario Domenico Barbaia, almost immediately invited Weber to compose an opera for the spring season of 1822. According to Weber's Diary, he received Barbaia's invitation on 11 November 1821, the date that thus formally marks the commencement of the project that eventually resulted in *Euryanthe*.[3]

[1] This is the date traditionally given for the première in Vienna. The most recent and thorough catalogue of opera performances at the Kärtnerthortheater, Franz Hadamovsky, comp., *Die Wiener Hoftheater (Staatstheater)*, Part II (Vienna, 1975), pp. 160 and 607, however, gives 4 November as the date of the première.

[2] The censored text used at the Vienna première is preserved in an extant manuscript libretto in the music collection of the Österreichische Nationalbibliothek in Vienna (S. m. 32151 Musik-S.). For Weber's dismayed reaction to these cuts see his letter of 9 Dec. 1822 to C. E. F. Weyse in Matthias S. Viertel, 'Zur Wirkungsgeschichte des "Freischütz" im 19. Jahrhundert', in *Carl Maria von Weber. Werk und Wirkung im 19. Jahrhundert* (Kiel, 1986), p. 62, note 8.

[3] Weber's Diaries, which he kept from 1810 until his death in London in 1826, have never been published in full; in 1956 they were permanently loaned by Weber's heirs to the Deutsche Staatsbibliothek, Berlin (DDR), where they are now catalogued as Mus. ms. autogr. theor. C. M. von Weber WFN 1. I wish to extend my sincerest thanks to Hans-Jürgen Freiherr von Weber and Dr Wolfgang Goldhan of the Deutsche Staatsbibliothek for allowing me to consult a photographic facsimile of Weber's diaries (Mus. 276.3 (Fot.)) as well as a typescript transcription of the diary made by Franz Zapf. A description of the diaries is given by John Warrack in 'Carl Maria von Weber in his Diaries', in *Slavonic and Western Music: Essays for Gerald Abraham*, ed. Malcolm Hamrick Brown and Roland John Wiley (Ann Arbor, Mich. and Oxford, 1985), pp. 131–8. See also Eveline Bartlitz, comp., *Carl Maria von Weber. Autographenverzeichnis*, Deutsche Staatsbibliothek Handschrifteninventare, 9 (Berlin, 1986), pp. 57–61.

Weber's reaction to Barbaia's invitation and the succeeding events that led him to settle upon *Euryanthe* as the subject for his new opera are actually more difficult to document than one would suspect from the traditional accounts of the earliest phase in the opera's history. According to Weber's most important biographer, his son Max Maria von Weber (1822–1881), Barbaia's letter requested that the new opera be written 'in the style of the *Freischütz*', but Weber, who at the time was engaged in the composition of the comic opera *Die drei Pintos*, saw the new commission as a chance to silence critics who had belittled the success of the *Freischütz* and expressed doubts about his ability to succeed with a more ambitious work in the serious style. Anxious to demonstrate his full competence, Weber is alleged to have resolved immediately that only a 'grand opera' would be in order.[4] The origins of *Euryanthe* in the decision to undertake the composition of a 'grand opera' are therefore usually attributed to Weber's sensitivity to contemporary criticism.

As I have argued more fully elsewhere, Max Maria von Weber's account, which has been appropriated by nearly every succeeding biography of the composer, suffers from a lack of documentation and heavy-handed use of extant materials.[5] For one thing, Barbaia's letter to Weber was probably no longer extant at the time Max Maria was writing the biography; that Max Maria did not know the date on which the letter was written and that he did not refer to the contents of the letter beyond the phrase 'im Style des Freischützen' certainly suggest that he did not have first-hand knowledge of the letter. It is in fact likely that Barbaia's initial letter left Weber with complete freedom in the matters of style and choice of libretto, for in his reply of 20 November 1821, Weber expressly asked whether Barbaia preferred a comic or serious opera, an unlikely question if Barbaia had already requested a work in the style of the *Freischütz*. Significantly, Max Maria omitted from his published version of the letter the one clause (underscored in the following

[4] Max Maria von Weber, *Carl Maria von Weber. Ein Lebensbild*, ii (Leipzig, 1864), 352; hereafter cited as *MMW*. This account is transmitted by all other important biographical treatments, e.g. Friedrich Wilhelm Jähns, *Carl Maria von Weber in seinen Werken. Chronologisch-Thematisches Verzeichnis seiner sämmtlichen Compositionen* (Berlin, 1871), p. 359; Lucy Poate Stebbins and Richard Poate Stebbins, *Enchanted Wanderer* (New York, 1940), p. 219; Julius Kapp, *Carl Maria von Weber*, 3rd edn. (Berlin, 1944), p. 189; and Warrack, *Carl Maria von Weber*, p. 256. For a discussion of the implications of the term 'grand opera' see below, Chapter III, section I.

[5] Michael C. Tusa, 'Weber's *Große Oper*. A Note on the Origins of *Euryanthe*', *19th-Century Music* 8/2 (Autumn 1984): 119–24.

transcription) that would call into question his interpretation of the origins of *Euryanthe*.[6]

Es ist sehr schwer ein interessantes Buch zu bekommen. Ich werde es allerdings selbst wählen. *Wird eine komische oder ernste Oper gewünscht, und* wird H. Barbaja den Dichter honoriren und mit wieviel? Oder soll der Componist das Buch auf eigene Rechnung nehmen. Für diesen Winter würde wohl die Frist zu kurz sein. Den Sommer 1822 aber darf H. Barbaja nur die Zeit ohngefähr bestimmen in der ihm die Aufführung der Oper am angenehmsten wäre.
(It is very difficult to acquire an interesting libretto. In any event I shall choose it myself. *Is a comic or serious opera desired, and* will Mr. Barbaia pay the poet's honorarium, and if so, how much? Or should the composer purchase the libretto for himself? There is not enough time to have the opera ready for the winter season. But Mr. Barbaia need only set an approximate time in the summer of 1822 in which the performance of the opera would be most agreeable to him.)

Max Maria's account must also be questioned on the matter of Weber's motivation to write a 'grand opera', in particular, his allegation that Weber hoped in this way to silence criticism of his compositional abilities. To be sure Weber could indeed be irked by unfavourable reviews of his work, and as late as December 1822 we find him piqued by assertions that the success of the *Freischütz* depended chiefly on the 'Teufelsspuk' in the opera.[7] However, none of the relevant correspondence for the autumn and early winter of 1821 shows Weber displeased with the critical reception of *Freischütz*, and it is probable that Max Maria's interpretation was based less on any hard evidence than on family tradition and the unreliable memoirs of Weber's student Julius Benedict.[8]

In fact, there is compelling evidence that Weber began to contemplate a project on the grand scale well over a year before the first performance of *Freischütz*. In a letter of 29 January 1820 to the Viennese playwright and theatre secretary Georg Friedrich Treitschke, the reviser of the 1814

---

[6] The published version of the letter is in *MMW* ii. 354. The manuscript version of the letter is contained among a group of papers preserved in the *Weber Familien-Nachlaß* in the Deutsche Staatsbibliothek. These papers are autograph drafts (*Konzepte und Entwürfe*) for Weber's essays, business letters, and official correspondence; see Bartlitz, op. cit. n. 3 above, pp. 64–71. Apparently Weber kept the first drafts and sent fair copies of the letters to the recipients, and in many cases the draft represents the only known preserved version of a letter. The entire collection of *Konzepte* was catalogued and itemized by Jähns and is now catalogued as Mus. ms. autogr. theor. C. M. v. Weber WFN 6; following Bartlitz, the collection will henceforth be referred to as 'WFN-Handschriftliches'. The present letter is found in WFN-Handschriftliches, Konvolut XI, Bl. 75a/v.

[7] See Weber's letters of 18 and 26 Dec. 1822 to his friend, the zoologist Hinrich Lichtenstein in *Briefe von Carl Maria von Weber an Hinrich Lichtenstein*, ed. by Ernst Rudorff (Braunschweig, 1900), pp. 114 and 120; hereafter cited as *Lichtenstein-Briefe*.

[8] Tusa, op. cit. n. 5 above, pp. 121–2.

Fidelio libretto, Weber expressed a real interest in writing a grand opera for Vienna:

> I am now in the final stages of my *Jägersbraut* [Weber's working title for *Freischütz*], with which the new theatre in Berlin will be opened. I should also be glad to have the opera performed at the court theatre in Vienna and therefore await your response. In general I should be very pleased to write a grand opera specifically for your stage. Would your management agree to that? I lay this wish entirely in your hands...[9]

A little over a year later, and still before the première of *Der Freischütz*, Weber again indicated that a through-composed opera was among his plans for the near future. On 28 March 1821, he wrote to his good friend Johann Gänsbacher:

> I am now working on a grand comic opera [*Die drei Pintos*]; then I'll turn to a serious one, with recitatives throughout. Weren't you pleased that Dietrichstein and Mosel became directors of the court theatres in Vienna? At last the *Kaiserstadt* will again be open to native talent, and the truly good will be preferred, without always turning everything into Rossini [*nicht immer alles Rossinisirt sein*].[10]

It is possible that Weber here refers to a specific project, an opera on the medieval Spanish epic, *El Cid*, for which Friedrich Kind, the librettist for *Der Freischütz*, had submitted a plan on 23 January 1821.[11] It is significant that Weber turned in this letter immediately from the mention of the projected opera to the subject of operatic conditions in Vienna, as if he still associated that city with his grand opera. Taken together, the letters to Treitschke and Gänsbacher indicate that Weber's attraction to grand opera predated any possible adverse criticism of *Freischütz* and suggest moreover that he linked the composition of such an opera with a first performance in Vienna, the ancient imperial capital and the leading centre for music and opera in the German-speaking world.

To this long-standing ambition must also be added the fact that after the immense success of *Freischütz* in Berlin and Vienna Weber seems indeed to have felt challenged to surpass his prior accomplishment in the new opera. Writing to his wife Caroline on 15 and 16 March 1822, from Vienna, where he had gone to inspect the personnel of the opera company and to submit the text of *Euryanthe* for the censor's approval, the composer eloquently expressed his hopes for the new work.

[9] The letter is published in the *Wiener allgemeine Musik Zeitung* 7 (1847): 441; hereafter cited as *WaMZ*.

[10] Ludwig Nohl, ed., *Musiker-Briefe* (Leipzig, 1867), p. 275.

[11] Jähns, op. cit. n. 4 above, p. 451. The projected *Der Cid* opera was perhaps dropped because another opera on the same subject, *Rodrigo und Zimene*, by Johann Kaspar Aiblinger, premièred on 1 May 1821 in Munich.

Yesterday I contracted to sell the rights to the piano reduction of *Euryanthe* for 150 Ducats, so that the finished opera will bring in over 1200 Thaler just from the Viennese revenues. May God give His blessing that the work be worthy of me and that it surpass *Freischütz*. To be sure, it is impossible for it ever to be more popular than *Freischütz*, especially in view of the great variety in *Freischütz*: for there can be no Hunters' Chorus, or Bridal Song, etc. in *Euryanthe*. But that it might, in its own way, thrive. I shall not go too fast, and I've informed the management of the opera of this fact. May God grant ideas and strength to execute it.[12]

Thus there is reason to suspect that Weber did feel pressure to attempt a more ambitious type of opera. However, it seems that this pressure came (at least at first) not from without, but from within—not from the critics, but from a self-imposed responsibility to justify the fame that he had achieved and to continue to grow as an artist.

With Barbaia's invitation in hand, the composer's initial response was to orientate himself to the new theatrical conditions in Vienna, where the management of the court opera had only recently been reorganized by leasing the two main opera houses to the private entrepreneur Barbaia.[13] On 13 November Weber wrote to his two most important contacts in Viennese theatrical circles, Ignaz Franz von Mosel and Treitschke, asking for advice about the new administration and the manner in which he should approach Barbaia.[14] A week later Weber drafted his reply to Barbaia in the previously cited letter of 20 November, requesting that the première of the new work take place in the summer of 1822, rather than during the early spring as Barbaia, an impresario accustomed to the speed with which Italian operas were written, had evidently suggested. At this early stage Weber also left the matter of his fee up to the impresario.[15]

During these early negotiations with Vienna Weber began to search for a librettist and subject for his new opera, and it is likely that he considered several candidates from among his Dresden acquaintances as potential collaborators. A prime concern in the selection of a librettist must have been that the collaborator live nearby, in order to facilitate

---

[12] This is one of a number of unpublished letters in the Weber *Familien-Nachlaß* in the Deutsche Staatsbibliothek. Letter no. 11 of the series sent from Weber to Caroline during his trip to Vienna in 1822 (WFN Mus. ep. C. M. v. Weber 159).

[13] Barbaia's lease of the Kärntnerthortheater, granted on 6 Nov. 1821 and effective from 1 Dec. 1821, stipulated an obligation to produce good German operas along with ballets and Italian operas. The contract is summarized by Karl Glossy in 'Zur Geschichte der Theater Wiens. II (1821 bis 1830)', *Jahrbuch der Grillparzer Gesellschaft* 26 (Zürich, etc., 1920), p. 13.

[14] The letter to Mosel was published in *WaMZ* 6 (1846): 490; the letter to Treitschke was published in *WaMZ* 7 (1847): 442.

[15] *MMW* ii. 354.

the exchange of ideas and revisions. Perhaps Weber hoped that Friedrich Kind, the *Freischütz* librettist, would agree to furnish another text, for on 27 November, at a time when he desperately needed a new text, he attempted to repair a declining relationship with Kind, who felt that Weber had usurped the lion's share of recognition and credit for the success of the opera, by offering him a sum of money as a token of appreciation and gratitude for the *Freischütz* libretto.[16] If Weber intended by this gesture to reopen the possibility of collaboration with Kind, however, the poet's wounded pride and evidently nasty rejection of the gift effectively terminated any chance that the two creators of the *Freischütz* might ever work together again.

Another person to whom Weber turned as a possible librettist was the lyric poet Helmina von Chezy (1783–1856), an inhabitant of Dresden since 1817. Chezy later claimed that she initially offered Weber several possible subjects for operatic treatment as early as October 1821, in response to his standing request 'to think of him if she should find a magnificent subject'; among these was the *Geschichte der tugendsamen Euryanthe von Savoyen*, her own German prose translation of the thirteenth-century *Roman de la violette* of Gerbert de Montreuil, which she had published in 1804 in Friedrich Schlegel's *Sammlung romantischer Dichtungen des Mittelalters.*[17] While it is conceivable that Weber might have approached Chezy before he received Barbaia's commission—after all he was constantly on the lookout for new librettos—the fact of the matter is that the first mention of Chezy's name in Weber's Diary occurs in the wake of the crisis with Kind in an entry for 30 November 1821; that he misspelled her name as 'Chezi' in this first entry suggests that she was not a close acquaintance despite their common membership in the local literary circle, the Dresden *Liederkreis*, and perhaps also that this was his first formal contact with her.[18] By 2 December the new collaborators seem to have settled on the subject for the impending project, for Weber's diary for that date records the first mention of '*Eurianthe*'.[19]

Despite the great detail with which Weber normally recorded the

---

[16] The relevant letters are given in Friedrich Kind, *Der Freischütz, Volksoper in drei Aufzügen. Ausgabe letzter Hand* (Leipzig, 1843), Letters No. 33 and 34.

[17] Helmina von Chezy, 'Auch ein Wort über die "Euryanthe" von der Dichterinn', in the *Wiener allgemeine Theaterzeitung und Unterhaltungsblatt für Freunde der Kunst, Literatur und des geselligen Lebens*, 16, No. 134 (8 Nov. 1823), p. 536; this article is hereafter cited as Chezy 1823A.

[18] Diary entry for 30 Nov. 1821: 'Zu Frau von Chezi.' For an overview of the *Liederkreis* and its activities see Hermann Anders Krüger, *Pseudoromantik. Friedrich Kind und der Dresdener Liederkreis* (Leipzig, 1904).

[19] Diary entry for 2 Dec.: 'Zu Frau v. Chezy. *Eurianthe*.'

events of his day-to-day life in his Diary, exact dates for the earliest stages of the *Euryanthe* collaboration cannot now be ascertained. The two earliest documents—Chezy's scenario and Weber's revision, which we shall discuss in Chapter IV—do not survive in manuscript and are not explicitly mentioned in the Diary; nor are they transmitted with reliable dates in Chezy's later accounts. What is certain is that on 15 December Chezy gave Weber the first version of Act I, a unit of text that corresponds to materials divided between Acts I and II in the final version of the opera. Weber was evidently pleased with Chezy's first offerings, which he deemed 'splendid' ('trefflich') in his Diary and which he praised in a letter of 17 December to Treitschke: 'The libretto that Helmina von Chezy is writing for me will, I hope, become an excellent poem; the first act is already finished to my complete satisfaction.'[20] By this time too he had received a set of proposals from Vienna to which he responded point by point in a second, official letter of 17 December to Treitschke and the administration of the opera. It is clear from this letter that he had begun to think of the new opera in ambitious terms that justified the rather large honorarium he was requesting: 'The work that I plan to write for Vienna will be a very grand opera with ballet, etc. I therefore believe that I am not expressing anything inappropriate for the conditions in the imperial capital through my suggestion of a honorarium of 300 ducats.'[21]

By the end of the year Chezy had finished the first version of the second act and given it to Weber, who paid her 20 ducats (65 Thaler) on 31 December for the completed work, the same amount that he paid his previous Dresden librettists, Kind and Carl Theodor Winkler, for their respective librettos.[22] In his accompanying letter the composer also expressed his hope that the management of the Viennese opera would agree to a larger honorarium for the librettist, which he gladly would pass along to her, and promised to keep the poet in mind should *Euryanthe* prove to be as successful as the *Freischütz*. According to Weber's letter, Chezy would regain the rights to publish the libretto after a period of four to five years, a stipulation that he had also made in his contract

---

[20] *WaMZ* 7 (1847): 442. It is again characteristic of Max Maria von Weber that he reprints the letter (*MMW* ii. 366) but omits the clause in which Weber praises the first act, evidently to support his thesis that Carl Maria immediately recognized the faults of the libretto.

[21] *MMW* ii. 367–9; a draft version of the letter is in WFN-Handschriftliches, Konvolut XI, Bl. 75b/ v.

[22] Diary entry for 31 Dec. 1821: 'Frau von Chezy. Honorar für die Euryanthe 20 # [i.e. ducats]'.

with Kind for the *Freischütz* libretto and a point of some importance for the later history of the collaboration.[23]

Weber received a counter-offer on 2 January from Barbaia's representative in Vienna, Louis Duport, the details of which are not known; one can infer from Weber's letter of 3 January to Duport that Barbaia was not willing to pay 300 ducats as honorarium, but instead offered to sweeten a more modest honorarium with a later payment dependent on the success of the opera. Rejecting this plan, Weber suggested as a compromise a single payment of 240 ducats. Moreover, he was now convinced of the necessity of a trip to Vienna in February 1822 in order to observe the operatic conditions there and to orientate his work according to his findings; he therefore asked for an additional 60 ducats for travel expenses. Barbaia accepted these terms and the financial negotiations with the Vienna Opera were thus concluded to Weber's satisfaction.[24]

With monetary issues seemingly resolved, Weber and Chezy entered a new round of discussions about the libretto in order to put it into a form that could be submitted to the Viennese authorities during his upcoming stay in the *Kaiserstadt*. Incipient uncertainty about the libretto seems around this time to have led Weber to seek an outside opinion. On 22 January, for example, he consulted the Romantic author-critic, Ludwig Tieck, the *Dramaturg* of the Dresden theatre, about the *Euryanthe* text; we shall return in a later chapter to consider Tieck's possible influence on the libretto. On the same day Weber met Chezy and paid her an additional 10 ducats, which brought her total fee to 30 ducats; doubtless they discussed at this time alterations of the libretto.[25] As a result of such conferences, Chezy revised the text, giving Weber the first act on 31 January and the second act on 6 February, just five days before Weber began his journey to Vienna.

The impact of Weber's five-week sojourn in Vienna on *Euryanthe*

---

[23] The relevant passage of Weber's letter was excerpted in the catalogue No. 603 of the firm J. A. Stargardt of Marburg for the auction of 11 and 12 June 1974. I should like to thank Mr David Kilroy for bringing this catalogue to my attention. Weber's arrangement with Kind is spelt out in the Diary entry of 3 Mar. 1817: 'An Kind das Honorar auf 5 Jahre Eigenthum der Oper: die *Jägersbraut* für mich geschickt mit 20 # in Gold = 62 rth. 2 gr.'

[24] Weber's letter to Duport is printed in *MMW* ii. 388; the draft of the letter is in WFN Handschriftliches, Konvolut XII, Bl. 76a/ v–76b/ r. Weber's receipt for the honorarium, dated 31 Oct. 1823 (WFN-Handschriftliches, Konvolut XIII, Bl. 80b), shows that he indeed received 240 ducats as honorarium and 60 ducats as travelling expenses.

[25] Diary entry for 22 Jan. 1822: '... zu Tieck wegen Euryanthe. dann zur Chezy... Fr. v. Chezy noch nachträgliches Honorar mit 10 # gegeben.' Weber's Diary shows that he was reimbursed by the administration of the Vienna opera on 9 Mar. 1822 for the 30 # that he had paid Frau von Chezy.

is difficult to assess, since the primary sources of information about his visit, his Diary and his letters to his wife, still mostly unpublished, deal less with artistic issues than with the social and financial matters of his stay in the imperial capital and his health.[26] Moreover, the sojourn was probably less fruitful than he had hoped, since he was ill and bed-ridden during much of his stay. However, he did have a chance to observe the personnel of the German troupe in a number of perform-ances,[27] and he conducted two performances of *Freischütz*, whose tremendous popularity in Vienna began to loom as a potential threat for the success of *Euryanthe*; as he wrote in his Diary after the benefit performance for the young Wilhelmine Schröder, 'there can be no more enthusiasm, and I tremble for the future, since it is hardly possible for it to increase.'[28] He was also able to obtain the approval of the Viennese censor on 28 February for the version of the *Euryanthe* libretto that he had brought with him.[29] To the Viennese publisher Steiner he sold the piano-vocal score for the new opera for 150 ducats on 15 March. And before leaving the town he gave a concert for his own benefit. Obviously such activities left little time for composition, but during his illness, he seems to have started turning the libretto of *Euryanthe* over in his mind, for as he wrote to Caroline on 15 March '... out of boredom I have taken out *Euryanthe* and read it several times. She will therefore probably receive her first allotment of ideas in Vienna, and indeed how just that is ...'[30]

In Vienna Weber also consulted with friends, especially Mosel, about the libretto, and following his return to Dresden on 26 March, he went through it again with Chezy on 6 April. A visit from the young poet and critic Ludwig Rellstab on 6 and 7 April gave Weber another chance to test the libretto on a disinterested party, and Rellstab's suggestions

[26] A few of the letters were published by *MMW* and others by Julius Kapp in 'Der "Freischütz" in Wien', *Die vierte Wand. Organ der deutschen Theater-Ausstellung Magdeburg 1927* 14/15 (14 May 1927): 39–44.

[27] Weber's Diary records a number of impressions about the Viennese singers. For example, after a performance of *L'Italiana in Algeri* on 18 Feb. Weber commented: 'Mad. Schütz, Mezzo-Sopr: *Jäger*, sehr brav. Dlle. *Demer* hübsch. *Fröhlich* nichts. *Spizeder* gute Stimme, komik. *Seipelt*. Stimme schön will singen ...' On 26 Feb. he heard the *Barber of Seville* and found 'K[ammer] S[änger] Forti sehr brav.' After a visit on 27 Feb. with Caroline Unger, whom he perhaps was considering for either Euryanthe or Eglantine, he noted in his Diary: 'singt recht brav, aber für das Theater artikouliert sie nicht genug.' Despite his efforts to familiarize himself with the singers (or rather perhaps because of them?), only two of the singers that Weber heard in February 1822, Forti (Lysiart) and Seipelt (King Ludwig), were eventually chosen for the première in 1823.

[28] Diary entry for 7 Mar. 1822.

[29] See Chapter IV, section 4.2.

[30] The source for this letter is described above, n. 12.

were in fact incorporated into a new scenario for the conclusion of the opera that Weber sent Chezy on 9 April.[31] After the birth of his son, Max Maria, on 25 April, Weber and his family moved on 15 May to the summer country house at Hosterwitz that afforded him an atmosphere more conducive to composition. Within two days he began the written composition of the opera, drafting on 17 May the second section of Adolar's aria in A-flat major ('O Seligkeit dich faß' ich kaum'). By 20 May the draft of the number's opening slow section was finished.

Much to his dismay, however, Weber's progress with the opera was rather slower than he had anticipated. While he had originally hoped to compose the entire opera during the summer of 1822, in order to meet a deadline set for early fall, he actually finished only slightly more than one-third of the work by August.[32] Relatively early in the summer he realized that the opera would not be ready by the appointed time, for he wrote to Treitschke on 23 May to complain about his continuing ill health and the time lost in commuting several times each week between Hosterwitz and Dresden, where he had to assume the duties of an ill colleague, the court composer and director of sacred music, Franz Anton Schubert: 'There can no longer be any talk of completing *Euryanthe* by *Autumn*, and I admit that everything that I hear about Vienna doesn't exactly encourage me very much. The composer cannot do everything by *himself*, especially after one has heard such splendid singers [i.e. the visiting Italian troupe] and will praise them even more, when one no longer has them...'[33] Weber's displeasure with the state of affairs in Vienna is worth noting, for he feared that the vocal brilliance of Barbaia's imported Italian troupe would overshadow the more modest capabilities of the German company and thus put his new opera in a disadvantageous position when compared to works by Rossini and other Italian composers.

Because of his slow progress, Weber requested and obtained a postponement for the scheduled first performance of the new work. Exactly when the opera should have been ready under this first delay is not clear, since a gap in Weber's preserved business correspondence obscures his negotiations with the Vienna opera during the summer and autumn of 1822.[34] A letter to Chezy of 10 October 1822, unfortunately defective,

---

[31] See Chapter IV, section 5.

[32] The chronology of composition is summarized in Chapter VI, Table 7; extracts from Weber's Diary pertaining to the composition of *Euryanthe* are given in Appendix I.

[33] A manuscript copy of this letter is preserved in *Web.* Cl. II B 4, Suppl. 56.

[34] There is a gap in the *Brief-Konzepte* between 23 Jan. 1822 and 10 Oct. 1822. According to his Diary Weber wrote to Joseph Kupelwieser, the theatre secretary of the *Hofoper* and the older brother of the Viennese painter Leopold Kupelwieser, and the management of the opera on 31 Aug. 1822.

suggests that Weber had promised to finish the opera by the end of November; it also reveals that his patience with Chezy, who had been in Berlin since September and thus was not available for frequent consultation, was beginning to wear thin, as she appears by this time to have lost the desire to work seriously on revisions that Weber felt necessary for the libretto.

The more I rejoice over your serenity and peace of mind, most esteemed Friend, the more difficult it is for me to have to tear you out of this friendly frenzy; I entreat and implore you to abbreviate your sojourn and to return here. Remember that the opera really was supposed to be ready by now, [and] that only with effort did I obtain an extension until the end of November. Recently you were pressured by other matters and no longer had the heart, or rather interest for the matter, and I understand this after my ceaseless pestering. The conclusion of the first act, as you have sent it to me, bears somewhat the stamp of haste. I know that you aren't really angry; I can still [words missing] but I lack peace of mind [words missing] cannot have a good overview of the whole. What you tell me about your continuing delight in [words missing] however confirms my fear about [words missing] displeasure at writing, and that which you carry inside you I have to see on paper, otherwise there can be no composition. The conclusion that you have suggested may be good and I gladly concur . . .[35]

Weber in fact seems to have made a real attempt to finish the opera at the end of 1822, since in late October he resumed work on *Euryanthe* and even began to plan the disposition of the full score.[36] Whatever momentum he attained through this period, however, was soon dissipated by his obligations as Royal Saxon *Kapellmeister*. For the wedding of Prince Johann of Saxony with Princess Amalie Auguste of Bavaria he was required to compose incidental music to a *Festspiel* by Ludwig Robert, on which he worked between 29 October and 13 November. In addition, another of his colleagues, the Italian *maestro di cappella* Francesco Morlacchi, fell ill at this time, thereby once again increasing his duties at court. Realizing that he could not finish the opera by

---

[35] A copy of the letter is preserved in *Web*. Cl. II B 2 a, 31. Weber's letter of 29 Jan. 1823 to the intendant in Dresden, Geheimrat Hans Heinrich von Könneritz, cited in *MMW* ii. 473–4, indicates that the première had been initially rescheduled for January 1823.

[36] The Diary for 28 Oct. records the comment '*Euryanthe angefangen in Partitur zu sezzen.*' It is unlikely that Weber began to write out the full score of any pieces at this point; rather, this remark probably refers to his practice of noting in the composition draft a list of the instruments used in a given piece and the number of staves that they would occupy in the final score. See Chapter VI, section 4.

year's end, Weber wrote on 28 November to the administration of the Kärntnerthortheater, requesting that the première be postponed until the autumn of 1823 and expressing the hope that the delay would give the company time to acquire a satisfactory singer for the part of Eglantine, whose role in the opera had grown considerably since his trip to Vienna earlier in the year.

> The most desirable [arrangement], and the one most likely to insure success, would therefore be to postpone the opera until the autumn of '23. This is my most ardent wish, one built on long consideration of what would be mutually most advantageous for both of us. I probably do not need to mention how infinitely unpleasant it is for me to have to lose an entire theatrical year. Perhaps by then, however, I shall have finished my comic opera and the esteemed Administration will have acquired a powerful bravura soprano, who is actress enough to accommodate the role of Eglantine, which in the most recent version has gained infinitely in importance . . .[37]

While Weber may have seen some advantages in postponing the opera until the following autumn—for example, by giving the management time to strengthen the personnel of the German opera or by avoiding a direct comparison between his work and those performed in the spring by Barbaia's Italian troupe[38]—on the whole he was frustrated by the end of 1822 at not having made sufficient headway with the opera. As he wrote to Count Brühl, the Intendant of the Berlin opera, on 3 December, 'Things are going badly for my *Euryanthe*. Frau von Chezy has been in Berlin since September—the court festivities here, in which I had to take over all of the duties by myself, since Morlacchi quickly fell ill—all of this leads me unfortunately to regard this winter as a lost cause'.[39] Clearly, Chezy's continued stay in Berlin throughout the fall and winter was a major impediment to the completion of the opera. Weber was not yet satisfied with the libretto, and his poet was now too far away to respond quickly to his criticisms and suggestions, which

---

[37] WFN-Handschriftliches, Konvolut XII, Bl. 78a/r. The start of this letter, and thus the addressee, is lacking, but the Diary for 29 Nov. indicates that a letter, presumably this one, had been sent to Kupelwieser.

[38] See Weber's letter to Lichtenstein of 18 Dec. 1822: 'In March the Italians return to Vienna, with whom I'd not like to collide [*carambolieren*]; I have thus postponed the whole thing until autumn 1823 . . .' *Lichtenstein-Briefe*, p. 116.

[39] Letter of 3 Dec. 1822 in Georg Kaiser, ed., *Carl Maria von Weber. Briefe an den Grafen Karl von Brühl* (Leipzig, 1911), p. 36; hereafter cited as *Brühl-Briefe*. The editor, Georg Kaiser, incorrectly resolves the abbreviation for 'September', '7', as '7 [Nov.]', but as we have already seen, Chezy was in Berlin by 10 Oct.

he had to communicate by post.[40] It is to this period, however, that we owe the most interesting correspondence between the two collaborators, to which we shall return in Chapter IV.

After receiving confirmation from Vienna of the opera's postponement until September 1823[41] and supplying yet another occasional piece for a member of the royal family, a small birthday cantata for the Princess Therese, Weber resumed composition of the opera by 1 February at the latest, and from this point on his Diary details a relatively unbroken period of work on the remaining numbers of the opera. The text, however, still failed to win his complete approval, and again he turned to acquaintances from Dresden literary circles for advice. On 31 March he read the *Euryanthe* text aloud at the home of Tieck, and on the following day he sought out Carl Förster, the translator of Petrarch, for help with the denouement.[42] On the same day, 1 April, Chezy at long last returned unexpectedly to Dresden, thereby expediting the final revisions of the libretto, which concentrated on the Finale to Act I, much of which Chezy prepared as a *contrafactum* to music that Weber had borrowed from earlier compositions, and on various sections of the third act. Work on the libretto continued into the middle of the summer of 1823. In the meantime Weber had on 10 May again withdrawn to Hosterwitz where, in contrast to the previous summer, he made rapid progress with the remaining tasks in the opera, principally the composition of several pieces in Act III and the orchestration of the

---

[40] See Weber's letter to Chezy of 27 Feb. 1823, wherein he again pleaded with her to return to Dresden: 'Not to know the thing finished is unbelievably disturbing for me, I cannot contemplate it calmly, I can make no plan with certainty. Isn't that right? Dear Friend! March will bring you back to us? I shall speak no more of it, for I worry about worrying you...' Helmina von Chezy, 'Carl Maria von Webers *Euryanthe*. Ein Beitrag zur Geschichte der deutschen Oper', *NZfM* 13 (1840): 38; this long and important article is hereafter cited as Chezy 1840. The autograph of this letter, along with those for a number of other letters from Weber to Chezy, is in the Biblioteka Jagiellońska in Kraków, where it is part of the Varnhagen von Ense collection formerly held by the Prussian State Library. See L. Stern, *Die Varnhagen von Ensesche Sammlung in der königlichen Bibliothek zu Berlin* (Berlin, 1911), p. 870. I wish to extend my sincerest thanks to Dr Marian Zwiercan of the Biblioteka Jagiellońska for providing me with a microfilm of these letters.

[41] Weber acknowledged the new deadline in an unpublished letter of 19 Jan. 1823 to the Administration of the Kärntnerthortheater, the draft for which is in WFN-Handschriftliches, Konvolut XIII, Bl. 79a/v.

[42] Diary entries for 31 Mar.: 'Abends bei Tieck, Euryanthe vorgelesen'; and 1 Apr.: 'zu Förster wegen Euryanthe bis 4 Uhr.' An entry for 2 Apr. in Förster's diary paints a very sympathetic picture of Weber's predicament; see L. Förster, ed., *Biographische und literarische Skizzen aus dem Leben und der Zeit Karl Försters* (Dresden, 1846), p. 295.

entire opera.[43] By 29 August *Euryanthe* was finished except for the Ouverture, which, typically, Weber had saved for last.

As work on *Euryanthe* was drawing to a close in the summer of 1823, the personal relationship between Weber and Chezy, already strained by seemingly endless revisions of the text, began to deteriorate in much the same way that the relationship between Kind and Weber had soured. Chezy felt, namely, that the large amount of time that she had spent on revisions of the libretto entitled her to more than the thirty ducats that she had received, and she began to besiege the composer with requests for additional money. Weber, however, rejected any such extra payment on the principle that he had long ago honoured his contractual responsibilities towards her. Annoyed also by the fact that she had sold the text of the new opera, which according to the terms of their contract was to remain his exclusive property for an extended period, to the Viennese publisher Wallishauser for 25 ducats, Weber nevertheless held out to Chezy in a letter written on 5 June the prospect of additional remuneration after the première, should the opera prove as lucrative as the *Freischütz*.[44] Unpacified by Weber's offer, however, Chezy continued to press for a supplement to the honorarium. Weber attempted unsuccessfully to meet with her on 17 June,[45] and on 13 July she and he finally met in Dresden to settle their differences. The result of this meeting seems to have been a compromise; while Weber still firmly refused to pay her an additional fee, he did agree to attempt to incorporate into his contracts with theatres wishing to perform *Euryanthe* a clause whereby such theatres would have to pay a fee to the librettist upon acquisition of the work. As we shall see, even this unprecedented measure did not satisfy the poetess.

By 29 August 1823, Weber had completed the composition and orches-

[43] The score of the first act was written in twelve working days between 11 May and 25 May, a feat over which the composer himself marvelled in his Diary. On 28 May Weber had his first ideas for Euryanthe's Act III Scena 'Schirmende Engelschaar'. Act II was scored between 18 June and 17 July. On 6 July he finished the draft of the Act III Euryanthe–Adolar duet; the completion of the draft of the Act III Finale on 8 Aug. marked the end of work on the composition draft of the entire opera save the Ouverture. The score of Act III was then written out between 12 and 29 Aug.

[44] The letter is printed in Michael C. Tusa, 'Carl Maria von Weber's *Euryanthe*: A Study of Its Historical Context, Genesis and Reception', Ph.D. dissertation, Princeton University, 1983, pp. 198–200. The autograph of this letter is in the Biblioteka Jagiellońska in Kraków; the draft of the letter is in WFN-Handschriftliches, Konvolut XIII, Bl. 80a/v—80b/r.

[45] Two unpublished letters that Weber wrote on that date, one in the Biblioteka Jagiellońska (preserved in an *Abschrift*) and the other in the Bibliothèque nationale in Paris (Weber's autograph), document Weber's eagerness to resolve the increasingly bitter matter.

tration of the entire opera, except for the Ouverture, which he began
to compose on 1 September. Most of the work on the overture was
accomplished, however, in Vienna, where he arrived with his student
Julius Benedict on 21 September to begin the preparations for the première. Weber's progress with the Ouverture was slowed by a number
of factors that he described in his letters to his wife, who had remained
in Dresden. He still had to select the cast, and thus made another round
of visits to the theatre and with individual singers in order to familiarize
himself with the available talent. In addition to attending the nearly
daily rehearsals that began on 4 October, Weber also had to finish the
piano-vocal score that he had previously sold to Steiner. As a visiting
celebrity Weber was once again obliged to fulfil certain social duties
that further slowed the rate of composition.[46] Moreover, even in
Vienna he was not safe from Chezy, who by now was acting in an
openly hostile manner towards him. On 10 October he received two
letters from his librettist, who threatened legal action to block all produc-
tions of the opera outside Vienna if he did not pay her 600 Thalers.[47]
Weber immediately replied with a cool reminder of the agreement that
they had reached on the preceding 13 July and of his subsequent efforts
to make a poet's honorarium a condition for acquisition of performance
rights to the opera.[48] In another gesture designed to create a peaceful
atmosphere for his work, Weber offered on 12 October to lend Chezy
50 ducats as an advance against the fees that she could expect to receive
from theatres performing the opera.[49] Chezy refused the offer, but
she seems not to have carried out her threat to instigate litigation, perhaps
realizing that she in fact had no legally justified claim to more money
from Weber.[50] Despite such disturbances, he was able to finish the
draft of the Ouverture on 15 October, and on the next day he went
through it with Mosel. Always a rapid orchestrator, he completed the
score of the Ouverture on 19 October, less than a week before the

[46] Far and away the most significant of these social calls was his trip to Baden on
Sunday, 5 Oct. to visit Beethoven.

[47] Weber explained the new imbroglio to his wife Caroline in a letter of 10 Oct.,
published in *Reisebriefe von Carl Maria von Weber an seine Gattin Caroline*, ed. Carl
von Weber (Leipzig, 1886), p. 39; hereafter cited as *Reisebriefe*.

[48] The draft of the letter is preserved in WFN-Handschriftliches, Konvolut XIII,
Bl. 80b/v; it is printed in Tusa, 'Carl Maria von Weber's *Euryanthe*', pp. 201–2.

[49] Weber explained this arrangement to Caroline in a letter of 12 Oct. 1823 in *Reisebriefe*, p. 42.

[50] See Weber's letter of 22 Oct. 1823 to Caroline in *Reisebriefe*, p. 52. Weber in
fact kept his promise to stipulate an additional honorarium for the librettist in his
contracts with various theatres. See, for example, his letter of 15 Dec. 1823 to Friedrich
Ludwig Schmidt in his *Denkwürdigkeiten*, ed. Hermann Uhde, 2nd edn. (Stuttgart,
1878), ii. 302, and also the letter of 7 Jan. 1824 to Count Brühl in the *Brühl-Briefe*,
pp. 40–1.

first public performance of the opera, which took place on 25 October in the Kärntnerthortheater under the composer's own direction.

Since the focus of the present study is the genesis of the work, we shall not dwell on the later history of *Euryanthe*. Nevertheless, a few points are necessary to conclude our present overview. The most important of these is the fact that in performance the opera simply did not live up to expectations. Weber's initial response to the première, documented in his Diary and letters to his wife, was euphoric, but press reports and rumours soon began to circulate that the opera had not really been successful. Back in Dresden, Weber wrote to Lichtenstein on 13 November to refute claims that the opera had enjoyed only a *succès d'estime*, attributing negative reports to the envy of the Viennese critics,[51] and he reiterated this point of view in a letter to Gottfried Weber of 15 December 1823:

The effect that *Euryanthe* produces is exactly just as I had imagined. My overwrought friends this time lent their support to my enemies in that both camps ludicrously demand that *Euryanthe* should attract the *masses* in exactly the same way as *Freischütz*. How foolish! as if—without making a comparison—an *Iphigenia*, a *Don Carlos* could ever become box office attractions. The first three performances in Vienna, which I conducted, were truly received with an incredible enthusiasm; also the fourth, which I heard from a box in the loge, and I was again called out three times for bows, altogether 14 times. Up to the twelfth performance the applause was always the same in moderately full houses. That's as far as my reports go. N.N. has behaved like a real bastard-critic ['Recensenten-Schuft'], having written simultaneously in *his* newpaper, in the *Mode-Zeitung*, and in the *Sammler*, and seeking to draw down whatever he could; he isn't afraid of even the obvious lie, or of using cunning silence, in order to portray the success as doubtful. One must be prepared for envy...[52]

Nevertheless, as *Euryanthe* began to make the rounds of other German

[51]   *Lichtenstein-Briefe*, p. 131.

[52]   Werner Bollert and Arno Lemke, ed., 'Carl Maria von Webers Briefe an Gottfried Weber', in *Jahrbuch des Staatlichen Instituts für Musikforschung Preußischer Kulturbesitz 1972* (Berlin, 1973), p. 86; hereafter cited as G. *Weber-Briefe*. The *Mode-Zeitung* to which Weber refers was formally known as the *Wiener Zeitschrift für Kunst, Literatur, Theater und Mode*. The critic whose name was excised has frequently been identified as Joseph von Seyfried, one of the co-editors of the *Sammler*. However, the close parallels between the review in the *Sammler* and the *Allgemeine musikalische Zeitung mit besonderer Rücksicht auf den oesterreichischen Kaiserstaat* (hereafter cited as *AmZ (Vienna)*) suggest instead that Weber in fact believed that F. A. Kanne, the editor of the *AmZ (Vienna)*, had been the 'Recensenten-Schuft'. This supposition is perhaps confirmed by Weber's letter to J. P. Schmidt of 4 Dec. 1823, which was published by Wilhelm Altmann in 'Aus Gottfried Webers brieflichem Nachlaß', *SiMG* 10 (1908–9): 502 n. 4, where Weber used practically the same words to denounce the Viennese journalists. The 'Th. Kriin[?]' identified in that letter as author of the three different reviews is most probably the editor's misreading of 'Fr. Kañe'.

theatres with decidedly mixed results, Weber grew resigned to and in fact somewhat embittered by the ambivalent reception, and only the great success of the opera in Dresden, which he proudly described to Lichtenstein on 1 April 1824, seemed to restore his faith in the work and himself.

A marvellously disturbing time have I experienced; and perhaps it was well that my enormous workload (since I am still *alone*) did not allow me to think too much about it. But I could not prevent a great bitterness from taking hold of my heart. *Euryanthe* failed in Prague, in Frankfurt it caused a sensation. The truly vile scribbling of the Viennese gossip columns had strangely determined all sensibilities. I was therefore very curious about the effect that this work would have on our sober, basically cold, and well-read public. The mood was certainly rather against the work than for it.

Yesterday we performed *Euryanthe*, and I have experienced an indescribably brilliant triumph. I have never seen our public so taken, so full of enthusiasm. The excitement increased with every act. At the end I was called out, and then everyone, by a veritable storm... There is now complete agreement about how much higher this opera stands than *Freischütz*. Tieck, among others, was supposed to socialize after the opera, but explained that his spirit was too full, and said (to others, naturally) that there are things in this opera for which Gluck and Mozart would have envied me. I know dear brother that I can repeat such things to you without being misunderstood; I'd never dare repeat them to anyone else in the world.[53]

However, the failure of the work in Stuttgart in May 1824 under the watchful eye of his old friend and mentor Franz Danzi brought him back to the more widespread reality of the situation and the disillusioned conclusion that 'in the end one doesn't have to write operas anyway'.[54]

The early performance history of *Euryanthe* also entailed a number of revisions that deserve mention. Weber shortened a number of passages in the opera between the first performance and his death in 1826, perhaps a tacit admission that the opera in fact suffered from certain intrinsic problems. Immediately after the first performance in Vienna Weber abbreviated the recitative between Euryanthe and Eglantine in the first act and eliminated part of the G-minor section of Euryanthe's Act III Scena e cavatina No. 17. On 20 November 1823, shortly after his return to Dresden, Weber composed a shorter version of Euryanthe's *Vision* narrative in the first act, compressing the twenty-two measures of the original version into fifteen measures; possibly at this time he also abridged the opening ritornello for Adolar's Aria No. 12, although this cut may already have been made in Vienna. And at the request of Count Brühl, the theatre intendant in Berlin, Weber drastically compressed the scene

[53] *Lichtenstein-Briefe*, pp. 133–4.
[54] Letter of 26 May 1824, cited in *MMW* ii. 539.

between Adolar and Euryanthe at the start of the third act, significantly shortening the Duetto No. 15 and the surrounding recitatives. After each round of cuts, which in sum are modest compared to the unauthorized cuts made in German theatres throughout the nineteenth century,[55] Weber claimed that the opera had gained, but he perhaps betrayed his true feelings about them when upon learning of Brühl's request for additional cuts for the Berlin production he wrote on 23 January 1824 that 'to cut anything else would be tantamount to cutting Don Carlos out of *Don Carlos*... In an organically connected whole like a grand opera, one of the most difficult tasks of all is to remove something, if the composer has thought at all about his opera' ('wenn der Komponist von Haus aus etwas über seine Oper gedacht hat').[56]

Lastly, in order to satisfy a local custom for ballet in grand opera, Weber composed a brief *pas de cinq* in December 1825 for the Berlin production of the opera, which had been delayed nearly two years by the intrigues of the *Generalmusikdirektor*, Gasparo Spontini, who had never forgiven Weber for the success that the *Freischütz* had enjoyed at the expense of his own *Olympie* in Berlin in 1821.[57]

[55] See Jähns, n. 4 above, pp. 364–5, for a discussion of nineteenth-century cuts in the opera, as well as those that Conradin Kreutzer made in Vienna immediately following Weber's departure in 1823. Extant theatre scores that document such massive cuts include: (1) Dresden, Sächsische Landesbibliothek, Mus. 4689-F-38a, a score that Weber sent to the Nationaltheater in Frankfurt am Main, and (2) Vienna, Österreichische Nationalbibliothek, Mus. Hs. KT 139, a score from the archives of the Kärntnerthortheater (but not the score used for the première performance).

[56] *Brühl-Briefe*, pp. 41–2.

[57] For a discussion of the delays in the first Berlin performance of *Euryanthe* see Albert Maecklenburg, 'Der Fall Spontini-Weber. Ein Beitrag zur Vorgeschichte der Berliner Erstaufführung der *Euryanthe*', *ZfMw* 6 (1924–5): 449–65. The music for the *pas de cinq* was largely borrowed from earlier compositions; its ultimate source was recently discovered to be a Rondo in B-flat major for wind sextet composed in 1808. See Jähns, n. 4 above, p. 363, and Wolfgang Sandner, *Die Klarinette bei Carl Maria von Weber* (Wiesbaden, 1971), pp. 204–5 and 228–34.

II. Synopsis and Structural Overview

Because the following discussions of the genesis of *Euryanthe* require a certain familiarity with the characters, plot, and structure of an opera that admittedly is not a staple of the modern repertory, the present chapter offers a brief synopsis of the work interspersed with commentary to orientate the reader to a number of critical and historical issues. Despite numerous features that enhance the sense of continuity and articulate the opera into larger scenic units, *Euryanthe* is essentially conceived as a succession of discrete musical pieces. For ease of future reference, Table I lists the musical pieces in the opera with the titles given to them in Weber's autograph score along with their tonalities.[1] The titles not designated in the autograph are indicated in brackets; these have been supplied from the first printed edition of the opera, the Steiner piano-vocal score that Weber himself prepared.[2] As one can readily see, the titles in the autograph are almost exclusively Italian and sometimes differ from those found in the only printed orchestral score of the opera, an edition by Ernst Rudorff published in 1866.

I. OUVERTURE

As is customary in overtures of the late eighteenth and early nineteenth centuries, the Ouverture to *Euryanthe* is cast in a modified sonata-allegro form. Departing from Weber's usual practice, it eschews a slow introduction and instead begins immediately with the main theme of the exposition.[3] Even more unusual, the end of the exposition and the beginning

---

[1] Dresden, Sächsische Landesbibliothek, Mus. 4689-F-37. The autograph score was damaged by water during World War II and much of the red ink that Weber used to indicate stage instructions has faded badly.

[2] Titles in square brackets are taken from rubrics immediately above the relevant numbers in the first edition. Titles in curly brackets are taken from the table of contents of the first edition. The principal soloists for each number are given in parentheses.

[3] On Weber's overtures see: Paul Listl, 'Carl Maria von Weber als Ouvertürenkomponist,' Ph. D. dissertation, Ludwig-Maximilians-Universität, Munich (Würzburg: Konrad Triltsch, 1936); and Susanne Steinbeck, *Die Ouvertüre in der Zeit von Beethoven bis Wagner. Probleme und Lösungen* (Munich, 1973), pp. 31–40.

TABLE I. The structure of *Euryanthe*[a]

Piece		Key
Ouverture		E♭major
Act I		
No. 1	Introduzione; Tanz / :Ernster Reigen:/ Recit.	G major
No. 2	Romanza (Adolar)	B♭ major
No. 3	[Chor] Recit.	G major
No. 4	{Scene und Chor}	E♭ major
No. 5	Cavatina (Euryanthe) Recit.	C major
No. 6	[Arie] (Eglantine) Recit.	E minor
No. 7	Duetto (Euryanthe, Eglantine)	A minor; A major
No. 8	Scena ed Aria (Eglantine)	E major
No. 9	Finale	D major; B♭ major; D major
Act II		
No. 10	Scena ed Aria (Lysiart) Recit.	C minor; G major; C minor
No. 11	Duetto (Eglantine, Lysiart)	B major
No. 12	Aria (Adolar)	A♭ major
No. 13	Duetto (Euryanthe, Adolar)	C major
No. 14	Finale	F major; D♭ major; A major; A minor; C major; F minor

of the development proper are separated by a Largo section fifteen measures in length that at first glance appears to stand wholly outside the discourse of the movement. Like Weber's other mature opera overtures, it establishes the key with which the opera will conclude, E-flat major, and much of its thematic material derives from the opera; thus at certain levels of awareness it prepares the listener for several main

TABLE I. (contd.)

Piece		Key
Act III		
	Erste Scene. Recit. (Euryanthe, Adolar)	D minor; C minor
No. 15	Duetto (Euryanthe, Adolar)	A major; A minor; to E♭ major
No. 16	[Scena] (Euryanthe)	B major; to E♭ major
No. 17	Scena e Cavatina (Euryanthe)	G minor; G major
No. 18	[Jaegerchor]	E♭ major
	Recit.	
No. 19	Duetto con Coro (Euryanthe, King)	C minor
No. 20	Aria con Coro (Euryanthe)	C major/ C minor
No. 21	{Scene und Chor} (Bertha, Adolar)	A major; A minor
No. 22	{Chor} (Adolar)	B♭ major
No. 23	Hochzeitmarsch	D major
	Recit.	
No. 24	Duetto con Coro (Adolar, Lysiart)	D major
No. 25	Finale	E♭ major

[a] Broken rules denote changes of scenery

threads of the dramatic action.[4] However, the extent to which the *Euryanthe* Ouverture depends on themes drawn from the opera is considerably less than in the overtures to *Freischütz* and *Oberon*. Thus the rousing first period of the main theme (mm. 1–8) is unique to the Ouverture, although the rising triplet arpeggiation of the opening gesture may be linked to the E-flat major fanfares in the ensemble No. 4, at the point where Adolar accepts Lysiart's wager (mm. 9–10: 'Es gilt'), and more subtly to the rising E-flat-major arpeggiations at the very end of the opera.[5]

The most significant relationships between the Ouverture and the body of the opera involve three thematic complexes. First, the second

[4] An interpretation of the dramatic function of the Ouverture, coupled with analysis and a study of its genesis, is presented in Chapter X.

[5] This subtle relationship between the Ouverture and the end of the opera is reminiscent of Mozart's practice as discussed by Daniel Heartz in 'Mozart's Overture to *Titus* as Dramatic Argument', *MQ* 64 (1978): 29–49.

period of the first-theme group (mm. 9–25), an important idea that contributes significantly to many other sections of the overture, is based on the concluding section of the large ensemble No. 4, where it is heard as Adolar's heroic expression of faith in God and his betrothed, Euryanthe ('Ich bau' auf Gott und meine Euryanth''). A second important point of contact between the Ouverture and the opera lies in the second theme, which is drawn from the Allegro section of Adolar's Aria No. 12, where he sings it to the words 'O Seligkeit dich faß' ich kaum' as he blissfully awaits the arrival of his beloved. On its quiet first appearance in the exposition (mm. 61–86), the theme presents a lyrical contrast to the energetic and boisterous first group, but it is later reinterpreted in the recapitulation (mm. 226–49) through more brilliant scoring, louder dynamics, and extension of its final cadence. Lastly, the puzzling Largo episode between the end of the exposition and the beginning of the development (mm. 129–43) stems from music associated throughout the opera with the supernatural presence of Adolar's deceased sister Emma. Like its first two appearances in the opera (Act I, scene iii and Act III, scene v) this music is endowed with a number of features that seem calculated to suggest an otherworldly ambience: its slow tempo and quiet dynamics; its scoring for flute, muted solo violins, and tremolando ripieni violins and violas; the absence of bass instruments; the chromatic voice leading; and even the choice of B as tonic. That this section was originally inspired by a plan to open the curtain for a 'Pantomimische Prolog-Szene' during the Ouverture is a point that we shall consider in the following discussions of sources. That the curtain in fact is not raised at this point in the final version of the opera poses issues for analysis and interpretation that will be addressed in Chapter X.

2.   ACT I, SCENE i

The story opens in the year AD 1110 in a large hall in the castle at Prémery of King Louis VI of France. In the Introduzione (No. 1, G major) the knights and ladies of the court celebrate the recent restoration of peace with a choral song ('Dem Frieden Heil') and a solemn dance, the 'Ernster Reigen'. In the recitative that follows the King asks one of his leading nobles, Adolar, the young Count of Nevers and Rethel, why he has thus far remained aloof from the celebration. Adolar replies that since his betrothed, Euryanthe of Savoy, is not present, he may not participate in the festivities. Moved by Adolar's plight, the King requests that the young knight-troubadour sing a song in praise of his beloved. Adolar takes up his zither and in the strophic Romanza No. 2 addressed to the gathering Adolar recounts his first meeting with her on the banks of the Loire, describing her beauty and fidelity (B-flat major). At the final cadence of the song the nobles burst into a brief chorus in praise of Adolar and Euryanthe that recalls the music of No. 1 (No. 3, G major).

In the subsequent recitative the principal dramatic conflict begins. Lysiart, Count of Forêt, who has uneasily observed the foregoing, steps forward to question Euryanthe's fidelity, thereby scandalizing the ladies of the court, who leave the hall. Emboldened by their retreat Lysiart wagers that he will be able to seduce Euryanthe. Adolar's acceptance of the wager triggers the final piece in scene i, the Scene und Chor No. 4 (E-flat major), which begins with Lysiart offering his lands as collateral for the wager. Heeding not the warnings of the King and the nobles, Adolar stakes all of his possessions on the virtue of his beloved. In the concluding section of the ensemble Adolar reaffirms his trust in Euryanthe and divine justice ('Ich bau' auf Gott und meine Euryanth'), while Lysiart pledges to bring back sufficient proof of his conquest and the King and his knights implore God to protect innocence.

The opening scene of *Euryanthe*, one of the most brilliant and effective sections of the opera, demonstrates certain traits that are important for this work and for Weber's conception of operatic dramaturgy. With the exception of the one-act *Singspiel Abu Hassan*, all of Weber's operas from *Silvana* (1810) to *Oberon* (1826) begin with a choral number that immediately establishes the atmosphere and milieu of the opera.[6] In *Euryanthe* the opening chorus introduces a poetic idea as well, fidelity

[6] In this regard Weber's alleged comments to J. C. Lobe about the opening scene of the *Freischütz* are interesting. In his 'Gespräche mit Weber', first published in *Fliegende Blätter für Musik*, vol. i (Leipzig, 1855), pp. 27–34 and 110–22, Lobe claims in his youth to have discussed a number of critical points about the *Freischütz* with the composer. At one point, according to Lobe, he asked Weber why he had struck the two opening scenes, given to the hermit and Agathe, from Kind's original libretto for the *Freischütz*, to which Weber is said to have replied: 'If a dramatic work has a specific geographical, historical and moral background that contributes in part to the motivation of the action, it has always proven a good maxim to transport the spectator immediately at the outset to this particular sphere, to which he should devote himself and in which he should believe . . .' Doubt has been cast on the authenticity of Lobe's account by Hans Schnoor, *Weber auf dem Welttheater. Ein Freischützbuch* (Dresden, 1943), p. 143, and more recently by Ludwig Finscher, 'Weber's *Freischütz*: Conceptions and Misconceptions', *PRMA* 109 (1984): 88–90, who sees it as the 'work of a brilliant music critic and writer from the middle of the century, but not the work of Weber'. Lobe himself explained in 1869 that the conversation had taken place at the inn Zum Erbprinzen in Weimar, where Weber had stayed on the way to Bad Ems in July 1825; see 'Der Meister und der Jünger', in *Consonanzen und Dissonanzen* (Leipzig, 1869), pp. 337–46 and also *MMW* ii. 606–7. A close assessment of the authenticity of Lobe's account is one of the most pressing needs of current Weber scholarship; we shall return to this article in future references, bearing in mind, however, that it must be used with a certain degree of caution and scepticism.

(*Treue*), that is of utmost importance for the opera. As in the respective Introductions to *Silvana* and the *Freischütz*, the chorus is immediately followed by a pantomimic or balletic action, which further enhances the sense of public gaiety as a foil to the more private concerns of the principal characters. Adolar's Romanza No. 2 represents a well-established type of piece in French and German opera during the early nineteenth century, a strophic piece with a narrative text. Like many such pieces it is addressed as a song directly to the other players on the stage, conveying important information about the background of the opera. Typical of the genre, the orchestration of this piece is rather elaborately worked out. In the first stanza pizzicato strings emulate the sound of the zither with which Adolar accompanies his song. The second stanza employs the warmer sound of the divided cellos, now bowed instead of plucked, and arco sixteenth-note patterns in all of the strings accompany the final stanza. Winton Dean has suggested that Weber may have modelled this piece on a number from one of Méhul's most ambitious *opéras-comiques*, *Ariodant* (Paris, 1799), whose second act contains a strophic-variation *romance*, also in B-flat major and also emulating the song of a bard to his harp.[7] The placement of the Romanza as the second piece in the opera reflects another convention that became commonplace in French and German opera in the first half of the nineteenth century, that is, the opening gambit of an introductory chorus followed by a strophic song.[8] Perhaps deriving from Grétry's very well-known *Richard cœur-de-Lion* (Paris, 1786), this pattern had been used by Weber already in the Introduction to *Freischütz*, where Kilian's strophic *Spottlied* immediately follows the opening chorus and the march of the peasants.

In fact one may extend the parallel between the respective openings of *Euryanthe* and the *Freischütz* one step further if one considers the relationship between the Terzett mit Chor No. 2 of the earlier work with the Scene und Chor No. 4 in *Euryanthe*. Both pieces are scored for three male soloists and chorus and are descendants of a type of piece first pioneered in French *opéra comique* of the later eighteenth century, the *morceau d'ensemble*.[9] Both fulfil similar dramatic functions, since

[7] Edward J. Dent, *The Rise of Romantic Opera*, ed. by Winton Dean (Cambridge, 1976), p. 86, n. 10. Méhul employs a real harp in the orchestra to suggest the bard's harp.

[8] For later examples of this convention see the start of *Robert le Diable* (1831), *Les Huguenots* (1836), and the *Flying Dutchman* (1841); even the start of *Tannhäuser* betrays vestiges of the convention.

[9] On the early history of this genre see the unpublished, but seminally important dissertation by M. Elizabeth C. Bartlet, 'Étienne Nicolas Méhul and Opera during the French Revolution, Consulate, and Empire: A Source, Archival and Stylistic Study', (Ph. D. dissertation, University of Chicago, 1982), pp. 823–44.

in each work the soloists consist of a youthful protagonist (tenor), an older authoritarian figure (bass), and a villain (bass) who eggs the hero on to potential catastrophe. The result is that the overall shape of the first scene of *Euryanthe* closely resembles that of the opening two scenes of *Freischütz*, a fact that does not prove surprising when one considers that Weber himself was primarily responsible for the large-scale structure of the start of the later work (Table 2).

TABLE 2. Opening scenes in *Der Freischütz* and *Euryanthe*.

Der Freischütz	Euryanthe
Introduction No.1	Introduzione No. 1
a. Ritornello & Chorus	*a*. Ritornello & Chorus
b. Pantomime: *Bauernmarsch*	*b*. Dance: 'Ernster Reigen'
	Recitative
c. Lied (Kilian): 2 strophes	Romanza No. 2 (Adolar): 3 strophes
	Chor No. 3 (reprise of No. 1*a*)
Spoken dialogue	Recitative
Terzett mit Chor No. 2 (Max, Caspar, Cuno)	*Scene und Chor* No. 4 (Adolar, Lysiart, King)

Where the opening scene of *Euryanthe* goes beyond the comparable section of its older sibling is its greater cohesiveness. Although divided in the autograph score into four numbers with intervening recitatives, the opening scene of the opera in reality functions as a single introductory unit, and was in fact conceived and designated as a single piece, an Introduzione, up to the time of composition.[10] One element of coherence is thematic recall, since No. 1 is quoted briefly in the pantomime that precedes No. 2 and later extensively in the chorus No. 3. A second factor that gives the opening scene a sense of unity is the relationship between the Ouverture and No. 4, which returns to the key of the Ouverture and also recalls one of its most important themes.

3.   ACT I, SCENES ii–v

The setting changes to Adolar's castle at Nevers. It is dusk, and Euryanthe is alone in a garden, contemplating the beauty of the twilight and

[10] That the first four numbers of the opera were in fact initially conceived as a single Introduzione is confirmed by various preliminary scenarios and librettos, as well as by Weber's Diary. See Chapter IV.

longing for reunion with Adolar in her Cavatina No. 5 (C major). In accordance with German practice of the early nineteenth century, this cavatina is a slow aria in a single movement with relatively little color-atura.[11] Agathe's Cavatina No. 12 in *Freischütz* conforms exactly to this type as well; moreover, like Agathe's cavatina, Euryanthe's makes conspi-cuous use of obbligato solo instruments. In the following recitative (I, iii), Euryanthe is joined by her supposed friend and confidante, Eglantine of Puiset, the daughter of the defeated rebel, Hugh of Puiset. Her entrance is marked by the first appearance of an orchestral motive that not only recurs throughout this scene but that also functions as a musical symbol for Eglantine, and more particularly her feigned friendship for Euryanthe, throughout the opera (see Ex. 1).

Ex. 1. Eglantine's motive (Act I, scene iii).

Eglantine inquires about the cause of Euryanthe's melancholy, and the latter replies that her only happiness lies with the distant Adolar. As she recalls her first encounter with him, the orchestra introduces a second motive of great importance for the opera as a whole, one that recurs, rhythmically transformed as the main theme of the love duet in the second act (No. 13) and in the Act III finale. Eglantine admits that Euryanthe has been very kind to her, but complains that she has never really been privy to Euryanthe's trust. For instance, she believes that Euryanthe is troubled by a dark secret and asks her to share it as a sign of love. Euryanthe at first refuses, thereby prompting Eglantine's impassioned outburst in the short Aria No. 6 (E minor), wherein she complains that Euryanthe has not returned her love.

---

[11] See the definitions of the cavatina given by C. D. F Schubart, *Ideen zu einer Ästhetik der Tonkunst* (Vienna, 1806), p. 358 and H. C. Koch, *Musikalisches Lexikon* (Frankfurt am Main, 1802), col. 308. On the development of the cavatina in Italy at the end of the eighteenth century see Helga Lühning, 'Die Cavatina in der italienischen Oper um 1800', in *Colloquium. 'Die stilistische Entwicklung der italienischen Musik zwischen 1770 und 1830 und ihre Beziehungen zum Norden' (Rom 1978)*, ed. Friedrich Lippmann, ([Cologne], 1982) [*Analecta musicologica* 21], pp. 333–69.

Overcome by Eglantine's protestation of love, Euryanthe reveals the secret that she has kept to herself up to now. Every night she prays in the crypt of Adolar's deceased sister Emma, whose ghost had appeared to her and Adolar as they prepared to take leave of one another on the last day of May. Accompanied by the slow, chromatic music previously heard in the Ouverture, Euryanthe relates the words spoken by the apparition in a section of recitative that Weber referred to in his Diary as the 'Vision' (B major/minor). Distressed by the death of her lover, Udo, Emma had committed suicide by drinking poison from a ring that is buried with her in the crypt. Because of her sin, however, she may not have eternal rest; she will wander endlessly in the afterlife until tears of innocence cleanse the fatal ring, and fidelity repays murder with rescue, or in the convoluted words of the original:

O weint um mich! nicht eh' kann Ruh' mir werden,	O weep for me! I shall not have rest
Bis diesen Ring aus dem ich Tod getrunken	until the ring from which I drank my death
Der Unschuld Thräne netzt im höchsten Leid,	is dampened by guiltless tears [shed] in greatest sorrow,
Und Treu' dem Mörder Rettung beut für Mord!	and fidelity offers rescue to the murderer in exchange for murder.

Upon completion of this narration, Euryanthe suddenly realizes that she has broken a sacred oath of secrecy that she had sworn to Adolar. This recognition initiates the Duetto No. 7 (A minor/A major), at the start of which Euryanthe senses that her revelation portends her own demise. Eglantine reassures her that her secret is safe and the duet concludes with the two women affirming their mutual trust and love. During the orchestral postlude Euryanthe leaves the stage, accompanied by Eglantine.

The latter immediately rushes back on stage alone (I, iv) and launches into her Scena ed aria No. 8 (E major), a bravura piece that reveals her evil intentions. Despite its title, the structure of this piece is indebted in only a limited degree to the conventional multi-movement Italian aria form of the time.[12] In the opening recitative ('Bethörte, die an meine Liebe glaubt') Eglantine gloats to the accompaniment of her recurring motive that she now has sufficient information to destroy Euryanthe. She plans to search Emma's crypt for evidence that will prove that Euryanthe has betrayed Adolar's secret, and by discrediting Euryanthe in this manner she briefly entertains the hope of winning Adolar, who once had spurned her love. In an extended arioso within the Scena

---

[12] See the discussion of No. 10 below, and the literature cited in n. 14.

('O! der Gedanke löst mich auf in Wonne') she rapturously contemplates future union with him. Returning to reality (recitative: 'Hinweg, wahnsinn'ge Hoffnung'), she recognizes, however, that happiness is impossible for her and that her only course of action is to make Adolar just as miserable as he had made her, a sentiment that she sums up in the bravura concluding movement of the aria ('Er konnte mich um sie verschmähn!'), which again makes extensive use of her basic motive as an accompanying figure.

As she begins to depart she is detained by the sound of trumpets that herald the arrival of Lysiart and his men (I, v) and that connect her aria to the first-act Finale No. 9. This piece comprises three movements, the first and last of which are substantially borrowed from earlier compositions by Weber. In the first choral movement (D major), the peasants of Adolar's domain exchange joyful greetings with Lysiart's entourage, while Eglantine brings Euryanthe back on stage (I, vi). In the second movement (D major and B-flat major) Lysiart greets Euryanthe with the news that he has been sent by the King to accompany her to the festivities at Prémery, while his knights quietly comment on the villainy of Lysiart's real purpose. The finale closes with a pastoral ensemble (D major) in which all of the soloists and chorus express their pleasure at the thought of Euryanthe's impending reunion with Adolar.

Standing back from the second half of Act I, we can again note certain features of broader critical and analytical interest. By this point one already recognizes that the plot is not especially clear. Many of the premises on which the action turns involve relationships and events that precede the start of the opera and that therefore must be related through narrations of various kinds. The third and fourth scenes of Act I reveal in rapid succession the most important background elements. First, at the start of the opera Emma's tragic fate is known only to Adolar and Euryanthe, and for reasons not explained in the libretto, Adolar has sworn Euryanthe to secrecy on this matter and attaches great importance to the maintenance of this secret. Second, Emma can be redeemed from her limbo, but only through the fulfilment of certain conditions that are posed in vague and puzzling terms. And third, Eglantine's real hatred for Euryanthe grows from a motive as old as humanity; rejected at some prior time by Adolar, Eglantine's unrequited love has turned to jealousy and a thirst for vengeance.

Musically, the second half of Act I is notable for several features. A certain degree of unity arises through frequent reference to Eglantine's motive throughout the third and fourth scenes of the act, whether quoted in the original form in the recitatives or transformed and worked into the accompaniments of No. 6 and No. 8. It is also important to note that the pitch–class E is strongly established as a referential tonic for

Eglantine in the course of the first act, for both of Eglantine's solo numbers are in an E tonality, and E minor is also implied at the moment when she first appears on stage. As we shall see, tonal associations of this sort play an important role in the musical organization of the opera. Finally, the scenic unit that constitutes the second half of Act I approximates a long-range crescendo in so far as the sequence of numbers entails progressive intensification of mood, orchestral sonority, effect, and complexity. The static and slow Cavatina No. 5, which establishes the new setting, yields in order to the faster solo number (No. 6), a two-part Duetto (No. 7), an extended bravura Scena ed aria with expanded brass complement (No. 8), and a large Finale with chorus and stage instruments (No. 9). The sense of *Steigerung* throughout the unit is also enhanced by a quickening of dramatic pace, since the kind of extended recitative that separates Nos. 5, 6, and 7 is curtailed between No. 7 and No. 8 and omitted altogether between No. 8 and No. 9.

4. ACT II. SCENES i–ii

The second act begins at night on the same setting with which Act I had closed. As a storm develops in the distance,[13] Lysiart sings his great Scena ed aria No. 10, the largest aria in the opera and one that is closely related to Rossinian archetypes, with, of course, certain deviations that reflect Weber's distance from the Italian master.[14] The turbulent opening ritornello (Allegro con fuoco, C minor) and recitative ('Wo berg' ich mich? Wo fänd ich Fassung wieder?') express Lysiart's despair over the knowledge that Euryanthe will never succumb to his amorous advances. In the second, *cantabile* section (Andante con moto, G major) he attempts to calm his own passions, for he recognizes that her fidelity and innocence are all that Adolar had boasted; that, in contradistinction to Rossini's normal practice, this slow movement is not in the tonic key of the entire Scena ed aria is significant, for in this manner Weber underscores tonally Lysiart's change of mood. The *tempo di mezzo*, poetically marked by a change of versification at the twelfth line, is here treated with considerable ingenuity as the poem and music together make a gradual transition away from the resigned mood of the *cantabile* to the bloodthirsty mood of the cabaletta. The start of the *tempo di*

---

[13] A storm is not specified in the published score, but a manuscript libretto for the Viennese première that was proofed by Weber and Chezy (Vienna, Österreichische Nationalbibliothek, S. m. 32304) provides annotations for 'distant thunder' during Lysiart's opening monologue and loud thunder and lightning at the end of the Scena ed aria.

[14] On the archetypal aria form of the 'Code Rossini' see Julian Budden, *The Operas of Verdi*, vol. i (London, 1973), pp. 13–17, and Harold S. Powers, '"La solita forma" and "The Uses of Convention"', *Acta musicologica* 59 (1987): 68–9.

mezzo, Lysiart's contemplation of the worthlessness of life without Euryanthe ('Was soll mir ferner Gut und Land'), is set as a modulatory arioso—with gestural traits reminiscent of recitative—in the same tempo and triple metre as the preceding *cantabile*, but as his thoughts turn to revenge against Adolar ('Und er sollte leben?') the music shifts into a faster tempo for a section of more impassioned recitative. The intensification of emotion throughout the latter part of this recitative culminates in Lysiart's resolution to devote himself to vengeance ('So weih' ich mich den Rachgewalten'), a quatrain of lyric poetry set in triple metre (Andante con moto, C minor) that may be heard either as the last segment of the *tempo di mezzo* or as an 'extra' movement between the archetypal *tempo di mezzo* and cabaletta. Also indicative of Weber's independence from the Italian model, the last movement, Lysiart's bravura vow of revenge against Adolar (Vivace feroce, C minor), does not entail the literal repetition customarily found in the cabalettas of Rossini and his successors; instead, the two statements of the text are treated, somewhat unusually even for Weber, in the manner of a binary form with features of the sonata principle.

Eglantine emerges from Emma's crypt, unaware that Lysiart quietly observes all of her words and actions (II, ii). She has found the fatal ring and plans to use it as proof that Euryanthe has betrayed Adolar. As a flash of lightning illuminates the scene, Lysiart discloses himself and offers to aid her quest for vengeance and to make her the mistress of all of Adolar's lands. In the Duetto No. 11 (B major) the villains make their pact. Lysiart promises to be Eglantine's avenger and spouse, and together they call upon the dark night to be their accomplice in the evil deed that they contemplate.

5.   ACT II, SCENE iii–iv

A change of scenery shifts the action to the large hall in the palace at Prémery, where Adolar impatiently awaits the arrival of Euryanthe in his Aria No. 12 (A-flat major), a two-movement aria in the tradition of the late eighteenth-century *rondò*. Euryanthe suddenly appears (II, iv) and rushes into Adolar's arms during a brief orchestral transition that links the aria to the Duetto No. 13 (C major) in which the two lovers express their unbridled joy at reunion after a painful separation.

Of interest at the beginning of the second act are the ways in which details of staging and music are co-ordinated with the plot to create the so-called *Totaleffekt* that Weber viewed as a principal goal of German opera.[15] The change of scenery between No. 11 and No. 12 symbolically

---

[15] See below, Chapter III, section 3.

separates the world of evil from that of virtue, and important visual and musical elements underscore the spiritual gulf that separates the two pairs of lovers. The bright lighting of the interior of the palace contrasts markedly with the stormy darkness that surrounds the two villains at the close of No. 11. Orchestration is calculated to maximize the contrast between the two numbers. To suggest a 'dark' atmosphere commensurate with the villainy of the two conspirators, the Duetto No. 11 is scored for strings, two oboes, four horns, three trombones, and timpani, thereby omitting flutes, clarinets, and bassoons as well as the bright trumpets. In contradistinction, Adolar's idyllic and hopeful Aria No. 12 begins with a lengthy ritornello that employs only those woodwind instruments that had not been used in the duet (two flutes, two clarinets, two bassoons) in order to effect the greatest possible contrast of sonority. The juxtaposition of 'villainous' and 'virtuous' sonorities coincides with the shift from a strongly sharp key (B major) to a tonality with many flats (A-flat major); as we shall later see in Chapter VII, the choice of keys is consonant with the larger patterns of tonal symbolism at work in the opera.

6.   ACT II, SCENE V

The joyful reunion of Adolar and Euryanthe provides the foil for the catastrophe that finally unfolds in the Finale No. 14. In accordance with operatic practices at the beginning of the nineteenth century, this piece is the longest and most complicated number in the opera, a multi-movement composition that traces the apparent triumph of treachery over innocence. As Lysiart's Scena ed aria may be related to Italian conventions, so too the overall structure of the finale exhibits many points of contact with the Rossinian central finale, which, as described by Philip Gossett, normally entails four basic sections: (1) a dramatically active or 'kinetic' movement; (2) a Largo movement for contemplative reaction to the foregoing; (3) a second kinetic movement; and (4) a fast concluding movement, the *stretta*, that again is a basically static response to the developments of the third movement.[16] In a number of Italian works this scheme is expanded to a five-part form through an introductory ensemble or chorus of basically static content that sets the stage for the first 'kinetic' movement,[17] and it is this five-part scheme with opening chorus that provides the backbone for the Act II Finale in *Euryanthe*, which follows the basic paradigm: stasis (chorus)–action–

[16] Philip Gossett, 'The "Candeur virginale" of *Tancredi*', *MT* 112 (1971): 327. See also Powers, op. cit. n. 14 above, 68–69, 73.

[17] For example, the first-act finales to *Tancredi* and *Semiramide* both begin with choral movements.

stasis (slow ensemble)–action–stasis (chorus). The static segments are essentially self-contained pieces, all cast in ternary form. Nevertheless, as in Lysiart's Scena ed aria there are a number of divergences from the Italian archetype. For one thing, the active movements are expanded and articulated into sub-movements, which employ a variety of techniques ranging from recitative to arioso to fully extended composition, and as in Lysiart's Scena ed aria an extra movement is added to the archetype immediately before the final chorus (see Table 3).

TABLE 3: The structure of the Act II Finale

Mode	Section	Description	Key
Static	1*a*	Allegro moderato. 9/8 (mm. 1-48) (Chorus: The knights greet Euryanthe)	F major
	1*b*	[Allegro moderato]. 3/4 (mm. 49–71) (Arioso: The King and Euryanthe exchange pleasantries)	F major
Active	2*a*	Largo; Poco più moto. C (mm. 72–92) (Arioso: Lysiart comes forward to claim victory)	D♭ major
	2*b*	Allegro. C (mm. 93–320) (Ensemble: Adolar disputes Lysiart's claim; Lysiart supplies the proof)	D♭ major
Static	3	Larghetto. 3/4 (mm. 321–70) (Ensemble: Euryanthe prays for Divine help; others comment)	A major
Active	4	Con fierezza. C (mm. 371–89) (Recitative and arioso: The King bestows Adolar's lands on Lysiart)	A minor
Static	5	Allegro ma non troppo. C (mm. 390–488) (Ensemble: Adolar summons Euryanthe to follow; the vassals express their wish to accompany Adolar)	C major
Static	6	Con tutto fuoco ed energia. C (mm. 489–556) (Chorus: All condemn Euryanthe)	F minor

In the introductory chorus the knights enter the hall and greet Euryanthe with a song of praise (Section 1*a*: F major). Exchanging pleasantries with the King (Section 1*b*: F major) she notes with some concern that no women are present. Lysiart boldly steps forward and shocks everyone by claiming Adolar's lands as his prize (Section 2*a*: D-flat major), an announcement that triggers the long 'kinetic' movement (Section 2*b*: D-flat major). To counter Adolar's and Euryanthe's protestations that he is lying, Lysiart produces Emma's ring and clinches his claim by alluding to Emma's secret. When Euryanthe truthfully admits that she did break her oath by divulging the secret (without, however, explaining that she had revealed it only to Eglantine) Adolar is crushed and concedes defeat. This complex movement, essentially through-composed, is unified primarily by an energetic eighth-note figure in the orchestra that seems to stand for the conflict between Adolar and Lysiart; significantly, the motive disappears at the moment when Adolar concedes defeat. During the course of this movement two melodies are also quoted from earlier in the opera. When, early in the section Adolar comes to Euryanthe's defence ('Komm an mein Herz'), he reiterates the theme that in No. 4 had symbolized his complete trust in Euryanthe's fidelity. Later, Lysiart's claim to have conquered Euryanthe's affections ('Bewundernswürdig ist's gelungen') is accompanied by motivic reference to the Eglantine motive, a hint by the omniscient orchestra at the true link between Lysiart and Euryanthe.[18]

At the end of the kinetic section all of the assembled knights unite to condemn poor Euryanthe, who in turn inaugurates the slow, contemplative ensemble with a prayer for divine assistance (Section 3: A major) while the other soloists and the chorus ponder the tragic situation from their respective points of view. In the subsequent action (Section 4: A minor), the King bestows Adolar's lands on Lysiart, and the disconsolate Adolar decides to withdraw from society and go into the wilderness with Euryanthe (Section 5: C major). As they depart the assembly unites in the final chorus to condemn Euryanthe one last time in extremely harsh terms (Section 6: F minor).

Certain factors serve to weld the finale into a single number. Chief among these is the principle of tonal closure that is commonly observed in the multi-movement finales of the late eighteenth and early nineteenth centuries; however, the change of mode from F major at the start to F minor in the final chorus is an obvious means of signalling the unfortu-

---

[18] A subtle allusion to the *Vision* may also be heard in this movement. In Act I the narration of Emma's plight is prefaced by an E-flat minor triad; in the Act II Finale E-flat minor is again heard as Lysiart begins to divulge the spectral vision of Emma to the assembled court ('In heller Mondennacht am letzten Mai . . .'); it is only Adolar's intervention at this point with a diminished-seventh chord ('Vollende nicht!') that keeps Lysiart from continuing on to B major with an account of the *Vision*.

nate reversal in the fates of the principal characters. A fanfare motive—a falling octave scored for woodwinds and brass—recurs at certain ceremonial points in the number: (1) when Lysiart addresses the King to offer proof of victory at the beginning of Section 2a; (2) when Lysiart demands that the King confer upon him Adolar's lands at the start of Section 4; and (3) when the King bestows the new fiefs upon Lysiart at the end of the same section.[19] Finally, a poetic-musical refrain first sung by the chorus of knights at the end of Section 2b as their commentary on Euryanthe's alleged infidelity recurs throughout Sections 3 and 5:

Ha! die Verrätherin!	Ha! the betrayer!
O Unthat gräßlichste von Allen	O misdeed most horrible of all
Die jemals auf der Welt erhört!	that ever was seen upon earth!
Der Treue Bündniß frech zerstört,	The bonds of fidelity impiously destroyed
Von Himmelshöhn in Staub gefallen!	and fallen from heavenly heights into the dust!

Without doubt the second-act finale has always been the most controversial piece in the opera, both from dramatic and musical perspectives. We shall deal with the criticisms of the music when we attempt to understand Weber's style and operatic ideal, but the problems of the libretto should be obvious from this synopsis. Critics of the libretto have repeatedly wondered (and with good cause) about Euryanthe's failure to refute Lysiart's charge. Common sense would seem to dictate that she could easily clarify the matter by simply confessing that she had revealed the secret to Eglantine, who must have passed it on to Lysiart. The evidence that Lysiart adduces as proof of his conquest—his knowledge of the secret—hardly seems compelling documentation of Euryanthe's alleged infidelity; moreover, Adolar's sudden abandonment of Euryanthe and his subsequent inhumanly severe treatment of her seems in no way commensurate with the quality of the evidence. All of these problems turn on a single issue, the importance that Adolar and Euryanthe both attach to the secret of Emma's appearance, an issue that frankly is not adequately stressed in the final version of the libretto.

[19] The descending octave leap in the male chorus at the end of Section 5 may be heard as another reference to this motivic refrain. Interestingly, the composition draft for *Euryanthe* shows that Weber originally intended to repeat the ceremonial falling octave at the beginning of the last movement, perhaps to enhance further the sense of coherence. That he eliminated it in the final version can probably be attributed to the fact that at this point in the finale there is no ceremonial action for it to announce; Adolar and Euryanthe depart the hall in quite unceremonious fashion.

7. ACT III, SCENE i

The third act again opens at night in a wildly romantic setting, a desolate moonlit mountainous glen. During the orchestral ritornello (D minor) Adolar, dressed in black armour and carrying a large sword, slowly descends a precipice and pauses to meditate. An exhausted Euryanthe follows, and remaining atop the cliff she asks permission to rest after such an arduous journey (recitative: 'Hier weilest du? hier darf ich ruh'n?'). In a measured arioso Adolar announces that he has chosen this secluded spot as the site for her execution (C minor: 'Dies ist der Ort, so schaurig öd' und still'). Her assurances of fidelity fall on deaf ears, and in the Duetto No. 15 (A major/A minor) Adolar contrasts his former happiness in Euryanthe's love with his present sense of betrayal and his resolve to punish the faithless woman. She maintains her innocence but prepares to die with a benediction for him upon her lips.

As the Duetto ends Euryanthe suddenly spies a giant snake moving towards Adolar, and she hurries down the cliff to shield him from it with her own body. Pushing her aside, he goes off to fight the snake himself (recitative: E-flat major, 'Mit Gott will ich den Kampf besteh'n!'), and she ascends the cliff once again to witness the battle. Calling upon heaven to protect him, Euryanthe describes the deadly struggle in No. 16, a piece without title in Weber's autograph (B major); with his victory she rejoices. Adolar returns from the combat, and Euryanthe is now prepared to die (recitative: 'Nun laß mich sterben!'), but he has now changed his mind. Because she had offered to sacrifice herself to protect him, he now feels that he cannot execute her. He therefore commends her to God's protection, and the scene ends with an extended orchestral ritornello (E-flat major), during which he departs, abandoning her to her fate.

Fluidity of construction, already observed in many examples in the first two acts, becomes one of the dominant characteristics of Act III. Distinctions between recitative and more lyrical vocal styles become less sharp, and numbers flow into one another with few opportunities for complete stops. Thus the opening part of the scene frequently shifts between recitative and measured arioso styles, and a definitive conclusion for the Duetto No. 15 is averted by a deceptive cadence, corresponding to Euryanthe's sudden perception of the snake, that initiates a transition in arioso style to No. 16.

8. ACT III, SCENES ii–iii

Left alone, Euryanthe ponders her fate in the Scena e cavatina No. 17 (G minor/G major). Now homeless, she decides to die on the spot where Adolar has left her, so that one day, when he returns to the place, the willows and flowers will whisper to him that she was indeed faithful. As day begins to break,[20] the echoing sounds of horn calls are heard offstage, and in the Hunters' Chorus No. 18, a strophic song in praise of the joys of the hunt, the royal hunting party emerges from the forest in pursuit of game (III, iii). The King and his retinue see the slain snake and a weeping woman whom, to their surprise, they recognize as Euryanthe. In the Duetto con coro No. 19 (C minor) Euryanthe requests to be left alone, but the King asks her to come with him to atone for her guilt, which she denies by explaining Eglantine's treachery (with reference to Eglantine's motive in the orchestra). Wishing to discover the truth of the matter, the King entices Euryanthe to return with him by holding out the promise of reunion with Adolar, should she in fact prove innocent. Excited by the prospect, Euryanthe bursts into the Aria con coro No. 20 (C major) to hasten her return to Adolar. Overcome by exhaustion and the vast emotional swing that she has undergone, however, she collapses at the end of the aria; fearing her to be dead, the hunters sorrowfully carry the inanimate body from the scene to the now sombre sound of their horns (C minor).

The opera's tendency to treat what is nominally a pair of numbers as a single unit can be observed most conspicuously in the coupling of No. 19 and No. 20, which share a common tonal centre (C). Continuity between the numbers is enhanced by the fact that No. 19 does not close in the tonic but rather ends with a long dominant pedal-point that resolves at the start of No. 20. The C-minor conclusion of No. 20 also looks back to the start of No. 19. As is often the case in *Euryanthe*, this complex progresses from a slower tempo to a faster one, and from a reduced orchestral complement (pairs of woodwinds, a pair of horns, and strings) to a fuller one that adds trumpets, timpani, and three trombones.

9. ACT III, SCENES iv–vi

The setting returns to Adolar's former castle at Nevers, in front of which a number of countryfolk prepare for a wedding (Scene und Chor No. 21). Bertha, one of the women, leads the peasants in a strophic song to celebrate the start of May and the fidelity of the two lovers (A major). An unknown knight with lowered visor interrupts the song to complain that there is no fidelity in the world (A minor). It is of course Adolar, who has returned to his native land. Recognizing their former master,

---

[20] This important scenic effect, specified in the Viennese manuscript libretto cited in n. 13 above ('Ritornell. Morgenröthe steigt empor.') and various preliminary drafts for the libretto, is not indicated in the printed score.

the peasants plead with him to liberate his lands from the tyranny of their present rulers. Adolar is surprised to learn of Eglantine's union with Lysiart and begins to suspect that there may have been foul play. Encouraged by his former subjects, Adolar prays for divine assistance against the forces of evil (No. 22: B-flat major).

An offstage fanfare announces the approaching wedding procession of Eglantine and Lysiart (Hochzeitmarsch No. 23: D major). As Adolar and the peasants observe the procession, Eglantine's demeanour betrays signs of great stress. Suddenly she interrupts the procession (recitative: 'Ich kann nicht weiter'). As the orchestra recalls the music that had accompanied Euryanthe's narration about Emma, Eglantine herself is haunted by a vision of the angry ghost demanding the return of the fatal ring. In her delirium she turns to Lysiart to reassure him that their secret is still safe. As the crowd reacts to this hysteria with astonishment, Adolar realizes that there indeed had been treachery. He reveals himself to the villains and threatens them with retribution, whereupon Lysiart orders the knights to seize the interloper. However, the vassals refuse to arrest their beloved former master and instead turn against Lysiart, who prepares to do battle with Adolar (Duetto con coro No. 24, D major).

The sudden arrival of the King and his retinue interrupts the altercation between Adolar and Lysiart and marks the start of the Finale No. 25. Like its counterpart in Act II, the third-act finale is a complex, multi-movement composition that details a number of actions that wind down the opera; in contradistinction to the earlier finales, however, the movements of No. 25 are relatively short and tend not to be self-contained compositions. First, the King calls for a halt to the violence, since he wishes to adjudicate the matter himself (Section 1: 'Laßt ruh'n das Schwert!'). Adolar complains to the King that everyone had been deceived (Section 2: E-flat major to A-flat minor); the King counsels him to steel himself, since Euryanthe has passed away. Upon hearing this news, Eglantine bursts forth with wild exultation (Section 3: E major, 'Triumph! gerochen ist meine Schmach!'), and she taunts Adolar for having sent an innocent woman to death. In the process she reveals her role in the conspiracy and the motivation behind it. Nervously, Lysiart attempts to silence her, but she scornfully replies that she has no more use for him, since he was but a tool in her plan for revenge against Adolar. Outraged, Lysiart stabs her to death. The King orders Lysiart's execution, but Adolar requests that he be set free, since he feels himself to have been the most culpable in the betrayal of Euryanthe (Section 4: C minor, 'Nein! gebt ihn frei!'). Nevertheless, Lysiart is led away, presumably to his death, as Adolar sinks in deep remorse. The offstage horns sound once again (Section 5: E-flat major), and the hunters rejoice that Euryanthe is alive after all. Euryanthe appears, carried by the hunters, and Adolar rushes to her. As the King and subjects look on, the two lovers reiterate the pledge of eternal devotion with which they had greeted each other in the second act (Section 6: C major, 'Hin nimm die Seele mein'). Following their embrace, Adolar mystically perceives that Emma has been freed from the curse and that she and Udo are now reunited in heaven (Section 7: C major, 'Ich ahne Emma! Selig ist sie jetzt'). The opera ends with a general chorus celebrating the triumph of virtue and fidelity over evil and the union of Adolar and Euryanthe (Section 8: E-flat major, 'Nun feiert hoch in vollen Jubeltönen').

Seen as a whole, the concluding scenes of *Euryanthe* again demonstrate the fluidity of construction observed in the opening scenes of the third act, but now to an even greater degree. For one thing, the size and relative weight of the individual numbers play an important role in the forward momentum of the scenes. Unlike earlier sections of the opera, which frequently comprise substantial multi-movement numbers, scenes iv–v of Act III contain only short single-movement numbers (Nos. 21–24), none of which significantly delays the unfolding of plot. More importantly, the musical pieces in the closing scene make a special point of avoiding closure to drive the action forward, as none of the last five pieces is allowed to come to a full stop before the final curtain. As in earlier instances within the opera, such continuity is prompted by dramatic interruptions and surprises. The expected final A-major cadence at the end of the third stanza of the May Song in No. 21 is interrupted by the sudden reappearance of the distraught Adolar in A minor. The third scale degree in the final cadence of No. 22, D, is reinterpreted as a new tonic by the stage trumpets that announce the approach of the wedding procession of Lysiart and Eglantine in No. 23. Eglantine's delirious vision of an angry Emma interrupts the wedding procession and thus motivates the deceptive cadence to the relative minor, B minor, at the conclusion of the Hochzeitmarsch. The abrupt entrance of the King at the height of the confrontation between Lysiart and Adolar is harmonically underscored by a violent wrench from the D-major cadence of No. 24 to a C-minor triad at the start of No. 25.

The blurring of stylistic distinctions also contributes to the fluidity of the final scenes. The only passages actually designated as recitative in the concluding scenes occur in Eglantine's delirium between Nos. 23 and 24. Even here the boundaries between recitative and measured song are greatly obscured, since the style of singing and the complexity of the orchestral accompaniment transcend the traditional norms for accompanied recitative, and the passages of recitative constantly alternate with passages in arioso style. Weber's use of arioso through the final scenes as a substitution for recitative is particularly noteworthy, in that it allows him to compose blocks of dialogue, such as the dialogue between Bertha and Adolar (scene iv) in a style that approximates that of the surrounding numbers. Hence, towards the end of the opera the dichotomy between number and recitative is smoothed out into a more consistent style.

Certain other details of the final scenes deserve special attention. The use of the chorus as an active participant in the drama is particularly conspicuous throughout these scenes, either as a commentator on events, or as an independent interlocutor, as in the scene following No. 21, in which the chorus as a whole attempts to convince Adolar of Euryanthe's innocence. Doubtless it was precisely scenes such as this that Weber had in mind when, three months before the long-delayed first Berlin performance of the opera, he wrote to the intendant of Berlin theatres, Count Carl von Brühl, requesting that he start the choral rehearsals as soon as possible, because 'the choruses in this opera are throughout so essentially participatory, as perhaps in no other opera, and must be quite securely memorized if they [the chorus] are to be effective as a personage in the play [*mitspielende Person*]'.[21]

Musical recall also plays an extremely important role in the structure of the final scenes. The music associated with Emma's ghost recurs during Eglantine's delirium in its original B tonality (although unlike its appearance in Act I, scene iii it now begins with a B-minor triad instead of a B-major triad, perhaps to suggest the more sinister context) and with its characteristic scoring. The concluding sections of the finale present a complex of musical recall. Euryanthe's awakening offstage elicits a brief allusion to the hunting fanfares previously heard in No. 18 in the same key as before, E-flat major. The following reunion of Adolar and Euryanthe recalls slightly modified versions of the music originally heard at the first reunion of the two lovers in the second act, the transition between Nos. 12 and 13, and the Duetto proper. Finally, Adolar's premonition of Emma's redemption and reunion with Udo is accompanied by a thoroughgoing transformation of the *Vision*, signifying her attainment of peace in the afterlife, as the original chromatic version is reinterpreted by a tonal shift to a purely diatonic C major and by a number of changes in the orchestration that evidently are intended to make

---

[21] Letter to Brühl of 5 Sept. 1825 in *Brühl-Briefe*, p. 46. The Berlin première took place on 23 Dec. 1825. Thirteen of the twenty-five pieces in *Euryanthe* involve the chorus in one way or another.

it sound less sinister or agitated: eight muted solo violins instead of the original four—a doubling perhaps symbolic of the union of Emma and Udo?—are now accompanied by violas that no longer employ the agitated and spooky tremolo.

III. Perspectives on Euryanthe

An essential feature of Western art and literature is that certain canonical works are constantly reinterpreted by succeeding generations in the light of ever-changing cultural and intellectual climates. One thing that characterizes great art in fact is its ability to strike different chords in men of different epochs and adapt to the new layers of meaning imposed upon it by successive eras. Yet, the historically orientated critic feels a certain responsibility to build bridges between his own present-day sensibilities and those of the time in which and for which a work was originally conceived, thereby enriching his own understanding of the work and allowing it to act as a conduit to the past. As a work that lies outside the canonical repertory of Western music, *Euryanthe* probably holds little meaning for audiences of the later twentieth century, and yet as a major cultural artifact of a bygone era it too offers a valuable pathway to the past. Thus, before embarking on a close examination of the surviving sources for the genesis of the opera, let us consider three broad topics that round out our introduction to the time, place, personalities, and sensibilities that originally produced and received the opera; these issues will then condition much of the approach in the remainder of the present study.

I. EURYANTHE AS A 'GRAND ROMANTIC OPERA'

One of the central issues that must be addressed in any study of *Euryanthe* is the fact that it eschews spoken dialogue in favour of orchestrally accompanied recitative and arioso as the connective tissue between the set pieces. It is the only opera by Weber so constructed, and it is indeed one of relatively few German operas before Wagner to employ a continuous musical setting. As writers have pointed out, the means by which this continuity is achieved entail a number of innovations in the treatment of recitative and scenic construction,[1] but equally significant is the fact that *Euryanthe* represented a new kind of through-composed opera, in effect a new genre. We may begin to understand this essential novelty by considering the composer's own designation for the opera. In sources

[1] For instance, see Anna Amalie Abert, 'Webers "Euryanthe" und Spohrs "Jessonda" als große Opern', in *Festschrift für Walter Wiora*, ed. Christoph-Hellmut Mahling (Kassel, 1967), pp. 435–40.

that have some claim to authenticity one encounters various descriptions of the work. Certain sources, notably two librettos associated with the first Viennese production—the first printed libretto and a manuscript libretto proofed by Weber himself[2]—call the work a 'romantische Oper', while several of the draft librettos that we shall discuss in Part II describe it as a 'große historisch-romantische Oper'. Weber's autograph score lacks any designation at all, and in his correspondence he informally referred to the work simply as a 'große Oper' ('grand opera'). However, 'official' sources that are demonstrably close to the composer, including the Steiner piano-vocal score prepared by Weber himself and manuscript copies of the score prepared in Dresden under his supervision for distribution to other German theatres,[3] designate the opera 'eine große romantische Oper', that is, a 'grand romantic opera'.

It is this last designation that best reflects one of the fundamental novelties of the work, the commixture of two genres, 'grand opera' and 'romantic opera', that for the most part had previously been kept apart because of their particular stylistic and structural idiosyncracies. Of course, this mixture later became commonplace, especially in the so-called 'French Grand Operas' of the July Monarchy and Second Empire,[4] but, as Carl Dahlhaus points out, at the time of *Euryanthe* a strong sense of generic proprieties still obtained, with the result that not all subject matters and not all types of pieces were considered appropriate to all genres of lyric theatre.[5] To understand this phenomenon, we may turn first to Weber's own insightful discussion of the stylistic principles of 'grand opera' in an appreciation of *Der Wettkampf zu Olympia*, a 'grand opera' by the Bavarian composer Johann Nepomuk von Poissl. Written in 1820 to introduce the work to Dresden audiences, this essay is an important barometer of Weber's sense of stylistic distinctions and current operatic tendencies at a time when he was first showing

---

[2] See Chapter II, note 13.

[3] Two such sources, both signed by Weber, are: (1) Dresden, Sächsische Landesbibliothek, Mus. 4689-F-38a, a score prepared for use by the Nationaltheater at Frankfurt am Main; and (2) Bremen, Universitätsbibliothek, Mus. ms. 223, a score prepared for the Gesangverein of C. Grabau in Bremen. This latter source is *not* the autograph score, as claimed by Wolfgang Sandner, in *Die Klarinette bei Carl Maria von Weber* (Wiesbaden, 1971), p. 266.

[4] On this point see Karin Pendle, *Eugène Scribe and French Opera of the Nineteenth Century* (Ann Arbor, Mich., 1979), a summary of which is provided in 'Eugène Scribe and French Opera of the Nineteenth Century', *MQ* 57 (1971): 535–61. See also Heinz Becker, 'Die historische Bedeutung der Grand Opéra', in *Beiträge zur Geschichte der Musikanschauung im 19. Jahrhundert* (Regensburg, 1965), pp. 151–9.

[5] Carl Dahlhaus, *Die Musik des 19. Jahrhunderts* (Wiesbaden, 1980), p. 59.

interest in writing such an opera himself[6] and is therefore crucial to any assessment of his aims in *Euryanthe*.

There has been a great deal of controversy about the exact nature of the so-called grand opera, and the basic principles that underlie it have never been ascertained. I content myself therefore only to cite the meaning of the adjective 'grand' that at present is tacitly accepted and understood, namely, an opera in which the musical numbers are connected by continuous accompanied recitative, and in which consequently music holds court as mistress, surrounded by all of her crown servants who are set into uninterrupted activity.

With this definition is also associated the idea that in the choice of subject matter only the grandiose may be employed. Generally, grandeur of this kind is understood to mean only that which can be borrowed from the ancient classical times of the Greeks and Romans. These concepts are not only related to the basic principles of French tragedy, they are in fact directly derived from them, since to the best of my knowledge, the French are the inventors of this grand opera, which Gluck has brought to a level that to the present time remains unattained.

We in Germany do not have very many original works that belong to this class of opera, and the spirit of the times that especially now inclines toward the Romantic will make the proliferation of such works increasingly difficult. Apart from the splendidly conceived *Salem* and *Cyrus* of Herr von Mosel in Vienna and a few other essays in the genre, it is Herr von Poissl who has dedicated himself to the genre and won applause and recognition with several successful works.[7]

The implications of these comments for Weber's understanding of operatic genres are clear. First, Weber assesses the primary attribute of 'grand opera' to be a compositional feature, the fact of continuous orchestral accompaniment (through-composition) for the entire opera, which therefore separates a 'grand opera' from the types of opera that use either spoken dialogue (*opéra comique* and traditional German opera) or so-called 'simple recitative' accompanied only by the continuo instruments[8] (*opera buffa* and Italian *opera seria* before Rossini's *Elisabetta regina d'Inghilterra*) as the connective tissue between lyric pieces. Second, Weber describes certain stylistic assumptions for grand opera—in particular, its association with subject matters derived from Greco-Roman antiquity and French neo-classical tragedy—and implies that these are not in tune with the 'romantic' *Zeitgeist* of his own day, which partially explains why there are relatively few such works in Germany.

---

[6] See Weber's letter of 29 Jan. 1820 to Treitschke, cited above in Chapter I.

[7] *Sämtliche Schriften von Carl Maria von Weber*, ed. by Georg Kaiser (Berlin and Leipzig, 1908), pp. 310–11 (hereafter referred to as *Sämtliche Schriften*). The article first appeared in the Dresden *Abendzeitung* on 16 Mar. 1820.

[8] On the term 'simple recitative' see Thomas Bauman, 'Benda, the Germans and Simple Recitative', *JAMS* 34 (1981): 119–31.

Weber's brief discussion of 'grand opera' opens up vistas that are extremely important for an understanding of *Euryanthe*. For one thing, his assertion that 'grand operas' were normally based on subjects from classical antiquity is for the most part confirmed by the repertoire of his day, since the relatively few German grand operas of the era tended in fact to draw on a rather restricted range of neo-classical and biblical subject matters. Poissl's *Athalia* (Munich, 1814), the most successful German recitative opera in the decade before *Euryanthe* and Spohr's *Jessonda*, was based on a biblical play by Racine; I. F. Mosel's *Salem* (Vienna, 1813), a far less popular work, attempted to disguise its origins in Voltaire's *Olympie* by changing the names of the characters and moving the setting from the empire of Alexander the Great to ancient Persia.[9] The text of Mosel's second recitative opera, *Cyrus und Astyages* (Vienna, 1818), was an adaptation of Metastasio's *Ciro riconosciuto*. Poissl, frustrated by his inability to find adequate librettos for his operas (a very common problem in early nineteenth-century Germany), made his own adaptations of Metastasian originals for three grand operas: *Der Wettkampf zu Olympie* (Munich, 1815), *Nittetis* (Darmstadt, 1817), and *Issipile* (composed 1818, unperformed).

Beyond the basic issue of subject matter, however, Weber's comments direct us to further features of the traditional grand opera. According to Weber grand operas exemplify 'only the grandiose', by which he probably meant that such works usually were entirely serious and exalted in tone, a fact that is emphasized in Mosel's opera treatise, basically an attempt to codify the principles of Gluck's grand operas, which states unequivocally that only a 'simple tragic or heroic action' would be suitable for the through-composed opera.[10] In contrast, practically all of the genres that mixed spoken dialogue with musical pieces employ sentimental and/or comic elements as a foil to the more serious main plot. Simply put, characters like Marzelline and Jacquino in *Fidelio* or Kilian and Ännchen in *Freischütz* would have no place in a grand opera of the early nineteenth century. An important structural distinction, not discussed by Weber, also separated 'grand opera' from other German operatic genres, including the so-called 'romantic opera'. Because it grew out of eighteenth-century genres that employed spoken dialogue, early romantic opera made extensive use of the strophic song forms, whether they be called 'Lied', 'Romanze', or even 'Aria'. Such strophic genres, traditionally associated with the sentimental, comic, or folk elements, evidently were not deemed serious enough for the heroic and elevated grand opera; again, according to Mosel, the character of such a work

[9] This fact was noted by the anonymous reviewer of the work in *AmZ* 15 (1813), col. 367.

[10] I. F. Mosel, *Versuch einer Aesthetik des dramatischen Tonsatzes* (Vienna, 1813), p. 12.

was that 'one should expect no *Lieder* in an "opera"'.[11] In the four most important works of this type by Mosel and Poissl, all known by Weber, there is only one strophic number at all, the Act II Romanze for the child Joas-Eliakin in Poissl's *Athalia*, a number probably inspired by the two *romances* in another, much more famous biblical work, Méhul's *opéra comique Joseph*.[12] In this respect, German practice paralleled that of early nineteenth-century France, where one is also hard pressed to find strophic *couplets* and *romances* in works performed at the Académie royale de musique. The mixing of styles and genres characteristic of the mainstream of German opera with spoken dialogue—*Singspiel*, *heroisch-komische Oper*, *romantische Oper*—is therefore not a feature of early nineteenth-century German 'grand opera'.

It has been necessary to go over the main points of Weber's commentary on 'grand opera' at some length since it provides an important key to an appreciation of his intentions and *Euryanthe*'s place within the history of German opera. For one thing, the epithet 'große romantische Oper' that accompanies *Euryanthe* in authentic sources is no empty term, but rather a precise description of the composer's aims in the work. Certainly the story of *Euryanthe* does not fit the mould of neo-classical materials usually employed in through-composed opera, but instead qualifies as a 'romantic' subject according to the criteria of early nineteenth-century literary criticism, that is, one drawn from the 'modern', Christian era.[13] Its medieval milieu reflects the early Romantic fascination for the Middle Ages, exemplified elsewhere in the writings of Novalis, Tieck, and Sir Walter Scott, and in the story of Emma's otherworldly existence the opera exploits another element commonly regarded as the property of the 'romantic', the supernatural. The inclusion of the peasant characters Bertha and Rudolph too marks an important departure from the normal grandeur and elevation of traditional 'grand opera'.

But *Euryanthe*'s divergence from the norms for *große Oper* goes beyond its unorthodox subject matter. As we have seen in Chapter II, *Euryanthe*

[11] Mosel, 'Vaudeville, Liederspiel, Singspiel, Oper', in *AmZ (Vienna)*, 4 (1820), col. 691.

[12] The fact that the opera was probably originally composed and perhaps even produced as an opera with spoken dialogue may help explain this exception. This fact has never been noted, but the manuscript sources in the Bayerische Staatsbibliothek strongly suggest that the recitatives were added at an early revival of the work.

[13] Doubtless the term 'Romantic' has over the years come to mean all things to all men, but the common connotation of the term at the beginning of the nineteenth century as an opposition to eighteenth-century neo-classicism is well documented by René Wellek, 'The Concept of Romanticism in Literary History', in his *Concepts of Criticism* (New Haven, Conn., 1963), pp. 128–99. See also M. H. Abrams, *The Mirror and the Lamp* (New York, 1953).

encompasses a wide variety of styles and types of pieces, ranging from simple, syllabically set strophic songs, used as musical symbols for unproblematic, idyllic life (the nascence of love in No. 2, the joys of the hunt in No. 18, and a simple peasant wedding in No. 21), to bravura multi-sectional arias and composite finales in which the dramatic complications unfold.[14] A mixture of solos, ensembles, and choruses obtains. Moreover, many of the pieces represent operatic types of diverse national origins. Adolar's Romanza No. 2 derives from the traditions of French *opéra comique*. The large ensemble No. 4 can be related to the French *morceau d'ensemble*. Though not identified as such in the autograph score, Euryanthe's No. 16 is a prayer—so called in Weber's correspondence with the librettist—whose opening section invokes famous antecedents in French operas by Gluck and Spontini. The extensive use of recurring music was pioneered in French *opéra comique*, and the quotation of the Act II love duet in the Act III Finale is a device that may have been borrowed from Spontini's *La vestale*. Elements of Italian origin are also easy to find in the opera. Euryanthe's two cavatinas ultimately look back to the Italian opera of the later eighteenth century,[15] as do also the bravura rage arias for the villains and the slow-fast form of Adolar's Aria No. 12. Of course, by the time of *Euryanthe* these types had become widely adopted in German opera, but Weber also adapted more recent developments in Italian opera for his own purposes, despite his critical opposition to many aspects of Rossini's art. Lysiart's Scena ed aria No. 10 appropriates the most up-to-date Italian aria type. The multi-sectional finales of course derive at much greater distance from the so-called *Kettenfinale* of eighteenth-century *opera buffa*, but the Act II Finale again reveals a more specific kinship to newer types of Italian finales.

At first glance, idiosyncratically German genres are harder to identify as such, precisely because few types actually originated within German opera. The Jaegerchor No. 18 builds on the tradition for all-male choral singing that blossomed in early nineteenth-century Germany and to which Weber himself made significant contributions, and the May Song in the third act may be thought of as a long-range descendant of the simple strophic Lieder that characterized the rebirth of German opera in the bourgeois comic operas of Hiller and Weisse of the 1760s. More

---

[14] Dahlhaus, *Die Musik des 19. Jahrhunderts*, p. 59.

[15] On the eighteenth-century developments in the cavatina see: Wolfgang Osthoff, 'Mozarts Cavatinen und ihre Tradition', in *Helmuth Osthoff zu seinen 70. Geburtstag*, ed. Ursula Aarburg and Peter Cahn (Tutzing, 1969), pp. 139–78; and Helga Lühning, 'Die Cavatina in der italienischen Oper um 1800', in *Colloquium. 'Die stilistische Entwicklung der italienischen Musik zwischen 1770 und 1830 und ihre Beziehungen zum Norden'* (*Rom 1978*), ed. Friedrich Lippmann ([Cologne], 1982) [*Analecta musicologica* 21], pp. 333–69.

to the point, however, it is the very heterogeneity of genre and style that in fact identifies the work as a German opera, since to a greater or lesser extent *all* German operas of the later eighteenth and early nineteenth century were characterized by their appropriation of genres, styles, and techniques of French and Italian opera.[16] As Weber himself pointed out to the opera-going public in Dresden, the lack of a single well-defined tradition for German opera actually constituted an artistic advantage: 'The Italians and French have shaped for themselves an operatic form in which they peacefully move around. Not so the German. Out of a desire for knowledge and a demand for constant progress, it is uniquely characteristic of him to draw to himself that which is excellent from all others.'[17]

In fact, *Euryanthe*'s proximity to the traditions of German opera with spoken dialogue is underscored by a number of close relationships between it and its immediate predecessor, *Der Freischütz*. As we have seen, the succession of pieces at the start of the opera structurally bears striking resemblance to the start of the *Freischütz*. Euryanthe's Cavatina No. 5 is a close relative of Agathe's by virtue of its mood and scoring. Similarities in style, structure, poetic content, and dramatic context link Bertha's May Song No. 21 to the famous Volkslied No. 14 in *Der Freischütz* and the Jaegerchor No. 18 to the celebrated hunters' chorus in the *Freischütz*. And even though Lysiart's Scena ed aria can be related to the 'Code Rossini', one should not overlook two important points of contact with *Freischütz*. With respect to vocal style, it clearly looks to Caspar's similarly motivated demonic Aria No. 5, which uses nearly identical coloratura figurations stated, like Lysiart's, twice shortly before the final cadence. And with respect to structure, Max's Scena ed aria No. 3, another aria motivated by despair, shares with it not only the same tonality, C minor, but also expands the Rossinian form with an additional *cantabile* movement ('Jetzt ist wohl ihr Fenster offen') between the recitative of the *tempo di mezzo* and the fast 'cabaletta'. These similarities by no means exhaust the relationships between *Freischütz* and *Euryanthe*, and in the course of the present study we shall continue to pay close attention to the relationship of these two siblings.

To sum up: a number of German grand operas antedate *Euryanthe*, but no prior work of comparable stature had ever attempted to bring 'grand opera' into the nineteenth century with such a vengeance, by

---

[16] The developments in the North German sphere are traced by Thomas Bauman in *North German Opera in the Age of Goethe* (Cambridge, 1985). For the parallel but different development of German opera in Vienna see Robert Haas's introduction to *Ignaz Umlauff: Die Bergknappen*, DTO 36 (Vienna, 1911), pp. ix–xxxiv.

[17] *Sämtliche Schriften*, p. 277. Such sentiments of course had already been espoused by eighteenth-century writers like Quantz.

fusing its one salient compositional feature with the stylistic, dramaturgic, and aesthetic principles of early romantic opera. For this reason, the opera is perhaps the most important forerunner for the kind of generic cross-fertilization that took place less than a decade later in the French grand operas based on Scribe's librettos. As we examine the preserved sources for the genesis of the opera we shall pay special attention to the evidence for Weber's awareness of this fundamental novelty during the planning and execution of the work.

2. ELEMENTS OF RECEPTION

For opera, the most public of all musical genres, success is primarily a function of audience acceptance, which determines the life or death of the work. *Euryanthe* certainly did not succeed like the *Freischütz*, either in terms of immediate acceptance by audiences of the 1820s or in terms of longevity within the operatic repertory. To be sure, judged by norms of the era, the opera was not a total failure at the box office. Unlike hundreds of operas that do not survive one or two locally isolated performances, *Euryanthe* did spread to most of Germany's important opera houses within the remainder of Weber's lifetime and eventually did attain the status of repertory opera in certain German theatres in the nineteenth century. Its widely recognized influence on works by Marschner, Meyerbeer, and Wagner also attests that the work was an important part of German operatic consciousness. Yet, in comparison to works like *Zauberflöte*, *Freischütz*, or *Tannhäuser*, its record of public performance can be described at best as only modestly successful. Moreover, it is clear from Weber's correspondence that he himself was disappointed with and embittered by the response that the opera elicited from early audiences and critics.

The reasons why an opera may fail to generate enthusiasm are naturally manifold and, of course, difficult to determine with any degree of certainty, especially when one is separated from the event by more than a century; after all, our own reactions to a work are not likely to be identical to those of a bygone public. This historical public, by no means a uniform entity, responds not only to the music and text of the work, but also to the numerous elements of presentation—the singers, sets, staging, and orchestral playing—that cannot be replicated. Moreover, prejudices and expectations based on prior knowledge and reputation also influence the way in which an audience views and judges a work. Yet it is important for us to attempt to understand why *Euryanthe* failed to win widespread and enthusiastic support during the early years of its existence, since the reactions of Weber's contemporaries not only shed an interesting light on taste in that era, but also raise a number of basic issues that must be confronted in any study that attempts to assess the opera historically and critically.

2.1. *Unfavourable circumstances*

To a certain extent conditions attending the early performances of the opera were not entirely favourable. Weber himself believed that *Euryanthe* had been doomed from the outset by the unreasonably high expectations aroused by the unprecedented success of the *Freischütz*. Having observed the fanatical reception of the *Freischütz* in Vienna in March 1822 he alluded to this concern several times during the composition of the new opera. Even before he left Vienna Weber began to prepare his wife Caroline for the more limited appeal of the new opera,[18] and over a month after his return to Dresden, he complained to his friend Hinrich Lichtenstein that the 'cursed *Freischütz* will make things difficult for his sister *Euryanthe*, and I sometimes get hot flushes when I consider the fact that the applause cannot really increase any more.'[19] On 22 December 1822, he wrote to Thaddäus [Ignaz] Susann that 'the excessive applause that the *Freischütz* has received is a dangerous enemy of all of my succeeding operas . . .'[20]

Thus Weber interpreted the ultimate ambivalence of contemporary audiences as a prophecy come true; finding their expectations of a second *Freischütz* frustrated by a different kind of work, the audiences were naturally disappointed. We have already seen his letter of 15 December to Gottfried Weber. Less than a month later Weber complained with undisguised bitterness to his long-time friend Friedrich Rochlitz:

The expectations were so immoderately set for something never before heard, electrifying [*blitzblau hinaus Leuchtendes*], and completely different that my uncomprehending friends truly lent their aid to my enemies. The former demanded, that *Euryanthe* should be—entirely contrary to its nature and intention—just as popular [*volkstümlich*] as the *Freischütz*, and the latter helped themselves to the fine phrase, 'yes, you see, that really isn't a *Freischütz*.'[21]

And to his friend and mentor Franz Danzi Weber confided on 1 March 1824: 'The expectations of the masses were stirred up beyond reason through the miraculous success of the *Freischütz*; and now appears the

---

[18] See the letter of 15 and 16 Mar. 1822 cited in Chapter I, n. 12.

[19] Letter of 28 Apr. 1822 in *Lichtenstein-Briefe*, p. 111.

[20] Robert Hernried, 'Discoveries in Vienna: Unpublished Letters by Weber and Liszt', *MQ* 32 (1946): 540–1.

[21] Letter of 7 Jan. 1824, published in Georg Kinsky, 'Ungedruckte Briefe Carl Maria von Webers', *Zeitschrift für Musik* 93 (1926): 485.

simple, serious work, that seeks nothing but truth of expression, passion and characterization, and dispenses with all of the manifold variety and stimulants of its predecessor.'[22]

The fact that the opera was first performed in Vienna at the height of the 'Rossini-fever' was viewed by many of Weber's contemporaries as another unfortunate circumstance that proved injurious to the new opera's reception. Weber himself envied the brilliance of the Italian troupe that Barbaia had brought to Vienna and doubted the ability of the German troupe to impress audiences accustomed to such great singers as Joséphine Fodor-Mainvielle and Luigi Lablache, and in fact several contemporary reviewers of the Vienna *Euryanthe* did point out the deficiencies of the tenor Haitzinger for the role of Adolar.[23] More fundamentally, a number of observers feared that the Viennese taste had become so thoroughly captivated by Rossini's magic as to be rendered insensitive to anything different, an opinion stated most forcefully by the anonymous reviewer 'Th.' in the *Wiener allgemeine Theaterzeitung*, who felt that 'the continual repetition of beautiful but vacuous and comfortably heard melodies has made us all nearly incapable of enjoying serious, solid, and substantial music; Weber's music will therefore certainly be completely recognized, but perhaps not until later.'[24] Needless to say, a number of Viennese critics themselves were quick to rebut this charge by pointing to the warmth with which *Freischütz* had been received by the city. A. B. Marx of Berlin also linked the coolness with which audiences around Germany reacted to the early performances of the opera to the ambivalent reception of the Viennese première, since the authority that Vienna had earlier attained as a great musical centre was still strong enough to influence opinions in other German cities. Yet Marx felt in this case that the Viennese press had misrepresented the work to the world at large: 'If one must speak of a misconception on the part of Weber and his poet, it is that they had their opera first performed in Vienna, where no attempt was made to illuminate his ideas and intentions—where one has been content with shallow reviews that either praise or insult.'[25]

---

[22] *MMW* ii. 549.

[23] According to Friedrich Kanne's review in *AMZ (Vienna)* 7 (1823), col. 704, the part lay too low for Haitzinger, whose voice was more comfortable in the high tenor parts of Rossini's operas; the anonymous reviewer in the *Wiener Zeitschrift für Kunst, Literatur, Theater und Mode*, 8, No. 135 (11 Nov. 1823): 1112, admitted that 'recitative lies outside his sphere'.

[24] *Wiener allgemeine Theaterzeitung* 16 (1823): 524.

[25] *Berliner allgemeine musikalische Zeitung* (hereafter referred to as *BamZ*), 3 (1826): 5.

2.2. Weaknesses in the libretto

If circumstances played a role in the rather cool reception accorded the work, most contemporary comments suggest, however, that the real obstacles to widespread acceptance lay in the opera itself. For one thing, Weber's contemporaries were just as acutely aware as later commentators of numerous problems in the text, and some observers were in fact inclined to see these as the primary reason for the failure of the opera. This was clearly Goethe's assessment, according to whom Weber 'ought not to have composed *Euryanthe*; he should have seen immediately that this is a bad subject that would lead to nothing'.[26] The anonymous reviewer in the *Wiener Zeitschrift für Kunst, Literatur, Theater und Mode* summed up most of the problems that were mentioned time and time again in the contemporary press and that have continued to be restated in the subsequent century and a half. Explaining the source of the libretto to be a diffuse medieval romance that typically did not lend itself well to dramatic adaptation, the reviewer continued:

Moreover, that which is especially lacking in the dramatic action is the necessary clarity, whose deficiency is most painfully sensed in the principal motive, in the very point on which the drama really turns. This is Euryanthe's narration about the appearance of Emma, the sister of her betrothed, and of the fabulous poison-ring, from which the departed once drank her death, but which in future, rinsed by the tears of innocence, and when 'Treu dem Mörder Rettung beut für Mord' (very harsh and extremely peculiar) is to become the sign of reconciliation. This circumstance, which is stated only a single time in recitative, has in addition to the obscurity that surrounds it yet other faults, and the substitution with the circumstance mentioned in the romance,[27] however necessary it may have been, cannot be considered successful. In the first place the marvellous appears as a highly foreign component in an action that otherwise makes no use of it. Second, the admission of this vision is not sufficient grounds for the most shameful suspicion. Euryanthe ought but to have said a single word, just confess—there certainly is enough time and opportunity for her to do it—and the betrayal would thus be discovered. The danger is more significant in the romance, where the unfortunate girl does not know how it has happened and can only assert her innocence without having the means to prove it. The jealousy of the treacherous Eglantine is an equally unfortunate invention, since she could hope to win Adolar's hand after the separation of the lovers is brought about, and consequently should not give her hand to Lysiart so hastily; it would be entirely different, if she were driven to it for her own self-interest. Her intimate relationship with Euryanthe brings to her expressions of tenderness a cutting tone, which becomes all the more

---

[26] Johann Peter Eckermann, *Gespräche mit Goethe in den letzten Jahren seines Lebens 1823–1832*, ed. Eduard Castle (Berlin, etc., 1916), vol. i. 121.

[27] i.e. a violet-shaped mole on Euryanthe's breast; the relationship of the libretto to its literary source is discussed below in Chapter IV, section 2.

repulsive, because the ambiguous character that these utterances must have cannot be brought to life through music. In addition almost all of the relationships in this drama are too little motivated, and the events are never sufficiently prepared ... With respect to characterization, the sympathetic Euryanthe is nevertheless too suffering, Adolar appears too weak, too much as a troubadour, the King is insignificant; Lysiart is most successfully drawn, even if he at times does sigh too much and then again rages too violently. The verses are excellent, if one does not consider their musical purpose. For the most part they have euphony and poetic charm. If one considers them from the other side, they occasionally present puzzles that another cannot solve so easily, and the bouncing, ringing, overly sweet, and lovely qualities that predominate are little suited to musical setting. Leaving aside these faults, the piece still distinguishes itself from many others both through its romantic character as well as it noble bearing.[28]

These comments by no means exhaust the litany of criticisms directed against the libretto. Many commentators were disturbed by the unchivalric harshness with which Adolar treats *Euryanthe* and his barbarous decision to leave her to her fate in the forest after she had saved his life; the Viennese critic-composer F. A. Kanne found the violence with which the King and knights condemned Euryanthe at the end of the Act II Finale equally difficult to justify. In a long footnote to the highly critical discussion of the libretto by Stephan Schütze in *Caecilia*, Gottfried Weber went so far as to consider the libretto completely offensive to standards of moral propriety, a criticism that might not occur to twentieth-century opera-goers accustomed to works like *Salome* and *Lulu*.[29]

2.3. Weber's critics vs. Weber's aesthetics: 'lack of melody', 'musical prose', and 'dramatic truth'

Yet, unlike most twentieth-century observers, who have maintained that the libretto was the primary stumbling block to the work's acceptance and have therefore sought to rescue the opera for the stage by revising or even replacing the libretto, few writers of Weber's own day laid the cause for the public's indifference to the work solely, or even principally at the feet of the libretto. Such a premiss in fact is rendered suspect by the successful works in the history of opera whose librettos in no way stand up to close scrutiny of logic in plot development

[28] *Wiener Zeitschrift für Kunst, Literatur, Theater und Mode*, 8 (1823): 1102–3. For the most extended and severe criticism of the libretto see St. Schütze, 'Ueber den Text der Oper Euryanthe', *Caecilia* 2 (1825): 42–65.

[29] *Caecilia* 2 (1825): 52–6. Carl Maria must have seen a pre-publication copy of Gottfried's comments, for on 11 Oct. 1824 he wrote somewhat vexed to Gottfried 'But tell me for God's sake where did you get your *terribly virtuous* views. In this matter you're wrong, for what would have become of Shakespeare's "Cymbelline", "Romeo and Juliet", and 100 other works?' G. *Weber-Briefe*, p. 89.

and characterization. Instead, recurring threads in the early assessments of the opera make it evident that many of Weber's contemporaries found the music to *Euryanthe* as problematic as the text, if not more so, indeed unsatisfying and even disturbing. The anonymous reviewer of the *Lettere del Professore Carpani sulla Musica di Gioacchino Rossini* in the *Allgemeine musikalische Zeitung* of Leipzig questioned whether the music to *Euryanthe* could claim to be music at all: 'Just listen to a very considerable portion of [Weber's] *Euryanthe*, for example the large vocal pieces of the second act as they occur in order. Expression—yes indeed, lots of it: but is that song? is it melody? indeed, one might even ask to a certain extent at many passages (in all of the accompanied recitatives): is that harmony? and at times even: is that music?'[30] A more extreme case in point is found in the diary of the Viennese playwright Franz Grillparzer:

Yesterday again at *Euryanthe*. This music is *disgusting*. This inversion of euphony, this rape of the beautiful would have been punished by the state in the good old days of [ancient] Greece. Such music is illegal; it would create monsters, were it ever possible that it gradually could find general acceptance. . . . This opera can only please fools, or lunatics, or scholars, or street thieves and assassins . . . [31]

At first glance, one might be tempted to dismiss both the *AmZ* reviewer and Grillparzer as critics of Weber, since they both seem to represent an extreme, pro-Italian, pro-Rossini bias that potentially predisposed them to be hostile toward German opera and especially toward a composer who was generally viewed as the German antipode to Rossini.[32] Yet the very vehemence of these comments leads one to wonder what in this music could provoke such violent distaste. Fortunately, more restrained and reasoned critiques point to specific elements in the music that disturbed early audiences and critics and worked against popular acceptance.

For one thing, the fact that the opera was through-composed seems to have alienated audiences on several accounts. The *AmZ* correspondent in Prague found the very presence of recitatives problematic since 'they are unfamiliar to a portion of the public, and on the other hand our singers, like all German singers, always have difficulties with the performance of recitative, and certainly four-fifths of the audience left the theater,

[30] 'Fragen an die, welche zu antworten wissen', *Allgemeine musikalische Zeitung* (hereafter referred to as *AmZ*), 28 (1826), col. 800.

[31] Franz Grillparzer, *Tagebücher und literarische Skizzenhefte. Zweiter Teil. 1822 bis Mitte 1830*, ed. August Sauer, in *Sämtliche Werke*. Part II, vol. viii (Vienna, 1916), pp. 128–9.

[32] On Grillparzer's pro-Italian leanings see Richard Batka, 'Grillparzer und der Kampf gegen die deutsche Oper in Wien', *Jahrbuch der Grillparzer Gesellschaft* 4 (Vienna, 1894), pp. 119–44.

without having understood the plot'.[33] The Viennese critic Kanne also noted that Weber's attempts to enhance continuity by linking the ends of pieces with the beginning of the following recitatives appeared 'in many scenes to be an obstacle to the unimpeded stream of applause, since the spectator believes his noise might interrupt the flow of beautiful musical moments'.[34] Critics consistently acknowledged the great care that Weber had lavished upon the recitatives in terms of accuracy of declamation, interesting modulations, and instrumentation; Rochlitz, for one, found the recitatives to be 'incomparable and a true spiritual feast for him who knows how to recognize and enjoy such things'.[35] But a number of commentators also suggested that such efforts were, in the final analysis, counter-productive. For Kanne, Weber's attempts to make the recitatives consistently interesting placed excessive demands on the singers that detracted from the effectiveness of the pieces that followed,[36] and the reviewer in the *Wiener Zeitschrift für Kunst, Literatur, Theater und Mode*, one of Weber's harshest critics, found the recitatives themselves burdened by their own efforts at rhetorical precision:

Because he wishes to give to every part of a period and sometimes to every word its value and appropriate accent with the greatest precision and the most rigorous correctness, the progress has become somewhat dragging and uniform, the rhythm not infrequently ponderous and the dramatic declamation has been subordinated to a tedious accentuation. Just listen to the recitative in the *Magic Flute*! or to *Titus* and Gluck's *Iphigenia*!—What truth of expression, and what lively, powerful motion![37]

Critics and contemporary observers adduced a number of additional reasons to explain the public's ambivalence towards the work. Kanne found the work too gloomy and somewhat cold, and thus it 'does not fill the soul of the listener with the rapture that is awakened by the divine spark that inhabits all beautiful works of great masters'.[38] Various writers pointed to the extreme demands of intonation that the opera made on the singers and the orchestra, especially the first violins; accordingly, the *AmZ* correspondent from Prague asserted that this was the most difficult opera ever written, and Sir George Smart was of the opinion that the opera could only be successfully performed in Dresden

[33] *AmZ* 26 (1824): 406–7.

[34] *AmZ (Vienna)* 7 (1823): 710–11.

[35] Rochlitz's views on *Euryanthe* were communicated to Weber in a letter of 25 May 1825, published in full in the *Lichtenstein-Briefe*, pp. 233–9. For the comment about recitative, see p. 238.

[36] *AmZ (Vienna)*, 7 (1823), col. 710–11.

[37] *Wiener Zeitschrift für Kunst, Literatur, Theater und Mode*, 8 (1823): 1110.

[38] *AmZ (Vienna)*, 7 (1823), col. 713.

under the composer's direction.[39] Most commentators expressed admiration for the compositional skill and learning—especially in the harmony and instrumentation—that Weber had demonstrated in the opera, and because of this, Smart felt that 'the audience should be professors [i.e. professional musicians] of the first rank' and that 'to understand the whole opera, it must be heard at least half a dozen times';[40] as Rochlitz pointed out to Weber in his letter of 25 May 1825, however, repeated hearings of an opera are normally possible only if the work generates sufficient public interest at the first few performances.[41] In general, however, the critics found that the opera's intellectual demands ultimately tempered the audience's enthusiasm. For instance, the critic in the *Sammler* (probably Kanne) was of the opinion that Weber had lost widespread support by giving 'more space to a greater diligence, to a more tedious elaboration than was nececessary, than in general the free unfolding of genius should permit. In the entire work this is attested by the all too many enharmonic shifts and frequent wrenches in the harmony, which are just as disadvantageous to the clarity of the composition as the exaggerated accentuation of tone in the declamation.'[42] The critic in the *Wiener Zeitschrift für Kunst, Literatur, Theater und Mode* wondered aloud whether a desire on Weber's part to surpass the *Freischütz* might not have led him to strive unsuccessfully to go beyond the natural limits of his own talent:

They [the part of the Viennese public not satisfied by *Euryanthe*] say that the composer of the beloved, highly praised *Freischütz* overstepped the boundaries of his talent by leaving the sphere of folk-like, German life and character that suits him in order to try his talent successfully on the heroic—if this term can be applied to *Euryanthe*—and sensing this with a modest feeling of his own ability, he fell into a disturbing concern and an effortful endeavour to make the new work equal the older one, indeed, in accordance with the demand, to surpass the earlier work by a wide margin, to offer something entirely original, uncommon, extraordinary, which in its smallest parts would remind of nothing earlier, which in no trait, not even the smallest, would betray a similarity with another work, and that the stamp of calculating reason was all too noticeably imprinted on his newest work through this care-ridden effort, even in its most successful parts.[43]

[39] H. Bertram Cox and C. L. E. Cox, ed., *Leaves from the Journals of Sir George Smart* (London, 1907), p. 145.

[40] Ibid.

[41] See Rochlitz's letter of 25 May 1825 in *Lichtenstein-Briefe*, pp. 236–7. Rochlitz's discussion of the necessity of making concessions to the operatic public is omitted in the lengthy excerpt of the letter published in Jähns, op. cit. ch. 1 n. 4 above, p. 370.

[42] *Der Sammler* 15 (8 Nov. 1823), p. 536

[43] *Wiener Zeitschrift für Kunst, Literatur, Theater und Mode* 8 (1823): 1109.

And even the sympathetic Berlin critic Amadeus Wendt admitted that the opera was in fact too tiring for even the most cultivated and sympathetic audiences, since:

> the great, mighty exertions and the restless *progression to constantly new portrayals* in this composition ultimately affect the receptivity of the listener in the same way that the physical activity of the singers and actors must find itself affected at the end. It is impossible for a *cultivated listener*, who attentively follows the change of moods and situations of the characters, to be *bored* by this opera, but he can easily be deeply and variously moved by it and still be exhausted.[44]

The frequency with which commentators addressed the 'lack of melody' in *Euryanthe* is especially striking and perhaps suggestive of the main reason for public coolness towards the opera. According to Joseph von Spaun, Franz Schubert frankly told Weber that 'there was a conspicuous lack of melody' in *Euryanthe* and that 'because of this, he was forced to consider this new work greatly inferior to the splendid *Freischütz*'.[45] The Saxon ambassador to Vienna, Georg August von Griesinger, reported back to Dresden that the opera had failed in Vienna primarily because it 'lacked the magic of *Melos*, without which music finds no salvation'.[46] To begin to understand what this criticism meant we may turn again to the diary of one of the opera's strongest detractors, Franz Grillparzer.

> What I already sensed at the appearance of the *Freischütz* appears now to be confirmed. Weber is admittedly a poetic mentality, but not a musician. No trace of melody, not just of pleasant [melody], but of melody in general. (I however name as melody an *organically* connected sentence [*Satz*], whose individual components necessarily condition one another musically.) Fragmented thoughts, held together only by the text and without internal (musical) consistency.[47]

This appraisal brings us to the heart of the matter, the recognition that much of the music in *Euryanthe* was not the self-sufficient, self-contained type that developed out of itself and pleased in its own right. Hence the failure of Weber's music to measure up against the yardstick of the organic metaphor, as defined by Grillparzer. Even a staunch supporter of German opera like the critic and aesthetician Amadeus Wendt, who felt compelled to refute the widespread charge that *Euryanthe* 'lacked

[44] Amadeus Wendt, 'Über Weber's *Euryanthe*. Ein Nachtrag', *BamZ* 3 (1826): 55.

[45] Otto Erich Deutsch, ed., *Schubert. Memoires by His Friends*, translated by Rosamund Ley and John Nowell (London, 1958), p. 27.

[46] Griesinger's comments on the preparations for and reception of *Euryanthe* in Vienna were published by Ludwig Schmidt, 'Zeitgenössische Nachrichten über Carl Maria v. Weber', *Die Musik* 18, No. 9 (June, 1926): 653–9.

[47] Grillparzer, *Tagebücher und literarische Skizzenhefte. Zweiter Teil. 1822 bis Mitte 1830*, p. 128.

melody', nevertheless had to concede that the opera's music was not exactly the kind of self-contained melody that one normally expected:

I find this reproach [*Euryanthe*'s alleged lack of melody] unfounded, if one is speaking of melodic clauses [*melodischen Sätze*] in general, in that, on the contrary, I find such a great wealth of novel melodic ideas in this work, that I would scarcely know another recent work that could compare with it. On the other hand, one can indeed miss a *flowing of melody* in this work; that is, the *internal development* of melodic clauses *out of one another* and out of large basic melodic thoughts (which musicians often call development [*Durchführung*] or elaboration [*Ausführung*] of the theme) is to be observed in this work much more rarely.[48]

For Wendt, only Nos. 1, 2, 5, 6, 9, 12, 17, 18, 20, and 21, the second half of No. 7, and the andante section of No. 10 revealed a composer interested in sustained, developed melody, and he concluded that this particular aspect represented the '*weaker* side of the music' in the opera.[49] In a similar vein, the severe critic in the *Wiener Zeitschrift für Kunst, Literatur, Theater und Mode*, while admitting that the opera contained a plethora of melodic ideas, nevertheless explained 'that the ideas all too often lack development and unity, that overly bold and daring transitions and artificial harmonic interconnections often interrupt the progress of ideas, too frequently steal clarity from the stream of melody and song and inhibit its free course'.[50]

Nor was this line of criticism confined to the immediate era of *Euryanthe*'s première, for it continued in the writings of no less a figure than Richard Wagner, one of Weber's greatest admirers. In his first published essay of 1834, 'Die deutsche Oper', the young Wagner, at the time admittedly under the sway of Bellini and the anti-Romantic 'Young German' movement, lamented the fragmentation of melody in *Euryanthe* as evidence of the unfortunate tendency of German composers to aspire to erudition:

What fussy hairsplitting in the declamation—what fastidious use of this and that instrument to support the expression of some word! Instead of dashing off a complete sentiment with a single stroke, he dissects the impression of the whole through fussy details and individual pedantries. How difficult it is for him to breathe life into his ensembles: how lame the second-act finale is! Here an instrument, there a voice wishes to say something very learned, and in the end no one knows what it is saying. And since people must admit when it's over that they have not understood any of it, all find at least one consolation in the fact that they can regard it as remarkably erudite and may

---

[48] *BamZ* 3 (1826): 55–6.
[49] Ibid., p. 56.
[50] *Wiener Zeitschrift für Kunst, Literatur, Theater und Mode* 8 (1823): 1109.

therefore have great respect for it.—Oh, this unfortunate *erudition*—this fount of all German evils![51]

Even in the more mature and closely argued *Opera and Drama*, Wagner concluded that the primary reason for the audience's failure to embrace the work warmly was the disintegration of its melody into a 'declamatory mosaic'.[52]

In essence, then, many nineteenth-century commentators, whatever their ideological stance, observed that the music in *Euryanthe* works not according to the logic of autonomous musical development—Grillparzer's 'organically connected sentence'— but instead represents an approach that Wagner described as a 'mosaic' and that Grillparzer elsewhere had characterized as 'musical prose'.[53]

It is important to recognize that many of the criticisms brought to bear against the music of *Euryanthe* cover precisely those points where Weber seems most closely to have approximated his ideals of operatic dramaturgy and that the opera aroused antipathy in large measure because it realized principles with which the era was not wholly sympathetic. To be sure, Weber was never a systematic aesthetician, but his critical writings and correspondence supply hints that suggest that *Euryanthe* was planned as a practical realization of long-held ideals that must be understood if one is to approach the work sympathetically. And in many ways, what Grillparzer, Wagner, and others perceived negatively as 'prose-' or 'mosaic-like' qualities of the music to *Euryanthe* was in fact a direct consequence of principles that Weber stressed repeatedly in his writings on opera, namely, that dramatic music should above all be 'truthful' and 'characteristic'. In Chapter VIII we shall attempt to put flesh on these concepts by an examination of the *Euryanthe* score, but for the present it is sufficient to record that for Weber, self-contained beauty was not the sole nor even the primary consideration for dramatic music. Thus he admitted to being charmed by the autonomous beauty of Rossini's music, but faulted it repeatedly for its seeming disregard

---

[51] Richard Wagner, *Sämtliche Schriften und Dichtungen*, 6th edn. (Leipzig, 1912), xii. 2.

[52] *GSD* iii. 290–1.

[53] Grillparzer's notion of a 'musical prosaist' as a composer who mechanically sets words to music without concern for the independent inner life of melody appears in a diary entry from *c* 1820–1, where the target of criticism is the Viennese composer-aesthetician I. F. von Mosel. See Hermann Danuser, *Musikalische Prosa* (Regensburg, 1975), pp. 33–50. Danuser brings Grillparzer's *Euryanthe* criticism into the discussion of 'musical prose', but goes somewhat awry in limiting his interpretation of what Grillparzer would have considered 'prosaic' to Weber's approach to recitative in the opera (pp. 40–3). For Grillparzer and his contemporaries the problem lay as much if not more so in the issue of coherence and development within supposedly lyric movements, a point to which we shall return in Part III of the present study.

for situation and characterization.[54] In contrast, he described his own *Euryanthe* to his long-time friend and fellow composer Franz Danzi as a 'simple, serious work, that seeks nothing other than truth of expression, passion and characterization'.[55] Although Weber most likely would not have equated this approach with a musical 'prose', he doubtless recognized, however, that his own bias for a consistently 'truthful' and 'characteristic' music did not produce music of a type that would or could be complete and satisfying in and of itself as music. In a letter of 20 December 1824 he explicitly forbade a concert performance of *Euryanthe* by the Akademischer Musikverein of the University of Breslau precisely because he felt that the music of the work would be wholly ineffective if divorced from its dramatic context:

Accept my most cordial and sincerest thanks, esteemed sirs, for the honour bestowed upon me in your communication of the 15th of this month. It truly pains me that I cannot so joyfully respond to this ambitious [*strebensfrohen*] and trusting summons. *Euryanthe* is a *purely dramatic* essay, building its hopes *only on the united collaboration of all of the sister arts*, and surely ineffective if robbed of their assistance. I was already convinced of this before numerous requests like yours (which I unfortunately partially satisfied) reached me, or the arbitrary desire introduced the public to pieces or the whole thing without asking. The experience confirmed my conviction. The work yielded not just coolness, it in fact aroused displeasure, for the public sympathetic to me brought no small expectations with it. Permit me to ask, not for the sake of comparison but only as an example, if you could count on the effect of the most successful performance of one of the *Iphigenias* by Gluck in your concert hall? And this is a *recognized* masterpiece, generally *known*, such that the imagination of the listener can work to complete and add [to the music]. Sirs, you in your pure zeal for art would not be able to forgive yourselves if you found my words confirmed and were forced to reproach yourselves for having significantly shattered the faith in German dramatic art by this concert performance.[56]

In effect, then, Weber was something of an anomaly for his time, for by subjugating musical values to 'truth of expression' and 'characterization', he chose a path that was not only unpopular with opera-going audiences and critics, but that also brought him into direct confrontation with important premises in both traditional music aesthetics and in the newer Romantic view of music as well. With regard to the former *Euryanthe* sacrificed 'beauty' for the sake of expression and characteriza-

---

[54] See, for example, Weber's criticism of Meyerbeer's attempt to copy Rossini's style in his Italian opera *Emma di Resburgo*: 'Who does not listen gladly to Rossini's lively storm of ideas and to the piquant teasing of his melodies? But who is also so blinded as to wish to concede him dramatic truth?' *Sämtliche Schriften*, p. 397.

[55] See above, note 22.

[56] *MMW* ii. 585–6. The draft of the letter is in WFN-Handschriftliches, Konvolut XIV, Bl. 84b/v.

tion, whereas from the Romantic point of view the opera's music failed in its mission as music precisely because its close alliance to specific characters and situations diminished the autonomy from concrete ideas that made music the perfect vehicle for the expression of the ideal and transcendant. From the perspective of many of his contemporaries, the 'problem of *Euryanthe*' was thus a fundamental failure to reconcile the traditional demands for musical coherence and sensual gratification on the one hand with the desire for dramatic expression and truth on the other, a view most directly expressed by the critic in the *Wiener Zeitschrift für Kunst, Literatur, Theater und Mode*:

Do character and correctness exclude melody and song? or do they also command that the latter are always subordinated to them? Is song, in the final analysis, always only a hollow jingle? No one will dare to maintain this. To justify their demands, [Weber's critics] invoke *Don Giovanni*, *Figaro*, indeed even that work of genius, *Fidelio*; in this last piece, despite all ingenuity and boldness, despite the most significant and most profound harmonic complications, ubiquitous clarity and far more melody and song predominate than in *Euryanthe* ...[57]

In the eyes of many, then, the music to *Euryanthe* suffered not so much in comparison to Rossini's, but rather in comparison to that of the recent past, especially Mozart's music for the stage, which for many Germans of the early nineteenth century represented the only true model for operatic music because it was both dramatically appropriate *and* musically satisfying.

3. 'Organic Opera': Theory and Practice

In the preceding section we saw how Grillparzer criticized the music in *Euryanthe* because it lacked qualities of 'organic' growth and development. Such a comment was of course rooted in what was perhaps the most widespread metaphor for creativity and criticism in the early nineteenth century. And in point of fact, viewed solely as music, many pieces in *Euryanthe* do not exhibit qualities of phrase balancing, motivic-thematic work, harmonic predictability, and rhythmic 'flow' that writers of Weber's time interpreted as musical manifestations of organicism. Nor does Weber's music seem to evince the kind of interrelationship between detail and structure that a number of recent analyses have unco-

---

[57] *Wiener Zeitschrift für Kunst, Literatur, Theater und Mode* 8 (1823): 1110.

vered in the music of eighteenth- and nineteenth-century Austrian-German composers as yet further embodiments of the organic metaphor.[58]

Though Weber freely acknowledged that the music to *Euryanthe* could not be divorced successfully from its dramatic context and in so doing implicitly admitted its limitations as autonomous music, nevertheless, as a Romantic in his own right he himself was by no means a stranger to the organic metaphor. Instead, he seems to have interpreted it at a different level than did his critics, for whereas Grillparzer and other commentators viewed the individual piece or even passage as the 'organism', Weber applied the concept to the opera as a whole. One of the most conspicuous tenets in his writings is that an opera ought to represent a unified work of art. Of course this precept has become a commonplace since the time of the Romantics,[59] but it is well to recall that operas were long considered primarily as agglomerations of individual parts that could be and indeed normally were replaced by other parts as the need arose. In Weber's time, in fact, this older view of operatic structure continued unchallenged in Italy, where composers like Rossini pragmatically accommodated their works to the demands of singers and popular taste.[60]

Throughout his writings Weber's aesthetic of operatic organicism is expressed in a number of ways, although three basic meanings emerge from various discussions. In one sense, 'unity' implied the melding of different arts in an opera. Hence, Weber spoke of the 'fusion of all means into a total effect' in his discussion of orchestration in Cherubini's *Lodoïska*.[61] He elaborated the same idea at greater length in his most important operatic manifesto, a review of the Berlin première of E. T. A. Hoffmann's *Undine* that was published in the widely read *AmZ*: 'It goes without saying that I speak of *the* opera that the German desires—an art work complete in itself, in which all sections and the contributions of the related arts that have been utilized disappear in the act of blending together, and in being destroyed after a fashion—form a new world'.[62]

---

[58] I have in mind here Schenker's 'verborgene Wiederholungen' as well as the kinds of relationships between melodic detail , harmony, and tonal structure that are brilliantly demonstrated in Charles Rosen's analysis of the *Hammerklavier* Sonata in *The Classical Style* (New York, 1971), pp. 407–34.

[59] Though recent revisionist discussions of nineteenth-century opera, especially those dealing with the Italian tradition, have sought to mitigate the search for large-scale coherence. See James Webster, 'To Understand Verdi and Wagner We Must Understand Mozart', *19th-Century Music* 11 (1987): 175–93, especially 177–9 and 191.

[60] On the concept of the 'work' in Rossini's operas and the resultant implications for editorial policy see Philip Gossett, 'The Operas of Rossini: Problems of Textual Criticism in 19th-century Opera' (Ph. D. dissertation, Princeton University, 1970).

[61] *Sämtliche Schriften*, p. 298.

[62] Ibid., p. 129.

Weber also stressed a second type of unity, the sense that all of the successive segments of an opera are subordinated to the impression of the whole. Again the clearest statement of this idea occurs in his review of *Undine*, where he admits that most operas succeed because of 'individually outstanding musical pieces' that rarely are subsumed into the 'great feeling of the whole [*Allgefühl*] at the end, as really should be the case, since one must first come to love the entire form and then through closer familiarity rejoice in the beauty of the individual parts from which it is composed'.[63] In fact, he praised *Undine* precisely because it was 'truly of *one* piece' such that 'after the first hearing one has really comprehended the whole and the individual disappears in true artistic innocence and modesty'.[64]

In yet a third interpretation of the concept, Weber pointed to consistency of characterization as a means to unity, both in the sense that individual characters receive consistent treatment and in the sense that the entire work should exude a dominant character or colouring. In Spohr's *Faust*, which he introduced to the world in Prague in 1816, Weber detected a 'beautiful colouring of the entire work'.[65] He praised Méhul's *Joseph* for the way that it projected 'truly patriarchal life and colouring',[66] and he noted that the same composer's *Helene* possessed a *Kolorit* of its own that differed from that of *Joseph*.[67] Again, Hoffmann's *Undine* elicited special praise for the consistency with which certain characters, especially the supernatural beings Kühleborn and Undine, were depicted[68] and yet also for the way in which they were integrated into a single atmosphere: 'As differentiated and accurately drawn the various characters of the *dramatis personae* appear, nevertheless a spooky, story-telling life surrounds them, or rather arises from the whole, whose sweet excitations of horror are characteristic of the fairy-tale'.[69]

From Weber's own letters one may safely infer that he intended to embody his ideals of coherence in *Euryanthe*. He explicitly applied the organic metaphor to the opera in order to protest the additional cuts requested by Count Brühl for the Berlin production,[70] and as we have just seen, Weber explained to the Akademischer Musikverein of Breslau that *Euryanthe* was wholly dependent on the 'united collaboration of all the sister arts' for its effectiveness. Exactly how this organic ideal was realized in *Euryanthe* is one of the central topics of the present

[63] Ibid.

[64] Ibid., pp. 131–2.   [65] Ibid., p. 274.

[66] Ibid., p. 280.   [67] Ibid., p. 286.

[68] Weber called attention to the way in which Hoffmann had characterized the earth-spirit Kühleborn in the opera *Undine* 'through choice of melody and instrumentation that, always remaining true to him, announces his eerie proximity'. Ibid., p. 132.

[69] Ibid., p. 132.

[70] See Chapter I, n. 56.

study. The overview presented in Chapter II has brought to light a number of features that can readily be interpreted as manifestations of the organic metaphor as Weber seems to have understood it. For one thing, the very fact that *Euryanthe* does not use spoken dialogue but relies instead on orchestrally accompanied recitative and arioso to advance the plot, one of the primary reasons why the opera commands such exceptional interest in the history of German opera, must be considered an important factor in the unity of the opera, for as writers have long stressed, an opera that is sung throughout naturally projects a more uniform image than one that alternates between two modes of expression, spoken dialogue and music.[71] Another element that obviously contributes to the sense of overall unity is the recurrence of certain themes and motives throughout the opera for symbolic purposes (see Table 4), since through such recall the listener is compelled at some level of consciousness to relate the immediate experience of present action to some earlier moment in the opera; Weber's critical writings clearly reveal the significance that he attached to such recurring themes as agents of unity.[72] Of course he did not invent this practice, since by the time that he began to incorporate a significant amount of thematic reminiscence in his operas, the technique had already long been established in works of his French and German predecessors.[73]

Particularly relevant to Weber's notions of operatic organicism is the fact that *Euryanthe*, despite its organization as a series of discrete pieces, evinces a number of features that work to consolidate many of the pieces and intervening connective materials into larger complexes that

[71] For Jean-Jacques Rousseau the alternation of spoken and sung passages was an abomination: 'The passage from conversation to song, and vice versa, is too disparate; it is shocking to both the ear and verisimilitude; two conversationalists should either speak or sing; they ought not to alternate between the one and the other'. *Dictionnaire de musique* (Paris, 1768), p. 400 [s. v. 'Recitatif']. Spohr's 'Aufruf an deutsche Komponisten', a manifesto coeval with both his first 'grand opera', *Jessonda*, and *Euryanthe*, challenged German composers to tackle the problem of the recitative opera for precisely this reason: 'Another question is, however, whether we Germans should not at long last elevate the opera as a work of art to a greater unity by transforming the [spoken] dialogues into recitative. If the aestheticians reject opera as an artwork and call it monstrous, it is primarily the alternation of speech and song that justifies their so doing'. *AmZ* 25 (1823), col. 463.

[72] See especially Weber's discussions of his own *Preciosa*, Poissl's *Athalia*, and Spohr's *Faust* in *Sämtliche Schriften*, pp. 219, 270, and 275.

[73] Because of its eventual significance for the operas of Wagner there is an enormous bibliography on the history of the recurring motive in opera. For Weber's predecessors and contemporaries see especially: Ernst Bücken, *Der heroische Stil in der Oper* (Leipzig, 1924); Karl Wörner, 'Beiträge zur Geschichte des Leitmotivs in der Oper', *Zeitschrift für Musikwissenschaft* 14 (1931–2): 151–72; and Robert Tallant Laudon, *Sources of the Wagnerian Synthesis: a Study of the Franco-German Tradition in 19th-Century Opera* (Munich, 1979).

TABLE 4: Summary of musical recall in *Euryanthe* (excluding the Ouverture)

Item and First Appearance	Recurrence(s)
No. 1 (G major)	1. Ritornello preceding No. 2 (G major)
	2. No. 3 (G major; abbreviated and accelerated)
No. 4: *Con fuoco* (E♭ major; with text 'Ich bau' auf Gott und meine Euryanth')	Act II Finale, No. 14 (mm. 108–23) (D♭ major; with different text)
Eglantine's motive	
Act I, scene iii: Recitative (several statements)	1. Aria No. 6 (m. 37)
	2. Recitative (following No. 6)
	3. Scena ed aria No. 8
	4. Finale II (mm. 138–9, 142–3)
	5. Duetto con coro No. 19 (mm. 17–19)
Love Duet: main theme	
Act I, scene iii (E♭ major)	1. Duetto No. 13 (C major)
	2. Finale III (mm. 188–210, C major)
Emma (Vision)	
Act I, scene iii (B major/minor)	1. Act III, scene v (B major/minor: Eglantine's delirium)
	2. Finale III (mm. 216–23, C major, transformed)
Transition between No. 12 and No. 13	Finale III (mm. 174–87)
Jaegerchor No. 18 (E♭ major)	Finale III (mm. 166–73, E♭ major)

function as musico-dramatic units corresponding to primary articulations of dramatic structure, a trait that has been recognized by a number of prior commentators.[74] The first four pieces function as and in fact were composed as a multi-movement Introduzione setting the wager between Adolar and Lysiart in motion. The next three pieces and intervening recitatives (Nos. 5–7) develop Euryanthe's misplaced confidence in Eglantine. In the second act, the Aria No. 12 and the Duetto No.

[74] See A. A. Abert, 'Webers "Euryanthe"', p. 439, and René Leibowitz, 'Un opéra maudit: "Euryanthe"', in *Les Fantômes de l'opéra. Essais sur le théâtre lyrique* (Paris, 1972), pp. 145–74, translated as 'Eine verachtete Oper: Euryanthe', in *Musik-Konzepte*, 52, ed. Heinz-Klaus Metzger and Rainer Riehn (Munich, 1986), pp. 48–71. Reiner Zimmermann points out that in the autograph score Weber carefully distinguishes between thick double bars, used only at the conclusion of pieces that mark the end of large scenic units, and thin double bars that mark the ends of pieces within a scenic unit. See 'Zwei Blicke in die Quellen', in *Musik-Konzepte*, 52, pp. 77–8.

13 are obviously linked to one another and may also be heard as components of a larger structure that includes the Finale No. 14 as well, a large-scale scenic entity in its own right. The third act contains three multi-piece complexes: the revival of Euryanthe's hopes after the nadir of depression (Nos. 17–20); Adolar's first inklings of Euryanthe's innocence (Nos. 21–2); and a portrait of the villains that convinces Adolar of their guilt (Nos. 23–4). These latter two complexes are in turn yoked to one another and to the Act III Finale to effect a continuous sweep from No. 21 to the end of the opera.

Various consistencies obtain in the shaping of these larger complexes. First, as we shall discuss in Chapter VII, the scenic units for the most part exhibit logical tonal relationships predicated on root movement by third or fifth. Second, continuity within a given scenic complex is often enhanced by the avoidance of closure at the ends of set pieces; in such cases the vocal part normally makes an authentic final cadence in the tonic, following which the concluding ritornello becomes the starting point for a transition to the next section; when a situation within a scene is interrupted by a particularly startling turn of events, as happens so often in the third act, the end of one piece may be linked more abruptly to the succeeding unit by means of a deceptive cadence or brusque harmonic twist as a way to highlight the dramatic disjunction. Again, Weber himself explained the significance of such techniques in his important discussion of Hoffmann's *Undine*,[75] which elicited his praise precisely for its attempts to create a greater sense of forward motion at the expense of effective and crowd-pleasing final cadences.[76] Mozart's *Idomeneo*, the operas of Gluck, and the *opéras comiques* of Méhul also afforded Weber a number of precedents for procedures of this type.[77] Third, the scenic units are shaped by a fairly consistent three-part paradigm for structure, consisting of: (1) an opening, static piece that establishes a basic mood, colour, or situation; (2) a recitative, arioso, or set piece that redefines the situation; and (3) a culminating piece that sum-

[75] 'As a result of the form which is its right, each musical piece gives the impression of an independent, organic, self-contained entity. Yet as a part of the whole, it must disappear when the whole is beheld; at the same time, displaying several surfaces simultaneously it can and should be many-sided (especially if it is an ensemble piece), a Janus head to be taken in at a glance.' *Sämtliche Schriften*, pp. 129–30; I have adapted the present translation from Oliver Strunk, comp., *Source Readings in Music History* (New York, 1950), pp. 803–4.

[76] *Sämtliche Schriften*, pp. 132, 135. It is of course not without irony that the critic Kanne attributed the coolness of Viennese audiences to the first performances of *Euryanthe* in part to the 'immer rasch wieder einfallenden Recitative', in other words, the frequent avoidance of closure throughout the opera.

[77] On the structural innovations in *Mélidore et Phrosine* and *Ariodant* see Bartlet, op. cit. ch. 2 n. 9 above, pp. 1246–59 and 1384–99.

marizes the new situation. Coupled with this plan is the tendency to intensify the emotion and hence the musical activity in the course of the unit, such that the scene progresses from relatively slow to relatively fast, from relatively quiet to relatively loud, and from relatively small performing forces to relatively large performing forces. Orchestration is particularly calculated to reflect the emotional *Steigerung* within the scenic unit, as the most brilliant scorings are typically reserved for the climactic last piece in the major dramatic units. Thus in the opening scene at Prémery the sonority of No. 4 is much greater than that of any of the preceding movements, thanks principally to the introduction of the three trombones. In the second dramatic unit of Act I, the relatively subdued orchestrations for Nos. 5, 6, and 7 are exceeded by that of No. 8, which employs four horns, and which itself in turn is eclipsed by the addition of trumpets and timpani in the first-act Finale No. 9. The orchestration of the second dramatic unit of Act II, from Adolar's Aria No. 12 to the end of Finale No. 14, is also carefully laid out to correspond to the intensification of mood—further underscored by increases in tempo and the progression from aria to duet to ensemble with chorus—throughout the scene. In the third act, No. 20 and No. 24 are similarly treated as the climactic goals for their respective dramatic units and for this reason employ much fuller sonorities than the pieces that precede them. Naturally, the tendency to build up the *Instrumentarium* through the course of a scene at times runs counter to the more symbolic uses of sonority that are observed at various points in the opera; brass instruments, especially the trombones, are used as much for their power to punctuate the end of a dramatic unit as for any associative value.[78]

Given the fact that Weber placed a premium on overall consistency of character in an opera, which he described with terms like 'Kolorit', 'Farbengebung', 'Allgefühl am Ende', and 'Haupt- und Totaleffekt', questions of unity in the opera must ultimately turn to considerations of character. Beyond the technical means that make *Euryanthe* an 'organisch verbundenes' work, does the opera possess a colouring or identity that can be apprehended and described? For *Euryanthe* this question is perhaps more difficult to answer than for any other of Weber's mature stage works. Consider, for example, the opera's medievalism: does the music to *Euryanthe* seek to portray its twelfth-century milieu? As we have seen in his discussion of Méhul's *Joseph*, Weber clearly valued the ability of an opera to suggest the time and place of its action, and it

---

[78] On the symbolic uses of orchestration in *Euryanthe* see Chapter VIII. The potential conflict between the symbolism of instruments and the desire for climactic sonority is discussed by Frits Noske, 'Semantics of Orchestration', in *The Signifier and the Signified* (The Hague, 1977), p. 121.

is well known that he implemented this ideal in a number of his works by resorting to obvious devices of *couleur locale*: the quotation of 'authentic' exotic melodies in the early *Overtura chinesa* and *Oberon*; the use of conventional 'Turkish music' in *Abu Hassan*; the allusions to Spanish dance rhythms in *Preciosa* and *Die drei Pintos*; and the evocation of simple village life in *Freischütz* through self-consciously square rhythms and diatonic melodies. In contrast, *Euryanthe* makes few if any direct or obvious allusions to the music of the European Middle Ages, at least none that would be recognized as such by a twentieth-century listener with even a passing acquaintance with medieval music. Admittedly, practically nothing was known about medieval music during the early nineteenth century, and thus a composer like Weber would have had few sources to which to turn for 'authentic' melodies.[79] But neither does the opera strive at self-conscious archaisms to suggest the Middle Ages, as Grétry had done in *Richard cœur-de-lion*.[80] The one musical feature in *Euryanthe* that perhaps betrays an obvious attempt at medieval colour is the conspicuous use of the zither as a stage prop in the first act. Not mentioned at all in the proximate source for the libretto, Chezy's translation of the *Roman de la violette*, the zither may have been suggested to Weber and Chezy as an authentic touch of local colour by Forkel's *Allgemeine Geschichte der Musik*, where it is equated with the medieval 'rote' (rocta, rotta), one of the instruments that Forkel associates with the medieval minstrels.[81]

Nevertheless, *Euryanthe was* received by a number of Weber's contemporaries as a medieval opera. Henry Chorley noted a 'chivalresque' tone throughout the entire opera and found in the opening chorus a 'chivalrous strain'.[82] Amadeus Wendt felt that the Introduzione had portrayed 'the feeling of untroubled rejoicing, restrained, however, by the noble

manners of chivalry' and that the composer had in Adolar's Romanza No. 2 'masterfully struck the noble tone of the knightly troubadour, and differentiated it from the folk-like [tone], of which he has elsewhere produced so many successful examples'.[83] A. B. Marx was particularly impressed by the medievalism of the opera, which he felt to be a

[79] Weber seems to make no use of the *trouvère* chansons published in Jean Benjamin de Laborde's *Essai sur la musique ancienne et moderne*, vol. ii (Paris, 1780; facsimile reprint: New York, 1978).

[80] For Grétry's self-conscious efforts to create a vivid image of the Middle Ages see David Charlton, *Grétry and the Growth of Opéra-Comique* (Cambridge, 1986), pp. 232–40.

[81] Johann Nicolaus Forkel, *Allgemeine Geschichte der Musik*, vol. ii (Leipzig, 1801; facsimile reprint: Graz, 1967), pp. 743–4.

[82] Henry Chorley, *Modern German Music* (London, 1854), i. 304.

[83] *BamZ* 3 (1826): 21.

faithful interpretation of the time and the place in which the event occurs. The south of France in the heyday of the age of knights—that is the content of the music, just as it is of the poem. The song-like tone at the beginning of the *Introduction*, which speaks as a '*Blüthenweis*' or '*Frühlingsweis*', and the solemn *Reigen* before the King's throne, in which knightly pride and *courtoisie* are united with noble adornment and lap up as in joyful waves: both direct our imaginations to that specified point [in time]; and Adolar's *Minnelied* makes us feel at home there.[84]

In another writing Marx went so far as to claim that 'in his *Euryanthe* Weber had the credit of being the first among all composers to strive with the most fortunate success toward truth and unity of the character of its time and place (which Mozart had only intimated in the choruses of the *Entführung* and in the Fandango in *Figaro*).'[85]

However, these writers were probably responding less to concrete details of compositional technique and 'authentic' medievalism than to their own poetic image of the Middle Ages, one rooted in the romantic literature of the day, that pictured the European Middle Ages as an 'age of chivalry' replete with court pageant, solemn oath-taking, and trial-by-combat, in which duty and honour were more important than life itself, in which warriors were also sensitive poet-musicians and graceful dancers, in which conduct was guided by a refined code of etiquette and morality, in which women were placed upon a pedestal as objects of love and admiration and at the same time held to a severely strict code of fidelity and chastity, and in which the supernatural still communicated with the living world.[86] Presumably Weber shared this image as well, for he had, after all, selected the story and moulded a libretto that embodied all of these 'romantic' clichés about the Middle Ages. The artificiality of language throughout the libretto seems calculated to strengthen the impression of an extremely formal and courtly age. And to a certain extent, Weber seems also to have subtly aimed at a musical style that would correspond to this fanciful image of life at court. Thus in comparison to the examples in *Der Freischütz* and the norms for genres like the Lied and *romance*, the strophic pieces in *Euryanthe* are rather self-consciously complicated compositions filled with harmonic and rhythmic artifices and 'unusual' turns perhaps to suggest the refinement of courtly life. Adolar's Romanza No. 2 avoids the lilting compound metre normally associated with more folk-like examples of the genre, turning instead to a graceful triple metre somewhat

[84] *BamZ* 3 (1826): 10–11.

[85] A. B. Marx, *Die Kunst des Gesanges* (Berlin, 1826), p. 232.

[86] On the purportedly authentic details in the stage action and properties see Gaynor Gray Jones, 'Background and Themes of the Operas of Carl Maria von Weber' (Ph. D. dissertation, Cornell University, 1972), pp. 135–6.

evocative of eighteenth-century court dances. Melodic chromaticism and rhythmic irregularities certainly make the May Song a more complicated wedding song than the Volkslied No. 14 in the *Freischütz*, and the Jaegerchor in *Euryanthe* also exhibits unusual quirks of syncopation, phrase organization, and harmony that again suggest a more elevated and artificial world than that of village life in seventeenth-century Bohemia.

Yet, it is perhaps fundamentally futile to seek much further for traces of musical medievalism in the opera, for as Weber repeatedly insisted, from well before he composed a single note to long after the première, in this one opera he felt compelled to eschew the 'popular' devices and variety that had aroused such enthusiasm in *Freischütz* and concentrate instead on human passions. In part this austerity may have stemmed, as Max Maria von Weber claimed, from the composer's desire to show that he could succeed without the 'Teufelsspuk' of the *Freischütz*; I think it more likely, however, that the composer's ambition to conquer 'grand opera', the acme of operatic genres, brought with it notions about elevation and severity of style that not even a 'grand romantic opera' could violate. The great 'grand operas' of Gluck and Spontini had focused primarily on the passions of individuals, and so too would *Euryanthe*. Thus Weber's characterization of the opera to Danzi after the work had begun to make the rounds of German theatres with varying degrees of success remains perhaps the best assessment of the work's peculiar 'Farbengebung': a 'simple, serious work that seeks nothing but truth of expression, passion, and characterization'.

The foregoing considerations have touched briefly upon certain aspects of the finished work that seem to respond to Weber's goal of operatic organicism, and at many points in the following study of the sources for the opera we shall observe other ways in which the opera is 'organically connected', for nearly all stages of genesis prior to the drafting of individual pieces bear witness to the composer's concern for large-scale organization and coherence. Indeed, in Weber's approach a good grasp of the whole seems to have been an indispensable precondition for the contemplation and composition of individual pieces; as he later explained to the English impresario Charles Kemble in connection with his last opera, *Oberon*: 'Before I know the extent and character of all the musical pieces, I can calculate neither the increase of the effects, nor the complection of each individual piece. Without the sure survey of the whole, my phantasy can not possibly develop itself, or be chained down to minutes . . .'[87]

[87] Letter of 6 Jan. 1825, published in *MMW* ii. 588. Weber's draft of this letter is in WFN-Handschriftliches, Konvolut XVII, Bl. 90a.

PART II: THE LIBRETTO

IV. The Sources for the Libretto

I. WEBER AND HIS LIBRETTISTS

The biographical overview presented in Chapter II makes it readily apparent that the final form of the *Euryanthe* libretto was reached only after an extremely prolonged period of gestation and revision, which stretched from the initial drafts of the winter of 1821–2 to the final emendations made after Chezy's return to Dresden in the spring and early summer of 1823. Carl Förster had heard that the libretto had been revised nine times by 1 April 1823, and Chezy herself claimed shortly after the première that the final version of the libretto represented the eleventh revision of the text.[1] Exactly why was the libretto altered so frequently and to what kinds of revision was the text subjected? Previous attempts to answer these questions have rested primarily on two published accounts, both of which prove to be problematic when subjected to closer scrutiny. Of the two, the more widely known version is the one presented by Max Maria von Weber,[2] whose reliability we have already had cause to question. Potentially more informative is the lengthy memoir published in 1840 by Chezy in the *Neue Zeitschrift für Musik*,[3] an account that reproduces letters and scenarios drafted by Weber during the genesis of *Euryanthe* as well as a few examples of text alterations suggested by the composer. Certain considerations, however, lead one to question the objectivity of Chezy's article. For one thing, she wrote her memoir almost a generation after the fact, and her vague treatment of dates and chronology suggests that much of the article was based on dim impressions of the past. Her description of a harmonious working relationship between herself and Weber conceals the considerable bitterness that prevailed towards the end of the collaboration and that arose primarily through her demands for more money.[4] On this point it is instructive to compare the tone of the 1840 article with the rancour evident in two articles that she published

[1] Förster, op. cit. ch. 1 n. 42 above, p. 295; Chezy 1823A.
[2] *MMW* ii. 356–63, 371–80, 461–2.
[3] Chezy 1840.
[4] For instance, Chezy withheld from publication the stern letters from Weber that concern her claims for more money and that thus put her in an unfavourable light; their presence in the Varnhagen collection along with other letters that she did publish assure that they were in her possession at the time of the 1840 article.

in Vienna immediately after the première.[5] Finally, the motivation behind all of her published accounts of the collaboration is easy to discern. Consistently claiming to have followed Weber's every whim in the revisions of the text, Chezy's memoirs attempt to exculpate the librettist from the charge that she had undermined the success of the opera and to shift the blame for commonly criticized elements of the libretto onto Weber.

To be sure, there is no reason to doubt that Weber was the moving force behind the numerous revisions of the *Euryanthe* libretto, for he seems habitually to have played an active role in the shaping of his libretti and to have viewed such control over textual matters as an indispensable part of his prerogatives and responsibilities as an opera composer.[6] To judge from the available evidence, Weber's influence over his librettos extended to all aspects of the text, from structural decisions like the deletion of the opening two scenes with the hermit in *Der Freischütz* to questions of versification and poetic metre. Even in the case of *Oberon*, an opera written in a foreign language and for an unfamiliar audience with a different set of expectations, Weber attempted to rectify matters that ultimately were out of his control.[7] Unfortunately, the full extent of Weber's participation in the selection and execution of his libretti in most cases can no longer be fully ascertained. Unlike the famous collaborations of Strauss and Hofmannsthal or of the mature Verdi and his librettists, which were carried on through correspondence and have thus been largely preserved for the scrutiny of posterity, Weber preferred to work with librettists who lived close at hand so that he might have direct and immediate access to them. His operatic collaborations have thus left behind precious little evidence for his engagement with questions of the libretto, which must be deduced from the memoirs of his librettists, the few letters that do survive, and most importantly,

---

[5] Chezy 1823A, and 'Erster Entwurf eines Scenariums der Euryanthe, Operndichtung für Carl Maria von Weber', *Wiener Zeitschrift für Kunst, Literatur, Theater und Mode*, 8/137 (15 Nov. 1823): 1128–31, and 8/138 (18 Nov. 1823): 1137–44; hereafter cited as Chezy 1823B.

[6] Weber's words to Friedrich Kind, the *Freischütz* librettist, perhaps best exemplify the critical stance towards the libretto that led him not only to reject numerous texts offered to him, but also to bend those texts that he did accept more to his taste: 'Do you believe that a proper composer simply accepts a libretto the way a schoolboy [accepts] an apple? that he accepts everything with his eyes shut and blindly pours tones over it, happy to be able to unleash that which has been held back so long?' Letter of 28 July 1821, in Friedrich Kind, *Der Freischütz, Volksoper in drei Aufzügen* (Leipzig, 1843), p. 165. See also the testimony of Carl Theodor Winkler, the librettist for *Die drei Pintos*, in Theodor Hell [i.e. Carl Theodor Winkler], ed., *Hinterlassene Schriften von Carl Maria von Weber* (Dresden and Leipzig, 1828), p. lxix.

[7] See Weber's letters to the English librettist, J. R. Planché, in James Robinson Planché, *Recollections and Reflections*, new and revised edition (London, n.d.), pp. 50–5.

the extant manuscript librettos made before the composition of the operas, which sometimes contain alterations in his handwriting.[8]

With *Euryanthe*, however, the preserved evidence does allow a fairly detailed reconstruction of the collaboration between composer and librettist. Relevant letters exist because, much to Weber's dismay, Chezy spent the period between September 1822 and the beginning of April 1823 in Berlin, thereby necessitating the correspondence that Weber normally would have preferred to avoid. The negative response that the libretto elicited from critics provoked her to publish three different articles about her collaboration with Weber. Finally, the fact that the libretto was revised so many times gave rise to a number of manuscript drafts for the text. At the present time it is impossible to account for all of the eleven versions that Chezy claimed to have made, but there still exist several preliminary drafts that document various stages in the evolution of the libretto between the winter of 1821–2 and the summer of 1823. Most of these preliminary manuscripts are now located in the *Weberiana* collection of the Deutsche Staatsbibliothek in Berlin (DDR), with additional materials preserved in the Österreichische National-bibliothek, Vienna, the archive of the Deutsche Akademie der Wissen-schaften, Berlin (DDR), and the Biblioteka Jagiellońska, Kraków; the relevant sources are outlined in Table 5. Although the existence of the most important of these manuscripts has been known since the publica-tion of Jähns's thematic catalogue in 1871,[9] they have largely been overlooked in the literature on Weber, doubtless because the final text of the libretto has been held in such disrepute as to discourage investi-gation of its sources.[10] These manuscripts in fact have never been system-atically described or evaluated. In so far as they potentially illuminate an important aspect of Weber's compositional routine, his role as col-laborator on librettos, these sources deserve greater attention than they have thus far received. Moreover, Weber's aesthetic of *Totaleffekt* makes it imperative to take the origins and development of the libretto seriously, especially since many fundamental decisions about the musical approach

---

[8] For a provisional listing of extant preliminary librettos for the operas other than *Euryanthe* see Michael C. Tusa, 'Carl Maria von Weber's *Euryanthe*: A Study of Its Historical Context, Genesis and Reception' (Ph.D. dissertation, Princeton University, 1983), pp. 456–7.

[9] Jähns, op. cit. ch. 1 n. 4 above, p. 361.

[10] Brief descriptions of the librettos with traces of Weber's handwriting in the *Weberiana* collection of the Deutsche Staatsbibliothek are offered by Bartlitz, op. cit. ch. 1 n. 3 above, pp. 36–7; the earliest surviving libretto, *Web.* Cl. II A g 13 is, however, not listed there because it contains no sign of Weber's handwriting. Limited use of the preliminary *Euryanthe* librettos for interpretive purposes is made by Wolfgang Becker, *Die deutsche Oper in Dresden unter der Leitung Carl Maria von Webers* (Berlin, 1962), pp. 145–50.

were worked out at this stage of the genesis; in many ways the history of the libretto reveals as much about Weber's notions of operatic dramaturgy as do the extant musical sketches and drafts. The following discussion is therefore an attempt to trace the history of the *Euryanthe* libretto through an examination and correlation of extant sources, letters, and memoirs, with special attention paid to the question of Weber's influence on the libretto.

2. THE SOURCE FOR THE LIBRETTO

The starting point for any consideration of the history of the *Euryanthe* libretto is most naturally the literary source on which the libretto was based. As mentioned in Chapter I, Chezy claims to have offered Weber a choice of several subjects for operatic treatment when he first approached her in the autumn of 1821. Of these alternatives we know from Chezy only that they included the Spanish comedy *Mejor está que estava* by Calderón de la Barca and her own German translation of an early printed prose version of the thirteenth-century *Roman de la violette* of Gerbert de Montreuil.[11] Weber never explained his reasons for selecting the *Euryanthe* text as the source for his new opera, although in a letter written in 1824 to his friend Gottfried Weber, he defended the choice of subject on musical grounds: 'Of course I myself chose the libretto of *Euryanthe*; I make nothing according to an ordered mould. If *you* don't recognize the musicality of the situation and so forth, then who should?'[12] Certainly in Chezy's translation the *Roman*, a story closely related to the sources for Shakespeare's *Cymbeline* and the *novella* 'Bernabò da Genova e la moglie Zinevra' in Boccaccio's *Decameron*, incorporates a number of decidedly musical elements. Gerhard, the protagonist and model for Adolar, is a noble youth equally well versed in combat and courtly song, and his songs form an important part of Chezy's translation of the *Roman*. Chivalric pomp and ceremony abound in the story, and

[11] Chezy 1840, p. 5. According to *MMW* ii. 355, Chezy also suggested *Melusine*, *Magellone*, and *Wigalois* as alternative subjects, but there is no documentary confirmation for this assertion. With respect to Chezy's translation of the Euryanthe story, Chezy claims not to have known the original verse version of the *Roman de la violette* at the time she made her translation, and she instead based her translation on an early printed prose version that she found in the Bibliothèque royale in Paris. Two sixteenth-century prints therefore come into question as the possible source for her translation; see Francisque Michel's preface to *Roman de la violette, ou de Gerard de Nevers*, by Gerbert de Montreuil (Paris, 1834), pp. xxv–xxxiii. For a summary of the *Roman* and a discussion of its thematic relationships to other medieval romances see: Gaynor Gray Jones, 'Background and Themes of the Operas of Carl Maria von Weber', Ph.D. diss., Cornell University, 1972, pp. 107–19.

[12] Letter of 19 Mar. 1824, in G. *Weber-Briefe*, p. 87.

TABLE 5. Sources for the *Euryanthe* libretto collaboration: an overview

A. The earliest sources (all published in Chezy 1823B)

Source	Date
1. Chezy's scenario	Nov. 1821?
2. Weber's scenario	Nov. 1821?
3. Libretto fragments	Dec. 1821

B. Manuscript libretti (all in Deutsche Staatsbibliothek, Berlin (DDR) unless otherwise specified)

Source	Date	Description, comments
1. *Web.* Cl. II A g 13	Dec. 1821/Jan. 1822	Chezy holograph. Composite libretto of entire opera.
2. *Web.* Cl. II A g 3	Jan. 1822	Copyist's libretto, with annotations by Weber. Examined by the Viennese censor in Feb. 1822.
3. Vienna, ONB S.m. 32305	Feb. 1822	Copy of *Web.* Cl II A g 3.
4. *Web.* Cl. II A g 6	Spring 1822	Weber holograph. Libretto of Act I (i.e. Acts I–II)
5. *Web.* Cl. II A g 4	Summer 1822–summer 1823	Chezy holograph, with annotations by Weber. Composite libretto (see Table 6).
6. *Web.* Cl. II A g 7	early 1823	Weber holograph. Scenario for the conclusion of Act III.
7. *Web.* Cl. II A g 5	Apr./May 1823	Copyist's libretto, annotated by Weber. Includes two insertions by Chezy.
8. Berlin (DDR), Akademie der Wissenschaften, Zentrales Archiv	Summer 1823	Copyist's libretto with comments by Chezy; fragments of Act III. Probably from the *Stichvorlage* for the first edition of the libretto.
9. Vienna, ONB S.m. 32304	Summer 1823 (before 28 Aug.)	Copyist's libretto. *Regiebuch* for première, proofed by Chezy and Weber.

C. Extant correspondence between Weber and Chezy

Author/addressee	Date	Location (publication)
1. Weber to Chezy	31 Dec. 1821	(Stargardt auction catalogue No. 603)
2. Weber to Chezy	9 Apr. 1822	Kraków, BJ (Chezy 1840, p. 33)
3. Weber to Chezy	10 Oct. 1822	*Web.* Cl. II B 2a, 31 [Abschrift]
4. Weber to Chezy	11 Nov. 1822	Kraków, BJ (Chezy 1840, p. 37)
5. Chezy to Weber	Nov. 1822	*Web.* Cl. V, Abt. 2, 14
6. Weber to Chezy	28 Nov. 1822	Kraków, BJ (Chezy 1840, pp. 37–8)
7. Weber to Chezy	22 Dec. 1822	Kraków, BJ (Chezy 1840, p. 38)
8. Weber to Chezy	27 Feb. 1823	Kraków, BJ (Chezy 1840, pp. 38–9)
9. Weber to Chezy	5 June 1823	Kraków BJ; WFN Handschriftliches, XIII, 80 [draft]
10. Weber to Chezy	17 June 1823 (1st letter)	Kraków, BJ [Abschrift]
11. Weber to Chezy	17 June 1823 (2nd letter)	Paris, BN; WFN Handschriftliches, XIII, 80 [draft]
12. Chezy to Weber	20 July 1823	*Web.* Cl. V, Abt. 2, 15
13. Weber to Chezy	? Summer 1823	Kraków, BJ
14. Weber to Chezy	10 Oct. 1823	WFN Handschriftliches, XIII, 80 [draft]

the opening feast at the court of Louis VI must have struck Weber as an ideal scene with which to establish the courtly tone of the opera.

Whatever Weber's reasons for preferring the *Euryanthe* subject to the alternatives, it must have been clear from the outset that a great deal of tailoring would be necessary to convert the *Roman* into a libretto. For one thing, the *Roman* is long, typically including a number of fanciful episodes that retard rather than hasten the resolution of the central story. Chezy's version of the romance is divided into forty-one unnumbered sections, the first nine of which develop: (*a*) the wager between Gerhard and Lysiardus on the fidelity of Gerhard's beloved, Euryanthe (sections 1–2); (*b*) the betrayal of Euryanthe by her old servant Gundrieth, who allows Lysiardus to observe the bathing Euryanthe and thereby to discover her jealously guarded secret (sections 2–4); (*c*) Lysiardus's claim and proof that he had seduced Euryanthe (sections 5–8); and (*d*) Gerhard's attempt to execute Euryanthe in the forest of Orléans as punishment for her alleged infidelity, thwarted at the last moment by the attack of a large snake (sections 8–9). In the thirteenth section Gerhard, disguised as a travelling minstrel, learns of Euryanthe's innocence and sets out to find her, and most of the remainder of the poem deals with Gerhard's various deeds as he roams northern France and the Rhineland seeking his beloved. Along the way he himself is made untrue to Euryanthe by a magic love potion with which the beautiful Eglantine of Cologne wins his love. Only in the thirty-fourth section is he actually reunited with Euryanthe, who in the meantime had been rescued from the wilderness by the Duke of Metz and taken to his castle, where she again had been falsely accused of another evil deed. Gerhard defends Euryanthe's innocence in two trials by combat, first at Metz (section 33) and then at King Louis's court (section 40), and the story ends with the executions of Lysiardus and Gundrieth and the marriage of Gerhard and Euryanthe, who, we are told, eventually have two sons.

While the numerous episodes presented no real problem to operatic adaptation—due to their extraneous nature they could be excised without damage to the central story—one key element of the core plot presented an insurmountable obstacle to nineteenth-century sensibilities. In the original version of the story, the secret that Euryanthe preserves as a sign of fidelity to Gerhard is that she bears a violet-shaped mole on her right breast. Only she and Gerhard are ever to know this secret. Lysiardus, having observed the mole while Euryanthe bathed, is able to offer his knowledge of that secret as convincing proof of Euryanthe's faithlessness. In view of the fact that the new opera was to be written for Vienna, where the notoriously strict censor had already mutilated the *Freischütz*, Chezy and Weber both agreed that some other device would have to be substituted for the rather indelicate secret in the source.

3. EARLIEST STAGES IN THE COLLABORATION

No manuscript materials are known to survive for the earliest stages of the collaboration, and to trace the steps that immediately followed the selection of subject matter one must therefore rely primarily on materials that Chezy published in 1823 and 1840—the early scenarios and fragments of her first attempt at a libretto as well as certain anecdotes about comments and advice that Weber allegedly passed along *viva voce* to his apprentice librettist.

3.1. *First scenario*

With Chezy's first scenario for the opera, a prose précis of the plot, we see the influence of the foregoing considerations for length and moral propriety.[13] Chezy presented Weber a three-act plan that generally keeps very close to the elements of the core story outlined above, reducing the number of characters and episodes to those required by the central theme of Gerhard and Euryanthe. Act I closes with the eighth section of the *Roman*, Adolar's and Euryanthe's departure from court following Lysiart's successful claim of victory, and Act II concludes with Gerhard's discovery that all had been deceived by Lysiart's treachery, the substance of the thirteenth section of Chezy's translation. The third act in Chezy's scenario then compresses the remainder of the *Roman* into a single *Gotteskampf* for Euryanthe's honour. Gerhard appears as an unidentified knight and defeats Lysiart, who confesses all as he dies; Euryanthe pardons Eglantine.

Beyond the elimination of the later episodes devoted to Gerhard's adventures and Euryanthe's misadventures in Metz, several substantial changes in the plot can be observed in the scenario, perhaps as a result of the earliest discussions between Weber and Chezy. First, to facilitate the condensation of the story, Euryanthe is discovered in the wilderness by the King instead of the Duke of Metz, and it is he who, unconvinced of Euryanthe's guilt, orders the trial by combat in Act III. Second, in place of the evil old servant Gundrieth, Chezy substituted the character of Eglantine, borrowed from the later episodes of the *Roman*, as a young confidante, perhaps to motivate the confidante's hatred for Euryanthe through the jealousy of unrequited love for Gerhard. In the scenario Euryanthe forgives Eglantine after the demise of Lysiart. Most significantly for the future of the opera, Chezy's first scenario substituted for the secret of the violet-shaped mole a more complicated sign of fealty between Gerhard and Euryanthe. Haunted by the ghost of a male ancestor (*Ahnherr*), Gerhard once revealed to Euryanthe under solemn oath

---

[13] Originally printed in Chezy 1823B; reprinted in full in *MMW* ii. 371–4 and Tusa, 'Carl Maria von Weber's *Euryanthe*', pp. 467–70.

of silence a family secret, and because of this oath Euryanthe prays at the ancestor's tomb every night. Although Euryanthe does not betray this secret to the false friend Eglantine, she does give her enough information to allow her to discover it. And the nature of the secret? While not completely specified in the scenario, proximity to the earliest libretto fragments (see below) suggests that Gerhard's solemn secret turned on the unfortunate fate of the ancestor who, having murdered his wife for falsely alleged infidelity and then committed suicide with the same weapon, a dagger on which the whole story was inscribed, is now condemned to wander the nights as a ghost. According to the scenario, Eglantine finds the blood-flecked dagger in the crypt and eventually reveals the secret to Lysiart, who uses this knowledge as proof of his conquest of Euryanthe.

It is generally agreed that the substitution of Gerhard's family secret for the simpler device of the violet represented no improvement in the story, since it complicates the plot by shifting several of the most crucial events to times before the start of the opera, such as the ancestor's murder-suicide, the ghost's appearance to Gerhard, and Gerhard's relation of these events to Euryanthe. Moreover, Lysiart's knowledge of Gerhard's secret hardly seems as compelling evidence of Euryanthe's infidelity as did his knowledge of the birthmark. Nevertheless, the replacement secret does bring the story of *Euryanthe* into close relationship to a genre currently fashionable in the spoken German drama, the so-called *Schicksalstragödie* or tragedy of fate. Particularly noteworthy are the similarities between the story of Gerhard's *Ahnherr* and the plot of *Die Ahnfrau* by Franz Grillparzer (1791–1872), published and first performed in 1817. Both stories develop from ancestral sins of passion punished by death, ghosts who cannot find peace in the afterlife, and murder weapons, in both cases a dagger, which function as prominent stage props. In the original *Euryanthe* scenario, too, the fact that Gerhard almost repeats the fatal mistake of his ancestor, the murder of an innocent lover, lends to the story the motive of the hereditary curse, a customary device in the *Schicksalstragödien* of Zacharias Werner and Adolf Müllner, and one particularly important in *Die Ahnfrau*, where the last descendant of the *Ahnfrau* unknowingly kills his father and enters into an incestuous relationship with his sister. In view of the fact that the *Ahnfrau* was written and first performed in Vienna, where it was immensely successful, it is not improbable that both Chezy and Weber saw in the substitution of a family secret with supernatural overtones for the indelicate motif of the violet-shaped mole a chance to capitalize on one very fashionable and successful tendency in the spoken drama of the day.

One final comment about Chezy's first scenario for *Euryanthe* is relevant, for it leads us to the next stage. Chezy's complete inexperience with opera, which she claims to have admitted to Weber when he first approached her about the project, is evident from the scenario's almost total lack of provision for musical numbers. Apart from two songs in the opening scene, both suggested by the *Roman*, Chezy's only attempt to specify a musical number in the scenario is a very tentative suggestion that the end of Act II close with Gerhard, Lysiart, and Eglantine singing together.

3.2. *Weber's correction of Chezy's scenario*

Having received Chezy's scenario, Weber proceeded to rework the plan himself into what he considered a more serviceable form. With regard to the plot, he seems not to have cared for the conclusion as Chezy had outlined it, and he suggested a new ending that deviated further from the original story than Chezy had dared. For one thing, Weber desired that Euryanthe's rescue from the forest by the King be followed by a riding accident that apparently kills Euryanthe; according to Chezy, Weber felt that such an event would enhance the suspense, increase Gerhard's remorse, and also provide the basis for an interesting musical effect at the end.[14] Euryanthe's apparent death would also motivate the new denouement that he suggested. Instead of bringing the treachery of Lysiart and Eglantine into the open through a trial by combat, which according to Chezy Weber felt to be a hackneyed dramatic situation,[15] he proposed a final scene in which Eglantine confesses the treachery after learning of Euryanthe's reported demise. Euryanthe is then carried onto the stage on a bier, but her recovery and reunion with Gerhard signal the happy conclusion of the work. Regarding the fate of the two villains, however, Weber was himself unsure, and he left that question open to Chezy: 'Should Lysiart murder Eglantine, or she him? Or what happens to both of them?'[16] Weber also significantly trimmed the *dramatis personae* of Chezy's scenario; as he allegedly remarked to Chezy: 'There are too many characters; we can specify only five acting personages, for *Euryanthe* must be played on all stages. There are many of these where one can barely manage a soprano, a second soprano, a bass, a tenor, and a baritone. We must arrange the pomp in such a way that one can display it profusely, but also that one can omit it. Small theatres can then chuck the spectacle away.'[17]

In structural matters, too, Weber's scenario considerably altered and refined the material that Chezy had first brought him. By eliminating

[14] Chezy 1840, p. 9.   [15] Ibid.
[16] 'Soll Lysiart die Eglantine ermorden, oder sie ihn? oder was geschieht mit Beiden?' Ibid., p. 10, and Chezy 1823B, p. 1131.
[17] Chezy 1840, p. 10.

the *Gotteskampf* of Chezy's third act, Weber was able to condense the opera into a two-act structure. Faced with Chezy's obvious ignorance of opera, Weber found it necessary to indicate in his scenario the placement and types of musical numbers that he wanted in the work. From the first, then, it was he who was responsible for the disposition of the numbers, and since his scenario represents the start of serious consideration of structural problems in the opera, it is relevant here to examine this draft more closely.[18] The following outline is an attempt to reconstruct the original structure proposed by Weber, with numbers in square brackets supplied to clarify the succession and number of items; broken rules indicate changes of scenery.

Act I

i	1.	*Introduction. Fest bei Hofe.*
		Tanz mit Chor
		Hymne (Gerhard)
		Beifalls-Chor
		[Wager]

– –

ii	2.	*Arie.* (Euryanthe alone)
iii	3.	*Duetto.* (Euryanthe, Eglantine)
iv	4.	[*Ensemblestück*] (Lysiart mit Rittern.

[18] Chezy published Weber's scenario in both Chezy 1823B, pp. 1130–31 and Chezy 1840, p. 10; both versions are reprinted in Tusa, 'Carl Maria von Weber's *Euryanthe*', pp. 470–4. It is highly unfortunate that Weber's manuscript cannot at present be located, since the two versions of the scenario that Chezy published do not agree with one another in all details, and it is thus difficult to know which of the two is closer to Weber's original plan. The autographs of the letters that Chezy published in 1840 were formerly in the Varnhagen von Ense Collection of the Prussian State Library and are now in the Biblioteka Jagiellońska in Kraków; Dr Marian Zwiercan of the Biblioteka Jagiellónska informs me, however, that the scenario does not appear to be among the holdings in Kraków. The version published in 1840, which according to Chezy was 'copied faithfully according to Weber's original draft', seems rather incomplete and jumbled, especially in the first act, where the scenario presents two conflicting series of numbers for the musical pieces; in contrast the version published in 1823 is very orderly, filling in gaps that are present in the 1840 version and avoiding its conflicting numeration. My surmise is that the 1840 version in fact *is* a diplomatic transcription of Weber's outline, but that it actually embodies at least two stages of evolution, hence the confusion in the numbering of musical pieces in the first act. By 1840, Chezy could no longer remember exactly what the two stages were and made no attempt to differentiate between them or explain the discrepancies. The 1823 version, however, published at a time when the details of the collaboration were still fresh in her mind and yet also when she was most openly hostile towards Weber, represents an edited version of the outline, with Chezy filling in, omitting, and clarifying for the sake of the Viennese public elements in the manuscript that would have been incomprehensible to an outside observer. For these reasons the outline presented here is principally based on Chezy 1840.

		Bewillkommungschor)
v	5.	*Aria*. (Lysiart)
vi	6.	*Duetto*. (Lysiart, Eglantine)

| vii | 7. | *Aria*. (Gerhard) |
| | 8. | *Finale*. |

Act II

i	1.	*Duett* (Euryanthe, Gerhard)
ii		(Euryanthe goes to the spring to refresh herself; Gerhard sinks down exhausted)
iii		(Euryanthe returns warning Adolar of the monster)
iv	2.	*Arie* (Euryanthe sees the battle with the monster; Gerhard leaves her)
[v]	[3]	*Scene und Arie* (Euryanthe alone)
[vi]	[4]	*Ritornell* (Daybreak, hunting signals in the distance, King and retinue find Euryanthe)
	[5]	*Arie und Duett mit Chor*.

[vii]	[6]	*Chor mit Solo's, Tanz?* Mädchenchor, Festesfreude.
[viii]	[7]	*Cavatine*, des Schmerzes (Gerhard)
[ix]	[8]	*Terzett mit Chor* (Eglantine, Lysiart, Gerhard)
[x]	[9]	*Finale*

Much of the outline seems in certain ways rather traditional. With the exception of the more active, multi-movement introduction and finale, the numbers of the first act, as sketched by Weber, are relatively static crystallizations of mood and situation, and each scene, defined by the entrance and/or exit of one or more characters, is originally built around a single number. In contrast, the plan for the second act is less clearly defined (note the abandonment of numbers for the successive scenes and musical pieces), probably because Weber was at this point more concerned with alterations in the plot than he had been in the first act, where he followed Chezy's scenario closely; on the whole, however, the pieces suggested for the second act appear to be more 'kinetic' than those of the first act, a fact of some consequence for the future development of the libretto. The wide range of types of pieces in Weber's plan is completely characteristic of the variegated nature of German opera, although no strophic numbers are specified as such. Almost as significant as what Weber put into the scenario are elements that he did not include in his outline. No solo numbers seem to be assigned to the character of Eglantine in the original layer of the scenario; this is perhaps understandable, however, when one considers that Gundrieth, the model for Eglantine in the *Roman*, really is a minor character, whose villainy is wholly unmotivated. Second, no musical provision is made for Euryanthe's revelation of Gerhard's secret to Eglantine or for the supernatural elements that this part of the story entails. Presumably Weber left such narrations for Chezy to compose as recitative, if, in fact, he and she had by this time agreed to write a 'große Oper'. There is little indication in Weber's draft that the opera should be through-composed, and only the 'Ritornell' of hunting horns at daybreak in Act II suggests a musical transition between the numbers. Weber's early outline for a 'große Oper' is therefore hardly distinguishable from one for an opera with spoken dialogue, except perhaps in its provision for balletic movements in both the first and second acts.

3.3 *Published fragments of the earliest libretto*

With Weber's outline in hand, Chezy began the versification of the opera, a process in which she claims to have been guided by Weber's instructions to make the verse as interesting and difficult as possible:

And now as regards the poem I beseech you, my friend: do not cut out the verses according to the old operatic pattern. Summon up instead your entire imagination and skill, and don't try to protect me! Pile up difficulties one on top of another, contemplate metres that would give one reason to despair; that will inspire me and give me wings! *Euryanthe* must become something entirely new, and stand completely alone on its own level![19]

Exactly what Chezy brought to Weber as a first attempt at a libretto cannot at the present time be determined in full, since the preserved manuscripts seem not to include the original libretto, with the possible exception of the first scene of Act I (see below). However, Chezy published selected passages from her first manuscript in 1823 that provide certain useful points of comparison with later developments. By the time of the first version, for example, Gerhard's name had been changed to Adolar, allegedly because Weber wanted a more lyrical sound.[20] The treatment of Adolar's secret closely follows Chezy's original scenario; Euryanthe does not reveal the entire secret to Eglantine, but in a short unrhymed dialogue presumably designed for treatment as recitative, she only mentions that Adolar had once entrusted her with a secret imparted to him in dreams by the ghost of his ancestor, Guy of Nevers. In the parts of the Act I Finale printed by Chezy, Lysiart offers as proof of his conquest the dagger that Eglantine had stolen from Guy's crypt, and he gives it to the King, who reads from it an inscription describing the history of Guy's murder and suicide.

---

[19] Chezy 1840, p. 13.   [20] Ibid.

King (takes the dagger and reads):

'Mit diesem Dolch hab' ich, verblendet durch Verrath,	With this dagger, blinded by betrayal,
'Mein treues, süsses Weib getödtet.	I killed my faithful, sweet wife.
'Die ihr den Dolch entdeckt, o, betet	You who discover the dagger, pray
'Für mich, und hüllt in Schweigen meine That!	for me, and keep my deed secret!
'Weil diesen Dolch nun auch mein Herzblut röthet.'	Because my heart's blood now also reddens this dagger.

In all of these published fragments, the wording differs considerably not only from the final version of the text, but also from the earliest extant manuscript versions.

According to Chezy, Weber submitted this first draft not only to his own scrutiny, but also to that of 'a prominent poet', whom she later identified as Ludwig Tieck.[21] Her assertion is confirmed by Weber's Diary, which, as previously mentioned, records that he consulted Tieck during the early phases of the libretto. Chezy reports that Tieck found Euryanthe's mention of Adolar's secret to be too casual and objective ('similar to a newspaper report'), and he and Weber evidently both agreed that the secret and its resolution should somehow be more closely tied to Euryanthe's personal fate.[22]

4. EARLY EXTANT MS LIBRETTOS

4.1. *Web. Cl. II A g 13*

That Chezy attempted to follow Weber's and Tieck's suggestions can be inferred from the earliest surviving manuscript of the libretto (*Web. Cl. II A g 13*), a heavily revised two-act draft of the opera completely in her handwriting. A close inspection reveals that this libretto is actually a composite manuscript incorporating three slightly different layers in the history of the text: (1) a draft for the start of Act I containing the text of the opening scene, scene ii, and the first 11 lines of scene iii. It is conceivable that this bifolium survives from the first version of Act I that Chezy gave Weber on 15 December 1821, but there is no way to prove or refute this conjecture; (2) a complete draft of Act II containing several revisions that aid in establishing a relative chron-

---

[21] Chezy 1823A; Chezy 1840, p. 18.

[22] *MMW* ii. 461, and following him Jähns, op. cit. ch. 1 n. 4 above, p. 361, and Warrack, op. cit. introduction n. 1 above, p. 284, all give the impression that Tieck advised Weber to revert to the original form of the story, or to bring it closer to Shakespeare's *Cymbeline*. Chezy's account, confirmed by the date of Weber's discussion with Tieck and the evidence of the earliest librettos, seems more plausible and indicates that the arch-Romantic Tieck pushed for an expansion of the supernatural element.

ology. The original layer of text in this draft refers to a dagger with which an unspecified ancestor was buried. Revisions by Chezy in this draft change the dagger into a goblet from which poison was drunk by Adolar's unfortunate relative, whom Chezy converts into Adolar's sister Emma;[23] (3) a continuous draft from Act I, scene ii, to the end of the first act. Since this section of the libretto consistently refers only to the goblet and to Emma, who poisoned herself because a faithless lover, Otto, had broken her heart, one may conclude that this section of the manuscript postdates the draft for the second act. Exactly when the three sections of the manuscript were written is not known, but the textual relationships between this manuscript and the next surviving libretto, *Web.* Cl. II A g 3, suggest that even the latest section of Cl. II A g 13 must have been finished by mid-January 1822.

The placement and type of musical numbers are seldom indicated in this earliest complete libretto, and we must attribute this lack once again to Chezy's inexperience with opera. The fact that much of the dialogue in this libretto (and in all of the succeeding versions) is written in rhymed metrical verse also blurs the distinction between texts intended as numbers and those intended for setting as recitative.[24] Nevertheless, it is not too difficult to ascertain the structure of the libretto, and the following overview shows that *Web.* Cl. II A g 13 is formally still close to the plan that Weber had outlined for Chezy. Items marked with an asterisk seem to be additions to Weber's scenario, and items in square brackets are not titled in the libretto.

Act I

i	*Introduction*
	Chorus of Ladies and Knights. Ernster Reigen.
	'Minnelied' in praise of Euryanthe (Adolar)
	Chorus applauds Adolar
	Wager

- -

ii	[Cavatina] (Euryanthe alone)
iii	*Romanze* (Euryanthe.)★
	Duo (Euryanthe, Eglantine)
iv	[Ensemble] (Lysiart's arrival with knights)
v	[Duet and Chorus] (Bertha, Rudolph)★

[23] Chezy at first named the ghost Mathilde; whether Mathilde was to have been the innocent victim of Guy's jealous rage, or in fact the suicidal prototype for Emma is unknown.

[24] In general the dialogues between musical numbers are not rhymed (e.g. the Eglantine–Euryanthe dialogue in the first act), whereas dialogue passages within the multi-movement pieces (e.g. Introduzione, Finales) are rhymed.

vi   *Aria* (Eglantine alone)★
vii   [Aria] (Lysiart)
viii   [Duet] (Lysiart, Eglantine)
----
ix   [Aria] (Adolar)
x   [Duet] (Adolar, Euryanthe)★
xi   *Chor*
          Finale[25]

Act II
i   *Aria No. 1* (Euryanthe sees Mathilde/Emma)
          Aria (Euryanthe describes battle with dragon)
ii   [Scene and aria] (Euryanthe alone)
iii   *Ritornell.* (Daybreak, hunting calls)
          Chor der Jaeger
          Duo (Euryanthe, King, chorus)
----
iv   [May Song] (solos, chorus)
v   (Adolar and Chorus)
vi   (Lysiart, pursued by Eglantine)
vii   [Trio and chorus] (Adolar, Lysiart, Eglantine)
[viii]   [Finale] (the above, King, Euryanthe)
          [May Song]

The revisions that can be inferred from a comparison of this text
with the two scenarios and the published fragments of Chezy's earliest
libretto, however, do seem to betray traces of the influences that Chezy
attributed to Weber and Tieck. For example, Chezy had originally concluded Act I with a chorus of knights and ladies consoling the distraught
Euryanthe:

Was auch den Sterblichen bedroht   Whatever endangers mortals,
Der Herr ist Hort in Noth und Tod!   the Lord is our refuge in death and
                                       distress!

Allegedly Weber wrote on the draft of the finale: 'Perhaps here an
ending that breathes despair, contempt and vengeance, where everything
topples upon poor Euryanthe, would be more effective than the magnifi-

[25] In this and in a number of subsequent librettos, Chezy indicates that the 'Finale'
begins with Lysiart's words 'Mein König!' Thus the preceding Euryanthe–King dialogue
is set in the unrhymed pentameters characteristic of passages between musical numbers.

cent, but too reassuring words given above.'[26] Subsequently in *Web. Cl.* II A g 13 the end of the Act I Finale replaced the conciliatory Schlußchor with a quatrain that, following Weber's instructions, does condemn Euryanthe more violently.

Du gleißend Bild! du bist enthüllt,	You glistening image! you are exposed.
Schnell folgte Strafe deinen Thaten!	Punishment quickly followed your deeds!
Weh dir! So schnöder List erfüllt,	Woe to you, who are filled with base deception;
Weh dir, die Lieb und Treu' verrathen!	woe to you, who have betrayed love and fidelity!

One other change in the Act I Finale can perhaps be related to Weber's desire for a more drastic presentation of Euryanthe's predicament. Whereas Chezy's first libretto had allowed Euryanthe to appear at court with her ladies-in-waiting, who sympathize with her after Lysiart discloses the secret, the version presented in Cl. II A g 13 eliminates the *Frauenchor*, so that Euryanthe's isolation from the other guests in the hall (all male) is complete.

The supernatural element is allotted a greater role in Cl. II A g 13 than in the earlier versions. Instead of the mere mention of a secret in her scene with Eglantine (I, iii), Euryanthe now relates the story of the ghost's appearance to Adolar in a separate musical number, a strophic, narrative Romanze not specified in Weber's earlier plan. The suffering, restless ancestor has been changed into a female, Adolar's sister Emma, perhaps to facilitate a sympathetic relationship between her and Euryanthe, and in converting the blood-stained dagger into a poison-filled goblet, Weber and Chezy may have sought to conceal one obvious similarity in plot between their opera and Grillparzer's *Ahnfrau*. Emma's ghost (originally named Mathilde) actually appears in the first scene of Act II as Euryanthe prepares to die at Adolar's hands, and the text of an additional aria given to Euryanthe at this point vaguely suggests that Euryanthe's suffering has somehow redeemed the spirit from eternal wandering. Thus, Cl. II A g 13 does show some attempt to tie together the fates of Emma and Euryanthe.

In comparison to the two early scenarios, the text of Cl. II A g 13 also gives greater prominence to the character of Eglantine. In Act I, scene vi, Eglantine is given an aria text, derived from one of the lyrical interpolations in Chezy's translation of the *Roman*, expressing

---

[26] Chezy 1823B, p. 1141.

the anguish of her unrequited love for Adolar and her desire for revenge. As she runs out of Emma's crypt at the beginning of Act I, scene viii, she addresses the goblet that she has stolen in a rhymed text possibly designed for treatment as an aria. Finally, in the scene between Eglantine and Euryanthe (I, iii), a marginal notation in the manuscript indicates that three lines of Eglantine's recitative are to be replaced by a 'Cavatine', the text for which we shall find in the next surviving manuscript.

Web. Cl. II A g 13 exhibits several other points of divergence from earlier stages of development. It includes, for example, a scene (Act I, scene vi) and presumably a set piece as well for two betrothed servants, Bertha and Rudolph, thereby adding an element of *Volkstümlichkeit* to the generally serious and courtly atmosphere of the opera; their unproblematic relationship may be seen as an idyllic foil to the more complicated female–male relationships that extend above them on the social scale (Emma/Otto, Euryanthe/Adolar, Eglantine/Lysiart). This scene was subsequently excised in this manuscript, but it does show up again in several of the later versions. The love duet between Euryanthe and Adolar, very close to its final form, and following directly upon Adolar's aria, evidently represents an accretion to the plan as outlined earlier in Weber's scenario. A chorus of hunters (Act II, scene iii), not specified in the scenario, also lends a dash of colour to the libretto, although the text in its earliest form—for divided chorus in the heat of the chase—is not that of the final version. Euryanthe's apparent death, caused by an off-stage riding accident in Weber's scenario, is now presented on stage as a result of her excessive excitement at the thought of being reunited with Adolar. Weber's uncertainty about the end of the opera is here resolved in favour of a conciliatory *lieto fine*, for the villains repent at the sight of Euryanthe on the bier; upon awakening, Euryanthe forgives them, and she and Adolar are finally reunited. One suspects that this version of the ending was more representative of Chezy's rather than Weber's conception. The Schlußchor in this early version, another strophe for the May Song first sung in Act II, scene iv, reveals a plan to conclude the opera with a corresponding musical reprise.

One last point about the earliest manuscript libretto: with respect to poetic structure, a number of pieces in the first act of Cl. II A g 13—the Introduzione, Euryanthe's Cavatina, the Euryanthe–Eglantine Duetto, Lysiart's Scena ed aria, the Eglantine–Lysiart Duetto and the Act I (i.e. Act II) Finale—are very close to the corresponding pieces in the final version of the opera. As we have seen, Weber's scenario had already dictated the broad outlines of the Introduzione along lines suggested by his earlier operas, and it seems probable that for fairly conventional pieces like Lysiart's Scena ed aria and the first-act finale Weber also pointed the inexperienced Chezy to extant models for large-scale form. In contrast, the texts in Act II are not at all close to those of Act III in the final version of the opera.

4.2. *Weberiana Cl. II A g 3*

The libretto that Weber took to Vienna in February 1822 (*Web.* Cl. II A g 3) is a copyist's manuscript containing a number of entries in Weber's handwriting. As the libretto that Weber officially submitted to the opera management in Vienna, it represents a version of the text that he and Chezy at the time probably viewed as definitive. According to Chezy, the version that accompanied Weber to Vienna was already the eighth reworking of the text.[27] In most respects, Cl. II A g 3 is similar to the Chezy autograph just described.[28] The two-act structure with the conciliatory ending is retained. There are, however, a few important differences between Chezy's manuscript and the libretto taken to Vienna. An additional piece for Eglantine appears in Cl. II A g 3, the cavatina mentioned in Cl. II A g 13 ('Ja, mein Leid ist unermessen') through which her feigned claims of wronged friendship compel Euryanthe to divulge her secret. A completely different text for Adolar's aria was originally copied in Cl. II A g 3, but Weber himself reinstated the earlier text ('Wehen mir Lüfte Ruh'). The Bertha–Rudolph scene deleted from the earlier libretto does not appear in the manuscript, but it too was restored as the sixth scene of Act I by the time Weber left Vienna, now placed after rather than before Eglantine's aria, perhaps to provide a moment of respite prior to Lysiart's revenge aria.[29]

A number of discrepancies between Cl. II A g 3 and Cl. II A g 13 indicate that the Emma story was still a cause for concern. For one thing, the Vienna libretto clarifies in some respects the question of Emma's redemption, in that the terms for her release from endless unrest—Emma can only be redeemed through the suffering of a wronged innocent—are now more explicitly stated, both in the Romanze and in the Act I Finale.[30] Nevertheless, Emma's actual attainment of redemp-

---

[27] Chezy 1823A.

[28] A complete transcription of this libretto is given in Tusa, 'Carl Maria von Weber's *Euryanthe*', pp. 483–532.

[29] Primary evidence for the restoration of the scene is a copy of the libretto that seems to have been made from the manuscript that Weber took with him to Vienna in 1822. The manuscript (Vienna, ONB, S.m. 32305) includes the peasant scene as Act I, scene vi. The scene was evidently pasted into *Web.* Cl. II A g 3, since this manuscript still has a stub where a leaf had been inserted, and since the remaining scenes in Act I after this point were renumbered by Weber.

[30] In the Romanze, for example, Emma is reported to have told Adolar: 'Rastlos, allnächtlich muß wandeln mein Geist, | Bis mich die Unschuld dem Abgrund entreißt.' In the Act I Finale Lysiart clarifies the mechanism of redemption somewhat: 'Und Ruhe kann sie nimmer haben, | Bis Unschuld sühnet sündiger Liebe That.'

tion still is left open, all the more so since she no longer appears to Euryanthe in the first scene of Act II; perhaps consideration for the technical difficulties of staging such an appearance led the collaborators to substitute for Emma's appearance only a lighting effect that coincides with Euryanthe's rather oblique textual reference to Emma's peace. The desire to clarify the relationship between Emma, Euryanthe, and Eglantine further led to the most interesting innovation in Cl. II A g 3, one that almost certainly was prompted by Weber.[31] The original layer of the manuscript taken to Vienna calls for a 'Pantomime und Gemählde während der Ouvertüre', which Weber retitled as a 'Pantomimische Prolog Szene während der Ouvertüre'. Set in Emma's crypt, the scene, planned to be shown during the overture, presents a tableau depicting Euryanthe praying at the coffin of Emma, whose ghost hovers overhead; Eglantine secretly observes the whole sequence.[32] In approving the libretto for performance, the censor in Vienna expressed reservations about this introductory pantomime, on which he promised to make a final decision at the time of the dress rehearsal.[33] But as of February 1822, over 18 months before the Ouverture was composed, the prologue was a part of the opera, evidently with the complete approval of the librettist.

Weber's own entries in the manuscript pertain mainly to the correction of obvious copying errors and omissions, although several of his entries, such as the reinstatement of the earlier form of Adolar's aria, are more significant. While correcting the libretto he also paid particular attention to the gestic elements in the drama, since he added a number of stage directions for the singers; it is perhaps characteristic of Weber's notion of theatricality that many of these added indications call for gestures of a violent or extremely emotional nature.[34] Finally, Weber divided

[31] Chezy 1840, p. 21; and Ludwig Rellstab, 'Carl Maria von Weber', Caecilia 7/25 (1828): 11–12.

[32] The original layer of the libretto gives the following stage instructions: 'Schauplatz, das Innere von Emmas Gruftgewölbe. Ihre Bildsäule, kniend neben ihrem Sarge, über den ein schöner Baldachin mit Säulen im Styl des zwölften Jahrhunderts, (Vide Museum de Augustius) sich erhebt. Eine Lampe hängt am Gewölbe.' Weber added to this description the following description of the action: 'Euryanthe betet am Sarge. Emmas Geist schwebt flehend vorüber. Eglantine belauscht das Ganze pp.'

[33] On the last page of the libretto the censor wrote: 'Die Aufführung wird mit dem Bedeuten gestattet, daß der Censur-Inspections-Commissär bey der General-Probe insbesondere die pantomimische Prolog-Scene zu beachten habe.'

[34] For example: I, iii: 'Euryanthe (Im Schauer der Erinnerung vor sich hinstarrend)'; I, iii: 'Euryanthe (fährt entsetzt auf)'; Finale I: 'Euryanthe sinkt in ihrer Frauen Arme'; II, iii: 'Euryanthe (in Entzücken ausbrechend)'; II, iii: '(Sie sinkt in höchster Erschöpfung nieder)'. See W. Becker, Die deutsche Oper in Dresden, pp. 144–51, for changes in ideals of operatic acting during the early decades of the nineteenth century that brought a more violent style into the theatre.

the text of the second act into seventeen sections, doubtless representing the compositional units that he envisioned for that act. The fact that no such divisions are indicated in Act I of Cl. II A g 3 suggests that Weber partitioned the text of Act II some time after his return from Vienna, at a time when he already possessed a new and similarly divided text for Act I, the manuscript *Web.* Cl. II A g 6, which we shall consider shortly.

5. DEVELOPMENTS IN THE SPRING OF 1822

During his stay in Vienna and immediately after his return to Dresden on 26 March, Weber showed the libretto to various friends and colleagues, including I. F. von Mosel in Vienna and the young critic Ludwig Rellstab, who visited him on 7 April. Rellstab, and evidently Mosel also, found the libretto inordinately long; the text presented to the Viennese authorities comprised over one thousand lines. Rellstab expressed other concerns, too, particularly about the pardon of Eglantine and Lysiart at the end of the opera and about the treatment of Euryanthe's apparent demise. In an article published in 1828 he claimed to have drafted a revised scenario that Weber later presented to Chezy as representing his own ideas in order not to hurt his librettist's feelings.[35]

Rellstab's claim is largely substantiated by a letter written on 9 April 1822 from Weber to Chezy, a revised outline for the conclusion of the opera that incorporates all of Rellstab's purported suggestions: the demise of Eglantine and Lysiart; the appearance of Emma's ghost at the end of the opera; and Euryanthe's subsequent reawakening through Emma's presence.

In accordance with your wishes, esteemed Friend, here are my fragmentary thoughts. Lysiart's and Eglantine's appearance drives away the peasants. Adolar remains. Trio: violent quarrel. Various rude remarks. Adolar as a contrasting, muffled voice. Lysiart's scorn angers Eglantine, such that she wishes to betray everything and ruin herself along with him. Lysiart, impudently resolute, draws the dagger against her; she calls for help and flees; Adolar leaps into the fray, but the deed is done. The onrushing crowd prevents the battle between Adolar and Lysiart. The dying Eglantine briefly confesses her deed, testifying more to Euryanthe's innocence than to her own guilt. With her last words the King enters with his retinue. Adolar rushes towards him—'The beloved is innocent' etc. The King sends Lysiart to his death. Chorus: 'Hail to the King' etc. Adolar rushes toward him, likewise the jubilant chorus. The King stands serious and taciturn, and suddenly interrupts with a 'Stop!' 'Silence the sound of joy, master your pain like a man' etc. Euryanthe is no more. Exclamation of fright. Profound silence. Funeral music in the distance. Euryanthe upon

---

[35] Rellstab, op. cit. n. 31 above, pp. 11–12.

a bier adorned with roses. Adolar at her feet. A quiet chorus in a few words. Everyone is bent over her. Emma's spirit, unseen by all, hovers over Euryanthe.—Euryanthe opens her eyes etc. etc. etc. and the matter is resolved...[36]

That Weber solicited revisions of other sections of the text from Chezy soon after his return from Vienna is demonstrated by the manuscript *Web*. Cl. II A g 6, a complete draft of the first act of the opera (in the two-act arrangement) entirely in Weber's hand and containing numerous alterations in red ink.[37] According to the testimony of Julius Benedict and Caroline von Weber, he made this copy of the libretto to carry with him on walks as he began to contemplate the musical setting of the text.[38] As in the second act of the preceding libretto (Cl. II A g 3), Weber's holograph copy of Act I is divided into compositional units, in this case twenty-three, and from textual comparisons and references in his Diary to the units indicated in this libretto, one may be sure that he used this libretto as the *Textvorlage* for some of the pieces composed during the spring of 1822.[39]

This version of the libretto departs from the text approved in Vienna in a number of important ways. The major difference between Cl. II A g 6 and Act I of the preceding libretto, Cl. II A g 3, is one of length; whereas the Vienna libretto had allotted 577 lines to Act I, not counting the Bertha–Rudolph scene that was omitted in the original layer of that manuscript, Weber's copy covers in 476 lines the same ground as well as the reinstated scene between the two servants. With respect to plot and structure, the most interesting difference between Weber's copy and the libretto taken to Vienna lies in a thorough reworking of the scene between Euryanthe and Eglantine (I, iii). In place of the strophic Romanze in the earlier librettos, Weber's copy now gives Euryanthe a recitative text in blank verse through which she relates

---

[36] Chezy 1840, p. 33.

[37] For a complete transcription of this manuscript see Tusa, 'Carl Maria von Weber's *Euryanthe*', pp. 533–46.

[38] Cf. Jähns, op. cit. ch. I n. 4 above, p. 363, and the manuscript copy of Benedict's reminiscence in *Web*. Cl. V.5 B. No. 65a.B, p. 15.

[39] For example, the Diary entry for 21 June 1822, 'No. 1–6 vollendet entworfen', refers not to Nos. 1–6 of the final version of the opera but to the first six units in Weber's copy of the libretto, which correspond to Nos. 1–4 in the final score; at the time of composition these six units together constituted the multi-movement Introduzione. *MMW* ii. 437 misconstrues the significance of the Diary entry and thus assigns the composition of Eglantine's Aria No. 6 to this early date. Jähns, p. 363, is also in error when he states that this manuscript indicates the succession of tonalities along with the division of the text into units; the only such tonal indications are found on a separate copy in Weber's handwriting of the final version of the text of the Act II Finale, a bifolium in the WFN-Handschriftliches, Konvolut XX, Bl. 116, which is described more fully in Chapter VII.

Emma's misfortune. Along with the change of musical approach, there are also important changes in the details of Emma's story: (1) Euryanthe now claims that Emma appeared on the last day of May to both herself and Adolar, so that she has learned the tale first-hand from the ghost. (2) The reason for Emma's suicide is no longer Otto's faithlessness, but rather the fact that he had died in battle, and that she could not bear to live without him. In this manuscript Weber subsequently changed Otto's name to Udo. (3) As originally copied, Emma is reported to have drunk poison from a phial; another change in red ink by Weber converts the *Phiole* into a ring filled with poison and all references to an inscription on the poisonous object are omitted. (4) The conditions for Emma's redemption from endless wandering are made more explicit than in the earlier versions (though admittedly they are still cryptic): tears of innocence must moisten the phial (*sive* ring) from which she had drunk the poison, and an act of pure love must be shown toward a murderer. Corresponding alterations in Lysiart's revelation of the secret in the first-act finale subsequently bring that section of the libretto into agreement with the new details of Emma's story; unlike earlier versions of the libretto, however, Lysiart does not reveal the full story to the assembled court, for he is interrupted by Adolar, who concedes defeat before Lysiart can divulge all of the details. As a result of these changes in Act I, scene iii and the first-act finale, Weber's copy of the libretto presents a version of Emma's story that is very close to the final treatment of that important strand in the plot.

In fact, in most respects—plot, versification, disposition of numbers and length—the text of Weber's new copy of Act I is very nearly that of the final version of Acts I and II, so that the basic work on the first half of the libretto was completed by the spring of 1822. However, two major features of this manuscript distinguish it from the final version. First, the draft still includes the sentimental scene between the two servants (I, vi). Second, Weber's manuscript still divides the opera into two acts. These features therefore seem to have persisted in Weber's conception of the work at least up to the time when he began the composition of the music.

6. LATER STAGES IN THE GENESIS OF THE LIBRETTO

In considering the later stages in the history of the *Euryanthe* libretto, one encounters an extremely complex array of sources. Along with complete and nearly complete drafts of the libretto, there also exist a number of isolated drafts for separate scenes and numbers. In cataloguing these materials Jähns treated them as three entities: (1) *Web.* Cl. II A g 4. A miscellany of loose bifolios and leaves written on a variety of papers;

all are in Chezy's hand, and most items contain additional comments by Weber. Various paginations and foliations appear throughout the papers; for the purposes of the present study we shall refer to a numeration in blue ink that labels each separate piece of paper, whether bifolio or leaf. Under this system there were once 32 items, of which Nos. 6, 7, and 16 were already missing at the time that Jähns acquired them; in addition, there is one unnumbered leaf among the papers. (2) *Web.* Cl. II A g 7. A bifolium in Weber's handwriting that contains a detailed outline of the conclusion of the last act, from the wedding march (final version, Act III, scene vi) to the end.[40] (3) *Web.* Cl. II A g 5. A copyist's libretto with two inserted items in Chezy's handwriting. Numerous entries appear in Weber's handwriting. This manuscript is presently incomplete, since the gathering on which the first four scenes of Act III had been written has been removed.[41] Although these three manuscripts are not dated, it is possible to infer the relative chronology of most of the later sources by means of textual comparisons and the physical evidence of paper type, and with the help of Weber's Diary and correspondence one can affix more definite dates to certain of the documents, thereby providing a framework for the chronology. Table 6 presents in synoptic form the results of the present study of these sources, showing the relative order of the documents and indicating, where possible, fixed points to which the drafts can be assigned.

As one can readily see in Table 6, the composite manuscript *Web.* Cl. II A g 4 comprises materials drafted over the span of an entire year, from the summer of 1822 to the summer of 1823, and presents, in conjunction with the other two sources and extant correspondence, a running commentary on the progress of the opera up to the time of its completion. It would be too tedious to belabour here every point in that commentary, but the major developments documented by these sources are traced in the following discussion.

[40] According to Jähns's notation in the manuscript, he once also owned a fair copy of this draft, also in Weber's hand, that he gave to the Viennese manuscript collector, G. A. Petter. This manuscript, which I have not located, was at one time contained in the collection of manuscripts owned by Wilhelm Heyer. See *Musikhistorisches Museum von Wilhelm Heyer in Cöln. Katalog von Georg Kinsky.* vol. iv. Autographen (Cologne, 1916), p. 213 (fn.).

[41] A note by a certain 'G. P.' added to Jähns's description of the manuscript claims that the missing pages were to be found in the 'Nachlaß der Dichterin im Literatur-Archiv der Akademie der Wissenschaften'. The Zentrales Archiv der Akademie der Wissenschaften der DDR in Berlin, the repository of a substantial portion of Chezy's literary *Nachlaß*, does possess three manuscript leaves of the third act of the libretto written by the same copyist as *Web.* Cl. II A g 5. However, closer inspection reveals these leaves *not* to be the missing leaves of *Web.* Cl. II A g 5, but rather to have been part of a later manuscript that Chezy sent to the Viennese publisher Wallishauser as the *Stichvorlage* for the first printed edition of the libretto.

TABLE 6. Later sources for the *Euryanthe* libretto

Date	Source	Description
Before July 26, 1822[a]	Cl. II A g 4 Items 1–3, 8–9	Continuous Draft of Act I (i.e. I + II)
Before early August 1822[b]	Cl. II A g 4 Item 10	Act II, i–ii (i.e. III, i–ii)
	Cl. II A g 4 Item 11	Act II, iii (i.e. III, iii)
	Cl. II A g 4 Unnumbered leaf	Variants for II, i (i.e. III, i)
November 1822[c]	Cl. II A g 4 Items 12, 22	Draft of III, iv–III, vii
	Cl. II A g 4 Item 17	'Einige Varianten' for III, iv and III, v.
	Weber's letter of 11 Nov. 1822	Critique of Items 12, 22 and Item 17
	Cl. II A g 4 Items 20, 19	Draft for III, v
	Cl. V. Abt. 2, No. 14	Undated letter from Chezy to Weber
	Cl. II A g 4 Items 13, 23–4	Draft for III, iv–conclusion
	Cl. II A g 4 Item 21	Variants for III, vi
	Weber's letter of 28 Nov. 1822	Critique of Items 20, 19, Items 13, 23–4, and Item 21
	Cl. II A g 4 Item 14	Variants for III, v
Between 28 November 1822 and early April 1823[d]	Cl. II A g 7	Weber's scenario for the denouement
Spring–summer 1823 (after 1 April)[e]	Cl. II A g 4 Items 30–1	Revised draft for III, v–conclusion
	Cl. II A g 5	Copyist's libretto
	Cl. II A g 4 Item 25	Final version of Scena No. 16
	Cl. II A g 4 Item 27	Worksheet for Scena e cavatina No. 17
	Cl. II A g 4 Item 26	Final version for No. 17
	Cl. II A g 4 Item 27a	Final version of Jaegerchor No. 18
	Cl. II A g 4 Item 29	Worksheet for Duetto con coro No. 19
	Cl. II A g 4 Item 28	Final version of No. 19
	Cl. II A g 5 Inserted bifolium A	Revision for Finale I
	Cl. II A g 4 Item 32	Variants for Finale III Schlußchor
	Cl. II A g 5 Inserted leaf B	Final version of concluding section of Finale I (Fröhliche Klänge)
	Cl. II A g 4 Item 5	Variants for I, iii (20 July 1823)
Uncertain Chronology	Cl. II A G 4 Item 4	Revision for I, ii–iii and Finale I (new style): October, 1822?[f]
	Cl. II A g 4 Item 15	Draft for III, i and III, ii
	Cl. II A g 4 Item 18	Variants for III, v (after 11 Nov. 1822)

See notes to table opposite.

6.1. *Division of the opera into 3 acts (summer 1822)*

The earliest papers in Cl. II A g 4 pick up where Weber's holograph (Cl. II A g 6) had left off. As copied, they incorporate most of the revisions that Weber had made in red ink in the earlier copy of the first act; moreover, they still include the scene between Bertha and Rudolph and treat the opera as a two-act structure. Entries in Weber's handwriting indicate, however, the removal of the servants' scene and

TABLE 6. (*contd.*)

[a] The *terminus ante quem* for this draft is given by the fact that this manuscript was the *Textvorlage* for the *Vision* narration, which was drafted on 26 July 1822.

[b] The items assigned to this group all predate the decision to reorganize the opera in three acts, a step taken by 5 Aug. 1822 at the latest. The *terminus ante quem* for Item 11 is also given by the composition date for Euryanthe's Aria con coro No. 20, which was started on 5 Aug. 1822. The unnumbered leaf seems to have been written as an alternative to Item 11.

[c] All of the items assigned to this group can be related to the preserved correspondence between Weber and Chezy from the month of Nov. 1822. I have attempted to arrange them in an order suggested by a close reading of the correspondence, since Weber's letters respond to certain details in the drafts. The drafts that I have designated as Items 12, 22 and Items 13, 23–4 constitute obvious entities on the basis of paper type and continuity of poetic content. Items 20, 19 probably were also conceived as a continuous draft.

[d] Weber signalled his intention to draft a new denouement himself in a letter to Chezy of 28 Nov. 1822. An entry in the Diary for 20 Mar. 1823 ('den 3: Akt der Euryanthe redigiert') most likely refers to this scenario.

[e] The items that I have assigned to the spring and summer of 1823 seem to have been written after Chezy's return to Dresden at the beginning of April since the draft Cl. II A g 4, Items 30–1, was written on paper with DRESDEN watermark, and since all of the other items are on the basis of content demonstrably later.

[f] This leaf possibly contains Chezy's first attempt at a finale for the new first act that Weber criticized in his letter of 10 Oct. 1822.

the division of the opera into three acts. Exactly when these decisions were made is not known, but references to a three-act format may be found in an entry for 5 August in Weber's Diary and again in a letter to Mosel written on 19 August.[42] Hence, the earliest items in Cl. II A g 4 represent the state of the libretto by mid-summer 1822 at the latest. It is unfortunate that these papers do not include a complete text of the final act; the preserved portions of Act II (i. e. Act III) that can be dated to the summer of 1822 diverge considerably from the final text, with the single exception of the text for the aria 'Zu ihm!' that Weber began to set on 5 August.

6.2. *Concern for the denouement (autumn 1822)*

As we have noted, Weber outlined a revised denouement for the opera in April 1822, and after Chezy's departure for Berlin in September 1822, the two collaborators devoted a great deal of attention to the resolution of the plot, a process attested by the correspondence that they exchanged during the month of November and six extant versions of the denouement that Chezy sent to Weber at various times in November 1822. These drafts and letters illuminate several important aspects in the history of the text. For example, even the earliest of the drafts (Items 12, 22), which Weber seems to have received immediately before his letter of 11 November, differs markedly from the text taken to Vienna in February

[42] Diary entry for 5 Aug. 1822: 'Idee zu der Arie der Euryanthe im 3. Act. "Zu ihm!" gefasst.'

1822, and presents the earliest form of many features associated with the final text, such as: (1) a piece at the end of Act III, scene iv in which the peasants exhort Adolar to reclaim his birthright ('Vernichte kühn das Werk der Tücke'); (2) the wedding procession for Eglantine and Lysiart (here accompanied by a choral text); (3) Eglantine's delirious vision of Emma; and (4) her defiant confession of the treachery. Between February and November, therefore, Eglantine's role in the concluding scenes had become more prominent, and we can see why Weber wrote to the Viennese authorities on 28 November that the part of Eglantine had gained immensely since his previous trip to Vienna.[43] Another draft (Items 13, 23–4), probably written between 11 and 28 November, specifies that Emma's ghost appear at the end of the opera at the point where Adolar and Euryanthe are reunited, and we may find in this detail a descendant of Weber's suggestion of 11 April 1822 that Emma hover over the unconscious Euryanthe and yet another attempt to indicate Emma's attainment of peace in the afterlife.

Yet Weber's detailed responses to Chezy's offerings reveal an increasing level of frustration with her lack of sympathy for and inability to understand his conception of the drama. She seems to have opposed throughout the history of the libretto Euryanthe's apparent death, to which he adamantly clung. The extant drafts also clearly document her difficulty in reconciling herself to Weber's conception of the denouement. Thus Weber was displeased by the sequence of events in the draft of Act III, scenes iv–vii that he received in early November (*Web. Cl. II A g 4*, Items 12, 22 and Item 17): (1) the arrival of the wedding procession prompts Adolar to go off to find help; (2) Eglantine has a delirious vision of Emma, which is therefore not witnessed by Adolar; (3) Adolar returns at the head of a procession of armed peasants and threatens Lysiart and Eglantine; (4) when Lysiart then orders the knights to seize Adolar, Adolar summons them as their 'true lord'; (5) Eglantine exults and reveals the villains' treachery; (6) Lysiart stabs Eglantine; and (7) the King arrives. Weber wrote to Chezy on 11 November, pointing out the poor light in which this version places Adolar and outlining the events that he desired:

It is very good that Bertha tells [Adolar] about Eglantine. But it displeases me that Adolar departs in order to get help; on the one hand he has lost his land to Lysiart, and he still only *hopes* [that Euryanthe is innocent], he cannot yet be *convinced*. For this reason he certainly seeks help only *within himself* and intends to summon [Lysiart] to a trial by combat; for this reason he should have to be restrained by the peasants from immediately rushing towards the couple. We should keep the scene that comes next [Weber probably

---

[43] See above, Chapter I, n. 37.

means Eglantine's delirium] just as it is. The other reading [Item 17?] might appear somewhat hasty. I should like to have Lysiart more occupied.

Adolar strides unrecognizable and alone towards him and curses the wedding procession, etc. Then Lysiart commands that the strange hothead be arrested. The crowd presses towards him, whereupon he opens his visor. (I hint here with only a few words approximately what I desire.) 'Wie! *mich* wollt *ihr* verderben?' ['What! *you* wish to harm *me*?'] Everyone then sinks at his feet, and in the next moment springs enraged against Lysiart. Lysiart stands heroically bold and defiant against the force. Adolar must say that he (Adolar) has sacrificed Euryanthe to his shame, and only now can Eglantine's jubilation occur, otherwise she destroys her work without learning of her success; I should find it very nice that she additionally scorns Lysiart and describes him as her tool, and Lysiart stabs her. I should like short, powerfully thundering words against Lysiart for the chorus. 'Trotze nicht! Verruchter!' etc.: in the midst of this storm the King now enters.

I cannot be dissuaded from the apparent death of Euryanthe. That is an *entirely different* situation from that in the *Freischütz*! . . .

As a postscript to the letter Weber wrote:

It suddenly occurs to me that it would be more horrible [*schauerlicher*] if the wedding procession came only with a march, without chorus, and [if] individual expressions of abhorrence from the peasants grouped at the front penetrate between these sounds of joy, likewise the barely contained rage of Adolar. What do you think?[44]

A tone of even greater exasperation can be sensed in Weber's letter of 28 November 1822, a response to several shipments that he had received since his last letter (*Web.* Cl. II A g 4, Items 20, 19, Item 21, and Items 13, 23–4) . For one thing, he was not at all pleased that Chezy had shown the libretto to various acquaintances in Berlin. And although the new materials did incorporate several of the ideas outlined in his letter of 11 November, on the whole Chezy seemed perversely obstinate in her refusal to follow other suggestions. In both Items 20, 19 and 13, 23–4, Adolar still summons the vassals to him as their rightful master. The fact that Chezy was uncomfortable with the violent ends for both Eglantine and Lysiart is attested by the fact that the new materials

---

[44] Chezy 1840, p. 37. In the original manuscript of this letter, in the Varnhagen von Ense collection in the Biblioteka Jagiellońska, Weber's last sentence reads somewhat differently from Chezy's published transcription: 'Da fällt mir eben noch ein, daß es mich schauerlicher dünkt wenn der Hochzeitzug blos unter einem Marsche *ohne* Chor käme, und einzelne Äußerungen des Abscheues der Vorn gruppirten Landleuten zwischen diesen Freudeklängen drängen, eben so Adolars mit Mühe zurück gehaltenen Wuth. Was meinen Sie?' I have based my translation of this postscript on Weber's autograph.

present three different ways of disposing of the villains,[45] despite the fact that Weber had specified as early as April that Lysiart should murder Eglantine and then be sent to death by the King. And in a fit of inspiration, Chezy suggested a new lighting effect for the end of the opera, a transformation of the scene through moonlight,[46] to which, however, Weber strenuously objected.

Esteemed Friend!
You have sent me much that is good. Thousand thanks. I now have an excess of materials. But it cannot remain exactly as it is. To be sure, I admit that those to whose judgement you have submitted it may be excellent poets, but they are hardly *musicians* and dramatists. Dear Friend, I should like to beseech you urgently not to communicate our work to so many people. You are guileless, but I have already had a number of bitter experiences. One allows himself advance judgements without having that right, which proceeds only from the *whole*. You have not read my most recent letters correctly, or have not considered my reasons sufficiently important.

*Adolar can in no way summon the **ceded** vassals to himself.* But that is a small matter. I shall send the whole thing to you in the shape that I believe to be most effective. I would have to write books to demonstrate everything with reasons.

Now to answer several details.

I myself had already made precisely the abbreviation of the scene between Euryanthe and Adolar that you sent along later. In just the same way I had long ago reinstated the old [version of the] prayer ['Schirmende Engelsschaar']; and was glad that you yourself now wish it.[47] Of course it is cold to lead Lysiart off to his death. But his fall at Adolar's hands and Eglantine's suicide shortly thereafter also produces an unpleasant effect. Lysiart must kill Eglantine and still present himself defiantly to the King and in any case go off combatively wishing to make his way, so that we may view him in a heroic fashion until the end, and yet be able to hope for his punishment. Eglantine's delirium was splendid in the first shipment, but in the second much too broad and

---

[45] In Items 20, 19 Lysiart stabs Eglantine and then falls in combat with Adolar before the King arrives. In Item 21 Lysiart dies as a result of the battle shortly after the King arrives; Eglantine then commits suicide. In Items 13, 23–4 the King halts the combat between Lysiart and Adolar, in accordance with Weber's suggestion of 11 Nov., but then Eglantine commits suicide after revealing Euryanthe's innocence, whereupon Lysiart is led off to his execution.

[46] In Items 13, 23–4 the effect is described as follows: 'Lysiart wird weggeführt, die Szene wird durch den, zwar nicht sichtbare Mond magisch, recht blau und in zarter Verklärung zauberhaft schön erhellt, und gewinnt ein geisterhaftes Aufsehen.' (Lysiart is led away. Though not visible, the moon magically illuminates the deep blue, tenderly transfigured, marvellously beautiful scenery, which acquires a supernatural appearance.)

[47] In both cases Weber here refers to an undated letter from Chezy (*Web.* Cl. V. Abt. 2, No. 14) evidently received on 27 Nov. 1822. Weber had already abridged the Adolar–Euryanthe scene at the start of Act III and reinstated the original 3-stanza form of Euryanthe's description of the battle in Cl. II A g 4, Item 10.

reminiscent of Ophelia.[48] The moonlight is also impossible. Have you forgotten that the act begins that way? We cannot repeat it, etc. . . .[49]

In his letter of 28 November Weber decided, as a last resort, to send Chezy an outline of the denouement in the form that he deemed most effective. The plan that Weber, true to his word, did draft is most probably the autograph previously mentioned, *Web.* Cl. II A g 7, an undated manuscript perhaps written on 20 March 1823.[50] This draft reveals that Weber specified precisely the order of events and musical numbers that he wanted in the concluding scenes. In this outline Weber retained as much of Chezy's versification as possible, piecing together in the order he desired the parts he liked best from the various drafts he had already received; where he could not draw on extant materials, he sketched in prose the general content of the passage and left the versification up to Chezy.

While most of the elements in Weber's draft are borrowed from earlier materials, certain features differ from anything seen before. For one thing, in order to clarify the question of Emma's redemption, Weber suggests that Emma and her lover Udo hover together at the end of the opera, reunited at the time of Adolar's reunion with Euryanthe. More provocative, however, are the musical implications of textual changes that Weber requested for the very end of the work. In all prior extant versions of the libretto the opera concludes with a stanza that clearly is meant to be sung to the music of the May Song first heard at the beginning of the fourth scene of the last act.[51] Weber's draft, however, specifies two different textual reprises with which to close the opera: (1) the Act II love duet between Adolar and Euryanthe at the moment of their reunion; and (2) a paraphrase of the line with which the opening scene of the first act concluded, 'Ich bau' auf Gott und meine Euryanth'.' Behind these textual changes it is not too hard to discern Weber's intention to build a broader pattern of structural

---

[48] In Items 13, 23–4 Eglantine is given an expanded version of the delirium, some of which is to be sung 'Im Balladenton'.

[49] Chezy 1840, pp. 37–8. The original of this letter is in the Varnhagen collection in the Biblioteka Jagiellońska. The name that Chezy removed in the published versions of the following paragraph of this letter and in the letter of 22 Dec. 1822 is that of the Berlin music dealer and publisher A. M. Schlesinger.

[50] Diary entry for 20 Mar. 1823: 'den 3: Akt der Euryanthe redigiert.' A complete transcription of this draft is presented in Appendix II.

[51] For example, in one draft that Weber received in November 1822 (*Web.* Cl. II A g 4, Items 13, 23–4), the opera concludes with the following text: 'Wir bringen dir, du holdes Paar | Das Opfer unsren Herzen dar. | Wohl wißt ihr zwey im grünen May | Wie selig Lieb und Treue sey. | *Chorus* Denn Lieb und Treu' krönt ew'ger May!'

musical recall into the opera, by relating the conclusion of the opera to significant moments in the first and second acts.

6.3. *Final stages in the collaboration (spring–summer 1823)*

With Chezy's return to Dresden on 1 April, the two collaborators entered the final stages of their work. Weber and Chezy conferred on 5 April, possibly to discuss Weber's scenario for the denouement, since one of the first things that Chezy did after her return from Berlin was to draft a new version of the final scenes (Cl. II A g 4, Items 30–1), following exactly the instructions that Weber had outlined in his plan. Having obtained the conclusion in the form that he had dictated, Weber seems then to have ordered a new fair copy of the libretto, the copyist's manuscript *Web.* Cl. II A g 5, which served as the *Textvorlage* for some of the pieces composed during the spring and summer and 1823.[52] Copied in the spring of 1823, the original layer of this libretto, now in three acts, reveals several interesting facts about the current state of the libretto: (1) As copied, the manuscript specifies the *Pantomimische Prolog Szene* during the Ouverture that Weber had introduced in February 1822; this tableau was at some later time deleted in this manuscript by Weber. (2) Although the wording of the Act I Finale, for which no earlier complete text is preserved, differs from that of the final version, the prosody of most of the verse corresponds to the final text; this phenomenon points to Weber's intention to borrow most of the music in the first-act finale from earlier compositions, to which Chezy had to fit a new text. (3) Despite the loss of several leaves at the start of the third act, circumstantial evidence allows us to conclude that the missing leaves of Cl. II A g 5 originally were textually identical to the revised layer of Cl. II A g 4, in which case the following numbers in Act III still had not reached their final form by early April 1823: (*a*) the Scena No. 16; (*b*) the Scena e cavatina No. 17; (*c*) the Jaegerchor No. 18;[53] (*d*) the Duetto con coro No. 19; (*e*) the Schlußchor. The copyist's manuscript and circumstantial evidence suggest, therefore, that the last elements to be fixed in the libretto were these five numbers in the third act and the Act I Finale, and this supposition is borne out by the existence of separate drafts in Chezy's handwriting for precisely these numbers (*Web.* Cl. II A g 4, Items 25, 26, 27*a*, 28, 32).

---

[52] Like *Web.* Cl. II A g 3 and Cl. II A g 6, the third act of Cl. II A g 5 is divided into numbered compositional units by Weber.

[53] Actually, the first stanza of the Jaegerchor had reached its final form in an earlier part of *Web.* Cl. II A g 4 (Item 11), but the second stanza was not added until the spring of 1823.

With these late revisions, which perhaps extended into July 1823, the text was finished in all aspects but two: the indication of Emma's redemption and the definitive wording for the Schlußchor. To be sure, Chezy continued to make suggestions for other parts of the opera, including those that Weber had already set. As late as 20 July, for example, she sent textual changes and scenic recommendations that she felt could clarify Emma's role in the opera.[54] A single leaf in Cl. II A g 4 (Item 5) in fact transmits some of the *Wortänderungen* that Chezy proposed at this late period, in this case extra lines for the recitative in Act I, scene iii, where Euryanthe speaks of Emma's fate. Having already composed the section, Weber adopted none of Chezy's late suggestions, but Chezy nevertheless proceeded to incorporate them into the librettos that she sent to Vienna in the summer of 1823, since they are contained in both the first printed edition of the libretto and in an extant manuscript libretto used for the first production (see below).

Regarding the treatment of Emma in the Act III Finale, Weber and Chezy seem to have agreed at some point in the summer of 1823 that Emma's redemption and reunion with Udo could be indicated more clearly through a short speech by Adolar than through the silent appearance of the reunited ghosts at the end; perhaps related to and contemporary with this decision was the removal of the *Pantomimische Prolog Szene* during the Ouverture. However, the collaborators seem not to have mutually settled the final wording of Adolar's speech, since the librettos that Chezy sent to the theatre and printer in Vienna in the summer of 1823 transmitted a different version of this speech from the one found in the final score. According to Chezy, the lines that Weber actually set ('Ich ahne Emma, selig ist sie jetzt') were his own invention, and they therefore represent one of the few instances in the opera where Weber demonstrably was responsible for versification.[55] The final

---

[54] The autograph of the letter is located in *Web*. Cl. V. Abt. 2. No. 15. The changes in Act I, scene iii that Chezy sent along are apparently contained on Item 5 in the libretto manuscript *Web*. Cl. II A g 4. Transcribed in Tusa, 'Carl Maria von Weber's *Euryanthe*', pp. 586–8.

[55] The first printed edition, the Viennese libretto proofed by Weber, and the fragmentary copyist's manuscript in the Chezy *Nachlaß* in the Akademie der Wissenschaften in Berlin all give Adolar a two-line speech not found in any of the manuscripts from Weber's possession: 'Erfüllt ist Emmas Wort: in Frieden wallt | Süß lächelnd hin die sel'ge Lichtgestalt.' In addition, the first edition of the libretto also gives the familiar version of the concluding lines ('Ich ahne Emma' etc.), explicitly attributing them to Weber. Chezy was apparently annoyed that Weber did not use her lines, but an undated, unpublished letter from Weber to Chezy in the Varnhagen collection in Kraków explains that he had lost Chezy's version of Adolar's speech and therefore had written the 'Ich ahne Emma' speech according to his recollection of the idea.

wording of the Schlußchor seems also to have rested with Weber, since his score and the librettos sent to Vienna diverge on this point too. In this case, however, he simply shortened and rearranged the revised Schlußchor that Chezy had given him earlier in the summer (*Web. Cl. II A g 4*, Item 32). Significantly, both the final version of the Schlußchor and its immediate predecessor dispensed with the textual refrain ('Vertrau' auf Gott und deine Euryanth'!') that Weber had earlier taken such pains to build into the concluding segment.

The fact that the last textual revisions in the opera were indeed made by the composer in the third-act finale suggests that they occurred to him as he composed the music for that number, the last section of the opera to be set to music. Weber completed the draft of the Act III Finale on 8 August 1823, and we may conclude that the text of *Euryanthe* was finished by that date too, since between the draft and final score Weber made no changes in the libretto. The frequent assertion that Weber continued to alter the libretto right up to the time of the first performance is consequently incorrect.[56] However, there is a logical explanation for the origin of this misconception. Two important librettos, the first printed edition of the libretto and an extant manuscript used for the first performance of the opera,[57] were based on sources that Chezy sent to Vienna in the summer of 1823 and differ at numerous points from the text set by Weber. While in Vienna, Weber learned of these discrepancies, about which he complained in a letter to his wife, written on 17 and 18 October: 'The compliance on the part of the directors and members is extraordinary, and I would be truly delighted if the damned Chezy were not here. Once again she has given the printer a libretto with thousands of minor deviations that must, however, serve as the libretto to *Euryanthe* ...'[58] Weber subsequently attempted to bring the deviant Viennese librettos into agreement with his text. The autograph alterations that he entered in the Viennese manuscript on 22 October and the few changes that he managed to make in the printed libretto therefore represent simple corrections. Such changes, however, were probably misconstrued by observers unfamiliar with the history of the text as a very late stage

---

[56] *MMW* ii. 462; Wilhelm Chezy, *Erinnerungen aus meinem Leben* (Schaffhausen, 1863), vol. i, part i, pp. 231–2; vol. i, part ii, p. 22.

[57] Vienna, Österreichische Nationalbibliothek, S.m. 32304. Copyist's manuscript written before 28 Aug. 1823 and containing corrections and changes by Chezy and Weber, as well as numerous later cuts in pencil and red crayon. Weber's corrections, entered on 22 Oct. 1823, are written in red ink. For a facsimile of the title-page of this manuscript, see Karl Laux, *Carl Maria von Weber* (Leipzig, 1978), p. 90.

[58] *Reisebriefe*, p. 49.

of revisions, thereby giving rise to the oft-repeated story that Weber kept changing his mind even after he arrived in Vienna to supervise the first production.

V. Weber's Role in the Revisions of the Libretto: An Assessment

Writing to Chezy on 5 June 1823, in response to her demands for additional remuneration, Weber praised his novice librettist for her diligence and willingness to follow his suggestions during the past eighteen months: 'I have never failed to recognize the boundless persistence with which you—a highly celebrated poet—spared yourself no effort to understand the essence of a genre unfamiliar to you; I have always praised the modesty that cannot be honoured enough, with which you permitted me to make my experiences your own ....'[1] Having surveyed the extant sources for the *Euryanthe* libretto, we are now in a position to understand what the 'experiences' were that Weber tried to impart to Chezy. Of course, one must approach the sources with a certain caution, for it cannot be shown, nor is it in fact even likely, that every textual alteration in every source is an expression of Weber's will. For example, the various versions of the denouement contained in the miscellany *Web.* Cl. II A g 4 all represent experiments by Chezy, none of which pleased Weber, and many changes of wording in the successive librettos probably reflect her sensitivity to language and versification; she was, after all, considered a competent lyric poet by her contemporaries. However, certain versions of the libretto must have pleased Weber, at least temporarily: his early scenario; the libretto taken to Vienna in February 1822 (*Web.* Cl. II A g 3); his holograph *Handexemplar* for Act I (*Web.* Cl. II A g 6); his draft for the conclusion of Act III (*Web.* Cl. II A g 7); the copyist's libretto from the spring of 1823 (*Web.* Cl. II A g 5); and, of course, the final version. Discrepancies between these versions surely indicate that Weber's conception of the opera changed over the course of the collaboration, and that his repeated demands for revisions did not stem solely from dissatisfaction with Chezy's efforts.

I. REVISIONS IN PLOT AND CHARACTER TREATMENT

Surveying the evidence of the collaboration, one can see that the revisions in the plot of *Euryanthe* essentially concentrated on the two parts of

---

[1] See above, Chapter I, n. 44.

the story that were not derived from Chezy's translation of the *Roman de la violette*: (1) the supernatural element, and (2) the denouement. Introduced as a replacement for the secret of Euryanthe's violet-shaped mole, the story of Adolar's deceased relative is an element completely foreign to its surroundings, and many of the successive revisions were attempts to integrate the alien substance into the original fabric, in other words to preserve the 'organic' quality that Weber deemed essential in opera. Concern for the denouement followed from the moment when Weber first discarded the *Gotteskampf* of the original version without himself knowing how to tie up the loose threads of the plot. In both cases fidelity to the original source clearly was not one of Weber's high priorities, but neither did he alter the original stories capriciously. We must assume that he did so with an eye towards making the plot in some way more stageworthy or more representative of his particular conception of operatic dramaturgy.

1.1. *The supernatural*

As we have seen, the initial impulse for altering the plot of the *Roman* was extremely practical; in its original form, Euryanthe's secret could not be put on the stage, especially not in Vienna, where censorship was extremely strict. In place of this all too indelicate device, the collaborators substituted a motif borrowed from the fashionable *Schicksalstragödien*, namely, the idea of a dark family secret with supernatural overtones. It is not clear who was responsible for this idea; Chezy later attributed it to Weber, but perhaps only in order to rid herself of blame for what was commonly perceived as the least successful aspect of the story.[2] What the preserved sources show, however, is that following its introduction as a somewhat ancillary element in the story, the supernatural became ever more important in the successive versions of the libretto.

One of the major concerns during the collaboration was to integrate the supernatural element more fully with the original story of Gerhard/ Adolar and Euryanthe. Chezy originally had devised the ghost story only as the pretext for the shared secret between Gerhard and Euryanthe, and in her first scenario no real interest was paid to the question of redeeming the unfortunate spirit from its endless wandering. The revisions of the libretto entailed, however, various attempts to resolve the spirit's dilemma and to make that resolution more pertinent to the main story, especially to Euryanthe's personal fate. For example, with the transformation of the murderer Guy of Nevers into Adolar's sister, Emma, the plot establishes a parallelism between the supernatural and human spheres, namely, the estrangements of Emma and Euryanthe

---

[2] Chezy 1840, p. 5.

from their respective lovers. The story was further revised to make Emma's redemption dependent on Euryanthe's suffering, and at one stage Weber suggested that Emma be the agent that revives Euryanthe from her death-like state at the end of the opera. To strengthen the bond between Euryanthe and Emma, various revisions altered both the prehistory of the plot and its denouement. While the early versions of the libretto relate that the ghost had appeared only to Adolar, Weber's autograph copy of the first act (*Web*. Cl. II A g 6) has the ghost appear to both Euryanthe and Adolar. In later versions of the libretto it is Emma's appearance to Eglantine that prompts the revelations that exculpate Euryanthe in Adolar's eyes. And Weber's scenario for the denouement (*Web*. Cl. II A g 7) and all later versions of the libretto co-ordinate Emma's reunion with Udo in the afterlife with that of Euryanthe with Adolar.

In order to accommodate these revisions, the space allotted to the ghost story grew considerably over the history of the libretto. In Weber's early scenario and the published fragments of Chezy's first libretto, no musical pieces were devoted to the supernatural element, and no mention was made of the ghost in the last act. By the earliest preserved manuscript adraft, however, a Romanze was added for the exposition of Emma's story and the ghost was made to appear to Euryanthe in the opening scene of the last act. Weber subsequently added the *Pantomimische Prolog Szene* during the Ouverture as another opportunity to put the ghost on stage. Finally, between the spring and fall of 1822 the supernatural element was further expanded with the addition of Eglantine's delirium in the last act, wherein she is haunted by a vision of the angry ghost.

As the role of the supernatural element within the opera grew, so too did the need to clarify Emma's role, whose deeds, after all, occur entirely before the start of the opera. Successive revisions of the libretto therefore embodied various attempts to make Emma's story as intelligible as possible. The exposition of Emma's deeds was converted from the added Romanze back into the *Vision* recitative, perhaps partly for reasons of text intelligibility, perhaps partly because Weber viewed the use of the Romanze for narrations of the supernatural as something of a hackneyed convention,[3] and perhaps also because he had conceived a new type of music to characterize the supernatural element (see below). In order to clarify the question of Emma's redemption, the terms of the conditions for her release from limbo became more explicit between the earliest preserved libretto (*Web*. Cl. II A g 13) and Weber's autograph copy of Act I (*Web*. Cl. II A g 6). Finally, to indicate her attainment

[3] Ännchen's Romanze und Arie No. 13 in *Der Freischütz* seems to parody the convention of the Romanze as a locus for narrations of the supernatural, in so far as the supernatural being that is described in this piece turns out to be the family dog.

of peace as unambiguously as possible, Weber eliminated her silent mimed reunion with Udo at the end of the opera and substituted in its place a short speech for Adolar ('Ich ahne Emma') that leaves no room for doubt on the subject. Various proposals for putting Emma's ghost on stage may be seen too as attempts to impress upon the audience the importance of Emma and to win sympathy for her. Yet, as the libretto approached the final version sometime in the spring or summer of 1823, all of Emma's on-stage appearances were removed, allegedly because of the technical difficulties in staging such effects.[4] It is more likely, however, that Weber came to view the visible representations of Emma as superfluous because the kind of music eventually associated with the ghost provided a much more subtle symbol for her ineffable, ethereal presence in the realm of spirits; in the final version of the opera Emma's purely spiritual presence is communicated only by her music, a quintessentially Romantic treatment of music as the 'natural' medium for the supernatural.[5]

1.2.   *The denouement*

With the story of Emma, therefore, one can observe a process whereby an element, grafted onto a body to which it did not initially belong, became more important and more closely related to the principal story as work on the libretto progressed. In contrast, the major revisions that Weber brought about in the denouement altered the basic substance of the original story. While the ultimate happy reunion of Adolar and Euryanthe was never in doubt, two questions do seem to have bothered Weber from the outset: (1) how to expose the treachery of Lysiart and Eglantine and (2) what to do with the villains at the end. Disposing of the *Gotteskampf* that Chezy's original scenario had derived from the *Roman*, Weber himself could offer no clear indication for the treatment of the two issues in his revised scenario of November 1821; in fact, he was completely unsure about the fate of the villains. This uncertainty

[4] *MMW* ii. 513 and Jähns, ch. 1 n. 4 above, p. 361, claim that both Chezy and the *Regisseur* of the Vienna opera, Gottdank, were opposed to the pantomime. Neither contention holds up to a scrutiny of the sources, since on the one hand Chezy's own claim to have fully supported the plans to put Emma on stage (Chezy 1840, p. 21) is verified by the evidence of the manuscript librettos, and on the other hand, the appearances of the spectre were removed long before Weber went to Vienna for the rehearsals and first performance. According to Chezy (ibid.), it was actually Weber's wife Caroline who convinced him to forgo the pantomimetic prologue during the Ouverture.

[5] Cf. E. T. A. Hoffmann's well-known description of music as 'the mysterious language of a faraway spirit world' in his essay 'The Poet and the Composer', translated in Oliver Strunk, ed., *Source Readings in Music History* (New York, 1950), especially pp. 788–9.

was responsible for the complete reversal of outcome between the earliest preserved version and the final text. The earliest librettos present a conciliatory conclusion in which Eglantine and Lysiart repent upon seeing the unconscious Euryanthe, who subsequently forgives them, but Weber's scenario of 9 April 1822 overturned this sickly-sweet ending and established two principles that guided all further revisions of the denouement. First, Eglantine should reveal the treachery and proclaim Euryanthe's innocence. Second, both villains should meet retribution.

Surveying the revisions of the denouement, one can see that the most significant are those that affect the role of Eglantine, who eventually came to play a much more potent and sinister role in the conclusion than she had in the original conception. Relegated in the first version to petty carping about Lysiart's reluctance to marry her, Eglantine later became the catalyst for the decisive events in the denouement. Haunted by a vision of Emma she reveals her theft of the ring in an extended monologue; upon learning of Euryanthe's alleged demise she exults triumphantly over the elimination of her rival and Adolar's misery, and in the process mocks and incriminates Lysiart, for whom she has no more need. Her death at Lysiart's hands consequently seems just retribution for the depth of her evil.

I.3.   *The villains*

The unrepentant demise of the two villains in the later drafts of the libretto reflects a more general tendency in the history of the collaboration to darken their characterization and to set them in sharper relief against the virtuous pair. Particularly noteworthy is the expansion of Eglantine's role. Weber and Chezy first conceived her as a minor figure, and his early scenario seems to make no provision for a separate solo number for her. Successive revisions added, however, a major revenge aria, a shorter solo number for her hypocritical expression of love for Euryanthe, and the two major speeches in the denouement that have already been discussed, her delirium and her triumphant outburst. Changes in details of the text further accentuated Eglantine's villainy and seem to have been calculated to remove any trace of weakness from the character that might give rise to sympathy in an audience. For example, the text of Eglantine's Scena ed aria No. 8 originally consisted of two strophes, of which the first was devoted to a self-pitying expression of unrequited love:

Early version (*Web.* Cl. II A g 13, f. 5v.)

Wer Minne kennt und ihre Pein	Let him who knows love and its pain
Der seh', was mich betroffen,	see what has befallen me;
Wohl grünt in Freuden Thal und	indeed the valley and field flourish in

Hayn,
Doch nimmer grünt mein Hoffen.
Die Turtel giert im Abendschein
O, Wehe!
Denn lauter Lust ist um mich her,
Doch härm' ich mich darum nur
    mehr!

joy,
but my hope never blossoms.
The turtle yaws in the evening's light;
alas!,
for nothing but pleasure surrounds me,
and yet for that reason I grieve all the
    more.

Der Stolze konnte mich verschmähn,
So muß ich ewig klagen!
O hätt' ich nimmer ihn gesehn,
Ich kann mein Leid nicht tragen!
Verhöhnet ward mein Liebesflehn,
O, Wehe!
Zerstört sey Liebe, Glück und Lust,
Nur Rache wohnt in meiner Brust!

I must ever lament that
the proud one was able to scorn me.
Would that I had never seen him,
I cannot bear my sorrow.
My entreaty of love was mocked;
alas!
Let happiness and delight be destroyed,
only revenge dwells in my breast!

With the removal of the first strophe, however, the focus falls solely on 'Rache.'

Final Version

Er konnte mich um sie verschmäh'n,
Und ich soll es ertragen?
In herbem Leid soll ich vergeh'n
In meinen Blüthentagen?
Er hörte kalt der Liebe Fleh'n,

He was able to to scorn me for her,
and I should endure that?
Am I to perish in bitter sorrow
during the bloom of my life?
He listened coldly to the entreaty of
    love—

Weh! Weh!
Mein Herz so bang, so todeswund,
Drum stürz' auch all' sein Glück zu
    Grund!

Alas! alas!—
my heart so anxious, so fatally injured;
therefore let all of his happiness crash
    to the ground!

Changes in the text of the Duetto No. 11 between Lysiart and Eglantine reverse the roles of the two villains and turn Eglantine into the leading figure in the relationship.

Early version (Web. Cl. II A g 13)

Egl. Wie du kannst, du willst mich
          rächen?
      Enden soll des Busens Qual?
Lys. Nimm mein feierlich Versprechen,
      Rächer werd' ich, und Gemahl!
Egl. In dich wähl ich zum Gemahl!
      Und du wirst dein Wort nicht
          brechen?
Lys. Nimm mein feierlich Versprechen,
      Heut' noch endet deine Qual!
Beide Ja ich wag es, nimm den Schwur,
      Nimm die Hand zum stillen

What? You can and wish to
    avenge me?
The bosom's torment shall end?
Take my solemn promise!
I shall be both avenger and spouse.
I choose you as my spouse!
And you will not break your
    word?
Take my solemn promise,
your torment ends this very day!
Yes, I'll dare and take the oath
and the hand of the secret

	Bunde!	alliance!
	Heut' noch schlägt der Rache Stunde,	On this very day strikes the hour of vengeance;
	Rache, Rache athm' ich nur!	I breathe only revenge.

Final version.

Egl.	Komm denn, unser Leid zu rächen,	Then come to avenge our sorrow!
	Enden soll der Seele Qual!	The soul's torment shall end!
Lys.	Nimm mein feyerlich Versprechen:	Take my solemn promise.
	Rächer werd' ich und Gemahl.	I shall be both avenger and spouse.
Egl.	Trostlos muß sie untergehn,	She must perish disconsolately
	Die mein Leben mir geraubt!	who stole my life from me!
Lys.	In dem Staub muß ich ihn sehn,	I must see him in the dust
	Der zu Sternen hob sein Haupt.	who raised his head to the stars.
Beide	Dunkle Nacht, du hörst den Schwur,	Dark night, you hear the oath.
	Sei mit uns'rer That im Bunde!	Be an ally to our deed.
	Ja es schlug der Rache Stunde,	The hour of vengeance has indeed struck;
	Rache, Rache athm' ich nur!	I only breathe revenge!

This change is of course entirely consistent with the revisions in the last act that convert Eglantine from a petty personality concerned only with holding Lysiart to his promise of marriage to a demonic figure of heroic stature for whom attainment of revenge unleashes voluntary self-destruction.

2. STRUCTURAL CONSIDERATIONS

To the extent that musico-dramatic structure in an opera may be divorced from plot, the history of the libretto reveals that a large number of revisions arose from structural considerations. This should come as no surprise, since Chezy began the project as an operatic novice, and her first scenario shows that she had no concept of musical structure. In addition, Weber had never before attempted a 'grand opera'. The history of the text therefore partly represents an attempt to discover the most effective framework for the story and for the kind of music that Weber envisioned.

2.1. *Length and division into acts*

At the most basic level, length and the division of the libretto into acts constituted grounds for revisions of the text. Weber initially conceived the opera as a two-act structure, and up until the summer of 1822 the opera was actually divided into two acts, perhaps because such an arrangement yields a symmetrical pattern of complication and resolution in the plot. That is, the serene and stable situation at the opening of the work is progressively disturbed by envy, jealousy, and treachery, and the end of Act I marks the nadir in the fortunes of the work's heroine, her condemnation by the assembled court and exile. Act II in Weber's original plan begins at the moment of Euryanthe's planned execution and then charts the progressive rehabilitation of Euryanthe's reputation and her eventual reunion with Adolar. The earliest librettos also show that Weber coupled with the decline and rise in Euryanthe's fortunes an important detail in the stage setting. In the two-act disposition, the first scene begins in full day. Twilight sets in on the scene between Euryanthe and Eglantine, and the first act closes at night. The second act reverses this procedure, with night giving way to day at the time of Euryanthe's rescue by the King's hunting party; the festive conclusion ends once again in the bright light of day. Such reinforcement of dramatic progress through scenic detail represents an important connection between the dramaturgy of *Euryanthe* and that of the *Freischütz*, where, as Weber himself is alleged to have pointed out, the opposition of good and evil is visually underscored by the progression from day to night to day.[6]

By August 1822, however, the opera had been split into three acts, perhaps out of concern for the comfort and attentiveness of potential audiences. Between Weber's first scenario and the version taken to Vienna in February 1822 the first act grew considerably through the accretion of several numbers: Eglantine's arias, the Romanze, the duet between Bertha and Rudolph, and the love duet for Adolar and Euryanthe. Whereas Weber's scenario had specified eight numbers in the first act, the libretto approved by the Viennese censor in February implied approximately fourteen numbers in the first act alone, just two less than the entire *Freischütz* score. A partitioned first act therefore presented less of an endurance test for the audience.

The division of the original Act I of course necessitated a finale for the new first act, for which purpose the scene of Lysiart's arrival at Nevers and his conversation with Euryanthe was adapted by the addition of a substantial closing movement for soloists and chorus that would bring the act to a satisfactory close. An early version of the start of the new finale, incompletely preserved in the miscellany *Web.* Cl. II A g 4 (Item 4), may in fact represent the remnants of the version that Chezy submitted to Weber in October 1822, and it is interesting primarily because its verse structure, twelve lines of trochaic tetrameter instead of the two quatrains of mixed iambic pentameter and tetrameter that had appeared at this point in earlier drafts of the libretto, hints that

[6] Lobe, 'Gespräche mit Weber', op. cit. ch. 2 n. 6 above, p. 33.

at this early date Weber already contemplated borrowing an extant instrumental piece, the *Marcia vivace* for ten trumpets (J. 288) as the basis for the opening movement of the finale. The second extant version of the new Act I Finale (the main layer of *Web.* Cl. II A g 5), from the spring of 1823, also points to a plan to borrow the last movement from the cantata that Weber had written in 1821 for the birthday of the Duchess Amalie of Zweibrücken (J. 283).[7] Why Weber decided to borrow much of the Act I Finale from prior compositions is not known, but his despair at having fallen behind contractual deadlines for completion of the opera doubtless played a role in the decision; perhaps too Chezy's departure for Berlin in September 1822 led him to consider using extant materials rather than count on her to return to Dresden in time to supply a poetically stimulating and satisfactory text for new composition.

One further consequence of the division of the first act seems to have been the definitive deletion of the Bertha–Rudolph scene, whose primary *raison d'être* had been to provide a moment of respite between the two great revenge arias; the new finale was shifted into the slot that this number had occupied, and in addition the two revenge arias would now be separated by the intermission between the first and second acts. On the whole Weber must not have mourned the loss of the peasants' number, since an ambivalence towards the scene had already surfaced in an earlier attempt to cut this duet from the opera. Doubtless he sensed that the sentimental and somewhat trivial tone of the duet was not congruent with the essentially serious and elevated tone of his 'grand opera.'

The concerns that seem to have brought about the division of the first act also led to a significant shortening of the libretto. In total length the two-act version of February 1822 was over 200 lines longer than the final three-act version. Most of the abbreviation was accomplished in passages of dialogue, presumably designed to be set as recitative. For example, a comparison of the undivided first act in *Web.* Cl. II A g 3 with the same unit in *Web.* Cl. II A g 6, where the situations basically remain unchanged, shows that compression of recitative texts for dialogues accounted for the elimination of about 70 lines; the amount of abbreviation in the texts of the musical pieces is, on the other hand, essentially negligible, except for the complete removal of the Romanze (20 lines) and the elimination of one strophe from Eglantine's Scena ed aria (see above). A comparison of different versions of the second

---

[7] Autographs of both items are included in the *Euryanthe* composition draft. For a discussion and edition of the *Marcia vivace* see Steven Winick, 'Trumpet Music by Carl Maria von Weber: A Tusch, a Canon, and a March', *Journal of the International Trumpet Guild* 12/ 4 (May, 1988): 11–15 and 19–21.

(i.e. third) act, though less precise because of more fundamental changes in dramatic situations, yields a similar shift in emphasis from dialogue to number, a point to which we shall return.

Of course, such cuts in the dialogue were not entirely beneficial to the presentation of the plot. *Euryanthe* is a very complicated story and much important information pertaining to the prehistory of the opera, such as Emma's story and appearance, Euryanthe's oath of secrecy to Adolar, and Adolar's rejection of Eglantine's love, must be related solely through narration. The abbreviation of the dialogue tended to obscure points that were relatively clear in earlier versions of the text. For example, in the final version of the dialogue between Eglantine and Euryanthe (I, iii) very little attention is devoted to the question of Euryanthe's oath of secrecy, precisely one line, in fact. In contrast, earlier versions of this dialogue had stressed the importance of the oath as a sign of fidelity and confidence between the two lovers. Hence the gravity of the secret in the final version is not adequately impressed upon the audience, to whom Adolar's and Euryanthe's violent reactions in the second-act finale to Lysiart's revelation of the secret must seem unmotivated. Knowing the story better than any audience possibly could, Weber underestimated the effect of this cut on the clarity of the plot.

2.2. *The structure of Act III*

A number of revisions made in the final act are especially suggestive of structural and musical considerations that guided Weber's alterations in the text. Over the history of the collaboration the final act was revised extensively, with respect to both the disposition of pieces and their texts. In contrast, the first two acts remained relatively stable, despite the fact that they were originally conceived as but one act. Two reasons seem to underlie this disparity between the opening and concluding acts. First, many of the alterations in the third act may be attributed to changes in the denouement that we have already discussed; no change of such a fundamental nature was ever made in the plot of the first two acts. This cannot be the full answer, however, since even sections of the last act not affected by changes in plot were subjected to significant rewriting. To explain this phenomenon more fully one must recall Weber's early scenario. In that outline, the structure of Act I had been defined with great clarity, thus forming the recognizable basis for the final version of Acts I and II. The history of the first half of the opera represents, as it were, only successive layers of accretions to and deletions from the basic framework of that early document. On the other hand, the treatment of the final act in that scenario had been much less precise in terms of musical structure, perhaps because Weber at that time was more concerned with matters of plot. Seen in this light, the revisions of the last act represent a necessary process of structural clarification. To demonstrate the musical impulses behind such changes one can point to the textual revisions of four scenes in the last act; for the first three the dramatic situations remain essentially unchanged from earliest to latest versions, and while changes of plot do affect the fourth example, structural alterations beyond those necessitated by plot can be observed that are consistent with those made in the three earlier cases.

(a) Act III, scene i (Euryanthe and Adolar in the wilderness)
Throughout the various versions of the first scene of the final act the basic sequence of events remains the same: (1) Euryanthe and Adolar arrive exhausted in the wilderness; (2) Euryanthe prepares to die at Adolar's hands; (3) just before her execution Euryanthe sees a giant snake—in subsequent drafts the animal variously became a lion, hyena, dragon, or monster[8]—and offers to sacrifice herself to it in order to save Adolar; (4) Euryanthe watches the battle between Adolar and the snake and describes it; (5) Adolar returns victorious and spares Euryanthe's life; (6) Adolar departs, leaving Euryanthe to her fate. These are the events much as they occurred in the ninth section of Chezy's translation of the fable. However, various elaborations of these events, particularly of the first three elements, differ considerably from the earliest version (in this case the published fragments from Chezy's first attempt at a libretto) to the final version.

Concentrating on the scene up to the point where Euryanthe sees the snake, we may summarize the evolution of the text in the following manner. The earliest surviving version (a published fragment from the original libretto) is essentially an extended monologue for Euryanthe, who is given nearly three-quarters of the text; Adolar is limited, with one exception, to short, angry replies, and there is no opportunity for the two lovers to sing simultaneously. Hence as originally constructed, the scene is rather more like a dialogue for the spoken stage than an operatic duet. By the time Weber left for Vienna in February 1822, however, the scene had changed drastically, presumably under the composer's influence. For one thing, it had more than doubled in length

[8] Chezy's translation of the *Roman de la violette* mentions a large snake, but her original scenario had already transformed it into a lion, and Weber's scenario mentions only a non-specified 'monster' (*Ungeheuer*). In the early librettos *Web.* Cl. II A g 13 and *Web.* Cl. II A g 3 the monster is made into a dragon (*Drache*). Only in the original layer of *Web.* Cl. II A g 4 is the 'snake' again specified. One leaf of indeterminable date in Cl. II A g 4 (unnumbered) transforms the monster into a 'Hyäna'. Chezy 1840, p. 18, claims that Weber was opposed to the snake because of the similarity to the *Die Zauberflöte*.

(42 lines in the original version of the scene, 89 lines in *Web*. Cl. II A g 3), articulating in the process a structure that, according to Weber's pencil annotations in *Web*. Cl. II A g 3, consisted of five compositional units up to the arrival of the 'dragon': (1) Euryanthe describes the journey with Adolar (monologue, 10 lines); (2) Euryanthe pleads for Adolar's sympathy (monologue, 7 lines); (3) Adolar reproaches Euryanthe and announces his plan to execute her (monologue with interjections for Euryanthe, 29 lines); (4) Adolar is firm in his resolve; Euryanthe asks to be allowed to pray ('Duett', 13 lines); (5) Euryanthe climbs the hill and observes nature for the last time; she perceives Emma's redeemed spirit and then sees a dragon (monologue, 30 lines). This version of the scene does redress in certain respects deficiencies that could be attributed to Chezy's original version. Adolar has a much more prominent role than before and a section that Weber himself labels a 'Duett' has been inserted into the scene. Finally, Euryanthe's descriptive monologue is greatly expanded, incorporating, moreover, an oblique reference to Emma's redemption. It should be noted, however, that none of these units closely corresponds to traditional genres. The monologues are not designated 'Aria' in *Web*. Cl. II A g 3, nor could they be, since their contents are essentially descriptive and conversational in tone, and the unit that Weber marked for treatment as a 'Duett' makes no poetic provision for simultaneous singing. In short, as taken to Vienna in February 1822 the scene between Adolar and Euryanthe still has no real opportunities for lyrical expansion.

Revisions of the libretto made between March and August 1822, however, entailed yet another complete reworking of this scene, which cast the dialogue between Euryanthe and Adolar into a form more conventionally duet-like than any of the preceding versions. As transmitted in the original layer of *Web*. Cl. II A g 4, the scene is segmented into three distinct stages: (1) a monologue of twelve lines for Euryanthe; (2) thirteen lines of dialogue between Adolar and Euryanthe; and (3) a concluding segment labelled 'No. 1 Duo' that itself is divided into four sections that alternate between passages of dialogue or extended monologue (the first and third sections) and passages designed for simultaneous singing (sections two and four). Not only is the scene considerably shorter in this revision, reflecting the general trend of coeval revisions elsewhere in the opera, but it is now structured around one number, the 'Duo', towards which the opening monologue and dialogue are aimed. Descriptive and conversational elements play a much smaller role; for example, Euryanthe's monologue about the landscape is reduced to about one-fifth of its previous length. Moreover, the revised duet itself follows a much more familiar pattern. An opening exchange between the characters leads to mutual reflection upon the situation, following which a change in the situation (here Euryanthe begins to descend the cliff and looks over the valley) leads to another round of mutual asides. Weber eventually removed the last ten lines of the duet text, eliminating Euryanthe's description of the landscape and the redundant expressions of sorrow in the final quatrain.[9] With this curtailment the text of the duet achieved its final form.

In contrast to the elements that precede the appearance of the snake, those that follow were revised very little between February 1822 and the final version; the order and type of elements involved were always constant, with significant revisions occurring only in the text of the aria in which Euryanthe prays for divine assistance and describes the battle. The earliest texts for this aria consist of three matched strophes:

Scena No. 16: Early version (Web. Cl. II A g 3)

Heiliger Engel Schaar,	Host of holy angels,
Wachend all, immerdar	ever watching
In tiefster Nächte Schoos	in the lap of deepest night
Ueber der Menschen Loos,	over the fate of men,
Blicke herab!	gaze down!
Schaue des Kampfes Wuth	Look upon the fury of the battle;
Qualmend in Dampf und Gluth	smoking with steam and fire
Dringet das Unthier ein,	the monster enters forcibly.
Wo, wo wird Hülfe seyn	Where will help be
In dieser Noth?	in this distress?
Wehe! der Drache siegt,	Woe! the dragon is victorious.
Wehe, mein Held erliegt—	Woe! my hero succumbs—
Nein!—sieh den Feind im Staub,	No! see the enemy in the dust;
Nicht mehr des Bangens Raub,	no longer prey to anxiety,
Seele, gieb Dank!	give thanks, my soul!

During the summer of 1822, however, Chezy and Weber began to move away from this strophic structure, perhaps because it seemed inappropriate to cast such an active text in a purely stanzaic form; in particular the content of the third stanza, the description of the battle and Adolar's victory, is emotionally far removed from the content of the first two stanzas. In the original layer of *Web.* Cl. II A g 4 (Item 10) the prayer is reduced to two matching stanzas by eliminating the third stanza and with it the description of the battle; Euryanthe announces Adolar's victory somewhat perfunctorily only after the piece is over and Adolar has returned. A variant on an unnumbered leaf in Cl. II A g 4 keyed to this version, probably made before August 1822, attempts

---

[9] See Weber's letter of 28 Nov. 1822 cited in the preceding chapter. Quite independently Chezy herself suggested the same cut in an undated letter of mid-November 1822 (*Web.* Cl. V. Abt. 2, No. 14).

to solve the problem by fashioning an asymmetrical structure of two unmatched stanzas, the first for the prayer proper, and the second for the description of the battle and its outcome:

No. 16: intermediate version (*Web.* Cl. II A g 4, unnumbered leaf):

Schirmender Engel Schaar	Host of protecting angels,
Wachend all immerdar	ever watching
In tiefster Nächte Schoos	in the lap of deepest night
Ueber der Menschen Loos	over the fate of men,
Blicke herab!	gaze down!
O, Schreckenskampf! Gott! wo wird Hülfe seyn!	Oh, fearful battle! God! where is help!
Wuthathmend dringt die Feindin ein,	Breathing fury the enemy enters forcibly.
Weh mir, daß ich jetzt wehrlos bin!	Woe is me, that I am now defenceless!
Vernicht euch mich, grausame Mörderin!	Destroy me, cruel murderess!
Ich athme wieder! Hochgeschwungen	I breathe again!
Blitzt meines Helden Schwerdt	My hero's sword flashes as it is brandished aloft.
Heil! es durchfährt	Hail! it transfixes
Des Unthiers Brust! Es ist gelungen.	the monster's breast! It is successful!
Ja, der Sieg ist ihm gegeben,	Yes, victory has been given to him.
Seele fühle ganz dein Glück,	Feel thoroughly your fortune, my soul;
O, was ist mein Leben	oh, what is my life
Gegen diesen Augenblick!	compared to a moment like this!

By November Weber and Chezy had, independently of one another, decided to restore the original version of the prayer in three matched stanzas,[10] perhaps because this last variant was poetically quite rough. Yet the asymmetrical conception eventually formed the basis for the final version of the text, achieved only by the spring of 1823, which grafts the first two stanzas of the original prayer onto a poetically refined version of the contrasting third stanza.

Final version.

Schirmende Engelschaar,	Host of protecting angels,
Wachend all immerdar,	ever watching
In tiefster Nächte Schoos,	in the lap of deepest night
Über der Menschen Los,	over the fate of men,
Blicke herab!	gaze down!
Schäumend in Kampfes Wuth,	Seething in the rage of battle,
Qualmend in Dampf und Gluth	smoking steam and fire,
Dringet die Feindinn ein;	the enemy enters forcibly.

[10] Weber's comment about restoring the 'das alte Gebet' in his letter of 28 Nov. 1822 is confirmed by an entry in his handwriting in *Web.* Cl. II A g 4, Item 10.

O, wo wird Hülfe seyn	Oh, where is help
In dieser Noth?	in this distress?
Wie sie dichter ihn umzingelt,	How she encircles him more tightly
Sich nach seinem Herzen ringelt.—	and coils towards his heart.—
Weh! er fällt!—	Woe! he falls!
Nein, mein Held	No, my hero
Ringt sich auf und hoch geschwungen	struggles up and brandished aloft
Blitzt sein Schwert—es ist gelungen!	his sword flashes. It is successful!
Heil! der Sieg ist ihm gegeben.	Hail! victory has been given to him.
Seele, fühle ganz dein Glück!	Feel thoroughly your fortune, my soul;
O, was ist mein Leben	oh, what is my life
Gegen diesen Augenblick?	compared to a moment like this!

In this version two matched stanzas are given to the prayer and Euryanthe's sense of helplessness, but at the decisive moment in the battle the controlled structure of the prayer breaks down. Moreover, in comparison to the purely strophic versions of the prayer, the final version also allots more space to and thus intensifies Euryanthe's ecstatic expression of jubilation at the victorious outcome of the battle. Of course, the compositional consequences of the non-strophic structure of the final version are obvious, since the drastic shift of poetic perspective and structure in the last stanza prefigures a correspondingly drastic shift of musical style, a point to which we shall return in Chapter IX.

(b) Act III, scene iii (Euryanthe and the King's retinue)

Without going into the same degree of detail we may observe that the tendencies evident in the revisions of the scene between Adolar and Euryanthe also played a role in the revisions of three other scenes in the last act. In Act III, scene iii, the dramatic situations remain constant throughout the preserved manuscript librettos. As transmitted in all extant versions of the text, the third scene may be outlined in five sections: (1) the royal hunting party emerges from the forest at daybreak (ritornello and chorus); (2) the King and his hunters discover Euryanthe (dialogue); (3) Euryanthe convinces the King of her innocence, and the King promises to help her (duet with chorus); (4) Euryanthe rejoices at the thought of reunion with Adolar (aria); and (5) Euryanthe collapses from emotional exhaustion. Structurally, however, the texts for the various component sections change in ways reminiscent of the history of the previous example. For one thing, there is a significant reduction in discursive or descriptive texts. The earliest version of the chorus is an active piece wherein the hunters describe the chase in which they are involved; by the summer of 1822 (*Web.* Cl. II A g 4), however, the chorus had turned into a purely static number extolling the abstract joys of the hunter's life. In the revised form, therefore, the chorus is much more like the Jaegerchor in *Freischütz* than the earlier versions had been, and this similarity subsequently becomes even stronger with the addition of a parallel second strophe with refrain in the spring of 1823. The duet, actually an alternating dialogue between Euryanthe and the King, is drastically shortened between the earliest and latest versions (42 lines in *Web.* Cl. II A g 13, 21 lines in the final version), and changes in the postlude following Euryanthe's collapse eliminate the dialogue between the fainting Euryanthe and the King, thereby retaining solely the hunters' expression of grief at her apparent demise.

Along with the reduction of conversational and descriptive elements, one notices a tendency towards intensification of the emotional content. Euryanthe's despair at the beginning of the duet is considerably deeper in the later versions, as a comparison of the opening lines shows; in the first version she thinks of consolation in the afterlife, but in the final version she can only think dismally of death as an end to her sufferings:

Early version of the start of Duetto con coro (Web. Cl. II A g 3).

Dort oben wohnt Erbarmen	Up there dwells compassion
Wohnt Liebe noch allein!	and love alone!

Final Version.

Laßt mich hier in Ruh' erblassen	Allow me to die here in peace;
Gönnt mir diese letzte Huld.	grant me this last favour.

At the other extreme, a completely new text for Euryanthe's contemplation of reunion with Adolar, the idea for which was allegedly suggested by Weber,[11] replaces the more controlled and somewhat incredulous expressions of hope of the earlier versions with an outburst of unbridled joy and urgency:

Early Version (Web. Cl. II A g 3).

Ruh' ich an seiner Brust?	Do I rest upon his breast?
Wird mich sein Arm umfangen?	Will his arm embrace me?.
O, Wonnevolles Bangen!	O anxiety filled with delight!
O, Schmerzerfüllte Lust!	O joy filled with pain!
Ihn soll ich wiedersehen	I am to see him again
Nach Todesqualen, Ach!	after the torments of death.
Dies Herz, das Schmerz nicht brach	My heart, which pain did not break,
Will nun in Lust vergehen!	wishes now to die in joy.

Final version.

Zu ihm! Zu ihm! O, weilet nicht!	To him! To him! O do not delay!
Wo bist du, meines Daseins Licht?	Where are you, light of my existence?
Zu ihm! daß ich ihn fest umfasse,	To him! that I might embrace him firmly

---

[11] Chezy 1840, p. 14.

Ihn nimmer, nimmer lasse   and never, never leave him,
So Herz an Herzen, Aug' in Auge,   and thus, heart on heart, eye to eye,
Aus seinem Blicke Leben sauge.   absorb life from his gaze.

Hence Euryanthe's emotional swing from despair at the start of the duet to ecstasy in the aria is considerably more pronounced in the final version of the scene. Euryanthe's subsequent collapse is made more abrupt in the revised version and represents another sudden change in situation, not unlike the unexpected arrival of the snake in the preceding example.

Revisions in the text of this scene thus ultimately create a more focused dramatic unit. By compressing the duet between the King and Euryanthe, inserting a brief transition at the end of the duet, and intensifying the level of emotion in the aria, the final version of the text provides the basis for treating the duet as an introductory movement to the climactic aria, so that the two numbers function together as the slow and fast parts of a single multi-movement number; this is in fact precisely how Weber handles the two numbers in his setting. An overview of the entire scene shows too that the final version of scene iii adheres to the same principles that shaped the revisions of the scene between Adolar and Euryanthe: introductory material of a conversational tone (the recitative and duet) leads to a climactic outpouring (the aria), following which an immediate change in situation undercuts the conclusion of the number. Added to the scheme is an opening colouristic movement, the chorus of hunters, which itself provides a sharp contrast with the immediately preceding situation, Euryanthe's private scene in the forest (scene ii).

(c) Act III, scene iv (Adolar and Chorus)

Entirely consistent with the changes in scenes i and iii of the last act are a number of revisions in the scene between Adolar and the chorus (Act III, scene iv). In the earliest librettos the picturesque May Song with which the scene begins is a strophic song of four stanzas sung by the peasants to Bertha and Rudolph, whose wedding day it is; appropriately the text, a rustic reflection of the courtly tribute to fidelity in the opening chorus of the Introduzione, is a celebration of the gifts of spring and the rewards of faithful love. As originally conceived each stanza is begun by a different soloist and completed by the chorus. In the two earliest librettos the fourth stanza of the May Song is then followed by another stanza for Bertha and Rudolph together, whose own happiness is spoiled, however, by melancholy thoughts about the misfortune that has befallen their beloved former mistress:

May Song. Fifth stanza. (Web. Cl. II A g 3).
Bertha, Rudolph.

Ich trete bangend zum Altar,	I approach the altar anxiously,
Noch nie das Herz so schwer mir war,	my heart was never before so heavy.
Mich freuet nicht der grüne May	I am gladdened by neither the verdant May
Noch Hochzeitlust, ich sag es frey	nor the joy of the wedding; I admit it openly,
Um Euryanth' klagt meine Treu'!	my fidelity laments Euryanthe!

At this point Adolar, who has entered unnoticed and unrecognized, laments bitterly the disappearance of fidelity in the world ('Giebt keine Treu auf weiter Erde mehr'). By the Autumn of 1822, the stanza for Bertha and Rudolph, which had effected a transition in mood from the innocence of the May song to Adolar's cynicism, was eliminated, so that Adolar's denial of the possibility of human faithfulness is juxtaposed immediately against the peasants' affirmation of fidelity. As in Act III, scene iii, therefore, a structural revision seems to have been calculated to intensify the emotional contrast between adjacent sections.[12]

Over the history of the collaboration the number of lines devoted to the dialogue between Adolar and his former subjects in the ensuing scene was significantly reduced (58 lines in *Web.* Cl. II A g 13; 35 in the final version). More interesting in light of the previous discussion, though, is the revision at the end of the scene. In the two earliest versions (*Web.* Cl. II A g 13 and *Web.* Cl. II A g 3), the rhymed dialogue between Adolar and the crowd continues consistently through the entire scene, for which there is no indication for structural subdivision, and the scene concludes with a three-line speech by Adolar.

Early conclusion of Act III, scene 4 (Web. Cl. II A g 3).

Adolar:	Entfernt euch alle, ohne Beben	Move out of sight, everyone. Without trembling
	Will ich durchschaun das Werk der Nacht,	I wish to see through the work of night;
	Dann sey des Lichtes Werk vollbracht!	then let the work of the day be accomplished!

By November, 1822, however, these three lines had been refashioned into a separate number for Adolar and the chorus.

---

[12] Two further changes in the text of the May Song are significant. First, the song was eventually further reduced from four stanzas to three by eliminating the original second stanza. Second, the song was eventually taken from the alternating soloists and given as a solo to Bertha, who sings it to an unidentified betrothed peasant couple. The fact that the motif of Bertha's and Rudolph's wedding was completely eliminated from the libretto in its later stages doubtless played a role in this decision.

Final version (*Web.* Cl. II A g 4, Item 12).

Chor:	Vernichte kühn das Werk der Tücke	Boldly destroy the work of malice;
	Vertrau der Unschuld und dem Glücke,	trust in innocence and fortune.
	Zum Schwert für dich greift jede Hand	Every hand seizes the sword for you,
	Wohlauf, zum Kampf für Euryanth'!	ready to battle for Euryanthe!
Adolar:	Ja, ich durchschau das Werk der Tücke,	Yes, I see through the work of malice;
	Der Liebe trau ich und dem Glücke,	I trust in love and fortune.
	Wohlauf, zum Kampf für Gut und Land,	Well then! onward to battle for property, land,
	Für Unschuld, Ehr, und Euryanth'!	innocence, honour, and Euryanthe!

Once again, the revision converts a relatively unstructured text into a scene in which dialogue develops a situation that is then summarized by a concise, well-defined number.

(d) Act III, scene v (arrival of Lysiart and Eglantine)

A structural analysis of the revisions in the scene that immediately follows is complicated by the fact that this section of the libretto was affected by significant plot alterations, as, for example, the inclusion of Eglantine's delirium. Beyond the changes in plot, however, the final version of the scene incorporates structural elements that resemble the revisions made in the preceding scenes of the last act. The early version transmitted in *Web.* Cl. II A g 3 can be outlined in four actions, which culminate in the arrival of the King that marks the beginning of the next scene: (1) Eglantine and Lysiart enter. Eglantine reminds Lysiart of his promise to marry her (duet); (2) Adolar confronts Lysiart, who summons the vassals to destroy Adolar (dialogue); (3) The vassals arrive to support Lysiart but then recognize Adolar and turn against Lysiart. The soloists comment upon this new turn of events (trio with chorus); and (4) Adolar challenges Lysiart to a battle (dialogue). At this stage in the history of the text the major number in the scene is the trio with chorus, an active number entailing motion, change of situation, and final contemplation. Between this piece and the chorus at the beginning of the final scene lies a short monologue for Adolar and Lysiart in irregular verse, hence certainly designed for treatment as recitative.

In the final version, based on Weber's draft of the denouement (*Web.* Cl. II A g 7), the scene is not only much more compact, but the dramaturgical plan is also simplified by clearer division of function between static and dynamic elements: (1) *Hochzeitmarsch No. 23.* Eglantine and Lysiart enter and the peasants look on with brief exclamations of horror. (2) *Recitative. Monologue and dialogue.* Eglantine is haunted by a delirious vision of an angry Emma, whereupon Adolar confronts the villains. Lysiart summons the vassals to arrest the interloper, but they recognize Adolar and refuse to carry out Lysiart's command. (3) *Duetto con coro No. 24.* The vassals threaten Lysiart as he and Adolar challenge one another to battle. As revised the shape of the scene is thus basically identical to those of the preceding scenes in the act. An opening number with primarily colouristic value (the wedding march) is followed by a more prosaic section exposing a new situation; the excitement of the new development then generates a climactic ensemble that Weber wished to be cast in 'kurze, kräftig donnernde' words.[13] As in the other revised scenes in the last act, the climactic moment in the revised version is interrupted abruptly, this time by the arrival of the King at the start of the finale.

Taken together, the textual revisions in the last act of *Euryanthe* represent a reworking of rather discursive scenes dominated by dialogue into units that more sharply separate the development of situation from lyrical reflection. In other words, whereas Chezy originally had given Weber a number of texts intended as lengthy, 'active' ensembles (see especially the duet with chorus for Euryanthe and the King and the trio with chorus for Eglantine, Adolar and Lysiart in *Web.* Cl. II A g 3), the revisions clarify the structure as an alternation of dramatically active texts designed to be set as recitative or arioso and more static texts destined for treatment as separate musical numbers. In particular, the revisions of the libretto create opportunites for emotionally charged numbers strategically placed as encapsulations of the preceding developments in the action. In this respect, then, the revisions in the last act seem to reflect traditional views on the nature and function of music in opera, based on the premiss that music is more appropriate for the expression of feeling than for description of events, as Weber's later admonition to the librettist of *Oberon* on the type of texts suitable for musical elaboration makes explicit:

Still I beg leave to observe that the composer looks more for the expression of feelings than the figurative; the former he may repeat and develope in all their graduations; but verses like—
    'Like the spot the tulip weareth
    Deep within its dewey urn;'

---

[13] Chezy 1840, p. 37.

or, in *Huon's* song—

'Like hopes that deceive us
Or false friends who leave us
Soon as descendeth prosperity's sun . . .'

must be said only *once*.[14]

The tendency to convert the texts for lengthy, dramatically active musical pieces into more compressed summations of emotion is perhaps also a tacit recognition on Weber's part that his own style of composition was more suited to the pithy definition of character through relatively short pieces than to the ongoing development of dramatic action through extended compositions; we shall return to this point in the next part of the present study.

Certain consistencies in the revisions of the last act suggest that Weber's thoughts about the large-scale structure of a 'grand opera' crystallized as work on the libretto progressed. For one thing, in their respective final versions, scenes iii, iv, and v of Act III are all shaped as three-stage progressions consisting of: (1) an opening, static piece that establishes a basic mood, colour, or situation; (2) a monologue and/or dialogue that redefines the situation; and (3) a culminating piece that emotionally summarizes the new situation. The text thus prefigures the treatment of the scene as a rudimentary, self-contained musical unit, framed on either end by set pieces and directed from a relatively simple opening movement to a concluding number of greater emotional intensity. Bearing in mind the fact that the structure of Act III crystallized after much of the opera had already been composed, one can see how the revisions of the libretto might have been influenced by Weber's experiences in composing other scenes of the opera. The three-part paradigm had already been tested in the first two scenes of Act I (Nos. 1–4 and Nos. 5–7), which both expand the model by including a brief number in the middle of the dramatically active second part. To a certain extent, the Act II Finale may also be seen as an expansion of the same three-part scheme, since its opening chorus corresponds to the mood-setting numbers that begin the scenic units in the last act, and its concluding movements are arranged in order of increasing intensity, ending with the violent choral condemnation of Euryanthe.

Weber's revisions in the last act also demonstrate a consistency of approach at a higher level of organization. In the final version of the libretto the scenic units are stacked back-to-back with no intervening dialogue. Such methods of construction strengthen the preponderance of closed number over more open-ended musical procedures, but they also shed an interesting light on Weber's ideas of operatic dramaturgy.

[14]Planché, op. cit. ch. 4 n. 7 above, p. 53.

In its final form, the third act is built on the principle of unmitigated juxtaposition of contrasting moods and situation. Hence, the 'colourful' numbers in the act serve primarily as foils that reverse the mood of what immediately precedes: the Jaegerchor immediately brightens the scene after the melancholy of Euryanthe's Scena e cavatina; Euryanthe's apparent demise at the end of No. 20 is followed by the serenity of the May Song; and the expressions of new-found hope in No. 22 are overturned by the sinister approach of the villains' wedding march. Contrasts of this sort are then intensified at other moments where abrupt twists in the action interrupt an emotional high-point, as, for example, the arrival of the snake at the moment of Euryanthe's planned execution, Euryanthe's collapse at the height of her ecstatic hope for reunion with Adolar, and the King's arrival in the midst of the dispute between Adolar and Lysiart. The act progresses, therefore, largely by the immediate opposition of contrasting elements, and the important dramatic consideration is the effect created by such unexpected turns. From the preserved documents, we may be quite sure that it was Weber, rather than Chezy, who was primarily responsible for this emphasis on sudden shifts of mood and situation. It was he who insisted, against Chezy's doubts, on Euryanthe's apparent demise and who suggested ways to make the Hochzeitmarsch 'schauerlicher', and his revision of the final scenes specified that the King appear at the moment of most intense confrontation between Adolar and Lysiart. In short, Weber's revisions of the last act emphasized abrupt contrasts and suggest that the composer essentially conceived the libretto as a succession of striking effects.

2.3.   Libretto revisions and musical recall

From the standpoint of musical organization one of the most interesting features of the history of the *Euryanthe* libretto is that the later versions of the text incorporated more opportunities for musical recall than did the earlier versions. For instance, Weber's revised scenario for the denouement (*Web*. Cl. II A g 7) specified that the opera close with citations of texts from two numbers heard earlier in the opera, the Euryanthe–Adolar Duetto No. 13 and the Scene und Chor No. 4, thereby laying the foundation for a broader pattern of musical recapitulation in the Act III Finale than had been planned in the early versions of the libretto. While the earliest libretti suggest that music heard earlier in the last act , the May Song, was originally contemplated as the concluding element in the Finale, Weber's revisions sought to tie the conclusion to important moments in the first and second acts.

Beyond this explicit provision for musical recall, however, implicit opportunities for the use of recurrent music were increased by the progressively greater importance given Eglantine and Emma. Eglantine's personal motive is built both into her own arias (No. 6 and No. 8) and into passages where other characters refer to her treachery (Act II Finale and the Duetto No. 19). As noted above, both of her solo numbers were accretions to the original scheme outlined in Weber's scenario of November 1821; further, the mention of Eglantine that prompts the appearance of the motive in the duet between Euryanthe and the King came about only in revisions made after Weber's trip to Vienna in February 1822. The music associated with the ghost of Emma occurs in the middle section of the Ouverture and at three points in the body of the opera: (1) as the music accompanying Euryanthe's recitative narration of Emma's story (I, iii); (2) during Eglantine's delirious vision of Emma (III, v); and (3) in the denouement, where, at the moment that Adolar becomes conscious of Emma's redemption, the music recurs in a transformed, diatonic version. Significantly, none of these moments were features of the earliest libretti; the Emma narration was treated in the early history of the libretto as a strophic Romanze, and the Act III allusions to Emma were fairly late additions to the libretto. Weber's plan to open the curtain during the Ouverture for a pantomimic scene in Emma's tomb, cautiously approved by the Viennese censor in February 1822, seems, however, to have suggested a certain type of music to him, one in which the orchestra rather than the voice would bear the primary responsibility for suggesting Emma's ethereal essence, and to have inspired him to rethink Emma's role and her musical treatment throughout the rest of the opera. Thus following his return from Vienna he soon had the Romanze recast as a recitative perhaps because the type of music that would characterize the sepulchral scene would not be compatible with the lilting rhythms of the Romanze text. Eglantine's delirium and the final redemption of the ghost were also added to the libretto only after Weber's return from Vienna in order to underscore the connection between Emma's fate and those of the main characters. Of course, Weber eventually abandoned all attempts to put Emma on stage as a visible presence, trusting entirely to music the task of suggesting Emma's invisible presence, but when he came to compose the Ouverture in September and October of 1823, he still incorporated the music that seems originally to have been inspired by the planned pantomime.[15]

It would not be too fanciful, then, to suggest that concerns for plot and musical structure were mutually influential in the evolving conception of Emma and Eglantine. Convention and precedent may have first

---

[15] See Chapter X, section 3.2, for a discussion of Weber's changing ideas about the use of the *Vision* within the Ouverture.

led Weber to identify these two figures through recurring music, for by associating motives most strongly with the villainous and supernatural elements in the opera, Weber was following models established in works like Méhul's *Euphrosine* and *Ariodant*,[16] Hoffmann's *Undine*, Spohr's *Faust* and *Zemire und Azor*,[17] and of course, his own *Freischütz*. But more than that, the possibilities for interesting musical effects that Emma and Eglantine presented may have captivated Weber's attention and led him to expand precisely those two figures into dominant elements in the final version of the text.

In the light of these implied opportunities for musical recall and our knowledge of the final score, we may turn again to Weber's revised plan for the conclusion of Act III (*Web.* Cl. II A g 7) and notice that it actually embodied the potential for the successive recall of four elements heard earlier in the opera, not just the two specified by textual reprise: (1) an off-stage cry of joy from the hunters (= Jaegerchor No. 18); (2) the reunion of Adolar and Euryanthe (= Duetto No. 13); (3) the celestial reunion of Emma with Udo (= *Vision* transformed); and (4) the Schlußchor (= Scene und Chor No. 4). Although the Ouverture was not yet composed, it also seems probable that by the time that he drafted the scenario for the denouement Weber already knew that it would incorporate several of the musical elements planned for use in the Finale, so that ties between Ouverture and Finale like those evident in his earlier operas would play a part in *Euryanthe* as well.[18] Of course Weber eventually abandoned his plan to close the opera with a melodic reprise based on Adolar's line 'Ich bau' auf Gott and meine Euryanth''; the final version of the Schlußchor omits the textual paraphrase 'Vertrau' auf Gott und deine Euryanth'' that would have facilitated such a thematic recapitulation. One can only speculate on the motives behind this evident change of plan. Perhaps the already heroic nature

---

[16] See David Charlton, 'Motive and Motif: Méhul before 1791', *ML* 53 (1976): 362–9; M. Elizabeth C. Bartlet, 'Etienne Nicolas Méhul and Opera during the French Revolution, Consulate, and Empire: A Source, Archival and Stylistic Study' (Ph.D. dissertation, University of Chicago, 1982), pp. 974–1010 and 1399–439; and Michael D. Grace, 'Méhul's *Ariodant* and the Early Leitmotif', in *A Festschrift for Albert Seay*, ed. Michael D. Grace (Colorado Springs, 1982), 173–94.

[17] For a recent discussion of recurring motives in Spohr's *Faust* see Clive Brown, 'Spohr, *Faust* and Leitmotif,' *MT* 125 (1984): 25–7.

[18] According to Chezy 1840, p. 13, Weber is alleged at some point early in the collaboration to have told her: '"Ich bau' auf Gott und meine Euryanth'!" das soll wie ein belebender Hauch durch die ganze Composition wehn, und schon in der Ouverture vorklingen ....' That Weber may have considered using the music of the love duet (No. 13) in the Ouverture is suggested by one of the extant musical drafts. See the discussion of Ex. 24 in Chapter X.

of Adolar's melody in No. 4 precluded its effective use as a musical symbol for the *lieto fine*; unlike Agathe's Aria in *Freischütz*, which could be musically intensified at the end of that opera as a symbol for the triumph of virtue, the original setting of Adolar's melody in No. 4 afforded the composer little room for such *Steigerung*.

3. CONCLUSION.

The picture that emerges from the history of the libretto is admittedly complicated and not readily susceptible to summary, but certain conclusions can be drawn. For one thing, Weber's responsibility for the final shape of the libretto must be seen as greater than Chezy's. Whereas Chezy was responsible primarily for the versification, Weber dictated the outcome of the story, the disposition of the numbers, the sequence of situations, and in many cases the forms of the individual numbers. To a large extent circumstances forced him to take control over these matters. Chezy had, after all, no experience as a librettist and evidently little prior contact of any kind with opera; nor was she an experienced playwright for the spoken stage. While Weber was always inclined to guide his librettists, it is doubtful that he exercised such complete control over the more experienced Kind or Hell in the other Dresden librettos. The genesis of *Euryanthe* therefore presents an exceptional case, even for Weber.

Precisely because Weber put so much of himself into the libretto for *Euryanthe*, however, the story of its genesis offers us the opportunity to form a better picture of Weber's conception of operatic dramaturgy. For example, a number of revisions in the libretto may be seen as attempts to implement Weber's ideal of 'organicism' in opera and thus serve to underscore the point that the musical 'unity' of an opera is a direct and natural consequence of unity within the text. Throughout the history of the libretto Weber and Chezy sought to integrate the supernatural pretext for the story more fully into the fabric of the opera, particularly by making the fates of Emma, Euryanthe and even Eglantine interdependent. And of course by building increased opportunities for musical recall into the libretto, Weber facilitated the use of musical devices that have an obvious unifying function.

Another side of Weber's outlook that emerges from the revisions of the libretto is a tendency to want the story painted in broad and colourful strokes. Through successive revisions the villains became more evil. Effects based on sudden changes of mood or situation proliferated. Emotions expressed by the characters became more intense and exaggerated. Even with respect to choice of words there is evidence that Weber made changes for the sake of more colourful and violent language. A large number of revisions therefore suggest that, for Weber, striking dramatic effects, unmitigated contrasts, and intense emotions formed the essential ingredients of operatic dramaturgy. Of course, to many critics such effects have seemed exaggerated and unmotivated by logical development of plot or character, 'Wirkungen ohne Ursache', to borrow a phrase that Wagner applied to the Scribe–Meyerbeer operas.

The genesis of the *Euryanthe* libretto also points up a strongly moralistic tendency on Weber's part. Revisions in the libretto sharpen the distinctions between the virtuous and evil couples, and the conclusion was rewritten to show that evil can only lead to its own destruction. As revised, the treatment of the villains in *Euryanthe* bears a marked resemblance to that of Caspar in the *Freischütz*. In both cases villainy is motivated by a combination of rejection and fear; Caspar and Eglantine wish to avenge unrequited love, while Lysiart and Caspar both fear the consequences of failure. The demise of the villains in the final version of *Euryanthe* runs a parallel course to Caspar's. Evil betrays its own kind in both operas; Samiel turns the seventh bullet on Caspar, Eglantine scornfully exposes Lysiart, Lysiart kills Eglantine. In both works the just sovereign metes out an ignoble end for the villain; while Caspar's corpse is thrown into the Wolf's Glen, Lysiart is led off to his execution. It is interesting to note that Weber for a time intended that Lysiart go to his execution with a defiant speech, which would, of course, have corresponded closely to Caspar's dying curse.[19] Only at a late stage of revision was this speech removed. By rewriting Chezy's conciliatory denouement, Weber therefore created parallels between *Euryanthe* and *Der Freischütz* that were not evident in the early versions of the libretto.

As a matter of fact, other echoes of the *Freischütz* seem to have reverberated in Weber's mind as he worked on the libretto, since many aspects of the *Euryanthe* libretto for which he was responsible descend from devices used in the *Freischütz*, and as the *Euryanthe* libretto was revised, many of these similarities were actually strengthened. The scenic progression from day to night and back to day was imposed on *Euryanthe* very early in the history of the collaboration, and the earliest librettos already contain situations and genres comparable to those in the *Freischütz*: a melancholy cavatina for the heroine; an aria of an expectant lover impatiently awaiting the arrival of the beloved in the second act; a rustic strophic Lied for a simple wedding celebration in the third act; and, of course, arias of revenge for the villains. Despite Weber's

---

[19] See Weber's letter of 28 Nov. 1822 to Chezy translated above in Chapter IV. In the manuscript libretto *Web. Cl.* II A g 5 Lysiart is in fact given a short speech as he is led off to his execution that is comparable to Caspar's dying curse: 'Auch sterbend pflück' ich noch des Sieges Palme, | Auf Trümmern deines Liebesglücks dich höhne | Versüßt den Tod!' Weber, however, did not set these lines.

protestation to the contrary, Euryanthe's collapse at the end of 'Zu ihm!' *is* reminiscent of the moment in *Freischütz* where Agathe is feared to have been killed by Max's shot. Later revisions not only strengthened the similarities between Caspar and the villains in *Euryanthe*, but also moulded the Jaegerchor into the same structure and function as the one in the *Freischütz*. Revisions in the text of the Act III Finale, whose final form was dictated by Weber's autograph scenario (*Web*. Cl. II A g 7), are strongly reminiscent of the third-act finale in *Freischütz*. The arrival of the King at the beginning of the Finale No. 25 in *Euryanthe* is a sudden, disruptive event, much like the shot with which the last finale in *Freischütz* begins. In both cases the concluding Finales therefore open at a moment of great excitement and confusion. Weber's plan to conclude the opera with melodies previously heard in the first and second acts adopts an important structural principle that he had realized in *Freischütz*. And of course, the supernatural element that was added to *Euryanthe* and subsequently expanded in successive revisions of the text invites comparison with the world of Samiel and the *wilde Heer*. Many of the 'experiences' that Weber attempted to impart to Chezy seem therefore to have been first acquired from the lessons he learned in working on the *Freischütz* and from their success therein.

That the final version of the libretto ultimately was not very successful should therefore come as no surprise. Chezy was no librettist, and, for that matter, neither was Weber. From the standpoint of logical and consistent development of plot and character, Weber's revisions hardly improved the libretto, and in some cases they were even detrimental to the intelligibility and plausibility of the story. Weber seems rather to have been interested in incorporating specific effects into the plot and in condensing the libretto into a series of powerful moments. In sum, we see that Weber as the collaborator for the text of *Euryanthe* was guided primarily by the instincts of a composer strongly conditioned by the prior success of the *Freischütz*. He gradually recognized what sort of music he wanted to write in *Euryanthe*, and stage by stage he rearranged the text to accommodate that music. Whether his musical approach was actually compatible with this style of libretto is, however, a question to which we shall turn in the next part of the present study.

PART III: MUSICAL ISSUES AND THE COMPOSITIONAL PROCESS

VI. The Euryanthe *Composition Draft*

I. INTRODUCTION: DESCRIPTION OF THE MANUSCRIPT

Though little studied since Jähns's catalogue of Weber sources, the composition draft for *Euryanthe* is arguably the best preserved and most direct source of information about how Weber composed.[1] It is known from his Diary that he routinely made preliminary drafts for all of his major works, following the completion of which he would proceed to a full score that he normally wrote out with great speed and calligraphic beauty. When Jähns catalogued the sources extant in 1871, however, he could find extensive drafts for only a very few works. For the operas, complete or nearly complete drafts existed for only *Euryanthe* and *Oberon* and for seven pieces of the unfinished *Die drei Pintos*; for the earlier operas up to and including *Der Freischütz* he found only a few sketches and drafts on isolated leaves. The intervening years have turned up only minor additions to what Jähns was able to locate. In contrast, a relatively high percentage of finished autograph scores have survived .

While we shall probably never know exactly what happened to the lost drafts, various pieces of evidence suggest that Weber himself for most of his life attached relatively little importance to them once he had finished a work. Unlike Beethoven, who after 1798 sketched in bound volumes that he kept to the end of his life, Weber seems frequently to have drafted on separate leaves and bifolios that he doubtless regarded as expendable scrap paper—for example, the versos and empty staves of orchestral and vocal parts for older works—perhaps a reflection of the frugality that led him to record fastidiously nearly every daily expense in his Diary. Then again, a number of the extant drafts up through those for the *Freischütz* apparently survived only because they happened to have been written on the empty leaves or staves of manuscripts that the composer preserved for other reasons. For example, one of the few surviving drafts for the *Freischütz*, a draft for the dialogue between Samiel and Caspar in the Act II Finale, appears on the verso of a draft for No. 3 in *Die drei Pintos*, which Weber of course had not orchestrated at the time of his death. The same reason for survival may be adduced

---

[1] Berlin, Deutsche Staatsbibliothek, *Web.* Cl. I, 30. The manuscript is described in Jähns, op. cit. ch. 1 n. 4 above, pp. 357–8, and briefly in Bartlitz, op. cit. ch. 1 n. 4 above, pp. 29–30.

for the one extant draft for the *Conzertstück* for piano and orchestra (J. 282), which appears on the verso of a draft for the Aria No. 2 in *Die drei Pintos*.

While the draft for *Die drei Pintos* may have survived only because Weber did not live to complete that opera, he does seem to have made a conscious effort to preserve a complete preliminary draft for *Euryanthe*, perhaps indicative of the special significance that the work held for him. With the exception of the opening ritornello of the *Introduzione* No. 1 and the last fifteen measures of Act III, scene i, nearly every measure of the opera is attested by at least one preliminary draft.[2] Weber assembled the sketches and drafts for this opera into a portfolio around which he wrapped a bifolium on which he wrote: 'Entwürfe zu Euryanthe | von mir Carl Maria von Weber | 1823.' Just as Jähns described it in 1871, the manuscript today consists of loose leaves and bifolios on assorted paper types; altogether there are 96 pages in this portfolio, paginated in red ink by Jähns.[3] The drafts are now arranged more or less according to the succession of pieces within the finished opera. Of course, it known from Weber's Diary that the individual pieces were not composed in consecutive order (see below), and in certain cases the present arrangement of the drafts is somewhat awkward, since the continuity of individual numbers is occasionally interrupted for the sake of overall order. It is not clear whether the manuscript's present organization derives from Weber or from Jähns. The only ordering obviously made by Weber was his pagination of the nine pages of the draft for the first scene of the opera. The composer also arranged the leaves and bifolios for the drafts for Act II into two gatherings. However, given Weber's penchant for assembling materials into consecutive order, a point that we shall discuss below, there is good reason to believe that the composer himself was largely responsible for the manuscript's present organization.

Along with the drafts for *Euryanthe*, the portfolio also contains work on other compositions. The autograph score and drafts for the music to the birthday cantata for the Duchess Maria Amalia of Zweibrücken (J. 283) doubtless found their way into the *Euryanthe* folder because Weber reused the finale of that earlier composition as the basis for the concluding section of the first-act finale No. 9; interestingly, the draft for J. 283 also contains a short sketch for the start of the Mermaid's

---

[2] Jähn's assertion (op. cit., p. 357) that the brief F-major movement in the Act II Finale from 'Ich grüss' Euch edles Fräulein' to 'Hoff' es fest' is not sketched is erroneous, since the section is present in an untexted pencil draft at the bottom of p. 66.

[3] Vestiges of an earlier, continuous pencil pagination of the portfolio are also occasionally legible.

Song in *Oberon*. The autograph of the *Marcia vivace* for ten trumpets (J. 288), which furnished much of the music for the opening movement of the Act I Finale, was probably included in the *Euryanthe* manuscript for the same reason. Sketches for the revisions of the Bassoon Concerto (J. 127) and the new Aria No. 8 in *Abu Hassan* ('Welch martyrvolles Loos') appear among the *Euryanthe* drafts because they were written during Weber's work on the opera. Appendix III summarizes the contents of the manuscript.

2. WEBER'S COMPOSITIONAL ROUTINE

The bulk of the *Euryanthe* portfolio comprises drafts on two or more staves in pen and/or pencil. In the terminology of recent Beethoven studies such drafts might be called 'continuity drafts', since they generally proceed from the beginning of a compositional unit—a set piece, a movement of a multi-movement structure or a segment of recitative—to its end.[4] Unlike Beethoven's single-line continuity drafts, however, Weber's composition drafts are normally laid out as short scores with a minimum of two staves, with one or more staves filled with music for the principal voice parts, and others reserved for occasional notation of the bass line, harmonic progressions, obbligato orchestral instruments, and chorus. 'Sketches' in the sense of isolated annotations of short ideas are rare, although Weber did occasionally write down melodic fragments, either to record a brief idea for later use, or in order to work out a specific problem. While Weber normally filled one page before starting another, he treated the openings of certain bifolios (pp. 2–95, 38–9, 74–5) as a single page and wrote continuously across the fold in the middle of the opening.

The preserved drafts exhibit a number of idiosyncracies of Weber's compositional routine. They frequently begin with the first measures of the vocal part and the final vocal cadence is often marked by a double bar in the sketch; thus in many instances the opening and closing ritornelli were notated demonstrably later than the vocal section of the piece. Revisions are normally entered directly over the original version, a practice that in some instances renders the first version practically indecipherable and that in other cases makes it very difficult to determine whether a revision has been entered immediately after the initial notation or whether it has been entered at a significantly later time. Texts for the vocal pieces are invariably entered after the musical line has been notated. Indications for dynamics, accents, articulation, tempo, and expression

---

[4] On the term 'continuity draft' see Lewis Lockwood, 'On Beethoven's Sketches and Autographs: Some Problems of Definition and Interpretation', *Acta musicologica* 42 (1970): 42.

appear frequently. Many drafts include parts for obbligato instruments, which are often identified through abbreviations; even where an instrument is not verbally specified, the choice of instrument is often clear from Weber's habit of writing instrumental parts in the transposing clef that is used in the full score. For most of the drafts Weber made marginal annotations indicating the number of staves that would be required to write out the vocal and instrumental parts in full score. These annotations do not seem to be coeval with the writing down of the draft, since an ink draft is often accompanied by a pencil listing of instruments and voices, or vice versa. One finds in almost all of the drafts vertical wavy lines written at irregular intervals over pre-existent bar lines. Again, these lines were made after the initial notation of the drafts on which they appear, and their purpose seems to have been to facilitate the transferral of music from the draft to the full score.[5] Finally, for several of the drafts Weber also indicated the amount of time that he estimated the finished piece would take in performance.[6]

At first glance the *Euryanthe* draft appears to offer relatively little grist for the study of the compositional process. Most of the compositions in *Euryanthe* are represented in the portfolio by a single preliminary draft, which normally differs from the final version in only minor details. Major revisions of form, phrase structure, and melodic contour within the drafts are extremely rare, and the great majority of revisions pertain to durational values of individual pitches. The preserved evidence thus initially seems to confirm the received view, derived from anecdotes of those who knew him and repeated throughout the major biographies, that Weber worked out most of the details of a composition in his head, often over an extended period of contemplation, and then wrote it down, once. The most extensive of such first-hand accounts comes from Julius Benedict, Weber's student during the period in which *Euryanthe* was composed.

Watching the progress of his *Euryanthe* from the first note to its completion, I had the best opportunity of observing his system of composing. Many a time might he be seen early in the morning, some closely-written pages in his hand, which he stood still to read, and then wandered on through forest and glen muttering to himself. He was learning by heart the words of *Euryanthe*, which he studied until he made them a portion of himself, his own creation, as it were. His genius would sometimes lie dormant during his frequent repetition of the words, and then the idea of a whole musical piece would flash

⁵ The drafts for *Die drei Pintos*, which were never orchestrated, lack both the wavy lines and the marginal annotations about orchestration.

⁶ E.g. p. 25 (end of No. 4): '9½'; p. 57 (end of No. 12): '4½M:'; p. 66 (F-major chorus at the start of the Act II Finale): '3M'; p. 67 (beginning of D-flat major movement of the Act II Finale): '15 Minuten'; p. 75 (end of No. 15): '8 Mi:'.

up in his mind, like the bursting of light into darkness. It would then remain there uneffaced, gradually assuming a perfect shape, and not till this process was attained would he put it down on paper. His first transcriptions were generally penned on the return from his solitary walks. He then noted down the voices fully, and only marked here and there the harmonies or the places where particular instruments were to be introduced. Sometimes he indicated by signs, known only to himself, his most characteristic orchestral effects: then he would play to his wife and to me, from these incomplete sketches, the most striking pieces of the opera, invariably in the form they afterwards maintained.[7]

By and large, many of Benedict's observations in this passage are accurate. We have already seen that Weber indeed prepared a 'closely written' copy of the libretto that he used during the early stages of composition (*Web.* Cl. II A g 6), and Benedict's description of the drafts corresponds closely to the actual state of affairs. Weber is also known to have worked out pieces in his head and performed them for friends before writing down a draft.[8] A close study of the *Euryanthe* drafts, however, brings to light two facts that suggest that the writing down of drafts was not quite the simple one-stage act suggested by Benedict and the following biographers. First, the use of both ink and pencil within a single draft points to different stages in which it was notated. Second, there is good evidence that a number of the extant drafts were in fact copied from earlier notated versions, some of which survive. Let us examine each of these points in turn.

2.1. *The uses of pen and ink*

One feature of the *Euryanthe* draft is that it is notated in both pen and pencil. Some drafts are written entirely in ink, a few entirely in pencil, and others alternate sections in pencil and ink. In still others, certain passages were originally notated in pencil and then traced over in ink, a process related to the recopying of pencil drafts discussed below. The uses of these different writing implements can be treated cautiously as evidence for the creative process, especially in drafts that combine pencil and ink annotations, for they make it possible to reconstruct the different stages in which a draft was entered—of great importance in the instances where only one draft for a given piece exists—and

---

[7] Julius Benedict, *Weber*, new edn. (London, n.d.), pp. 83–4.

[8] In a letter of 16 June 1817, during the early stages of the genesis of the *Freischütz*, Weber informed his bride-to-be Caroline Brandt that he had played the first couple of pieces for the librettist, Friedrich Kind, on the preceding day. Yet in his Diary he made a point of noting that he wrote down the first notes of the opera, presumably in draft, on 2 July. See *MMW* ii. 120. What relationship, if any, the extemporized pieces bear to the finished opera of course cannot be known.

potentially reveal something about the kind of compositional activity involved.

Consider, for example, the draft of Euryanthe's Aria con coro No. 20 on pages 80 and 81, where the alternation of pen and pencil in the draft, combined with other bits of evidence, reveals that the piece was composed in four stages that largely coincide with principal divisions of the structure. (1) The first fifteen measures, notated in ink, constitute a closed period in C major. Most likely these measures represent the 'Idee' for this aria that occurred to Weber on 5 August 1822.[9] The confident use of pen for this layer suggests that this idea was securely fixed in mind before Weber began to write it down. (2) The music between the pickup to measure 16 and the downbeat of measure 27 was originally notated in pencil and later traced over in ink. This passage is the bulk of the aria's middle section and entails a modulation to the dominant. Throughout the extant *Euryanthe* drafts the use of pencil is frequently associated with modulatory passages. (3) The resumption of ink drafting after the G-major cadence at measure 27 begins with a cadential gesture in the new tonic (mm. 27–29) and continues through a retransition on the dominant (mm. 30–37) into the reprise (mm. 38–60) and coda (mm. 60–70) of the piece. A double bar immediately after Euryanthe's final cadence in measure 70 suggests that Weber originally concluded the draft at that point. (4) The music following the double bar at measure 70 for Euryanthe's collapse, the chorus's reaction, and the final pantomime was also drafted in ink. That this epilogue was composed significantly later than the prior sections of the aria is suggested by the fact that the words of the choral lament on Euryanthe's presumed demise do not match the text in Weber's *Textvorlage* of the summer of 1822, the libretto *Web. Cl II A g 4*, which presumably supplied the text for the main part of the aria.

2.2. *Copying of drafts*

One reason that several of the drafts are nearly as neat as Weber's fair-copy autograph scores is that they were copied from earlier drafts. The most direct evidence for this assertion is the fact that some of the drafts demonstrably were copied from music first written out on other leaves that

[9] Diary entry: 'Idee zu der Arie der Euryanthe im 3: Akt *Zu ihm!* gefaßt.' It is probable that this diary annotation refers to the start of the draft on p. 80, because the six staves that immediately precede it on p. 80 contain sketches for the revision of Weber's Bassoon Concerto (J. 127), which the composer is known to have made between 1 and 3 Aug. The fact that the draft was begun on a piece of paper containing sketches for other pieces is typical for the notation of Weber's first ideas; at the time he notated the start of the aria he may in fact have planned eventually to copy it into a complete draft at some later time .

have survived. In other cases sections or passages of a piece were worked out in at least two surviving drafts. That Weber worked out other pieces in at least two preliminary drafts is also attested by the fact that certain pages of the *Euryanthe* portfolio are palimpsests. That is, certain pages contain passages, barely legible to the naked eye, that had originally been written in pencil and that were later erased so that the page could be reused for some other music, another sign of Weber's frugal use of paper. Doubtless because the original, erased pencil drafts are so faint, Jähns did not notice them, and consequently the phenomenon has escaped mention in the literature on Weber; thanks to modern technology, however, it has been possible to make photographically enhanced reproductions of the erased layers.[10] The most significant instances of this phenomenon are the following: (1) the *Vision* narration of Act I, scene iii was originally notated in pencil at the top of p. 32 and later recopied in ink on p. 31; p. 32 was then erased and used for the continuation for the draft of the Duetto No. 7. (2) The C-major section of the Act II Finale ('Wir alle wollen mit dir geh'n') drafted on pages 72 and 61 was preceded by pencil drafts of individual periods on p. 65 and p. 75. Page 65 was later reused for the Duetto No. 13, whereas p. 75 was eventually covered with a draft for Act III, scene i. (3) At the bottom of p. 65 Weber made a number of pencil sketches for the Duetto No. 13, probably as he was entering the main draft for the piece on the upper portions of the same page. These sketches were subsequently covered over by the concluding measures of the main continuity draft for the duet. In two other instances Weber wrote a final ink draft directly over a variant first pencil draft for the same piece, erasing those parts of the pencil draft that were not congruent with the final version: (1) the draft of the Duetto con coro No. 19 on p. 26, and (2) the draft of the introductory ritornello for Euryanthe's Cavatina No. 5 on p. 23.

Finally, various bits of circumstantial evidence suggest that several of the extant drafts were in fact copied from lost or discarded first drafts. In certain instances the dates of composition recorded in Weber's Diary conflict with the physical evidence of the draft. According to the Diary, for example, the slow first section of Adolar's Aria No. 12 was drafted after the fast section.[11] Yet, the lone draft for this piece (p. 60, p. 57) is notated as a continuous draft that extends from the beginning

---

[10] I must once again extend my sincerest thanks to Dr Wolfgang Goldhan of the Deutsche Staatsbibliothek and also to Mr Günter Schöneberg of the Criminology Division of the Humboldt University in Berlin for having made and provided me with these reproductions.

[11] Diary entry for 17 May 1822: 'Aria Adolar As dur entworfen'. Diary entry for 20 May: 'Aria in As Adagio notiert, und somit die Arie vollendet entworfen.'

of the vocal melody at measure 34 to the end of the aria. Rather than posit that Weber calculated precisely how much blank space to leave for the Larghetto non lento before starting with the Allegro, it seems much more likely either that the extant draft of the entire aria was copied from separate drafts for each of the two sections or that the extant draft of the Allegro was recopied in its structurally correct position after the draft of the slow first section. Similarly, Euryanthe's dramatic Scena No. 16 follows immediately upon the Duetto No. 15 in the draft on pages 74 and 75. However, the Diary records that the initial ideas for the piece came to Weber on 28 May 1823, well over a month before the draft for the A-minor duet was completed on 6 July.

In the case of the Eglantine–Lysiart Duetto No. 11, idiosyncracies of text suggest that the extant draft for the first section of the piece on p. 29 of the *Convolut* was notated significantly later than that of the concluding section. Whereas the text of the latter section ('Dunkle Nacht, du hörst den Schwur'), drafted on pp. 55–56, corresponds to a manuscript libretto, *Web. Cl.* II A g 6, that was very probably in Weber's possession at the time of composition recorded in his Diary (24–26 May 1822), the text for the first section ('Komm' denn, unser Leid zu rächen') corresponds only to the later libretto *Web. Cl.* II A g 4, which Weber seems to have received only after the composition of the *Introduzione* in the third week of June. In addition, an error in key signature at the start of the draft on page 29—Weber initially entered a key signature of two sharps and a time signature of common time in all four staves of the first system and then immediately corrected the key signature to B major, adding the verbal instruction 'H dur' for the sake of clarity—tantalizingly suggests that the draft of the B-major first section on p. 29 was recopied or revised from a discarded B-minor version of the corresponding section.

Why should Weber have copied over his first drafts? Here we can only speculate, but the practice does seem to follow a consistent pattern that casts some light on his compositional goals. In most of the cases of multiple drafts, the first draft was made in isolation on a separate page or leaf, whereas the second version of the same passage was copied into a more continuous context that connects it into the flow of a given piece or even of an entire scene. Perhaps the assembly of parts into longer units facilitated the sense for the whole that was such a major plank in Weber's aesthetic of opera, for the recopying of musical drafts into more continuous complexes may have aided his sense of timing, balance, and interconnections within the opera.

Needless to say, Weber's habit of copying drafts and then discarding or erasing the earlier versions presents an extremely vexing situation to the analyst, for whom the composer's initial responses and rejected ideas are normally more revealing than the fair copy final version. To be honest, though, the surviving first drafts tend not to exhibit profound differences from the final versions. The preliminary drafts for the Introduzione No. 1 and the Scene und Chor No. 4 are basically only less fully elaborated with respect to polyphonic texture than their respective successors, whereas the second draft of the Hochzeitmarsch copies only the leading melodic line from the more fully elaborated first draft into a continuous draft for the entire scene. The erased draft of the *Vision* on page 32 and the phrase drafts of the C-major Allegro of the Act II Finale on page 65 present no radically different alternatives to the published versions of the respective passages. Weber's error in notating the key signature for the first section of the Duetto No. 11 provides a tantalizing hint that the composer threw out a significantly different version of this piece, but unfortunately no trace of an earlier version survives.

The one instance among the vocal pieces where a preliminary draft does differ fundamentally from the final version is the pencil layer of the draft for the Duetto No. 19 on page 26, which presents a different continuation after measure 14 than the one known from the final version (see Example 2). But even here the discrepancy perhaps offers less than meets the eye, at least with respect to the study of compositional process, since on the one hand the first eleven measures of the draft up to the cadence in G major (mm. 3–13) are virtually identical with the final version—rests added to Euryanthe's line in the final version perhaps intensify the character of the situation—and on the other hand the divergent measures (mm. 14a–21a) set lines of text that were not taken over into the final version and thus cannot be compared to any second stage.[12] One is therefore left with little evidence for understanding why Weber abandoned the pencil draft or why he deemed the second version preferable to the first; indeed, it seems to me just as likely that the revision reflects dissatisfaction with the rather severe tone with which the King and hunters address Euryanthe in the excised lines as that it betrays musical self-criticism.

Yet even though they rarely entail major differences of conception, the first versions nevertheless consistently reveal more of the labour of creation than do the second drafts. And as we shall see in following chapters, the drafts occasionally suggest that Weber struggled with compositional decisions. Those extant drafts that indeed seem to represent a true 'composition draft', rather than a copy of one, therefore assume

---

[12] The additional lines are found in Weber's *Textvorlage* for the summer of 1822, *Web.* Cl. II A g 4, Item No. 11. This is the one instance in the preserved drafts where Weber began to set a text that differed structurally from the final version.

Ex. 2. The first draft of No. 19.

relatively great importance for the light that they shed on Weber's compositional procedures.

3. THE CHRONOLOGY OF COMPOSITION

For the most part, questions about the chronology of Weber's compositions are easily answered since he dated many of his musical manuscripts and normally recorded work on compositions in his Diary. The individual *Euryanthe* drafts are not dated, but we have already seen that the Diary contains numerous references to the progress of the opera.[13] However, the Diary furnishes only a starting point for precise chronology since it by no means provides complete information. It fails to mention a number of pieces (Nos. 6, 9, 17, 19, 22, and 23), and the *Vision* is the only segment of recitative or arioso that is cited; the Diary also refers ambiguously to a duet for Euryanthe and Adolar that could be either No. 13 or No. 15. For most of the pieces only one date is given, but as we have seen, several of the pieces assuredly were composed

---

[13] Entries pertaining to the composition of the opera are extracted in Appendix I.

in stages over a period of time; nor does the diary mention the recopying and revision of pieces evident in the preserved draft. Weber's reference in several instances to having conceived the 'Idee' for a particular piece on a given date also probably implies that the piece was elaborated into a complete draft at some later time. Thus the dates in the Diary in a number of cases may not refer to the surviving drafts. Table 7 summarizes the known information; the implications of this chronology for Weber's approach to composition will be taken up in Chapter VIII. Pieces not recorded in the Diary are enclosed in square brackets and assigned positions in the chronology on the basis of circumstantial evidence provided by paper type, continuity within a longer structural unit, or the history of the libretto. Weber's practice of composing on loose leaves and bifolios, however, precludes definitive assignments for a number of items in the opera, especially the recitatives, which are included in the overview only if the circumstantial evidence is strong enough to suggest an approximate date.

4. ORCHESTRATION IN THE COMPOSITIONAL PROCESS

One of the most crucial and frequently discussed aspects of Weber's art is his use of the orchestra as an integral part of the total conception of an opera, and in later chapters we shall pay considerable attention to the ways in which the orchestra in *Euryanthe* contributes vitally to the so-called *Totaleffekt*. As in so many other matters, however, the genetic record provides relatively little insight into Weber's decisions about the orchestration, since neither the extant drafts nor the autograph score reveal much about the way in which Weber's final decisions about scoring were made. On the one hand, the writing down of the full score was essentially a mechanical act, doubtless facilitated by the presence of a complete draft of the opera. According to his widow, the composer wrote out his full scores with the same ease as the writing of a letter, and Weber himself hinted in a letter about the *Euryanthe* Ouverture that scoring was a much easier task than invention.[14] The autograph score, unlike those of Beethoven, is a model of musical calligraphy, and the great rapidity with which Weber produced it also suggests that scoring was essentially a mechanical task for the composer. The inescapable conclusion is that Weber began the full score not only with a

---

[14] Jähns, op. cit. ch. 1 n. 4 above, p. 363. See also Weber's letter of 13–15 Oct. 1823 to Caroline (*Reisebriefe*, p. 46.), wherein he informed her that he would soon finish the draft of the Ouverture, effectively marking the end of his real compositional labours, since 'Das Instrumentiren geht hernach schon, wie Du weißt.'

TABLE 7. The chronology of composition

Piece		Dates recorded in Diary
Aria No. 12 (Adolar)	1822	17–20 May
Duetto No. 11 (Eglantine, Lysiart)		24–6 May
Introduzione (i.e. Nos. 1–4)		14–21 June
Vision (Act I, scene iii)		26 June
[No. 6 (Eglantine)]		? June–July[a]
[Recitative, Act I, scene iii]		? July
Duetto No. 7 (Euryanthe, Eglantine)		27 July
Aria con coro No. 20 (Euryanthe)		5 Aug, ['Idee . . . gefasst']
[Duetto con coro No. 19 (Euryanthe, King)]		? (first version)[b]
Scena ed aria No. 8 (Eglantine)		24 Oct.
Cavatina No. 5 (Euryanthe)		26 Oct.
Finale II No. 14	1823	1–25 Feb.
Scena ed aria No. 11 (Lysiart)		7–12 Mar.
[Recitative: Act II, scene ii]		after 12 Mar.
Jaegerchor No. 18		20 Mar. ['Idee']
Duetto [No. 13 or 15?] (Adolar/Euryanthe)		22 Mar. ['Idee'][c]
May Song [No. 21] (Bertha, Coro)		28 Mar.
[Hochzeitmarsch No. 23]		?[d]
[Chor No. 22]		?[e]
Duetto con coro No. 24 (Lysiart, Adolar)		9 Apr.
Finale I No. 9		? (by 3 May 1823)[f]
Scena No. 16 (Euryanthe)		28 May ['Ideen']
Duetto No. 15 (Adolar, Euryanthe)		6 July
[Scena e cavatina No. 17 (Euryanthe)]		?[g]
[Duetto con coro No. 19 (King, Euryanthe)]		?[g]
Finale III No. 25		completed 8 Aug.[h]
Ouverture		1 Sept.–15 Oct.

[a] Eglantine's Aria No. 6 probably predates the Duetto No. 7 because it immediately precedes it in a continuous draft on a single opening, pp. 30–1.

[b] The original pencil layer of No. 19 probably dates from the summer or autumn of 1822 because it is notated on a bifolium with drafts for No. 4 and the opening ritornello of No. 5; a more precise date is not possible. Since No. 19 functions as an introduction to No. 20, I suggest that its initial conception was approximately coeval with No. 20, a hypothesis that is not contradicted by any of the facts.

[c] The Diary annotation ('Idee: Duett Adol. Eury.') is ambiguous and could possibly refer to an initial idea for the A-minor duet No. 15, which in fact is preserved on p. 54.

[d] That the Hochzeitmarsch No. 23 predated No. 22 is suggested by the fact that Weber copied the march, already composed on p. 79, into a continuous composition draft for the dramatic unit immediately after No. 22 on pp. 84–5. Had the march not yet been composed at the time that he finished No. 22, he probably would not have taken the trouble to write it down twice.

[e] No. 22 seems to have been written after No. 21 since both of these numbers were written consecutively on the same bifolium.

[f] The Diary entry for 3 May 1823 ('Ersten Akt vollendet entworfen') clearly implies that the draft for the Act I Finale was complete by that time. The definitive text for the first and last movements of this piece were not ready until after Chezy's return to Dresden on 1 Apr.

[g] The texts for No. 17 and the ink draft of No. 19 were not finalized until after Chezy's return to Dresden in April 1823.

[h] According to the Diary the Finale No. 25 was the last piece to be composed, except for the Ouverture.

complete draft of the work's melodic content, but also with a fully formed image of its sonority.

This conclusion is certainly consonant with Weber's own utterances on the subject of instrumentation, which imply that decisions about orchestration were made at every stage of creation. Particularly revealing are his notes on Cherubini's *Lodoïska* that he published in 1817. According to Weber, instrumentation is not a separate stage of composition, grafted onto the melodic outlines of a work, but rather an integral part of conception and invention:

With [Cherubini's] manner of working the figure of speech, 'this or that musical piece is especially beautifully scored', which in any event is one-sided and divides the art-work miserably into two halves, is not at all applicable. In the moment of feeling a true master also has all of the means at his command as colours before his eyes. Like a painter, he scarcely conceives a nude figure that he only later dresses with brilliant materials and jewels. Indeed, one can discover beneath the rich folds the interior cause of the same in the muscle that produces it and so forth, but the *entirety* must be *entirely* thought out [*das* Ganze *muß* ganz *gedacht sein*]; otherwise it brings only a half measure before the eye or ear of the observer, is only a dressed-up mannequin and not a living figure.[15]

As noted, the calligraphic beauty of Weber's full scores and the apparent effortlessness with which they were written certainly suggest that the composer in fact practised the principle that he preached, namely, that invention and orchestration were inseparable parts of a single creative process largely completed before the production of the full score.

Yet the drafts themselves are again typically silent about Weber's approach to the orchestra. They surely conveyed more information to the composer than they ever could to anyone else, since they present only a very sketchy picture of the final orchestration. As we have seen, the drafts frequently indicate the presence of instruments and sometimes are quite explicit about instrumental effects that are in fact used in the final version. In addition, almost every draft is accompanied by a listing of the *Instrumentarium* that is envisioned for the work, with exact information about the number of staves required for each full system; in most instances it is clear that these lists were written down after the completion of the draft. Despite these indications, neither the definitive orchestration nor the exact harmony of the final version is so obvious that any professionally trained musician could take Weber's drafts and arrive at the final version automatically, a fact demonstrated by the diffi-

[15] *Sämtliche Schriften*, p. 298.

culties that both Meyerbeer and Benedict encountered in trying to complete *Die drei Pintos* from Weber's extant drafts.[16] Most of the instrumental motives are notated without any indication of instrumentation, such that only the wisdom of hindsight provided by knowledge of the full score lets us recognize whether a motive written in treble clef is intended for violin, flute, or oboe. And many of the most important instrumental motives do not appear at all in the drafts; thus Eglantine's motive is not once cited in the drafts for her Aria No. 6 or the cabaletta of her Scena ed aria No. 8. The drafts therefore record only the barest outline of a much more fully developed orchestral image that the composer must have carried in his memory between the fixing of the draft and the writing out of the full score.

And even where the drafts present relatively unambiguous evidence about choices of instrumentation, they seldom document the decision-making processes behind such choices. The few changes that are recorded do suggest certain criteria behind Weber's uses of the orchestra and will be discussed below, but there are too few of them upon which to rest an exhaustive theory of orchestration. As with other compositional issues, then, the critic must rely primarily on his analysis and sense of style and history to understand the work.

5. CONCLUSIONS

Ultimately, the *Euryanthe* draft leaves far more questions unanswered than it solves, for the dearth of significant compositional revisions makes it very difficult to interpret the criteria by which Weber arrived at his final decisions. To be sure, the sketches and drafts allow one to describe certain external, mechanical features of Weber's compositional routine, and these can convey certain insights into the nature of Weber's creativity. For example, the sources show that composition tends to begin with the invention of vocal melody, as Weber seems normally to derive the basic ideas for a piece from the affective content and rhythmic implications of a specific poem. The lack of orchestral detail in the drafts points up the fact that Weber does not conceive the orchestra

---

[16] On Meyerbeer's aborted efforts to complete *Die drei Pintos* see Heinz Becker, 'Meyerbeers Ergänzungsarbeit an Webers nachgelassener Oper 'Die drei Pintos', *Die Musikforschung* 7 (1954): 300–12. See also Birgit Heusgen, *Studien zu Gustav Mahlers Bearbeitung und Ergänzung von Carl Maria von Webers Opernfragment 'Die drei Pintos'* (Regensburg, 1983), pp. 60–4.

as a symphonic commentary on the poem, but rather as a homophonic support.[17]

Yet the drafts seldom open windows into the inner workings of creativity and the criteria by which decisions are made, for the simple fact that they rarely document the testing and rejection of compositional alternatives. In fact, the evident lack of creative struggle in the majority of Weber's surviving drafts might tempt one to conclude that Weber was a facile composer, to whom ideas appeared spontaneously and easily. However, certain facts tend to belie this interpretation of the compositional process. First, Weber was by no means a rapid composer, at least not by the standards that prevailed in the early nineteenth century. To a certain extent the relatively slow rate at which he composed was a product of the constant interruption of his compositional projects by numerous other obligations. Yet the fact remains that Weber could not simply produce at will, and by his own admission, there were periods in which ideas did not come easily.[18] Second, the substantial amount of self-borrowing in Weber's output points to a certain difficulty with thematic invention. To be sure, even extremely fertile composers like Bach, Handel, and Rossini frequently reused their earlier pieces, but the time pressures under which they operated were of a different magnitude than the comparatively leisurely rate at which Weber composed his operas.

Nor does the absence of substantial compositional revisions really betray a lack of critical reflection on the composer's part, but in a more positive light may be seen to reflect the premises from which Weber operated. As we shall see, if one approaches Weber's pieces from the point of view that that they are principally musical interpretations of specific texts and dramatic situations, they in fact make a great deal of sense and could only have arisen as the product of extended reflection and self-criticism; it was, after all, a matter of principle that a German

[17] Indeed, Weber's comments about Cherubini's *Lodoïska* (*Sämtliche Schriften*, p. 298) explicitly caution against copying that composer's symphonic treatment of the orchestra in vocal compositions, since 'he has frequently subordinated the normally accepted means of carrying out the real melody through the singer to the melody of the entire musical composition'. Weber does concede that Cherubini may have been forced into this approach by having had to compose for 'French singers, or rather screamers'. Here, as in other instances, Weber advocates a German approach that reconciles the expressive *vocalità* of Italian opera with the enhanced declamation and instrumental activity of French opera.

[18] In the fourteen-month period immediately following the première of *Euryanthe*, Weber, beset by deep depression and exhausted by illness and the demands of his position, composed practically nothing, complaining at one point to his wife Caroline from his cure in Marienbad that he would compose 'if I could get any ideas once again; presently nothing at all occurs to me and it seems to me as though I had never composed anything. Ultimately the operas are not at all by me.' *MMW* ii. 577.

opera composer like himself should take enough time to think through carefully all elements of composition.[19] And as we have seen, Weber's own contemporaries were in fact more likely to criticize him for excessive *Reflexion* than for not having thought out his works carefully enough. Yet whatever self-criticism and testing of alternatives took place, carried out perhaps at the keyboard or on the walks that the composer is known to have made with libretto in hand, were generally completed before he committed his ideas to paper.

The fact that the musical drafts do not provide strong evidence for Weber's self-criticism therefore poses a number of challenges to the critic-analyst-historian, who on the one hand should try to understand the relationship between compositional process and compositional aims and on the other hand must augment the scanty evidence of musical genesis to develop a sympathetic approach to the work that does justice to its particular ambitions and premises. Fortunately, in the case of Weber we have an articulate artist whose critical writings and letters supply some of the information missing from the drafts, in so far as they hint at principles that guided the compositional process. Moreover, the fact that *Euryanthe* triggered quite a bit of critical controversy and polemic can sensitize us to issues that we as late twentieth-century observers might otherwise overlook. Interpreted in the light of Weber's aesthetics and contemporary criticism, the composition drafts in fact do reflect in their own way the very premises from which Weber avowedly started and shed a limited amount of light on analytical and critical issues. The following chapters therefore outline certain key issues in Weber's compositional approach that are suggested by his own writings, contemporary criticism, and the extant drafts. This mixture of informants is in part a matter of necessity, since no one body of evidence explains the 'whole truth', and in this case it is more important to understand the work on its own terms than to force it into a single analytical mould or insist upon methodological purity. With these issues in mind we shall then be in a better position to return to a few selected drafts to attempt to understand Weber's compositional choices in action.

---

[19] As Weber wrote to Treitschke on 17 Dec. 1821, 'a *German* who takes the matter seriously, does not simply shake an opera out of his sleeve.' *WaMZ* 7 (1847): 442.

VII. Tonal Planning

One of the most important witnesses to Weber's approach to composition is a letter that the composer himself wrote in 1816 shortly after the first performances of his patriotic cantata *Kampf und Sieg* (J. 190). Hoping to clarify the aesthetic intentions behind the work and thereby rebut certain negative criticisms that had been brought to his attention, Weber furnished to friends and sympathetic critics a rather detailed account of the means by which he had realized his artistic vision of the Allied victory over Napoleon at Waterloo. Of vital importance for an understanding of his compositional procedures is his discussion of certain decisions made at the very outset of work. 'Before I proceeded to the execution of individual pieces, I drafted for myself the large outline of the composition by determining its principal colours in their individual parts, that is: I prescribed for myself the precise sequence of keys, from whose consecutive effect I felt sure of success, and I rigorously weighed the use of instrumentation ...'[1] Unfortunately, Weber did not go on to spell out the criteria by which he judged the efficacy of the succession of keys, whether key choices were determined primarily by reference to purely musical concerns for coherence, contrast, and smooth succession, by some unspoken doctrine of expressive key characteristics, or by a combination of both.

This reference to 'precompositional' decisions about tonality does not appear to be a unique case in Weber's output, but rather seems to reflect a practice that the composer consistently followed in the planning of large works, the devising of a master tonal scheme as a preliminary stage in composition. The genetic materials for the unfinished comic opera *Die drei Pintos* offer an instance where this procedure is clearly documented. Despite the fact that only seven pieces were ever drafted, there survives in the handwriting of the librettist Carl Theodor Winkler (pseud. Theodor Hell) an inventory of musical pieces for the entire opera in which each of the sixteen envisioned vocal pieces as well as the Ouverture is assigned a tonality; in addition, indications for metre and duration have been added to several of the pieces on the outline.

---

[1] *Sämtliche Schriften*, p. 200.

Hell can only have gained such information from the composer himself.[2]

In the case of *Euryanthe* no document survives that irrefutably proves that Weber also began this work with a large-scale tonal plan.[3] Nevertheless, the tonal choices in the finished work suggest that some predetermined key scheme furnished the starting point for the composition and guided a number of decisions made during the work on the opera. Simply put, *Euryanthe* manifests a network of tonal relationships in which the keys of individual pieces are determined not only by the logic of musically convincing relationships, but also by a well-developed system of symbolism, according to which keys act as signs for elements of the drama. To a certain extent this system also operates at lower levels of structure, informing the tonal choices for sections within multi-partite numbers like the finales as well as the succession of keys within sections of recitative. It is the purpose of this chapter therefore to explicate the principles of tonal organization within the opera. Since very little documentary evidence survives for this crucial aspect of composition—one of the most important ways by which Weber realized his ideal of an 'organically connected' opera—we shall have to deal primarily with the best evidence available, the work itself and the traditions for key usage in opera at the beginning of the nineteenth century. The few glimpses into tonal decisions afforded by the documents of the opera's genesis will then be evaluated for the light that they cast on the interpetations advanced on the basis of close reading.

I. KEY RELATIONSHIPS IN *EURYANTHE*

In many ways, tonal choices in *Euryanthe* seem to be guided by traditional concerns for satisfying autonomous musical relationships. At the largest level of structure, the opera is tonally closed, as E-flat major frames the start and finish of the work. Such closure figures prominently in Mozart's operas and other early German Romantic operas, and Weber consistently observes this practice in his other operas. Tonal closure for each of the finales also points to a tradition inherited from eighteenth-

---

[2] Winkler's table is on a loose leaf inserted in the drafts for the unfinished opera (Deutsche Staatsbibliothek, Berlin (DDR), Mus. ms. autogr. C. M. von Weber WFN 3). The document is printed in Jähns, op. cit. ch. I n. 4 above, pp. 425–6 with minor errors.

[3] Jähns, op. cit., p. 363, incorrectly states that the Weber autograph libretto of the first two acts (*Web.* Cl. II A g 6) indicates the succession of keys for the opera. This text is tentatively divided into musical units, but there is no indication of tonality.

Act I

Ouverture	No. 1	No. 2	No. 3	No. 4
E♭	G	B♭	G	E♭

No. 5	No. 6	No. 7	No. 8	No. 9 (Finale 1)
C	e	[B] a–A	E	D–B♭–D

Act II

No. 10	No. 11
c–G–c	B

No. 12	No. 13	No. 14 (Finale 2)
A♭	C	F–D♭–A–a–C–f

Act III

No. 15	No. 16	No. 17	No. 18	No. 19	No. 20
[d] A–a [E♭] B [E♭]		g–G	E♭	c	C–c

No. 21	No. 22	No. 23	No. 24	No. 25 (Finale 3)
A–a	B♭	D [B]	D	E♭–E–c–E♭–C–E♭

FIG. 1. Synopsis of key relationships in *Euryanthe*.

Note: Broken rules represent changes in setting within an act. Vertical lines within a setting reflect major articulations in action. Tonal areas in brackets are important tonicizations within passages of recitative.

century models, most prominently the great *buffa* finales of Mozart, and again normally followed in Weber's earlier operas.

Tonal successions within certain major subdivisions of the opera also seem to be controlled by relationships that make sense from a purely musical point of view and thus provide musical coherence to broad units of dramatic structure. That is, many of the principal dramatic units are organized around keys whose smooth succession is primarily assured by bass motion by fifth or progression between third-related keys that share tones in common (see Figure I). The first four numbers of the opera, together with the Ouverture, constitute a multi-partite structure framed by E-flat major. Internally this unit is articulated by a rising progression from the tonic (E-flat) through a third-related key (G) to the dominant (B-flat) and thence downward again by thirds to E-flat; the prominence accorded C minor at the start of No. 4 also allows us to hear G major as a subsidiary dominant within the unit. As we have already seen, Weber initially considered the first four numbers as a single 'Introduzione', and the tonal structure of the scene is reinforced by patterns of thematic recall that tie No. 4 to the Ouverture and No. 3 to No. 1. The second major dramatic unit of the opera, from Euryanthe's first appearance through her exit after the Duetto No. 7, moves from C major (No. 5) to E minor (No. 6) to A minor/A major (No. 7), which can be understood as motion from a tonic to its relative minor via a secondary dominant. The latter half of the scene in the forest in the third act, from the point where Euryanthe is abandoned by Adolar (No. 17) to the change of stage setting at the end of No. 20, again offers a logical succession when viewed in terms of traditional functions: a long-range dominant-to-tonic cadence in C (G minor/G major to C minor/C major) is filled in by descent through the relative major (E-flat major). Perhaps the most impressive of the extended key structures in the work, considered from the viewpoint of autonomous musical logic, is the second half of Act II, an entire scenic unit—the great hall in the palace at Prémery—that builds from Adolar's private anticipation of love (No. 12) through the joy of reunion with his beloved (No. 13) to the public ceremony, confrontation, and eventual catastrophe of the second-act finale (No. 14). Here the outer boundaries for the dramatic unit are framed by relative major–relative minor relationship (A-flat major–F minor). The F-major start of the finale is prepared by its dominant, C major, in the Duetto No. 20, a pattern that is replicated within the finale as the F-minor Schlußchor is preceded by an extended movement in C major. Lastly, the progressions within the first half of the finale articulate a descent through the augmented triad, F–D-flat–A, in which the tonic of the prior section is retained as the third of the following section.

2. TONAL SYMBOLISM IN *EURYANTHE*

Alongside these purely musical considerations for tonal structure, most of the key choices in *Euryanthe* are also determined by a well-developed network of key symbolism that, to a great extent, is rooted in traditional theories of key character and prior practice. For example, the key structure of the opera reflects long-standing traditions of opposing sharp keys and flat keys for symbolic purposes.[4] All of Adolar's major utterances are in flat keys—B-flat major (Nos. 2, 22), E-flat major (No. 4), and A-flat major (No. 12)—whereas the more sinister elements in the opera, the hatred of Eglantine (No. 8), the revenge duet (No. 11) and the sinister limbo that Emma inhabits (the *Vision*), tend to be set in the strongly sharp keys of E major and B major; thus a symbolic opposition of virtuous elements and their evil counterparts is inherent in the tonal structure of the opera. This contrast is in fact exploited at important junctures in the opera where the opposed worlds are presented back-to-back: between the villains' revenge Duetto No. 11 and Adolar's Aria No. 12 (B major/ A-flat major); between Adolar's despair at the news of Euryanthe's evident demise and Eglantine's wild outburst upon hearing that piece of information during the third-act finale (A-flat minor/ E major); and during the Ouverture, where, of course, the significance of the tonal juxtaposition (E-flat major/ B-minor) is completely intelligible only after one has become familiar with the body of the opera. A closer examination of *Euryanthe* reveals, however, that the work's system of tonal symbols is in fact more elaborately developed than the conventional sharp–flat dichotomy, as several prominent keys in the opera are endowed with more precise connotations that become evident when one considers the relationship between key and dramatic environment.

E-flat Major. Between its appearance in the Ouverture and the third-act finale, the keynote for the opera is used sparingly, but it does turn up at points that suggest an association with the Divine and the triumph of virtue over evil. In No. 4 the key is associated with Adolar's confidence in God and Euryanthe's fidelity ('Ich bau' auf Gott, und meine Euryanth''); as he rushes off to do combat with the giant snake before No. 16 he cadences in E-flat with another expression of trust in God's help ('Nicht verzage, mit Gott will ich den Kampf besteh'n'); and after the battle he departs in E-flat major, leaving Euryanthe in the protection of the Almighty ('Im Schütz des Höchsten bleibe hier allein!'). Later occurrences of the key reflect the actual interference of Providence to set matters straight, for it appears in the Jaegerchor No. 18 that signifies

---

[4] On this point see Rita Steblin, *A History of Key Characteristics in the Eighteenth and Early Nineteenth Centuries* (Ann Arbor, Mich., 1983), pp. 103–33.

Euryanthe's rescue from the wilderness and in the hunters' cry of joy in the Act III Finale when Euryanthe revives. The opera's *lieto fine* of course marks the triumph of virtue in E-flat major.

C major occurs prominently throughout the opera in conjunction with expressions of love, affection, and loyalty. It is most strongly associated with Euryanthe, the embodiment of the faithful woman who lives only for love, as two of her arias (Nos. 5 and 20), her duet with Adolar (No. 13) and its subsequent reprise at the original pitch level within the Act III Finale are set in this key. All of these instances stress the love that she feels for Adolar and her constant desire for union with him. That Adolar's subjects feel a similar kind of love for him is perhaps the reason that the penultimate movement of the second-act finale, in which Adolar's vassals express their desire to accompany him into the wilderness, is also set in C major. In a similar vein, at two points in the third act the returned Adolar is recognized by his former subjects, who lovingly greet him in C major.[5]

C minor assumes an important role as the sinister antipode to both C major and E-flat major. Whereas C major represents the bliss of the lovers' union, C minor in Lysiart's Scena ed aria No. 10 stands for his direct attack on that union. Adolar's annunciation of death to Euryanthe at the start of the third act, Euryanthe's despair and death wish in No. 19, and her apparent death (coda of No. 20, Act III Finale) are also represented by C minor. In these instances the theme of death, the most drastic and permanent sort of estrangement, is prominent.

E major and E minor are consistently associated with Eglantine. Her two arias (No. 6, No. 8) are both in E tonalities. E minor marks her very first appearance in the opera (I, iii), where the key is introduced along with the motive that symbolizes her deceit, and her final outburst in the Act III Finale, when she learns from the King that Euryanthe apparently has died and exults ('Triumph! gerochen ist meine Schmach!'), entails an abrupt assumption of E major that remains in effect until she is stabbed by Lysiart.

B major is a particularly ominous tonality throughout the opera, the more so as it rarely appears in a purely diatonic form but instead is normally inflected with pitches borrowed from the minor mode. On the one hand, it occurs in two pieces that present great dangers for the protagonists. In the Duetto No. 11 the two villains conspire to destroy Adolar and Euryanthe and take an evil oath to the powers of darkness to seal their pact; in No. 16 a giant snake nearly accomplishes that goal. On the other hand, a highly chromatic B tonality defines the spectre of the suffering Emma in Euryanthe's *Vision* narration in Act I and

[5] See the discussion of Act III, scene iv in the next section of this chapter.

Eglantine's delirious vision of an angry Emma in Act III.[6]   A very telling moment for the opera's tonal symbolism is therefore the penultimate section of the Act III Finale, at the point when Adolar senses Emma's redemption from the eternal night of restless wandering and her reunion in the afterlife with her lover Udo; paralleling the earthly reunion of Adolar and Euryanthe musically as well as dramatically, Emma's redemption is marked by a shift of the *Vision* music from its eerie chromatic B tonality to a purely diatonic C major, Adolar's and Euryanthe's love key.

A major/ A minor. The fact that A major and A minor are paired in three different numbers of the opera (Nos. 7, 15, and 21) is striking and hints that some sort of symbolism is at work. Dramatic context in each case suggests that the pairing is associated with the opposition of fidelity (A major) and faithlessness (A minor) and a secondary opposition of downfall (A minor) and renewal or upward motion (A major). This interpretation emerges most clearly in No. 21 from the juxtaposition of Bertha's A-major May Song, a wedding song about lovers' fidelity in May, the season of regeneration, and the defeated and embittered Adolar's following monologue in A minor wherein he bemoans the lack of fidelity in the world ('Giebt keine Treu' auf weiter Erden mehr'). The shift from A major to A minor in the Duetto No. 15 mirrors the turn from Adolar's remembrances of past happiness and belief in Euryanthe's love ('Wie liebt' ich dich!') to thoughts of Euryanthe's supposed infidelity and his present misery. In the Duetto No. 7 the direction of the modal change is reversed, but the essential dichotomy remains. After revealing Adolar's secret to Eglantine, Euryanthe at first feels remorse and impending doom at having broken her oath to Adolar (A minor: 'Unter ist mein Stern gegangen'), but Eglantine's reassurances bring the duet to a conclusion in A major, as Euryanthe places her trust in Eglantine's fidelity.

D major is conspicuously linked to chivalry, especially its more masculine aspects, in several situations: the chorus of knights who respond to the opening women's chorus ('Den Frauen Heil!') in the Introduzione; the first-act finale, with its arrival of Lysiart and his knights at Nevers; and the powerful confrontation between Adolar and Lysiart in the third act, the Duetto con coro No. 24 in which the former challenges the latter to a trial by combat. In all of these pieces the orchestral sonority is reinforced by the prominent use of brass instruments. The wedding

---

[6] Neither appearance of this music is marked by a key signature in the finished score, a concession to the norms for notating recitative. That the *Vision* was primarily conceived as a chromatically altered B major is attested by the erased first draft of the Act I narration on page 32 of the *Euryanthe* portfolio, whose pattern of accidentals clearly implies a B-major key signature.

march for Eglantine and Lysiart (No. 23) may be heard as an ironic use of this chivalric key, since it presents a chromatic mixture of D minor and D major.[7]

B-flat major is also associated with chivalry, although it seems to represent a more gentle and sensitive side to the courtly art. Thus in the Romanza No. 2 Adolar sings Euryanthe's praises in a troubadour song. In a memorable B-flat major period in the first part of the Ensemble No. 4 Adolar affirms his knightly duty to protect his lady's honour ('Mein König! Frauenehre schirmen, war die Höchste stets von allen Ritterpflichten!'). Lysiart's meeting with Euryanthe in the middle section of the Act I Finale, again set in B-flat major, effects one of the loveliest exchanges of *courtoisie* in all of operatic literature, as Euryanthe offers shelter to her guest ('Verschmähet nicht die ländlich stille Zelle') and Lysiart responds with an enthusiastic compliment to his host ('Wo du erscheinst, da wird die Wildnis helle'). In the Act II Finale Lysiart then seems to allude ironically to the chivalric B-flat, as he claims miraculously to have conquered Euryanthe's proud heart ('Bewundernswürdig ist's gelungen'). Finally, Adolar's former vassals exhort him to uphold his knightly responsibility to protect virtue and efface evil in No. 22.

G major. The three important uses of G major all convey a sense of calm or peace. In No. 1, the women of King Ludwig's court praise the return of peace after years of war. In the G-major section of Lysiart's Scena ed aria No. 10 ('Schweigt glühn'den Sehnens wilde Triebe') he attempts to still his passions aroused by Euryanthe's beauty, since he knows that she will never betray Adolar. And in Euryanthe's scene alone in the forest after she has been abandoned by Adolar (No. 17), she regains peace of mind as she accepts her fate to die quietly at the springs beside the willows ('Sie fand von Lieb' und Leiden Ruh').

3. LOCAL RAMIFICATIONS

The foregoing overview points up the fact that symbolic key associations in *Euryanthe* influence not only the selection of keys for entire pieces, but also tonal choices within certain units of structure, so that the plan for the whole is intimately tied to certain more localized details of composition. The tonal structure of the Act III Finale, for example, is predicated almost entirely on the succession of strongly associative tonalities, as each of the principal dramatic divisions within the finale save the first establishes a key appropriate to the main dramatic concept of the respective unit.

(1) *Maestoso con moto* (mm. 1–7): *no strong tonal centre.* The King interrupts

[7] The first draft of this piece on page 79 in fact gives the March a D-minor key signature, with the D-major inflections treated as accidentals.

the confrontation between Adolar and Lysiart. The C minor at the start of this unit does not really represent an established key, since it is not prepared but instead is heard as a brusque tonal interruption of the D-major cadence of No. 24; by the second measure it has vanished. The absence of a strong tonic for these introductory measures is itself an appropriate symbol for the confusion precipitated by the King's sudden and unexpected arrival. As order is restored, measures 6–7 prepare the tonic of the following section. (2) *Agitato* (mm. 8–47): *E-flat major.* Adolar discloses the villains' deception and seeks the King's help in locating Euryanthe in the wilderness. As a belated reaffirmation of her innocence, the tonal choice may be heard in reference to Adolar's original affirmation of faith in the Scene und Chor No. 4. When the King informs Adolar of Euryanthe's demise, the music leads towards A-flat minor in order to facilitate the connection with the following section. (3) *Con furia; Moderato assai; Poco piu moto* (mm. 48–106): *E major.* Believing her triumph complete, Eglantine's jubilant eruption is marked by the key of her revenge Aria No. 8. At two subsequent points in this remarkable monologue E is reasserted as tonic, first at measure 69, where Eglantine reminds Adolar of her unrequited love (E minor), and lastly at measures 101–3, where a thunderous cadence in E major underscores her death at Lysiart's hands. (4) *Molto passionato* (mm. 107–65): *C minor.* Adolar, overcome by grief, offers himself as another victim to Lysiart's treachery and then remorsefully realizes that he, more than Lysiart, had been responsible for Euryanthe's untimely fate. The choice of C minor refers both to Lysiart's vengeance Aria No. 10, as Adolar urges him to complete his deadly work ('Lasst ganz sein Werk ihn krönen'), and also to Adolar's own annunciation of death to Euryanthe in the forest at the start of Act III. (5) *Chorus of Hunters behind the scene* (mm. 166–73): *E-flat major.* Euryanthe's revival is symbolized by a brief allusion to the Hunters' Chorus in its original key. As in No. 18, the implications of divine intervention lie close at hand. (6) *Allegro; Animato* (mm. 174–215): *C major.* The lovers are reunited to the music that had accompanied their first reunion in the Duetto No. 13. C major again fulfils its function as the key most closely associated with love. (7) *Largo* (mm. 216–23): *C major.* Emma's music is 'elevated' from its original B tonality into the C-major sphere of fulfilled love as Adolar senses her otherworldly reunion with Udo. (8) *Presto marcato* (mm. 224–303): *E-flat major.* The Schlußchor celebrates the triumph of love and fidelity.

As in the large-scale organization of the opera, the succession of keys within the finale makes sense with respect to purely musical values. E-flat major works as the keynote for the entire finale, and as is often the case in this opera, its primary antipode is a third-related key (C major–minor) rather than the dominant. The only key in the finale that stands outside this axis, the E major of section (3), is heard not only as a referent for Eglantine, but also as an internally intelligible symbol for the shocking interruption brought about by Eglantine's outburst and revelations; at the same time, this 'distant' E major is also attained through root motion by third, a descent from E-flat major to C minor to A-flat minor to E major. Of course, for ears accustomed to and expecting cadential motion by fifth at pivotal points in the structure, such long-range progressions through third-related keys may seem musically unusual and unsettling, for they effect little sense of traditional resolution; thus Amadeus Wendt, for example, found that the abrupt juxtaposition of E-flat major and C major at the juncture between sections (7) and (8) made an 'unpleasant impression'.[8]

To a considerable extent, the recitatives in *Euryanthe* are also shaped by the tonal associations worked out for the key structure of the opera as a whole, as each recitative typically gravitates towards certain tonal goals that symbolically underscore the dramatic content. Four examples may serve to demonstrate this point.

1. *The recitative following No. 3 (Act I, scene i).* Lysiart's first speech concludes in A minor as he makes an ironic reference to Adolar's loss of patrimony ('Die Zither sorgt, daß nicht ihr Held verderbe!'); of course, it is precisely in A minor that Adolar's eventual 'downfall' is realized when he returns penniless to his native land in the third act. Adolar's defence of Euryanthe is marked by a cadence to a 'pure' C major ('Dort schließet dir mein Schwert, mit Gott, die gift'gen Lippen zu'), and Lysiart's confident assertion that he could win Euryanthe's affections under any circumstances is underscored by a cadence to the sinister key of B minor ('Die Liebe deiner Braut gewönn' ich mir, trotz deiner Rosenwang und gold'nen Zither'). The C minor that predominates at the end of the recitative belies Lysiart's words ('Du fromme Turteltaube, dein Glück zu stören trüg' ich Scheu!'), pointing, as it does, to his revenge aria of the second act.

2. *The Euryanthe–Eglantine recitative between No. 5 and No. 6 (Act I, scene iii).* The E-minor start of the recitative coincides with Eglantine's first appearance on stage. E-flat major suddenly appears at measure 15 as Euryanthe thinks back to her first encounter with Adolar, thus alluding to the key of No. 4 and the keynote for the entire opera. In both of these cases, the symbolism of the harmonic choice is reinforced by a symbolic motive in the accompaniment. The two occurrences of G minor (m. 13, 34) are allied to the poetic conception of abandonment and thus point ahead to Euryanthe's abandonment in the Act III Scena e cavatina No. 17 in the same key. C major, Euryanthe's key *par excellence*,

[8] BamZ 3 (1826): 55.

and one associated especially with her purity, innocence, and capacity for love, occurs twice, both times underscoring her innocent belief in Eglantine's friendship (m. 28, m. 37). The turn toward B minor and E minor near the end of the scene coincides with Eglantine's devious plan to unlock Euryanthe's secret. And the choice of D minor for the phrase at the very end of the scene with which Eglantine describes Euryanthe's activities at midnight is both tonally and motivically related to the ritornello at the start of Act III, where Adolar and Euryanthe are seen on a moonlit night.

3. *The scene in the third act in which Adolar is recognized by his former vassals (Act III, scene iv)*. Following immediately upon the A-major May Song, the scene begins with a lament for Adolar in A minor, a symbol for his downfall and disillusionment. The peasants recognize him, and their continuing affection for him is signalled by a cadence in C major, the key of love and fidelity ('Geliebter Herr, willkommen bei den Deinen!'). Adolar continues to protest Euryanthe's infidelity, effecting a cadence in D minor ('Du süße heil'ge Treue, du lebst, doch nicht in Euryanthens Brust!'), the key with which he had led her into the forest at the start of the third act. The peasants take up her defence, once again leading back to the purity of C major ('es wankten eh' des Himmels Sterne, als uns'rer süßen Herrin Treu!'). With the disclosure that Eglantine and Lysiart have entered a liaison, the music aims for a key strongly associated with Lysiart, C minor, which then easily leads through a dominant-seventh on F to the chivalric key of the next piece, B-flat major.

4. *Eglantine's delirium (Act III, scene v)*. Although a highly flexible structure consisting of recitative and arioso, the delirium does have a primary keynote, B, which seems to have been predetermined by the central dramatic element, Eglantine's tortured vision of Emma's ghost. Thus the scene begins in B minor, with motives that may be heard as distorted or 'deranged' reminiscences of the revenge duet. Eglantine's vision of Emma naturally entails quotation of the *Vision* at its original pitch level, with, however, the original B-major triad at the start replaced now by B minor, perhaps to suggest the more ominous or sinister tone of this moment. The major structural division at the close of Eglantine's first speech ('Sei ruhig! Nacht hüllt unsre Thaten ein') is marked by a half-cadence on the dominant of B minor, and the end of the scene prepares another half-cadence in B minor, which quickly turns to the 'chivalric' D major at the beginning of No. 24. Within this B-minor frame, two other primary tonicizations are heard as symbols in their own right. Thus in the first part Eglantine's attempt to drive away the ghostly vision is marked by a fortissimo cadence to the 'triumphant' key of her own Scena ed aria, E major ('Hinweg, hier bin ich Herrscher-

in geworden'), and in the second part of the scene, the vassal's joyful recognition of Adolar ('Heil Adolar! Heil in seiner Väter Hallen!') is set to C major, a symbol of love and devotion. The one other important key area within the second half of the scene, G major, seems not to have any strong symbolic value in and of itself, but rather was the musically logical choice to mediate between B minor and C major. Thus it is introduced as a deceptive cadence following Eglantine's half-cadence in B minor; the harmonic 'interruption' is certainly justified by the completely different perspective from which the crowd views the crazed Eglantine.

Because they tend to modulate between tonal goals chosen more for their associative, symbolic value than for purely musical connectivity, the recitatives in *Euryanthe* are often far removed from the traditional harmonic profile of recitative in late eighteenth- and early nineteenth-century opera, which normally progresses by falling fifth in the root until some dramatic interruption—a question, a surprise, the entrance of a new character, and so forth—motivates an 'unexpected' progression. To be sure, vestiges of the traditional fifth progressions may be heard throughout *Euryanthe*, but on the whole, the harmonic successions are far from predictable, a situation that perhaps gave rise to Chorley's observations that 'there is no prophesying, by the best practised listener, of the change or chord which is next to come'.[9] For this reason it is easy to understand how early nineteenth-century audiences accustomed to the conventional cadential structure of recitative and unaware of the peculiar tonal symbolism in the opera could and did find the recitatives in *Euryanthe* excessively learned and tiring. Thus the 'associative' logic of the harmonic choices is at once yet another reason why *Euryanthe* appeared to many of Weber's contemporaries as 'musical mosaic' or a piece of 'musical prose'.

4. THE CONVENTIONS OF TONAL SYMBOLISM

The use of tonality for connotative purposes in *Euryanthe*, in principle, represents no major innovation. Certain of the associations seem frankly conventional and may be related both to practical precedents and to the contemporary theoretical discussions of the characteristics of keys. The association of Divinity and E-flat major figures prominently in *Die Zauberflöte*, and C. F. D. Schubart's well-known description of tonal characteristics seconds this association: 'E-flat major, the key of love, of devotion, of intimate conversations with God; expressing the Holy

---

[9] Chorley, *Modern German Music* (London, 1854), i. 303–4.

Trinity through its three flats.'[10] That the key is also conceived as a heroic symbol, especially in the large ensemble No. 4, finds precedent in the writings of the Italian theorist Francesco Galeazzi and of course Beethoven's 'Eroica' Symphony.[11] Schubart's comments about the purity of C major ('C major is entirely pure. Its character is: innocence, simplicity, naiveté and the speech of children.') also agree with Weber's association of that key with Euryanthe's lily-white innocence, love for Adolar and naively trusting nature.[12] In a review written in 1812 of a song collection by G. W. Fink, Weber himself spoke of A-flat major as being appropriate to the character of 'a sensitive, faithful heart', an apt characterization of Adolar's frame of mind in his Aria No. 12.[13] Schubart described D major as a 'key of triumph, of Hallelujahs, of war-cries, or victory-rejoicing', and countless operas of the later eighteenth and early nineteenth centuries associate the key with heroic or martial, and hence by extension knightly, activities.[14] The choice of B major for the villains' revenge Duetto No. 11 seems to reflect Schubart's view of that key: 'Strongly coloured, announcing wild passions, composed from the most glaring colours. Anger, rage, jealousy, fury, despair and every burden of the heart lies in its sphere.'[15] The association of a mixed-mode B tonality with the supernatural element in *Euryanthe* may also be related to practice, albeit indirectly, since theory and practice seem to agree that B *minor* is also a sinister key. Beethoven's misgivings about B minor ('B minor, black key') are well known,[16] and the rarity of that key in the works of Mozart and Beethoven seems to indicate that composers did view it with circumspection.[17] When it does appear, the connotations very frequently are indeed sinister, as in Caspar's Drinking Song in *Der Freischütz*, or even demonic; such is the role played by B minor in Spohr's *Faust* (Prague, 1816), in which the music for

---

[10] Christian Friedrich Daniel Schubart, *Ideen zu einer Ästhetik der Tonkunst* (Vienna, 1806), p. 377. The present translation is adapted from Steblin, n. 4 above, p. 122.

[11] For Galeazzi E-flat was 'a heroic key, extremely majestic, grave and serious: in all these features it is superior to that of C'. Cited after Steblin, op. cit., p. 111.

[12] Schubart, op. cit., p. 377. The present translation is adapted from Steblin, p. 121.

[13] *Sämtliche Schriften*, p. 169.

[14] Schubart, op. cit., p. 379, cited after Steblin, op. cit., p. 124. In the Mozart canon one can easily cite examples of 'heroic' D-major pieces: the aria 'Fuor del mar' in *Idomeneo*; Pedrillo's mock heroic 'Frisch zum Kampfe' in the *Entführung aus dem Serail*; and the two revenge arias in *Le nozze di Figaro*.

[15] Schubart, pp. 378–9, cited after Steblin, p. 123.

[16] Beethoven's remark is written in the so-called Scheide Sketchbook at Princeton University Library. See Lewis Lockwood, 'The Beethoven Sketchbook in the Scheide Library', *The Princeton University Library Chronicle*, 37 (1976): 151–2.

[17] Galeazzi was quite adamant that B minor is 'banished from music of good taste'. Cited after Steblin, op. cit., p. 112.

the Blocksberg witches and other references to magic appear in that key.

Some of the other key choices may also have been influenced by repertoire that Weber knew or by his own prior practice. Thus the seed for a G-major chorus at the start of an opera might have been planted by Grétry's most famous opera, *Richard cœur-de-lion*. An A-major peasant wedding song in the third act of an opera could have been suggested by one of Weber's favourite operas, Cherubini's *Les Deux Journées*. Méhul's *Ariodant* contains a courtly strophic *romance* in B-flat major that, like Adolar's No. 2, varies the accompaniment from stanza to stanza. The C-minor entr'acte at the beginning of Act II of Cherubini's *Médée* possibly inspired the C-minor ritornello at the beginning of Lysiart's Scena ed aria, and the C-minor revenge aria of the villain Mafferu, like Lysiart a high bass, in Peter Winter's *Das unterbrochene Opferfest* (Vienna, 1796), one of the best known German works of the period, may also lie behind the key choice. In discussing Eglantine's No. 8 in a letter about tempo in *Euryanthe* Weber himself called attention to the E-major *aria di bravura* for the revenge-driven character of Elvira in *Das unterbrochene Opferfest*.[18] Slow G-minor arias about isolation, abandonment, or lost love occur in *Idomeneo* (Ilia's 'Padre, germani, addio'), *Die Entführung aus dem Serail* (Constanze's 'Traurigkeit ward mir zum Lose'), *Die Zauberflöte* (Pamina's 'Ach! Ich fühl's'), and Spohr's *Faust* (Röschen's cavatina 'Dürft ich mich nennen'). Doubtless a systematic study of tonal uses throughout early Romantic French and German opera would yield numerous antecedents for the tonal symbols in *Euryanthe*.

Weber's own *Freischütz* probably provided the most important model for the tonal symbolism in *Euryanthe*, since in the earlier opera three of the most important keys in *Euryanthe* function in entirely analogous ways. E-flat major, for example, stands for divine protection against the powers of darkness, both in Max's Scena ed aria ('O dringt kein Strahl durch diese Nächte') and in the Act III Finale where the appearance of the religious Hermit sets matters aright. C minor functions as its demonic antithesis, in both the cabaletta of Max's aria ('Doch mich umgarnen finstre Mächte') and in several sections of the Wolf's Glen scene, for example, the conversation between Samiel and Caspar and the storm that erupts after the casting of the sixth bullet. We have

---

[18] Letter to the Leipzig *Kapellmeister* Aloys Präger published in *Sämtliche Schriften*, p. 224. E major is the key of a number of conspicuous bravura soprano arias at the end of the eighteenth century and beginning of the nineteenth century: Fiordiligi's Act 2 *Rondò* in *Così fan tutte*; Leonore's 'Komm' Hoffnung' in *Fidelio*; Amenaïde's Act 2 Scena ed aria in Rossini's *Tancredi*; and of course Agathe's 'Leise, leise' from the second act of *Freischütz*.

already mentioned the sinister B-minor tonality of Caspar's drinking song. The association of recurring music with fixed tonality, represented in *Euryanthe* by Emma's music, finds a precedent in the Samiel chord, which always recurs at the same pitch level. Where *Euryanthe* differs from *Der Freischütz* in the treatment of tonality is primarily in the rigour of the musical logic of the key relationships, a phenomenon perhaps explained by the fact that a musically continuous opera like *Euryanthe* requires a greater attention to the succession of tonalities than would an opera where the numbers are separated by long stretches of spoken dialogue.

5. THE GENESIS OF THE TONAL PLAN: THE EVIDENCE AND SOME HYPOTHESES

Exactly how Weber arrived at the tonal plan for *Euryanthe* is a topic for which the extant record provides little documentary evidence. However, a few inferences about Weber's tonal decisions can be drawn provisionally from the evidence for the genesis of the opera. A particularly revealing document for Weber's approach to tonal planning is furnished by a surviving copy of his *Textvorlage* for the composition of the Act II Finale.[19] Prior to composing this crucial centrepiece for the opera, Weber wrote out in ink the text of the complete finale, following the emended version of the text in his current *Textvorlage* (*Web.* Cl. II A g 4); he also marked the major subsections of the finale. Alongside the text Weber noted in pencil preliminary indications for the tonal succession of the first few sections of the finale up through Euryanthe's prayer for divine protection ('Der du die Unschuld kennst, beschütz mein Leben'). The annotated *Textvorlage* thus represents a miniature version of the kind of tonal sketch that survives for *Die drei Pintos* (see Table 8).

There are several interesting features about the annotations on this leaf. The succession of principal keys—F–D-flat–A—does correspond to the tonal shifts by descending major third in the first half of the finale, although, as we shall see, the timing of the shift is rather different in the final version (Table 9). As in the final version, B-flat is singled out as a major point of internal articulation within a D-flat major section; its assocation with Lysiart's claim to have conquered Euryanthe's proud heart may signal an ironic reference to the Adolar's Romanza No. 2 and perhaps suggest as well that at the time of the composition of the Act II Finale Weber contemplated setting Lysiart's conversation with Euryanthe at Nevers in B-flat major. What is most significant about

---

[19] WFN-Handschriftliches, Konvolut XX, Bl. 116.

TABLE 8. Act II Finale: tonal structure (original plan)

Section	Key	Character	Corresponding line in the copy of the libretto
1.	F	Chor.	Leuchtend füllt die Königshallen...
2.	Des	Lysiart.	Mein König! *Chor.* Jezt schlägt der Entscheidung Stunde...
	B	Lys.	Bewund'rungswürdig ists gelungen...
	Des	Ad.	Zur Fehde! *Kön.* Nein, gebt wahre Kunde...
3.	A	Eur.	Der du die Unschuld kennst, beschütz mein Leben...

Note: Weber's orthography and German system for pitch nomenclature are retained.

this tonal plan, however, are the ways in which it deviates from the final version; to facilitate this comparison Table 9 aligns major tonal areas in the finale with the relevant lines of text.

TABLE 9. Act II Finale: tonal structure (final version)

Section	Key	Character	Corresponding line of text
1.	F	Chorus	Leuchtend füllt die Königshallen...
2.	D♭	Lysiart	Mein König!...
	B♭	Lysiart	Bewundernswürdig ists gelungen...
	C	Adolar	Zur Fehde!...
	A♭	Lysiart	Dies Unterpfand der Liebe reichte mir...
	G♭	Euryanthe	Der du die Unschuld Kennst, beschütz mein Leben!...
	D♭	Lysiart	Wer sonst als Euryanth' und du kannst sagen...
	d♭	Chorus	Ha! die Verrätherin!...
3.	A	Euryanthe	Laß mich empor zum Lichte wallen....

First, D-flat remains in effect much longer in the final version than Weber originally planned. While Weber's initial outline suggests that Euryanthe's prayer for protection ('Der du die Unschuld kennst') would mark the beginning of a new movement within the finale, the final version extends the D-flat section well past its original boundary, with a strong point of tonal reprise occurring at Lysiart's line 'Wer sonst als Euryanth' und du kannst sagen' and a final assertion of D-flat minor at the end of the segment in the chorus 'Ha! die Verrätherin!' Second,

Adolar's line 'Zur Fehde!' does not mark a return to D-flat major in the finished opera; rather, it is set in C major, perhaps symbolizing his continuing belief (at that point) in Euryanthe's fidelity. Third, in the final version of the opera, A major does follow D-flat, but it is withheld until Euryanthe's later prayer, 'Laß mich empor zum Lichte wallen', the slow concerted ensemble for the finale; the lines with which it was originally associated ('Der du die Unschuld kennst, beschütz mein Leben'), eventually came to be set in G-flat major, the only prolonged tonicization of that key in the opera. This shift of A major from one text to another is not as arbitrary as it might seem at first, since in both the original outline and the final version this key is associated with a prayer by Euryanthe. The decision to shift A major to the second prayer can perhaps be taken as a degree of confirmation of the prior interpretation of this key as a tonal metaphor for regeneration, renewal, and the uplifting of spirit, since its text explicitly describes an upward motion of the soul in terms that resonate with the image invoked by Euryanthe's line at the beginning of the A major section of the Duetto No. 7 ('Ja! es wallt mein Herz aufs Neue | Selig deinem Herzen zu.') As we shall see below, the corollary to this shift, the replacement of A major with G-flat major as the tonality for Euryanthe's first prayer, is fraught with implications about the near identity of expression for certain keys that seems to lie behind numerous key choices in the opera.

A few glimpses into Weber's tonal thinking may also be caught from the history of the libretto. If Weber started off with a fixed tonal scheme at the time that he began composition, he clearly was forced to adjust it substantially as the libretto continued to evolve long after the first pieces were written. The conversion of the narration of Emma's *Vision* from a Romanze into a special recitative may have entailed significant consequences for the tonal conception of that important element in the opera. The growth of Eglantine's role perhaps spread E minor and E major into areas where they had not originally been envisioned. The prominence accorded D major as a symbol for chivalry in the final version of the opera may not have been part of Weber's original conception, since all of the pieces that are in D major (the Act I Finale No. 9, the Hochzeitmarsch No. 23, and the Duetto con coro No. 24) were conceived very late in the history of the libretto.

The revisions of the concluding scenes of Act I probably prompted a certain amount of rethinking of tonal organization. Consider, for example, the three major structural differences between Weber's *Textvorlage* of June 1822, his autograph libretto *Web.* Cl. II A g 6, and the final version of the opera: (1) Like the librettos of February 1822, Cl. II A g 6 still divided the opera into two acts instead of three. Lysiart's arrival at Nevers, immediately following the Duetto No. 7 for Eglantine and Euryanthe, therefore was conceived not as a finale, but as a shorter piece approximately corresponding to the first two sections of the Act I Finale in the completed opera. Weber's pencil annotations in this libretto actually divide the scene into two units, a chorus for the arrival of Lysiart's knights and the exchange between Euryanthe and Lysiart, which is capped off by a single line for chorus. Whether these two sections were originally to have been set in the same key or in contrasting keys cannot be known, but in either case the tonal structure would have differed from the tripartite structure in the final opera. Possibly the greeting was planned from the outset in D major, a logical choice to follow the A-major conclusion of the Eglantine–Euryanthe duet, whereas the scene between Euryanthe and Lysiart may have been planned either as a tonally closed movement in D major or B-flat major or as a tonally open-ended section in the manner of a recitative or arioso; (2) In this version Eglantine's revenge aria follows, rather than precedes, Lysiart's arrival at Nevers. Perhaps E major had been determined from the outset as the key for this aria, since Weber would have found numerous E-major precedents for bravura arias for dramatic sopranos, such as those for Fiodiligi, Elvira in Winter's *Opferfest*, Leonore, and Agathe; (3) An ensemble in which the two peasants, Rudolf and Bertha, discuss their own impending wedding plans, was still planned to come between Eglantine's aria and Lysiart's aria; since, in the final version of the opera the peasants play a negligible role, it is not at all clear what key would have been chosen, although G major might have been considered as a 'simple' key, one long associated with rustic life,[20] that could also mediate effectively between the E major of Eglantine's piece and the C minor of Lysiart's aria. The final version of the opera perhaps betrays the way that the substantial changes in the libretto structure upset a plan for tonal relationships since the definitive key succession for the end of Act I, A major to E major to D major, is not nearly as elegant as those for the first two musico-dramatic units in the opera.

The drastic changes in plot and structure that were made in the third act after Weber began composition of the opera—especially in the concluding scene, in which only the May Song remained a constant feature from the earliest librettos to the final version—must also have entailed substantial modifications of any primitive tonal outline for the work. Of these the most suggestive for Weber's tonal thinking is the complete revision of the end of the opera documented by several of the draft

---

[20] Precedents for G-major peasant choruses occur in *Le nozze di Figaro, Don Giovanni*, and Grétry's *Richard cœur-de-lion*.

librettos. From the start of the project to the Winter of 1822–23, the opera was planned to finish with a final strophe of the May Song. The possible implications of this fact for the original tonal plan of the opera are summarized in Table 10, which outlines four hypothetical models for the original tonal choices envisioned for the Ouverture, the first stanzas of the May Song sung at the start of the last scene, and its reprise at the end of the opera; the final version is presented to facilitate a comparison.

TABLE 10. Tonality at the end of the opera

| | 'Original Version' (Hypothetical) | | | | Final Version |
	1	2	3	4	
Ouverture	E♭	A	E♭	E♭	E♭
May Song (st. 1–3)	A	A	E♭	A	A
May song (end of opera)	A	A	E♭	E♭	E♭ (not May Song)

Excluding the highly unlikely model presented in the first column, according to which the opera, for the first and only time in Weber's known operatic output, would have ended in a key other than that of the Ouverture, one is left with three possible tonal combinations. Either the Ouverture and all of the stanzas of the May Song were in A major (Model 2), they were all planned in E-flat major (Model 3), or the end of the opera entailed a transposition of the May Song from its original key of A major to E-flat major (Model 4). Models 3 and 4 seem more likely candidates than Model 2 because the sequence of keys established early on for the Introduzione (Nos. 1–4) strongly suggests E-flat major as the original key for the Ouverture.

The conclusion to be drawn from these latter two models, that the May Song could be set in either A major or E-flat major, is at first glance rather startling, for it implies a near equivalence of mood between major keys a tritone apart. However, this radical conclusion does seem consistent with the tonal logic of the entire opera. Consider, for example, the fact that the keys principally associated with Adolar's and Euryanthe's chief virtues—love, fidelity, and faith in God—are major keys that form a chain of minor-third relationships: E-flat, C, and A. Although the symbolic uses of these keys are subtly differentiated in the course of the opera, there are nevertheless two further clues, in addition to that offered by the revisions of the end of the opera, that suggest that Weber viewed the major-mode keys along this minor-third cycle as practical equivalents that could be used interchangeably as necessary for the representation of virtue.[21] Thus in the scene between Euryanthe and Eglantine in the first act Euryanthe recalls the first awakening of her love for Adolar as the orchestra introduces in E-flat major the motive that later, in C major, forms the main theme for the love duet, No. 13. And as we have seen in the prior discussion of Weber's initial tonal plan for the second-act finale, he eventually substituted G-flat major in place of the original A major for the setting of Euryanthe's prayer for divine protection ('Der du die Unschuld kennst, beschütz mein Leben'). Of course, G-flat major thereby completes a 'virtuous' cycle of major keys outlining the diminished-seventh chord A-C-E-flat-G-flat, a fact that students of Weber will note with some irony, since these are precisely the pitch classes that had been employed so ingeniously in *Freischütz* as the musical embodiment of the demonic, in both the 'Samiel chord' that is that opera's most important recurring motive and in the succession of keys in the second-act finale, the Wolf's Glen scene.[22] As in so many other ways, then, *Euryanthe* may been seen here also to build upon its immediate predecessor, by extending a matrix for tonal organization that had first been tried out as a guiding principle for a scene to an organizing principle for an entire opera. Naturally, a diminished-seventh cycle of practically interchangeable keys greatly facilitates the smooth succession of keys in the work, since the near equivalence of the members of the cycle makes it possible to relate any positive affection to almost any other key choice.

Whatever its flaws, *Euryanthe* clearly was one of the influential operas of the early nineteenth century. Chief among its lasting legacies to its successors in the German school is a concern for careful, large-scale tonal planning that seeks to reconcile a purely musical logic of key relations with a tonal symbolism, in part conventional, in part arbitrarily assigned. Clearly Weber had powerful antecedents for this task in the works of Mozart and in his own prior works,[23] but the brilliance and consistency of the solution in *Euryanthe* set it apart in degree if not in kind from what came before. Doubtless the necessity of organizing

[21] Similarly, another pair of keys a minor third apart, A minor and C minor, are strongly associated with misfortune and are thus practically interchangeable.

[22] See Robert Bailey, 'Visual and Musical Symbolism in German Romantic Opera', in International Musicological Society, *Report of the Twelfth Congress Berkeley 1977*, ed. by Daniel Heartz and Bonnie Wade (Kassel, Basle and London, 1981), pp. 440–3.

[23] Principles of tonal organization in Mozart's operas are discussed in two important articles by Daniel Heartz: 'Tonality and Motif in *Idomeneo*', *MT* (1974); and 'Constructing *Le nozze di Figaro*', *JRMA* 112 (1987), 119–31.

a 'through-composed opera', in which pieces had to be connected musically, prompted this extraordinarily well thought out scheme, which could and did provide the model for Wagner's achievements in the works of his maturity.[24]

[24] On the fundamental importance of 'associative tonality' in Wagner's works after *The Flying Dutchman* see Robert Bailey, 'The Structure of the *Ring* and its Evolution', *19th-Century Music* 1 (1977): 51–5. Building on Bailey's work, the present author has pointed out a number of parallelisms between the tonal organization of *Euryanthe* and that of *Tannhäuser* and *Lohengrin* in 'Richard Wagner and Weber's *Euryanthe*', *19th-Century Music* 9 (1986): 215–7.

VIII. Dramatic Truth

As we saw in Chapter III, many of *Euryanthe*'s early critics, pro-German and pro-Italian alike, were disturbed by what they felt to be Weber's willingness to sacrifice traditional values of independent musical development to a single-minded pursuit of dramatic effect. For modern analysis and criticism, Weber's insistence on 'truth' and 'characterization' as the primary criteria for dramatic music is in many ways as problematic as it was for his contemporaries. On the one hand, almost all analytical models of the nineteenth and twentieth centuries are predicated on the notion that great music is 'organically' conceived and thus susceptible to reductive processes that explain the coherence and cogency of the music in terms of simple generating principles.[1] Unquestionably, these models have yielded and will continue to yield powerful insights into the works of many eighteenth-, nineteenth-, and twentieth-century composers. But Weber's dramatic music was admittedly and intentionally not self-sufficient, and attempts to analyse it according to the organic metaphor are therefore doomed to produce unsatisfying and a priori negatively critical results. On the other hand, whereas twentieth-century theory has developed a number of sophisticated models for understanding the manipulation of pitch in music, we have no commonly accepted yardsticks by which to measure or discuss the communicative, expressive, and characterizing force of music. Yet, in order to approach Weber's music on its own terms, one must take seriously its claim to be an agent of dramatic expression and develop criteria for evaluating its success or failure in accomplishing this goal. This was, after all, what mattered most to Weber. Naturally, the fact that Weber's music was conceived with the ears, knowledge, and assumptions of an early nineteenth-century European musician in no way facilitates this challenge to understanding, for the work is therefore a product of a bygone cultural system whose similarities to our own disguise subtle and profound differences. Put another way, Weber probably felt that the truth of his musical utterance would be self-evident to his contemporaries, but the twentieth-century observer must rediscover the language of Weber's expressive vision.

---

[1] On the history of the 'organic metaphor' in music criticism and analysis see Ruth Solie, 'The Living Work: Organicism and Musical Analysis', *19th-Century Music* 4 (1980–1): 147–56. For a critique of the organic model see also Janet Levy, 'Covert and Casual Values in Recent Writings about Music', *Journal of Musicology* 5/1 (1987): 3–27.

It therefore falls primarily to the historian to attempt to reclaim something of the communicative content of the work, and what follows is an attempt to develop a rudimentary model for 'truth' and 'character' in *Euryanthe*. Admittedly this is a difficult and problematic task,[2] but a provisional attempt is necessary if we are to begin to do justice to Weber and his work.

I. DECLAMATION

Without question the single most important fact of dramatic composition for Weber was the presence of a text that stimulated his fantasy and guided a number of crucial compositional choices. As we shall see repeatedly throughout the remainder of this study, the text acts as a blueprint for a number of decisions, but nowhere is it more crucial than in its actual influence on melodic and rhythmic invention. For Weber, 'truthful declamation' was not only 'the first and most sacred duty of song',[3] but also a real source of melodic invention; as he explained in 1815 to Friedrich Wieck, 'the creation of a new form must be produced by the poetry that one composes. In my own songs only the greatest effort to reproduce my poet's declamation in a truthful and correct manner has led me to many a new melodic shape'.[4] Important elements of Weber's understanding of declamatory 'truth' are outlined in a lengthy discussion of text setting in his incidental music to Adolph Müllner's play *König Yngurd*. One of the vocal pieces for the play represented a novel experiment in heightened declamation, in which the notated melody provided only a sketch for performance. Müllner responded favourably to the song, but pointed out certain passages in which he felt that the musical setting had contradicted the correct scansion of the poem. Weber's reply to Müllner, evidently prepared for publication but never published during the composer's lifetime, clearly reveals that he had thought long and hard about problems of declamation in vocal music:

For the most part the composer runs into trouble because the poet does not always equate speaking accent with prosodic quantity. This dichotomy of versification and declamation is intensified by music, whose rhythmic members are bound to a far more precise motion in time than even the most scrupulous

---

[2] Important contributions to this topic include: Leonard B. Meyer, *Emotion and Meaning in Music* (Chicago, 1956); Carl Dahlhaus, 'Die Kategorie des Charakteristischen in der Aesthetik des 19. Jahrhunderts', in *Die 'Couleur Locale' in der Oper des 19. Jahrhunderts*, ed. Heinz Becker (Regensburg, 1976), pp. 9–21; Marlene Schmidt, *Zur Theorie des musikalischen Charakters* (Munich and Salzburg, 1981); and Carl Dahlhaus, *Realism in Nineteenth-Century Music*, trans. by Mary Whittall (Cambridge, etc., 1985).

[3] *Sämtliche Schriften*, p. 372.

[4] *Sämtliche Schriften*, p. 176.

declamator is capable of indicating, should he not wish to be ridiculously stiff. For this problem, however, music also possesses as aid and even solution—to a much higher degree than speech—the significant weight of higher or lower accentuation, and often the weight of the pulse must concede to the succeeding weight of a higher tone at least the same strength and effect, and therefore equality. Further, however, it is also in the first instance the proper concern of melody to reproduce and clarify the interior life that the word expresses; thus appears the great danger whereby anxiously researched correctness transforms the pollen of the interior truth of melody into stiffness and dryness. The decision, whether it falls to the one or the other, music or poetry, to predominate, is the great crag on which many a one has already shattered.[5]

Weber then went on to justify his compositional choices with detailed discussions of passages from the song.

According to Weber's own criteria, then, truthful declamation is more than just an accurate matching of relatively long and short durational values to relatively strong and weak syllables. It entails a comprehension of the meaning of the text as well as the attempt to reflect accentuation and expression through melodic contour. And to judge by criticisms voiced in the letter to Wieck cited earlier, it is also a matter of keeping the sense and syntax of the poem together in the organization of musical phrases and periods.[6]

In view of the primacy that Weber accorded correct declamation, it is initially surprising to find that the composition draft for *Euryanthe* provides so little evidence for the ways in which he translated this ideal into musical results. To be sure, the fact that he started the majority of vocal pieces with music for the first line of text of course follows from his principles, and almost every draft exhibits minor revisions of rhythm in individual phrases that betray a certain fussiness—the conversion of two notes of equal duration into a dotted rhythm and vice versa, the shortening of the last pitch in a phrase, the augmentation or diminution of durational values in a phrase of recitative—but rarely do such changes afford more than a tiny glimpse into the rationale behind

---

[5] *Sämtliche Schriften*, p. 372. The song, along with an explanation of the manner of performance, is printed ibid., pp. 368–9. Müllner's critique is published ibid., pp. 369–71. Georg Kaiser, the editor of Weber's collected writings, supposed that most of Müllner's comments were written not by the playwright, who admits to having no expertise in music, but by 'someone else who considered himself a specialist' (ibid., p. xcix).

[6] *Sämtliche Schriften*, pp. 176–7: 'Your declamation is occasionally very careless and tears apart the coherence of meaning.' Weber then went on to cite examples of the 'sinnentstellende Trennung der Worte' in Wieck's first and fourth songs.

decisions in text setting, on the one hand because the revisions rarely work through alternatives methodically and on the other hand because the revisions tend to be confined to isolated occurrences.

As an attempt to interpret declamatory truth along lines suggested by Weber's letter to Müllner, let us briefly consider the first twelve measures of the Andante con moto movement of Lysiart's Scena ed aria No. 10, to which our attention is drawn in the first instance by a number of small rhythmic revisions between the draft and the final version (see Ex. 3). The opening of the movement comprises four three-measure phrases (a–b–a′–b′) that set a quatrain of text.

Schweigt glühn'den Sehnens wilde Triebe,	Be still you wild desires of glowing yearning,
Ihr Auge sucht den Himmel nur.	her eye seeks only heaven.
In Ihr wohnt Unschuld, Anmuth, Liebe,	Innocence, grace and love reside in her;
Ganz Wahrheit ist Sie, ganz Natur.	she is entirely truthful and natural.

Following his own premiss that truthful declamation is more a matter of bringing life to the inner meaning of a poem rather than a mechanical realization of its metre, Weber rejects a stiff scansion of the poem as iambic tetrameter in favour of a more natural declamation emphasizing meaning. Thus at the very start 'Schweigt' is placed on a downbeat, an appropriate position of strength for a command, and 'Ihr' at the start of the second line is set as a strong beat, perhaps to underscore Lysiart's obsession with Euryanthe ('Ihr') rather than with any one of her physical attributes ('Auge'). Why the word 'Sehnens', originally set as a dotted rhythm corresponding to its natural accentuation, was revised into a spondee is unclear. A desire to variegate musically parallel passages for the sake of declamatory truth may be observed in the second period. By accepting the iambic implications of the words 'In Ihr' at the beginning of the third line as a weak–strong gesture, the start of the second phrase again emphasizes Lysiart's obsession with Euryanthe ('Ihr'). At measure 69 the rhythmic pattern of measure 63 is altered, perhaps because the noun 'Anmuth' deserves greater weight than was accorded the adjective 'wilde' in the first phrase. As originally drafted, measure 72 followed the rhythmic model of measure 66 but altered its melodic profile by dropping down to e on the second beat; although the precise effect of this change is hard to articulate, there can be little disagreement that the falling third is a great improvement over the repeated pitches in the original version of measure 66, which was revised retroactively to include the falling third. Eventually the rhythm of measure 72 was revised to effect a spondaic treatment of the words 'ist Sie', again giving weight to the object ('Sie') that haunts Lysiart.

Ex. 3 Rhythmic revisions in Lysiart's Scena ed aria No. 10
(Andante con moto).

2. OTHER ELEMENTS OF DRAMATIC TRUTH: A MODEL FOR 'CHARAKTER'

Of course 'truth' and 'Charakter' in dramatic music entail more than just correct declamation, but rather a matching of all musical elements to the situation and the emotion. Precisely because all elements are fused together into what Weber and his contemporaries often called *Totaleffekt*, it is difficult and arbitrary to separate the technical means of composition from one another and discuss them individually. This difficulty extends also to the study of Weber's compositional processes, since for the most part—the initial impression given by the drafts notwithstanding—composition seems to have entailed the simultaneous conception of many musical elements, a point that Weber himself emphasized in his commentary on Cherubini's *Lodoïska* cited above. For this reason, the following discussion of criteria for 'truth' and 'character' in *Euryanthe* is organized not by separate musical elements but instead according to types of musical symbolism. The criteria are suggested by Weber's own utterances, by Lobe's 'interview' with Weber about *Freischütz*, an example of early nineteenth-century criticism that, if not authentic, at the very least is geographically and chronologically close to the composer, by contemporary appraisals and criticism of *Euryanthe*, and by pragmatic observation of the relationship of music and drama in the opera. This discussion is meant in no way as a comprehensive treatise on 'Charakter' in music, but rather only as a point of departure for understanding Weber's approach.

2.1. 'Truth' as imitatio naturae

In traditional aesthetics of art before the nineteenth century, 'imitation' of the real, visible world was a primary goal of art. That 'imitation' should still constitute one of the means to 'truth' in a self-styled 'Romantic' opera is therefore doubly paradoxical, since on the one hand the conventions of opera distance it conspicuously from the real world in many ways, and on the other hand, the Romantic movement downplayed mimesis as the *raison d'être* of art and substituted instead an aesthetic rooted in personal expression of the artist.[7] Then again, the Romantic aesthetic of music's autonomy from the real world certainly finds little sympathy for traditional *imitatio*. To a certain extent Weber's own writings also seem to reject *imitatio* as a basis for characterization in

---

[7] This is the principal thesis in M. H. Abrams's study of the Romantic movement in literature, *The Mirror and the Lamp* (New York, 1953).

music, as he expressed distaste for realistic effects that brought music too close to the noises of the real world.[8]

Nevertheless, 'truth' in dramatic music, even in Weber's 'Romantic' opera, in some ways is still predicated upon imitation of the 'real world', especially through its ability to emulate real-life sounds. For example, in operatic conventions of the early nineteenth century strophic songs are often introduced as formal songs sung in the course of action to other characters on stage. In *Euryanthe*, Adolar's Romanza and Bertha's May Song both conform to this model of verisimilitude; the former is a troubadour song sung to the assembled nobles, whereas the latter is a memorized folksong sung as part of a peasant wedding celebration. The Romanza demonstrates another manner of imitation in that the pizzicato accompaniment in its first stanza simulates the sound of a plucked-string instrument, in this case the zither to which Adolar sings his song in praise of Euryanthe.

Even more obviously imitative is the use of stage instruments. According to long-standing operatic convention, situations that in real life employ musical instruments are those that justify the presence of instruments on stage, and *Euryanthe* employs stage instruments in precisely this manner. The trumpets that herald the arrival of Lysiart (No. 9), the hunters' horn calls in the forest (No. 18), and the band that accompanies the wedding procession of Lysiart and Eglantine (No. 23) not only provide a dash of spectacle but also reflect common uses of music in a courtly society. As Wagner pointed out in his conversations with his wife Cosima, the Act III horn calls and the subsequent hunting chorus in particular achieve an especially naturalistic effect, as isolated horn calls gradually coalesce into a sustained song in which all music comes from the stage.[9]

2.2. *Traditional expressive topoi*

Early nineteenth-century composers inherited a number of devices with well-established affective connotations, the vestiges of traditional *loci topici* of eighteenth-century music. Many of these may have originated in

[8] Weber made a point of avoiding overtly imitative effects in his *Kampf und Sieg* (*Sämtliche Schriften*, p. 200) and he was also critical of the special bellicose effects in Beethoven's *Wellingtons Sieg* (ibid., p. 81).

[9] In comparing the hunting chorus in *Freischütz* with that in *Euryanthe* Wagner told Cosima on 10 Oct. 1875: 'In the first ... Weber was still entirely a popular melodist (*Volkslyriker*) and he wrote a chorus as one sings it; in *Euryanthe* he is much more the dramatist, and he wrote the chorus as one hears it, coming out of nature.' Cosima Wagner, *Die Tagebücher*, ed. Martin Gregor-Dellin and Dietrich Mack, vol. i (Munich and Zurich, 1976), p. 941. See also ibid., vol. ii (Munich and Zurich, 1977), p. 509. On the resonance of this scene in *Tannhäuser* see my 'Richard Wagner and Weber's *Euryanthe*', *19th-Century Music* 9/3 (1985–6): 212–14.

imitatio naturae, but the important point here is that by the early nine-teenth century they were so firmly entrenched as expressive *topoi* that composers could draw upon them with the expectation that their mean-ing would be easily understood.[10] Examples of such phenomena include, but by no means are restricted to: (1) traditional rhythmic and melodic *figurae* for certain affections, like the dotted rhythms and triadic contours that carry royal, chivalric, or martial connotations, the fast 6/8 used as a symbol for the hunt, and the relatively slow compound-metre dances (especially the *siciliano*) traditionally associated with pastoral items in ba-roque and classical music; (2) conventional harmonic symbols for expres-sion, such as the affective opposition of the major and minor modes, the uses of dissonance to connote pain or instability, various cadence types to signal affirmation (full cadence) and questioning (half-cadence, 'Phrygian' cadence), and the use of drone basses to suggest pastoral set-tings—by Weber's time the diminished-seventh chord had clearly become established in the *Schreckensoper* of the French Revolution as a harmonic topos for anxiety or terror; (3) traditional symbolism of instru-ments, according to which, for example, horns stand for the hunt, trum-pets and drums for martial activities, trombones for religion and worlds beyond the grave, various woodwind sonorities for pastoral life, and the so-called 'Turkish' instruments for almost any non-European locale;[11] (4) conventional interpretations of key character, as discussed in Chapter VII; and (5) traditional associations of vocal style with character type, as, for example, the use of coloratura in eighteenth-century opera variously as a symbol for rage or heroism.

It is not at all surprising that a composer like Weber who stressed originality as a prime measure of genuine art[12] would fail to discuss the uses of such conventional devices for expressive purposes. Yet, *Euryanthe* is filled with topoi that are quite conventional. As we have seen, many of the key choices in the opera are frankly traditional symbols for specific *Affekten*. The major and minor modes are rather consistently used in their customary roles as affective opposites. A number of choices in the instrumentation, especially the uses of trumpets and drums for prominently chivalric moments (No. 1, No. 9, etc.) and of horns as

[10] George J. Buelow, 'The *Loci Topici* and Affect in Late Baroque Music: Heinichen's Practical Demonstration', *Music Review* (1966): 161–76. On the importance of one large category of such topics for Mozart's operas, dance rhythms, see Wye Jamison Allanbrook, *Rhythmic Gesture in Mozart's Music* (Chicago and London, 1983).

[11] Thus in Gluck's *Iphigénie en Tauride* the Turkish music serves to characterize the barbarous Scythians of antiquity, whereas in Spontini's *Fernand Cortez* the ensemble is associated with early sixteenth-century Mexicans.

[12] In a review of Joseph Weigl's *Das Waisenhaus* Weber criticized composers like Weigl and Peter von Winter for having repeated successful formulas rather than risk audience disapproval by experimentation. *Sämtliche Schriften*, p. 295.

a symbol for the hunt in the third act, represent traditional associations of sonority and symbol. Tremolando strings are employed as symbols for agitation in much the same way as they had been since the time of Monteverdi's *stile concitato*, as a number of emotionally charged moments are marked by furious, loud tremolo accompaniments, whereas the quiet string tremolo is used in many instances as a symbol for sinister, suspenseful moments.

Even a number of melodic-rhythmic patterns may be related to traditional musical symbols for expression. Some of these are limited to isolated occurrences. Thus in the middle section of the Act I Finale, Euryanthe's nervous excitement at being summoned to Prémery to join Adolar and the King ('Mit Wonnebeben ehr' ich dies Gebot') is conveyed through an orchestral pattern for 'trembling' that is entirely analogous to the pattern that Mozart used in Belmonte's Aria No. 4 in the *Entführung aus dem Serail* to depict the palpitations of the heart and his trembling; naturally this device could also be cited as an example of *imitatio*. The close of Eglantine's self-pitying Aria No. 6 (mm. 64–5) relies on two-note slurs that were traditional symbols for sighs or sobs. Other topoi are used more frequently and underscore similar dramatic situations or moods, thereby effecting a kind of consistency of expression that unifies the opera as a whole. For instance, throughout the opera dotted rhythms are present in passages that refer to chivalry, heroism, and knights. Thus the D-major trumpets and timpani that characterize *Rittertum* in No. 1 (mm. 45–59), No. 24 and the Hochzeitmarsch are heard in conjunction with dotted rhythms, and several of Adolar's heroic moments—the cabaletta of No. 4, the concluding section of No. 16 (mm. 36 ff.), and No. 22—are stamped by dotted rhythms. Even a fleeting reference to dotted rhythms can be significant, as in the last section of Euryanthe's Cavatina No. 5 (mm. 64–76), where they make an unexpected appearance at the mention of Adolar's name.

2.3. *Character defined through opposition*

In many cases, the characteristic content of music is established through opposition; if one musical element is by convention or association defined as a metaphor for one kind of expression, then its stylistic antithesis becomes a symbol for an opposed expression. It is of course a commonplace that the major and minor modes are conventionally treated as affective opposites. And we have seen how Weber relies on the conventional dichotomy of flat and sharp keys for establishment of a basic tonal symbolism. But musical contrasts of any kind—in tempo, melodic direction, durational values, texture, relationship of voices and orchestra, instrumentation and dynamics, for example—may be used to convey contrasts of character, emotion, and situation, as a number of examples can illustrate.

(a) Orchestration: woodwinds versus brass

One important principle for 'characteristic' orchestration is the use of contrasting sonorities to signal dramatic opposition. In No. 1, the women's chorus is answered by the chorus of knights; although these two bodies sing similar melodic material, they are supported by differentiated sonorities. The women are accompanied primarily by woodwind instruments in their upper registers, whereas the men are supported by brass (four horns, trumpets) and timpani; only the bassoons carry over from the prior wind ensemble.[13] To a certain extent, of course, the symbolism of this contrast is rooted in convention, since by Weber's time trumpets and timpani already had a long history as military symbols, and one can easily think of precedents in which woodwind sonority is associated with feminine attributes.[14]

More fundamental to the central dramatic conflict in *Euryanthe* is a general tendency to exploit the contrast of woodwind and brass sonorities as an analogy for the opposition of virtue and evil throughout the opera, a feature that has been pointed out in prior discussions of the opera.[15] The numbers that deal most directly with the love of Adolar and Euryanthe (Nos. 2, 5, and 12) all feature the woodwinds prominently, either in extensive introductory ritornelli (as in Nos. 5 and 12) or in instrumental interludes (No. 2). At several points in Act III a woodwind ensemble briefly stands out to underscore aspects of the heroes' love: in the ritornello immediately before the Duetto No. 15 as Adolar considers his past love for Euryanthe; later in the same piece as Euryanthe

---

[13] A subtle rhythmic nuance also serves to differentiate the feminine charms of the women from the more martial knights, since the woodwind ritornellos ('dolce e con grazia') inserted between the phrases of the women's chorus are 1½ measures long, thereby shifting the principal beat within the measure from beat one (m. 25) to beat 3 (m. 26, 27) to beat one again (m. 29); in contrast, the timpani and brass ritornellos between the comparable phrases in the knight's chorus are each but one measure long, thereby ensuring that the male chorus constantly stresses the first beat in each measure and confirming the impression of greater strength. As Daniel Heartz points out, a comparable technique for contrasting masculine and feminine characters through conflict of metric accent occurs in the opening *Duettino* of *Le nozze di Figaro*. See 'Constructing *Le nozze di Figaro*, *JRMA* 1 (1987): 90.

[14] For example: the woodwind sonorities that accompany the Countess in 'Porgi amor' and Susanna in 'Deh vienni' in *Le nozze di Figaro*; the lovely oboe solo that is the sounding equivalent of Florestan's delirious vision of his liberating angel Leonore in his great aria in the second act of *Fidelio* and in the subsequent *Melodrama*; or the introductory ritornello to Agathe's Scena ed aria No. 8 in *Freischütz*.

[15] Wolfgang Sandner, *Die Klarinette bei Carl Maria von Weber* (Wiesbaden, 1971), pp. 190–1.

offers her last breath as a blessing for Adolar (mm. 30–7, 'Mein letzter Hauch ist Segen für dich, mein letzter Herzschlag dir geweiht!'); and in Finale 3, as the King reports that Euryanthe had 'died' with a benediction for Adolar upon her lips (mm. 36–42, 'Dich segnend ist das treuste Herz gebrochen'). The woodwind sonority in the first movement of the Act II Finale may also be heard as a symbol for Euryanthe, whom the chorus greets and praises; similarly, only woodwinds accompany the joyful recognition of Adolar by his former vassals in the third act immediately before No. 24 (mm. 109–21, 'Heil Adolar!'). More generally, the prominent woodwind sonorities in the Introduzione and No. 9 reflect an innocent state of mind untroubled by the knowledge of evil. In contrast, the lower brass instruments colour the music given to the villains and the most sinister moments in the opera. Trombones are featured in Lysiart's challenge to Adolar at the start of No. 4 and his public humiliation of Euryanthe in the second-act finale ('Mein König'); they are also briefly present in Euryanthe's outburst immediately before No. 7 when she realizes that she has broken her oath to Adolar. The bass trombone is used again in the music accompanying the giant snake before and during the Scena No. 16. Four horns inform the sonority of both revenge arias, Eglantine's No. 8 and Lysiart's No. 10.[16]

The symbolism of the woodwind/brass dichotomy is most apparent at the change of scenery in the second act, poetically and visually the most extreme juxtaposition of the two opposed spheres in the course of the opera; the stormy nocturnal setting for the villains' revenge Duetto No. 11 is followed by the brightly lit hall in which Adolar expresses his expectant reverie in No. 12. To underscore this complete shift, the 'sinister' orchestral complement for No. 11 (2 oboes, 4 horns, 3 trombones, strings) yields to a radically different, 'virtuous', ensemble in the introductory ritornello to No. 12, whose first seventeen measures are played only by instruments absent from the duet (2 flutes, 2 clarinets, 2 bassoons). Of course, co-ordinated with this contrast of orchestration is a change in dynamic level and the important tonal shift from a sinister 'sharp' key to a virtuous 'flat' key. The draft of the opera provides one interesting glimpse into Weber's thinking at this crucial spot. On the draft of the first section of the Duetto on page 29 Weber made a list of the instruments and the number of staves to be allocated to each in the full score: 'Ob. / Fag. / 2 C: / 3 Trb / 4 Quar / 2 V'; this is Weber's shorthand for 2 oboes, 2 bassoons, 4 horns, 3 trombones,

---

[16] Naturally, the tendency to employ the lower brass instruments as a sonorous metaphor for the sinister elements in the opera is not operative in those pieces (No. 4, No. 20, No. 24, and the Schlußchor of the Act III Finale) where the full orchestra with expanded brass complement is used to mark the climactic final piece in a unit of scenic structure.

strings, and 2 voice parts. In a rare change of mind, the composer later crossed out the indication for bassoons. A plausible interpretation of this alteration is that Weber at first conceived the instrumentation in terms of a dark, low sonority in which bassoons would be appropriate, but later decided to omit them in order to maximize the contrast with the planned scoring of No. 12, which does employ the bassoons. This revision thus suggests that contrast of sonority rather than absolute sonority *per se* was in fact the guiding principle at this juncture in the opera.

(b) Melodic and rhythmic oppositions
Contrasts of rhythm and melodic contour also provide a basis for 'characteristic' opposition. Consider, for example, the relationship of No. 19 and No. 20, two pieces that portray one of the most conspicuous reversals of mood and situation in the course of the opera. Here the tremendous affective swing from Euryanthe's abject despair ('Laßt mich hier in Ruh' erblassen') to her ecstatic hope at the prospect of reunion with Adolar ('Zu ihm! zu ihm!') is conveyed by a number of obvious stylistic oppositions: minor mode versus major mode; slow tempo versus fast tempo; quiet dynamic versus loud dynamic. Another important opposition lies in the contrast of melodic profiles, as No. 19 features falling, stepwise contour, whereas No. 20 relies on rising, arpeggiated melody. Both of these types may ultimately be rooted in topoi, since the triadic melody of No. 20, coupled with its dotted rhythms and full brass complement, strongly suggests traditional heroic-martial imagery, while it is possible to relate the melody at the start of No. 19 to an eighteenth-century *figura*, the *Subjectum Catabatum*, associated by J. G. Walther with depictions of things 'vile, contemptible and worthy of scorn'.[17]

Melodic and rhythmic oppositions in a polyphonic texture may also work as symbols of characterization. Thus at two points in the Act II Finale Euryanthe and Lysiart, suffering victim and gleeful victor respectively, are pointedly set as opposite poles through contrasts of rhythm and melodic direction. In the A-major Larghetto movement he is distinctly set apart from the sustained lines of the suffering Euryanthe through an athletic, arpeggiated style of writing that expresses his glee at his triumph over Adolar (mm. 338–45, 'Triumph! mein Flehen ist erhört'), and in the subsequent C-major Allegro section Lysiart is again treated as Euryanthe's antipode, as his contour moves consistently in contrary motion to that of the heroine (cf. especially mm. 422–39). With respect to these two last-named passages, Weber's draft reveals that in both instances the composer first drafted Euryanthe's melody,

---

[17] Johann Gottfried Walther, *Musikalisches Lexicon* (Leipzig, 1832; reprint Kassel and Basle, 1953), p. 148, s.v. 'Catabasis'.

the basic determinant for the *Affekt* of the moment, to which he then added Lysiart's voice as an opposed counterpoint; the parts for Adolar, the King, and chorus were then filled in around the basic two-voice framework. This dialectical process seems to represent a basic impulse in Weber's compositional approach, one that we shall observe again at later points in the present study.

(c) Textural contrasts

The contrast between chordal and contrapuntal styles is also used symbolically. Thus the Euryanthe–Adolar Duetto No. 13 is set throughout in completely synchronous declamation, a conventional symbol for unanimity of feeling; in contrast, the Agitato movement of their Duetto No. 15, in which the two characters are completely estranged, is largely set as two rhythmically independent melodic lines. In a similar vein, the ubiquitous chordal style of choral singing that predominates in the opera and that Wagner criticized for its proximity to a well-trained glee club,[18] is a convention for expressing collective, communal sentiments of the *vox populi*, whereas the more contrapuntal, imitative style in No. 4 ('Vermessenes Beginnen') may be heard as emblematic of the knight's confused reaction to the start of the wager.[19]

With these principles in mind it is necessary to criticize the last movement of the first-act finale ('Fröhliche Klänge') for its lack of 'dramatic truth'. In the middle section of this movement (mm. 215–40), which was borrowed from the birthday cantata for the Duchess Amalie of Zweibrücken (J. 283) that Weber wrote in 1821, three of the four soloists, Euryanthe, Eglantine, and Lysiart, sing different texts expressing quite different emotions. On the one hand, their texts are all sung simultaneously, thereby making it impossible to understand them, and on the other hand there is no attempt to differentiate musically the conflicting points of view; the major-mode, compound-metre bucolic music of this section really only fits Euryanthe's joy at the prospect of seeing Adolar again. In the cantata, this homophonic style had been justified by giving all of the soloists the same text in praise of the Duchess. The fact that this piece was, by many accounts, one of the most popular pieces in the opera thus provides an ironic commentary on the importance of 'truth' in popular acceptance of dramatic music.[20]

---

[18] See Wagner's criticism in his late essay 'Über das Opern-Dichten und -Komponieren im besonderen', *GSD* x. 164.

[19] See Amadeus Wendt's review, *BamZ* 3 (1826): 21.

[20] According to Julius Benedict, op. cit. ch. 6 n. 7 above, p. 94, the closing section of the Act I Finale 'excited the public almost to frenzy'.

(d) Voice types and vocal style

Voice types and vocal style also play an important part in defining character in *Euryanthe*. As in the other areas that we have covered, certain features of their treatment are rooted in convention, but the force of characterization in the experience of the opera ultimately turns on sharply drawn dichotomies. Consider, for example, the ways in which the four principal characters are differentiated. Euryanthe and Eglantine are without question both 'first sopranos' according to Weber's categories of voice types,[21] but their contrasted treatments reflect the sharp contrasts of their personalities, much in the same way that Pamina and the Queen of the Night are distinguished in *Die Zauberflöte*. On the one hand, Eglantine is given extensive coloratura in her principal solo, the Scena ed aria No. 8, and in the Duetto No. 11 with Lysiart; the association of coloratura with a diabolical female of course reaches back to numerous eighteenth-century precedents, including the Queen of the Night and Elvira in Winter's *Das unterbrochene Opferfest*. Euryanthe, on the other hand, makes much less use of coloratura. The only significant florid writing for her part occurs in the concluding movement of the Act I Finale, and the fact that this piece was borrowed from the cantata J. 283 at an advanced stage in the composition of the opera suggests that Euryanthe's part had originally been planned without any coloratura, in order to accentuate her spiritual distance from Eglantine.

The vocal contrasts between the two principal male characters underscore their different personalities even more distinctly. The sensitive and lyrical Adolar is a 'first tenor', a voice type that Weber and German convention associated with youthful characters , the so-called 'Jugendhelden' and 'ersten Liebhabern'.[22] Behind this type lay youthful figures like Don Ottavio and Tamino, and it is important to understand that at the start of the opera Adolar, though already distinguished on the battlefield, is still an inexperienced and idealistic youth who must learn certain bitter realities of life in the course of the opera.[23] In sharp contrast, the worldly-wise, cynical, and presumably older, villain Lysiart is cast as a 'first bass', for whom evil characters like Pizarro in *Fidelio* and the Incan warrior Mafferu in Winter's *Opferfest*, not to mention Caspar in *Freischütz*, provided ample precedent. Again, style also serves to differen-

---

[21] *Sämtliche Schriften*, p. 40.

[22] Ibid., p. 40. For an overview of the voice and character types in German romantic opera see also Bernd Göpfert, *Stimmtypen und Rollencharakter in der deutschen Oper von 1815–1848* (Wiesbaden, 1977).

[23] The recurrent criticisms of Adolar's 'non-heroic' character are accurate but fail to observe that this is a significant point of the opera; Adolar must and does outgrow his youthful impetuosity and egocentricity in order to merit the love and fidelity of Euryanthe and his vassals.

tiate the two males, for Adolar's music is primarily lyrical and nearly devoid of coloratura, whereas Lysiart is frequently characterized by jagged contours and large leaps, a legacy of French *opéra comique* villains.[24] Like his female counterpart Eglantine, he also employs coloratura in his two most important pieces, the Scena ed aria No. 10 and the Duetto No. 11.[25] To a certain extent Lysiart's vocal style also reflects the cynicism and irony that colour his view of the world. In the opening scene (No. 4, mm. 32–5) he forsees Adolar reduced to a touring minstrel and mocks him through a leaping grace-note figure perhaps to caricature the sound of the zither that will become Adolar's sole companion after he loses the wager ('Wie schön wirst du mit Kranz und Zither wallen'), and in the second-act finale, his claim of having won Euryanthe's hand is set to an elaborate flourish on the word 'schönste' (mm. 190–2).

2.4. *Character as interruption or surprise*

The interruption of an established pattern and the non-fulfilment of an expectation are other means for the definition of 'character' in music. The premiss here is that musical surprises furnish equivalents to abrupt changes in mood and situation and serve to call attention to details of text and action that otherwise might be lost in music that flows along in a more predictable fashion. Such surprises potentially include abrupt shifts of dynamic level and the disruption of periodic phrase structure.

Especially important in *Euryanthe* are the deceptive cadences and other types of unexpected harmonic and tonal motion—unexpected, that is, according to the norms of the early nineteenth-century style—that frequently connote sudden and unforseen turns in plot and mood, as a few examples readily demonstrate. In the Scene und Chor No. 4 Lysiart's taunting provokes an angry, nearly uncontrolled response from Adolar that veers abruptly from the dominant of B-flat major to D-flat major (m. 37, 'Vermessener frohlocke nicht'). Euryanthe's attempt to reassure Adolar of her fidelity in the first scene of Act III is answered angrily by Adolar, and this abrupt shift of mood elicits a correspondingly brusque dynamic, rhythmic, and harmonic twist at mm. 85–86 (C^{b7}–e_4^6). Eglantine's interruption of the wedding procession with her delirious vision

---

[24] Warrack, op. cit. introduction n. 1 above, pp. 225–7.

[25] At first glance the use of coloratura for bass voice seems to contradict Weber's own earlier opinion, expressed in an 1815 review of the bass Siebert (*Sämtliche Schriften*, p. 64), that virtuosic coloratura was unnatural for the bass and best left to the soprano and tenor. It is, however, the very unnaturalness and excessiveness of the coloratura for both Lysiart and Eglantine that helps characterize them as deceitful and villainous characters, whereas the virtuous characters sing in a dramatically more 'truthful' (i.e. declamatory) style.

of Emma (Act III, scene v) undercuts the expected D-major cadence of the march with a turn toward B minor. The King's sudden arrival at the beginning of the Act III Finale interrupts the confrontation between Adolar and Lysiart and therefore entails a jolting shift from D major to a fortissimo C-minor triad.

2.5. *Music as a sign for physical motion or psychological change*

The fact that music regulates the experience of time makes it a particularly powerful medium to suggest various qualities of physical motion or emotional progression. For these different types of progression, music has at its disposal a number of elements of characterization. For example, a gradual change in dynamic level is an obvious way to suggest the approach or retreat of a person or group, a specialized case of *imitatio*. But other devices, such as acceleration of tempo, progressive foreshortening of phrase structure and melodic pattern, and rising progressions in the bass or upper voice may also function as more abstract signs for the approach of someone or something out of the distance; conversely, the liquidation of melody, as at the respective conclusions of the Waltz in the *Freischütz* and Schumann's *Papillons*, may be taken as a symbol for removal into the distance.[26]

Physical movement is featured at important transitional passages in *Euryanthe*, and in each case several musical elements combine to depict motion. The transition between Eglantine's No. 8 and the start of the Act I Finale uses rising sequence and quickening of phrase rhythm to suggest the approach of Lysiart's entourage. Eglantine's breathless emergence from Emma's crypt at the start of the second scene of Act II correlates physical motion with a rising bass progression. The transition between No. 12 and No. 13, during which Euryanthe runs into Adolar's arms, depicts physical motion through a nexus of musical devices: a rising four-note motive that grows out of Adolar's aria ('Sie ist mir nah!'); a bass progression that ascends chromatically from a-flat to c; progressive upward extension of the topmost line (e-flat^2–g-flat^2–b-flat^2–e-flat^3–g-flat^3–a^3); rhythmic compression and acceleration of tempo; and a crescendo. The transition between No. 17 and No. 18 similarly coordinates crescendo, incremental instrumentation, progressively faster rate of rhythmic activity and registral ascent in the accompanying strings to suggest two types of progression: the approach of the royal hunting party and the progression from night to day at daybreak. A different kind of motion—aimless wandering—is suggested at two places in the opera by a confused maze of chromatic harmony. In the *Vision* the quotation of Emma's words 'Getrennt von Udo, irr' ich durch die

[26] See Manfred Hermann Schmid, *Musik als Abbild* (Tutzing, 1981), pp. 11–26.

Nächte', is set as a slowly descending, chromatic chain of sequences to depict Emma's restless state.[27] In Euryanthe's Scena e cavatina No. 17, the description of Adolar's future inability to locate the precise place in the forest where he had left her ('und findet kaum die Stätte mehr') is set as another kind of maze, a rapid, colouristic chromatic sequence.

At a more purely psychological level, many of these same techniques stand in the service of portraying emotional progression. Thus, the use of rising progressions in transitional and modulatory passages may also suggest rising tension or excitement. The transition between No. 12 and No. 13 represents not only a physical approximation, but presumably also the quickening of adrenalin in the two long-separated lovers. Euryanthe's sudden remorse in the recitative immediately following her narration of the *Vision* is set to a rising sequence of diminished-seventh chords, thereby suggesting a heightening of anxiety over the betrayal of Adolar's secret. The modulatory middle sections of the two large ensembles, No. 4 and No. 24, are set to rising sequences, perhaps to signify the increasing tension of these two Adolar–Lysiart confrontations. In the D-flat-major Allegro of the Act II Finale, the chorus's anxiety at the possibility of Euryanthe's faithlessness (mm. 130–4, 'Weh! Euryanthe! Was hast du begangen?') and Adolar's later anxious questioning of Euryanthe (mm. 240–4, 'Mein reiner Engel kannst zu zagen?') are similarly set to rising bass progressions. In a different vein, the relative levels of harmonic tension in the transitional measures at the end of the Andante con moto movement of Lysiart's Scena ed aria No. 10 may also be seen as a barometer for psychological progression. As Lysiart's thoughts turn from Euryanthe's innocence and fidelity to his own hopeless plight and despair sets in, an orchestral motive in the lower strings becomes progressively less stable, moving from G major (m. 97), through C minor (m. 100) and F minor (m. 103), to diminished-seventh chords (m. 105, 110).

In Weber's approach modulation also plays an extremely important role in tracing psychological progression. The premise here is that tonal stasis is appropriate to psychological or emotional stasis, whereas modulation signifies psychological change; return to the tonic after modulation points up emotional equivalences between the opening section and later sections of the piece. This point was emphasized in the Lobe–Weber 'conversation', during which Weber is alleged to have remarked that he not only sought 'to find the corresponding main key for every principal mood' but also 'to follow faithfully every modified stirring therein with

[27] A similar progression in the opening ritornello of Lysiart's Scena ed aria No. 10 (mm. 18–20) perhaps serves to underscore the fact that he is standing in front of Emma's crypt.

modulation',[28] as well as in his letter of 1815 to Friedrich Wieck, in which he criticized the young composer for his failure to co-ordinate poetic content and modulation.[29]

As an example of the correlation between harmonic progression and mood, let us consider the first thirty-five measures of the cabaletta of Eglantine's Scena ed aria No. 8 (mm. 60–94), whose shifting poetic rhetoric is largely delineated by harmonic means. The opening line of poetry, an outcry of indignant jealousy (mm. 60–5, 'Er konnte mich um sie verschmähn!'), is stated twice over a progression that establishes the tonic (I–iv–ii$_{5\atop3}^6$–V); as we shall see below, the minor tinges in the subdominant and supertonic harmonies are relevant to Eglantine's sinister character. The second line introduces a rhetorical question (mm. 66–71, 'Und ich sollt' es ertragen?') that is set over a dominant harmony, a traditional musical equivalent for questioning. This question is followed by another question in the third and fourth verses, which shift the mood from anger to self-pity ('In herbem Leid soll ich vergehn | In meinen Blüthentagen?'). Accordingly the dominant does not resolve, but veers towards C-sharp minor (mm. 72–6), as the minor mode supplies a conventional metaphor for Eglantine's sorrow; once again, the question is punctuated by a half-cadence on the dominant of C-sharp minor at measure 79. Naturally, the poetic shift is also reflected by melodic and rhythmic means as well, since the more cantabile style of singing for this second period stands in contrast to the declamatory vocal style and pronounced martial rhythms of the first period and thus also contributes to the softening of mood during this brief excursion into self-pity. The third period, set to the fifth, sixth, and seventh verses, continues the basic image of a wronged and suffering Eglantine (mm. 80–6, 'Er hörte kalt der Liebe Fleh'n | Mein Herz so bang so todeswund | Weh! Weh!'), and accordingly it prolongs the 'sorrowful' key of C-sharp minor through diminished-seventh harmony, which throughout the opera is used as a symbol for grief. With the last line of the poem, however, Eglantine casts off her own sorrow and commits herself to revenge (mm. 87–94, 'Drum stürz auch all' sein Glück zu Grund'). The reappearance of the E-major triad at precisely this moment is thus a twofold symbol, for on the one hand in its capacity as tonic it marks her 'resolution' to action, and on the other hand as the key most closely identified with her it signifies the re-emergence of her true, vengeful character as well.

---

[28] Lobe, op. cit. ch. 2 n. 6 above, p. 118.
[29] *Sämtliche Schriften*, p. 176.

2.6. 'Charakter' as a breaking-away from norms

As Carl Dahlhaus points out in a recent discussion of Hegel's criticisms of the *Freischütz*, *Charakter*, especially that which is deemed to be particularly 'realistic' and thus offensive to traditional precepts of absolute musical beauty, often results from the stretching or bending of commonly accepted compositional-technical norms.[30] This principle can be extended in various directions to understand the 'truth' of a particular musical idea. For example, harmonic progressions that seem to violate the norms of 'textbook' harmony or offend the sense of the 'beautiful' may function as symbols for the sinister. Euryanthe's foreboding at the start of the Duetto No. 7 is set to a decidedly unorthodox chord progression (V–iv–I–♭II–V–i). In two of the most vitriolic and vengeful moments of the opera, Eglantine's Aria No. 8 and the Duetto No. 11, highly aberrant progressions may be taken as metaphors for uncontrolled hatred; in the former it is the progression from a prolonged V⁷/E to a first-inversion F-major triad (mm. 105–11), whereas in the latter it is a progression from vii°⁷/B minor to another first-inversion F-major triad at m. 124. Another instance of aberration of norms for expressive purpose is the chromatic contamination of the major mode to signify spiritual or moral corruption. In *Euryanthe* a number of passages strongly associated with sinister elements—the *Vision*, the cabaletta of Eglantine's No. 8, Lysiart's D-major address to Eglantine in the second scene of Act II ('Zur Sühne beut dir Forest seine Hand'), and the fast section of the revenge duet No. 11—are set in the major mode but entail strong minor inflections to betray the true colours of the situation. The 'resolution' of Emma's plight at the end of the opera in part turns on transformation of her highly chromatic music into a 'pure' diatonic version. The chromatic inflections in Euryanthe's prayer in the A-major Larghetto movement of the Act II Finale perhaps also suggest the sinister trap into which she has fallen.

The Hochzeitmarsch No. 23 offers a particularly good example of the ways in which a well-established type, a festive march, is distorted in order to cast a light on the unholy union of Lysiart and Eglantine; as we have already seen from his letter of 11 November 1822, the composer wished to make this passage as 'schauerlich' as possible. Thus the march's modal ambivalence—Weber in fact originally composed the march on page 79 of the composition draft with a key signature of D minor and treated the major-mode inflections as accidentals—is consistent with other portrayals of villainy in the opera and belies the traditional expectation for major-mode joy at a wedding ceremony. The curiously uneven and unpredictable rhythm of the march—it resolves

---

[30] Dahlhaus, *Realism in Nineteenth-Century Music*, p. 36.

itself into no convincingly regular phrase structure—seems particularly inappropriate for a piece that should regulate bodily motion, but in this case admirably suggests Eglantine's interior struggle, which of course eventually interrupts the cortège altogether.[31] And the harshness with which the piece is scored reflects the forced and unnatural gaiety of the situation.[32]

More generally, it is possible to see any deviation from established norms as a potential contributor to characterization, even in cases where the deviation is by no means a 'distortion' of or departure from good taste. For example, the character of the opening movement of the Act II Finale, in which the assembled knights greet Euryanthe ('Leuchtend füllt die Königshallen'), seems to reside in a reversal of expectations about voice-orchestra relationships. Whereas the norm in Weber's style is for the orchestra to accompany the dominating vocal parts, at the start of this movement the chorus cedes melodic primacy to the orchestra. The implication of this reversal is clear, for it is the woodwind-dominated orchestra that in this case represents Euryanthe's 'Wunderpracht' that so enraptures the chorus that greets her. Perhaps significantly, Weber seems to have abandoned his usual compositional routine in this case as well, for the draft of this movement begins not, as is customary, at the point where the voices enter, but instead with the opening ritornello. The complementary relationship between voice and orchestra in Euryanthe's Cavatina No. 5 presents another instance where greater than usual interdependence of voice and orchestra in the maintenance of melodic coherence seems to reflect a particular poetic image; we shall return to this piece in the next chapter for a fuller discussion.

2.7. Defined symbols and internal allusion

Lastly, the character of a musical phenomenon may also accrue from reference to a symbol that is arbitrarily defined within the context of the work. That is, once an element or set of elements is established and accepted, for whatever reason, as a symbol for a particular kind of expression, it may be used at will as a symbol in other contexts.

[31] In the manuscript libretto *Web*. Cl. II A g 5, approximately contemporary with the Hochzeitmarsch's date of composition, Eglantine is described at this point as 'Todtblaß', moving in the procession 'Mit Geberden des Schmerzes und der Verwirrung'.

[32] Amadeus Wendt called attention to the excellent demonstration of *Charakteristik* in the march, 'in which are fused in the most masterful manner external brilliance and internal conflict. The screeching instruments contribute to this; penetrating dissonances and a heavy rhythm announce "das Frevlerpaar"'. *BamZ* 3 (1826): 54. See also A. B. Marx, *Die Lehre von der musikalischen Komposition*, iv (Leipzig, 1847), pp. 557–8; and Alfred Sandt, 'Karl Maria von Webers Opern in ihrer Instrumentation', (Ph.D. dissertation, Frankfurt am Main, 1921), p. 212.

Because they recur in different pieces, such symbols contribute to the unity of the entire work, either by giving a character a specific type of music or by pointing up similarities of situation and mood at different points in the opera. Leitmotifs are obvious manifestations of such arbitrary symbols, and key character can be specified in this way as well. Close attention to detail in the opera suggests a number of more subtle ways in which arbitrarily defined symbols are at work.

For instance, certain melodic-rhythmic figures, too nondescript in themselves to be considered classical 'Leitmotifs', serve to define internal consistencies within the work. Throughout *Euryanthe* the diminished-seventh chord is used—perhaps overused—in passages of sinister content; of course, this harmony had already become a cliché for the representation of horror in the French Revolutionary operas of the 1790s and is thus another expressive topos inherited by Weber. However, one particular manifestation of the harmony, an arpeggiated descent through the chord, seems to be marked for rather specific use as a symbol for unbounded grief; first associated with Eglantine, Emma and Lysiart, in the course of the work this figure is transferred to the virtuous couple as they come to suffer the consequences of the villains' treachery. Thus it first appears in the Euryanthe–Eglantine recitative following No. 5 as Eglantine recalls the humiliation of her family and her father's flight ('Mich tödtet die Erinn'rung'). It next occurs as the opening orchestral motive in Eglantine's No. 6 (mm. 1–2), where it is explicitly associated with her protestations of unbounded sorrow ('O mein Leid ist unermessen'). In the ritornello that introduces the cabaletta of the Scena ed aria No. 8 (m. 58) the gesture is heard at the same pitch-class level, but now intensified through placement in a higher register and rhythmic diminution, perhaps because Eglantine truly is overcome with a sense of misery ('Ich weiß daß ich ganz elend bin'); in the course of the aria Eglantine sings another version of the topos (mm. 102–3, 'und ich sollt es ertragen!'). Lysiart's torment at the knowledge that he can never win Euryanthe's love evokes the figure in the Scena to his No. 10 (m. 47, 'Ihr Felsen stürzt auf mich hernieder'). The reversal of fortunes in the second-act finale shifts the figure from the villains to the heroes. Near the beginning of the finale Lysiart answers Adolar's defence of Euryanthe with a sung version of the topos, as he threatens the loving couple with a promise of proof (mm. 128–30, 'Beweise bring' ich dar'). The figure is next heard in the orchestra at precisely the point at which Adolar is convinced of Euryanthe's infidelity and concedes defeat (mm. 291–4, 'Vollende nicht, nimm' alles, alles hin, mein Leben mit!'). When Adolar's vassals attempt to encourage him with their show of loyalty, the disconsolate Adolar vents his grief by singing a variant of the figure with an appoggiatura before the final pitch (mm. 404–7, 'O laßt, kein Auge soll mich sehen'), and so too does Euryanthe with her last unheeded protestation of innocence near the end of the finale (mm. 521–4, 'Hört Niemand denn der Unschuld Fleh'n'). In the recitative at the start of the third act (m. 50) the figure appears once again in the orchestra as a symbol for Adolar's anger toward Euryanthe. Finally, Euryanthe's sudden collapse in the coda of her Aria con coro No. 20 (mm. 72–5) unleashes the figure in the orchestra as a sign of the hunters' anguish at her apparent demise.

In similar fashion, Lysiart and more generally his conflict with Adolar are associated throughout the opera with a characteristic figure that also approximates the status of a leitmotif, a rising step-wise gesture associated with the sound of cellos and basses in unison, occasionally doubled at the octave by the rest of the string complement. The first appearance of this figure in Act I, scene i coincides with Lysiart's agitation following Adolar's Romanza No. 2 (Ex. 4a) and the bulk of the ensuing recitative, during which Lysiart provokes Adolar into the wager, is dominated by the sonority of unison lower strings (Ex. 4b). At the very outset of the Scene und Chor No. 4 Lysiart's proposal of the terms of the wager is accompanied by fortissimo unison strings in a chromatic ascending stepwise gesture (Ex. 4c). The extended *tempo di mezzo* of his Scena ed aria No. 10 entails a succession of rising unison figures that trace psychological development: from a quiet, slow gesture associated with his despair at the impossibility of attaining Euryanthe's favour (Ex. 4d), to a faster one in sixteenth-notes as he decides to wreck Adolar's happiness (Ex. 4e), to the continuous thirty-seconds that accompany his definitive decision to devote himself to the powers of revenge (Ex. 4f). Lysiart's claim of victory in the Act II Finale ('Die Lande Adolars sind mein!') also unleashes a powerful unison motive, whose rising chromatic motion recalls the start of the wager at the beginning of No. 4. Dominating the D-flat major Allegro movement of the finale, this motive seems to function primarily as a symbol for the wager, an interpretation suggested not only by its association with certain passages of text, but also by the fact that it disappears at the very point where Lysiart convinces Adolar of Euryanthe's infidelity by invoking Emma's secret (Ex. 4g). In the third act Lysiart's anger is again underscored at two points by ascending gestures in the unison strings. First, when Adolar steps forward in his armour to threaten the villains with revenge, Lysiart orders the knights to seize and imprison the interloper (Ex. 4h). Second, Eglantine's delirious revelations swell Lysiart's rage past the breaking point, and he kills her; for the only time Lysiart sings this final variant of his gesture in unison with the fortissimo strings, perhaps a sign that he himself has now been overpowered by the rage that had driven him from the start (Ex. 4i).

Ex. 4 Orchestral figures associated with Lysiart.
 (*a*) Recitative, Act I, scene i.
 (*b*) Recitative, Act I, scene i.
 (*c*) Start of No. 4.
 (*d*) Lysiart's Scena ed aria No. 10.
 (*e*) Scena ed aria No. 10.
 (*f*) Scena ed aria No. 10.
 (*g*) Act II Finale, No. 14
 (*h*) Act III, scene v
 (*i*) Act III, Finale No. 25.

Another gesture typically associated with either of the two villains is rapid triplet motion. The most obvious instance of this is offered by the Duetto No. 11, which incorporates a number of prominent triplet figures, ranging from scalar motion and neighbour-note figures of the first section to the throbbing repeated triplets and wildly leaping ejaculations of the second. Menacing triplet figures in other passages in the opera may be heard in relation to this central portrayal of evil. In the first act Euryanthe's sudden and overpowering remorse at having broken her oath to Adolar in the recitative immediately before No. 7—a premonition of the evil that she has unleashed—elicits a massive sonority for sustaining winds and brass (the three trombones are included on the word 'Eid'), to which the strings add a fortissimo unison triplet neighbour-note figure. In the third act the approach of the giant snake in the arioso before No. 16 is signalled by rapid scales in triplets in the basses and cellos. Eglantine's delirium in the third act presents a distorted version of the leaping triplet figure of the Duetto No. 11, a symbol for the dark night into which she herself has fallen. Finally, upon learning of Euryanthe's apparent demise in the forest Eglantine's diabolical exultation is again set to the throbbing fortissimo triplet motion of the duet.

At least one gesture stands out as a referent for more positive elements in the opera, a cadential figure built from two-note slurs that descend step-wise from the sixth scale degree that is associated with love. In the Duetto No. 7, the figure appears as Euryanthe is melted by Eglantine's apparent affection (Ex. 5a). In No. 12, Adolar is deliciously tormented by the expectation of Euryanthe's arrival (Ex. 5b). Love is obviously the topic of the Duetto No. 13 (Ex. 5c), and in No. 20 Euryanthe is overwhelmed by her emotions at the thought of being rejoined with Adolar (Ex. 5d).

Whether Weber consciously planned these figures as unifying devices or whether they arose as instinctive reactions to similar dramatic situations is a question for which the preserved drafts provide typically little information. One revision, however, hints that Weber was aware of at least one of them. As originally drafted, the first section of the Eglantine–Lysiart Duetto No. 11 concluded with a slurred cadential figure closely related to the one associated with love (Ex. 6a). Perhaps recognizing that love plays no role in the villains' alliance, Weber later replaced the cadence with a new gesture that itself is more closely related to the falling diminished-seventh gestures that we have previously associated with expressions of pain (Ex. 6b); this is appropriate since the relevant text refers quite explicitly to the villains' torment ('Enden soll der Seele Qual'). Put simply, Weber substituted a suitable topos for an unsuitable one.

Ex. 5. Cadence figures associated with love.
  (a) Euryanthe–Eglantine Duetto No. 7.
  (b) Adolar's Aria No. 12.
  (c) Euryanthe–Adolar Duetto No. 13.
  (d) Euryanthe's Aria No. 20.

The compositional record also suggests another principle at work in the opera, the matching of sonorities in comparable dramatic situations. The draft for the introductory ritornello of Adolar's No. 12, notated on p. 56 immediately below the conclusion of the Lysiart–Eglantine duet and therefore some time after the body of Adolar's aria proper, is an extraordinarily detailed short score with numerous indications for orchestration. Measures 18–29 were originally drafted as a three-voice texture with melody for B-flat clarinet accompanied by an unspecified bass voice (presumably the bassoon of the final version) and obbligato middle voice moving in constant sixteenth-notes for '2do'; the transposition required of this part can only imply the second clarinet in B-flat. Later this clarinet part was replaced by a similar line for solo viola, the only use of a stringed instrument during the ritornello. Clearly, Weber's original plan was to score all of the ritornello in such a way as to 'negate' the scoring of the preceding Duetto by using only instruments that had not been heard in No. 11. What led him to break this pattern at measure 18 by introducing the viola, an instrument that is used in the duet? One possible explanation is that he wished to match the ritornello of Adolar's aria to the most comparable moment in the opera, the opening ritornello for Euryanthe's Cavatina No. 5. Like No. 12, No. 5 depicts a lover's quiet reverie, and the language and conceits

Ex. 6. Cadential phrase in the Eglantine–Lysiart Duetto No. II.
   (a) Original version
   (b) Final version

(a)

(b)

of both pieces are entirely analogous in that in both cases the protagonist hopes that Nature will convey some news of the 'distant beloved'. Euryanthe's cavatina is introduced by a lengthy ritornello that features not only the 'virtuous' woodwinds (a symbol in both her and Adolar's arias for the 'Lüften' to which they both eagerly attend?) but also two obbligato solo violoncellos. The obbligato solo viola in the analogous ritornello of Adolar's aria thus strengthens the bond between these two moments. Put another way, considerations for unity of the entire work in this instance seem to have taken precedence over considerations for a more local contrast.

3. CONCLUSIONS

The foregoing criteria for 'truth' and 'Charakter' in dramatic music are by no means mutually exclusive—indeed, in a style predicated on the notion of *Totaleffekt* their potential for overlap tends to reinforce the expressive determinacy of the music—and the model offered here does not claim to be anything more than an attempt to understand the means of expression in a single work. A model of this type is, however, necessary if we are to begin to understand the criteria that guided Weber's compositional choices and at the same time attune ourselves to the communicative elements in the work, and one advantage of the present model is that it can be applied to all levels within the work, ranging from relationships that span the entire opera to the succession of detail within pieces.

With respect to the former, the consistent association of certain musical elements—orchestral sonorities, melodic-rhythmic types, vocal styles—with certain emotions, situations, or characters, produces a number of consistencies of characterization that together give the work as a whole a particular identity, the concept that Weber called 'Kolorit' or 'Farbengebung'. At the global level, therefore, elements of characterization are largely synonymous with elements of unification, and in this light it is instructive to consider the relationship between the chronology of composition outlined in Chapter VI and the elements of characterization, especially in the earlier stages of composition, where the composer was more or less free to roam throughout the libretto and select pieces that spoke to him.[33] For one thing, the order of the earliest pieces, those composed up through the summer of 1822, suggests that at the outset of composition Weber was concerned with establishing the primary musical colours for characterizing the opera's four principal spheres: the love-filled world of the youthful, *sensible* troubadour Adolar (No. 12); the demonic realm of the villains (No. 11); the ceremonial domain of medieval chivalry (the Introduzione Nos. 1–4); and Emma's ethereal spirit world (*Vision*). The chronology also suggests a second, related principle that can be observed at numerous levels in the opera, namely, a dialectic of extreme opposition as a way to define the principal dramatic threads and musical colours. This is manifest at first in the juxtaposition of Adolar's Aria No. 12 and the villains' Duetto No. 11, and later in the concentration on the opposition of Euryanthe and Eglantine in Nos. 6, 7, 20, 19, 8, and 5. That Weber started at the middle of the opera with No. 12 and No. 11 seems particularly significant for the large-scale planning of the opera. These back-to-back numbers represent the most complete and unmediated juxtaposition of musical and dramatic opposites in the entire opera, and by composing them first Weber was

[33] In the later stages of work, from the start of 1823 on to the end, Weber filled in pieces approximately in the order in which they occur in the opera. Thus in February and March of 1823 he concentrated primarily on pieces from Act II and then moved on to Act III; as was customary, he composed the Ouverture last. The composition of much of the third act had to be postponed until the end because of Weber's continuing dissatisfaction with that part of the libretto, much of which was not finalized until after Chezy's return to Dresden on 1 Apr. 1823. For the same reason, the Act I Finale must have been composed—or rather pieced together from earlier compositions—at a relatively late date.

thereby able to delineate a number of elements that could be and in fact were extended throughout the opera to characterize the opposed worlds of vice and virtue. Thus Adolar's aria established the flat-key, woodwind-dominated, and primarily syllabic-lyrical world that he and Euryanthe inhabit. In contrast, the Duetto brings forward elements that consistently depict evil and harm in the opera: a strongly sharp tonality (specifically B); modal mixture; vocal coloratura; brass-dominated orchestration; and driving triplet figures. In addition, the association of high strings with Eglantine and low strings with Lysiart at work throughout the opera may also be traced to the first section of the Duetto. Weber's alleged comment to Lobe about beginning work on *Freischütz* by first defining the musical parameters of two opposed worlds,[34] Samiel's and the huntsmen's, is thus explicitly borne out by the written record of the genesis of *Euryanthe*, a fact that perhaps should lead us to re-evaluate the possible authenticity of Lobe's account.[35]

Within the individual piece and musical passage, however, the elements of 'dramatic truth', particularly those that mark shifts of mood through contrasts, surprises, and deviations from norms, potentially become agents for disruption, as the desire to depict the shifting rhetoric and feeling in a particular text or situation can and in many instances does interrupt the sustained development of musical thought. For example, the numerous harmonic effects that stand in the service of *Charakter*—deceptive cadences, modulation, dissonances, changes of mode, 'unusual' progressions, and so forth—continuously interrupt incipient forward momentum predicated on a certain predictability of harmonic progression, a fact that various writers of Weber's day recog-

---

[34] Lobe, op. cit. ch. 2 n. 6 above, p. 31.

[35] A third point suggested by the chronology of composition is the close relationship between the earliest pieces and the Ouverture. No. 12 supplies the second theme. The cabaletta for the Introduzione (No. 4 in the definitive numbering) furnishes the second half of the main theme and the principal tonality. The *Vision* is quoted at length at the start of the development section. Whether these pieces were from the start envisioned in relation to the Ouverture is again a question for which one may provide only tentative answers. As suggested by the evolution of the libretto, the *Vision* recitative was probably composed with its eventual use as a Pantomimische Prolog Szene within the Ouverture already in mind. It is impossible to determine whether Adolar's two melodies were predestined from the outset for use in the Ouverture, but at the very least, what can be said is that the impulses that led Weber to use elements from No. 12 and No. 4 in the Ouverture were probably the same ones that led him to compose them at the very outset of work, that is, a recognition that they embody or characterize two of the most central pillars in the opera, love (No. 12) and faith (No. 4).

nized and criticized as a sin against the nature of music.[36] And with respect to form the pursuit of dramatic truth and characterization produces in certain extreme examples—the introductory movement of No. 4, the D-flat major Allegro movement of the Act II Finale and most of the Act III Finale—a nearly through-composed patchwork of musical conceits with little claim to autonomous musical coherence; we shall return to this point in the next chapter.

Weber's approach thus does not invite the listener to succumb to the inevitable sweep of 'organically' unfolding melody, but rather forces him to confront each musical-dramatic event as it occurs on a moment-by-moment basis. His contemporaries were fully aware of this, and as we have seen many of them felt the result an unsatisfactory 'mosaic' or 'musical prose' because the elements of characterization break up the rhythmic, melodic, and harmonic strands that normally hold a piece together. Even an entirely sympathetic commentator like A. B. Marx admitted that Weber's approach was 'less inclined to fuse these elements into a unity' than to 'struggle selfconsciously with his entire being towards dramatic expression of the whole in every individual moment'. Hence 'one must faithfully follow the ingenious artist in every individual situation and for each of his creations keep in mind his essential goal, in order to do justice to his works.'[37]

Seen in the light of his insistence on dramatic 'truth' and 'character' as the principal criteria for dramatic composition, the evidence of Weber's compositional processes begins to make a certain amount of sense. Simply put, the notable absence of significant revisions throughout the *Euryanthe* drafts bespeaks an approach that places a premium on the invention of 'characteristic' ideas and accords relatively little value to the working-out of the individual piece according to primarily musical criteria. A comparison with Beethoven's compositional processes can perhaps illuminate this point, since Beethoven's sketches and drafts, even those of the slightest pieces, reveal a composer obsessed not only with perfection but with the continuous, interdependent adjustment of detail and structure—an approach to composition that readily lends itself to interpretation by the organic metaphor. In contrast, once Weber arrived at what he considered a truthful and characteristic musical idea, there were few reasons to compel him to alter it. Weber himself attests his

---

[36] Weber himself became sensitive to the charge of excessive modulation in *Euryanthe*, for in a letter of 26 May 1824 to Franz Danzi he wrote: 'Moreover I certainly did not wish to pay hommage to the spirit of the times; if I have indeed done so, then the devil drove me to it unconsciously, although I monitor myself very rigorously precisely on the question of modulation. But I shall certainly be even more vigilant, in case I ever allow myself to be seduced to write another opera.' *MMW* ii. 539.

[37] Adolph Bernhard Marx, *Die Kunst des Gesanges* (Berlin, 1826), p. 232.

difficulty in reconsidering his ideas in a letter to the poet Kannegießer, who had sent him a number of song texts for his consideration.

The *Schlummerlied* caused me a misfortune that in other cases would not have been one: namely, while reading the first stanza the music to it arose in my soul—but for four voices. Since I consider it nonsense if four men should love and address a beloved in the first-person singular, I must therefore probably leave it uncomposed, since I cannot rid myself of a melody once I have received it in this way, and in general can be *true* only once; and not even the prevailing taste for music can bring me to lie. With a heavy heart I must abandon the lovely item.'[38]

Considerations of a purely musical sort, such as contrapuntal sophistication, motivic development, and thematic interrelationship were in and of themselves unimportant, unless they contributed in some way to the 'truth' of the musical realization; hardly surprising, then, that Weber's composition drafts reveal no great expenditure of effort on the organic working-out of ideas. Moreover, in so far as Weber's manner of composition resembled a mosaic-like assembly of characteristic ideas rather than a more organic process of continuous re-evaluation of prior composition in light of what follows, there were fundamentally few musical reasons to alter ideas that had once been fixed; we shall come back to this point in the following chapter on form.

Yet it would be a mistake to fault Weber for a cavalier attitude toward composition or lack of thought, for as we have seen repeatedly, his compositional choices prove to be extremely well thought out from the point of view of characterization. As Weber's contemporaries pointed out, his music *is* intellectual, but the intellectuality is of a different order than that which one encounters in works composed from the premiss of musical autonomy.

---

[38] Letter of 2 Aug. 1819. The original German in preserved in a copy in the *Weberiana* collection, Cl. II B, 2a, No. 42.

IX. Form

As noted in Chapter VI, the *Euryanthe* composition drafts seem to indicate
that Weber rarely entertained second thoughts about the structure of
individual pieces. At first this may come as a surprise, since German
opera composers did not as a rule rely upon highly conventionalized
structures like those that facilitated certain fundamental decisions about
form in Italian opera of the early *ottocento*,[1] and it was in fact a matter
of principle for a German like Weber to be original. Yet, various reasons
may be adduced for the apparent confidence with which Weber confronted form in the preserved composition drafts. For one thing, it is
quite possible that we have lost a number of preliminary worksheets
on which matters of form were first tackled and settled. A surviving
worksheet for the C-major Allegro movement of the Act II Finale that
will be discussed in the next chapter documents at least one case in
which certain decisions about large-scale form were made before the
composer proceeded to a continuous draft of a movement; yet even
here, the worksheet does not suggest a different formal conception than
that encountered in the final version of the piece. Then again, many
facets of large-scale musical structure were in fact hammered out during
the shaping of the libretto. The basic succession of tempi in the large,
multi-sectional pieces like Lysiart's Scena ed aria and the Act II Finale
were established very early in the history of the libretto, probably by
reference to extant models for such pieces. The broad outlines of other
pieces, like Eglantine's Scena ed aria No. 8, Euryanthe's Scena e cavatina
No. 17 and the Duetto No. 15, emerged more gradually in the course
of libretto revisions. The revision of the text of Euryanthe's prayer No.
16 from a strophic structure to a non-strophic structure was doubtless
made with an eye on its eventual musical realization. As discussed in
Chapter V, the reshaping of the more extended scenic units in the

---

[1] The burgeoning scholarship on Italian opera from Rossini to Verdi has rightly
stressed that certain archetypes for dramatic structure were just as fundamental to the
way in which Italian composers and librettists conceived their works as was 'sonata-
allegro form' for the instrumental music of the classical style. From a substantial number
of relevant studies see especially Philip Gossett, 'Gioacchino Rossini and the Conventions
of Composition', *Acta musicologica* 42 (1970): 48–58; Julian Budden, *The Operas of
Verdi*, vol. i (London, 1973), pp. 13–20; Gossett, 'Verdi, Ghislanzoni, and *Aida*: The
Uses of Convention', *Critical Inquiry* 1 (1974): 291–334; Harold S. Powers, '"La solita
forma" and "The Uses of Convention"', *Acta musicologica* 59 (1987): 65–90.

third act also seems to have been dictated by an awareness of the large-scale succession of tempos, styles, and musical effects. To a certain extent, then, composition entailed the filling-in of large forms already worked out before the first notes were written down. But ultimately, Weber's apparent non-struggle with form must be related to basic elements of his compositional approach, and here two factors seem especially to have facilitated decisions about form: (1) a reliance on a ternary-form archetype for most of the extended lyrical movements in the opera; and (2) a through-composed, mosaic-like manner of construction for more kinetic movements that invents and assembles diverse melodic ideas according to the succession of moods or situations in the text.

I. TERNARY FORMS WITH ENHANCED REPRISE

Despite his frequent insistence on originality as a necessary attribute of valid art, Weber's decisions about form seem in many instances to have been guided by a fairly conventional template. That is, a high percentage of pieces and self-sufficient movements fall into an archetypal form, a clear ternary shape in which some climactic effect is reserved for the reprise. This archetype is present in: the single movements of Nos. 20, 22, and 24; the opening choral movement of No. 1; the 'cabalettas' of No. 4, No. 9, and No. 12; the slow G-major movement of No. 10; the final chorus of Finale 3; both sections of No. 7; and the F-major, A-major, C-major, and F-minor movements of the Act II Finale. Even the *Vision*, a recitative that by all rights could be through-composed, exhibits certain features of this archetype.[2]

Within the ternary-form pieces a variety of means are used to make the reprise more intense than the original statement. Thus in comparison to the start of a movement, the reprise may entail a fuller texture, a more richly scored accompaniment, an unexpected harmonic twist or acceleration of harmonic rhythm, a melodic peak not yet attained in the course of the piece, an added bit of coloratura, or an alteration of the original phrase rhythm; in most cases the reprise entails a combination of two or more of these effects. For example, the reprise in No. 1 (m. 66) adds strings to the original woodwind complement, the dynamic level is raised to forte and the previously separated female and

---

[2] Upon its first appearance in Act I, scene iii, the *Vision* has a tonal and thematic recapitulation in its nineteenth measure, where the words 'der Unschuld Thräne netzt in höchster Leid' are set to the same melodic contour and harmonic progression as the words 'Herz so selig weinet, hört mich an' at the beginning of the recitative. The fact that the words 'weinet' and 'Thräne' are both set as appoggiaturas over a diminished-seventh harmony points up a textual parallelism ('weep' and 'tears') that may have suggested the musical reprise in the first place.

male choruses are combined. In No. 4, Adolar's motto 'Ich bau' auf Gott und meine Euryanth" is reinforced upon its return at m. 159 by the addition of winds, brass, chorus, and additional soloists and brought to a more emphatic close by an extension of its final cadence through six measures of dominant pedal point (mm. 176–81). Even the pieces not in ternary form make use of elements of the ternary archetype, in so far as climactic events are reserved for the end of the work, as, for example, the upward extension of tessitura to a^2 at measures 71–2 in the Cavatina No. 5 and the shocking harmonic progression near the end (m. 124) of the Con strepito of the Duetto No. 11 (vii^{o7} of B to F^6). In the cabaletta of Eglantine's No. 8, a piece that we have already traced through its first thirty-five measures, the text repetitions in the last half of the piece involve both a violent harmonic jolt at m. 110 (V^7 of E major to F_4^6) and a gradual stepwise extension of the upper boundary of melodic motion from the $g\sharp^2$ heard at m. 88 through a^2 (m. 109) and b^2 (m. 115) to the climactic c^3 at measure 128.

In most instances the ternary forms and intensified restatements are justified primarily by the fact that the relevant text is either a static presentation of a single mood or *Affekt*, such as the celebration of peace in No. 1 and Adolar's rapture in the Allegro of No. 12, or a simultaneous conflation of contradictory sentiments, as in the concluding section of the Scene und Chor No. 4 or the Duetto con coro No. 24. Since these pieces as a rule do not entail any dramatic action or psychological progression (the *Vision* excepted), the large-scale repetition of ternary form is used not as a metaphor for dramatic recapitulation, as is so often the case in Mozart's reprises, but is instead justified simply by the traditional prerogative of music to extend or enhance a basic mood, a right that Weber explicitly defended in his letter to Müllner.[3]

2. THE TERNARY ARCHETYPE IN THE COMPOSITIONAL PROCESS

The guiding presence of the ternary archetype can be sensed in the extant drafts in certain ways. The first, erased pencil draft of the *Vision*

---

[3] 'I am especially encouraged that the famous poet does not object to the repetitions at the end [of Brunhilde's song], because I value highly and respect this prerogative of music, which in itself is so entirely magnificent but so often is misused to the point of disgust . . .', *Sämtliche Schriften*, p. 374. Weber evidently planned to discuss repetition in his unfinished novel *Tonkünstlers Leben*, but never did return to this important topic.

breaks off at the very beginning of its reprise, a tacit admission that what follows requires no further thematic invention. In the drafts for both No. 22 and 24, Weber switches from pen to pencil at precisely the moment where the reprise begins to diverge from the model of the original. The draft of the reprise of the Duetto No. 7 even reveals a certain amount of uncharacteristic indecision and second thought on Weber's part, a telling phenomenon in that in such an instance Weber is confronted with the task of variation or modest development of a given rather than invention of something new. In one other case, the draft of the Duetto No. 13, Weber seems to have started out with a rondo form in mind as an appropriate realization of the poetic structure of his *Textvorlage*, but in the act of composition he fell back upon the ternary archetype. Since for these two last-named pieces the genetic record supplies various insights into the compositional process, let us examine them at some length.

2.1. *The Duetto No. 7*

The reprise in the A-minor Moderato assai section of the Euryanthe–Eglantine Duetto No. 7 occasioned a small but interesting complex of revisions, with no fewer than three different versions for the music between measures 34 and 37. A first version of the reprise was notated as part of the continuous draft for the duet on p. 32 (Ex. 7a). As originally drafted the reprise already contained a number of features that can be associated with the ternary-reprise archetype. In contradistinction to the opening section of the duet (mm. 1–19), in which the two characters alternate solos, the reprise entails simultaneous singing. The three-measure phrases of the opening section are compressed into two-measure groups. In addition, Euryanthe's part unfolds a gradual step-wise ascent towards a climactic pitch on the word 'laut', $f\sharp^2$, which exceeds the peak pitch of the opening section, the $f\natural^2$ heard at measures 7–8 and 15.

Yet, by the time that Weber reached the concluding measures of the Moderato assai, in which the minor mode yields to A major as Euryanthe finally is calmed by Eglantine's reassurances, he seems to have felt that the first version of the reprise was deficient. He interrupted the continuous draft at measure 43 and drafted immediately below the first version a new continuation of the reprise as a replacement for measures 34a–41a of the original draft (Ex. 7b). This revision is three measures shorter than before, and it eliminates a certain harmonic redundancy of the first version, which had oscillated between F-sharp minor and the diminished-seventh chord on its leading tone. Telling too is the fact that the goal pitch of the original version, $f\sharp^2$, is not attained in the revised draft; the highest pitch in the new version is $f\natural^2$, perhaps in order to defer the arrival on $f\sharp^2$ until the turn to major at m. 41.[4]

While this second version established the length and harmonic progressions for the passage, a third version, sketched immediately below the second draft, altered the harmonic rhythm and melodic contour of measures 34–37 for the sake of text realization (Ex. 7c). Whereas in version 2 the peak pitch $f\natural^2$ was placed in the middle of m. 34 on the word 'sagt', the third draft reverts to the original plan to make the word 'laut' the local melodic climax, a logical realization of the text. The final version thus better reconciles a purely musical concern, the gradual stepwise ascent in the melodic line from the beginning of the reprise to the beginning of the Allegretto grazioso, with demands for declamation and text expression.

2.2. The Duetto No. 13

In the case of the Duetto No. 13, the ternary-form archetype seems during the course of composition to have replaced a rondo form that Weber initially envisioned for the text. The *Textvorlage* was presumably the Chezy autograph libretto *Web. Cl. II A g 4*, which presents the text as follows in three stanzas of four lines each:

Hin nimm die Seele mein,	Take my soul,
Athme mein Leben ein,	inhale my life;
Laß mich ganz du nur seyn,	allow me to be only you;
Ganz bin ich dein.	I am entirely yours.
Seufzer wie Flammen wehn,	Sighs blow like flames,
Seelig um Lindrung flehn,	blissfully pleading for relief;
Laß mich in Lust und Wehn	let me die in joy and sorrow
An deiner Brust vergehn.	on your breast.
Herb ist der Abschiedkuß	The kiss of departure is bitter
Wenn Lieb von Liebe muß,	whenever love must leave love;
Gieb mir den Tod im Kuß,	your kiss gives me a fatal blow
Wenn ich je scheiden muß!	whenever I have to depart.

As a finished piece, the Duetto constitutes a ternary form in which only the first two stanzas are set to music; the first stanza is employed in the main theme (mm. 1–32) and the reprise (mm. 52–76), and the second stanza is set as a contrasting middle section (mm. 35–51) and partially quoted as a new theme in the coda (mm. 77–83). Yet, two

---

[4] Although he had not yet drafted the music beyond m. 43, Weber perhaps already knew that the long-range ascent in Euryanthe's part would continue through the transitional section to $g\sharp^2$ at m. 44 of the final version. The climactic a^2 at m. 47 in the main theme of the Allegretto grazioso may therefore be heard as the completion of an upper-line octave ascent (a^1–a^2) that had started with the reprise in the minore section.

Ex. 7. The reprise of the Duetto No. 7.
   (a) First draft mm. 29–42
   (b) Revision of mm. 34–8
   (c) Final version of mm. 34–5

(b)

(c)

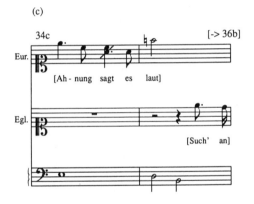

pieces of evidence suggest that Weber actually set out to compose a rondo structure employing all stanzas of the text. First, Weber did not delete the third stanza in his *Textvorlage*, which he presumably would have done if he had decided before composition to truncate the poem. Second, the extant draft and sketches for the piece support the notion that the decision to abridge the form was not made until well into the composition of the duet.

The Duetto was drafted on page 65, a page that, as we shall see in the following chapter, originally had been used for pencil sketches for the C-major Allegro section of the Act II Finale. In addition to the continuous ink draft for the duet, faint pencil sketches pertaining to the duet were notated on two systems near the bottom of the page (lines 15/16 and line 17) and then covered by the conclusion of the continuous ink draft; although the chronology of these two sketches cannot be demonstrated with absolute certainty, they seem to have been entered at the bottom of the page as provisional solutions to problems that arose during the composition of the ink draft. As before, the draft and the sketches reveal that moments of reprise tended to pose certain problems for the composer. To begin, the main theme (mm. 1–32) is conceived as two periods, each set to the first quatrain of the poem and each beginning with the same eight-measure melody. The first period (mm. 1–17) ends on a half cadence, whereas the second (mm. 18–32) brings the opening section to a full close that is underscored by the tutti ritornello. The first compositional decision that troubled Weber concerned the close of the second period, which, as a short-range reprise, Weber wished more brilliant than the first period. A number of features suggest that the pencil sketch on line 17 (Ex. 8a) was made as a first, tentative attempt to close the second period of the opening section with a local climax. First, the conclusion of the main theme is enjambed with a new continuation that disrupts the regular phrase organization (2 + 2 + 2 + 2) that has heretofore dominated. Second, the sketch's chromatic motion and an implied quickening of the harmonic rhythm effect a degree of intensification in comparison to the first period. Third, the sketch aims toward a melodic peak, g^2, from which a cadential gesture then falls stepwise to the tonic.

By the time that Weber reached the end of the second period in the ink draft, however, he had discarded this pencil sketch in favour of a new ending for the first section. As initially notated (Ex. 8b), this new ending clearly reveals its ancestry in the sketch on line 17 through the retention of certain basic features: the enjambed continuation of the main theme, the local chromatic inflections of the melodic line, and the faster rate of harmonic change. However, after notating only one measure of this new continuation, Weber reconsidered its placement within the metrical structure and added two extra beats of rest between the end of the main theme and the beginning of the continuation, thereby eliminating the prior enjambment. The continuation of the phrase was then made to lead to a new climactic pitch, a^2, before the definitive cadence. As a critique of the original sketch, this definitive version of the closing phrase points out two weaknesses of the earlier version. First, the original melodic peak, g^2, had already been attained within the main theme (m. 4, m. 15, m. 21) and thus presented no upward extension of register; in the definitive version, a^2 is the highest pitch yet heard in the melodic line. Second, the original stepwise descent from $\hat{5}$ to $\hat{1}$ at the cadence is particularly uninspired; what replaces it,

Ex. 8. Cadential phrase in the Duetto No. 13, mm. 22–30.
  (a) Pencil sketch
  (b) Continuity draft

(a)

(b)

however, is a typical gesture, a topos, similar to many cadences in 'blissful' pieces throughout the opera.[5]

The next recorded crisis in the composition of the Duetto occurred as Weber wrote out the large reprise of the piece. At a point corresponding to measure 60 in the final version, Weber at first notated a literal restatement of measures 9–16, whereupon he stopped the ink draft and sketched in pencil a new, canonic idea on the same system (Ex. 9a). As usual, it is difficult to interpret this sequence of events, but I should

[5] See Chapter VIII, Ex. 5.

suggest the following. First, the fact that Weber began to write out a literal reprise of measures 9 to 16 in the continuous ink draft suggests that he still had in mind a five-part rondo form as the way to realize the entire three-stanza text contained in his *Textvorlage*; according to this hypothesis, a second episode, based on the third stanza of poetry, would have followed a full restatement of the refrain. In the course of writing out what would have been the full refrain, however, Weber decided to curtail the form into a ternary structure and omit the third stanza altogether. Perhaps the reason for this is that the two periods of the refrain already encompass two statements of the main theme; thus a setting of all three stanzas in rondo form would be excessively repetitive. Second, the canonic pencil sketch that immediately followed the interruption of the ink draft seems to have been a first attempt at a closing phrase for the reprise. The relation of text to music is not at all clear for the first four measures of the sketch, but the last four measures identify its function beyond doubt. Again, the impulse to make the final statement of the reprise more emphatic may be noted, as Weber tries a new four-measure canonic passage over oscillating tonic and dominant harmonies as a way to enhance a texture that, up to this point, has been entirely homophonic. With respect to poetic content the canon still expresses the same 'truth' as the main theme, the unanimity of thought and sentiment of the two lovers. The sketch concludes with the four-measure cadential figure worked out earlier at the close of the first section; here, however, Weber returns to his original impulse to link the concluding phrase directly to what precedes as a way to intensify the push to the cadence.

Although Weber's final solution for the end of the Duetto, drafted in ink over the pencil sketch, did not adopt the canonic pattern (Ex. 9*b*), it does recall a number of ideas previously worked out. Thus measures 60–3 and 64–7 are derived from measures 9–10 and 11–12, respectively, altering the model by lengthening the phrase structure and extending the upper registral boundary to a^2 for climactic effect; the chromatic dotted rhythm figure at the end of each phrase may be heard in relation to the abortive canonic idea. For measures 68–71 Weber returned to the initial pencil sketch on line 17 for the close of the first section, salvaging from it the quarter-note curve from e^2 to a^1 back up to e^2 (cf. Ex. 8*a*). Lastly, the reprise closes with the four-measure cadential melody from the end of the opening section, but it is now linked without rest directly to the preceding phrase, as had been the case in the pencil sketch on lines 15 and 16. In the small detail of composition, then, Weber's approach may truly be seen to exemplify the 'mosaic' metaphor, for the end result is pieced together from melodic units previously worked out in isolation.

Ex. 9. The reprise of the Duetto No. 13.

   (a) Deleted measures in reprise and pencil sketch for new cadential phrase

   (b) Final version

3. THE MOSAIC OF THROUGH-COMPOSITION

As his contemporaries perceived in their charges that his music was not 'organic', 'lacked melody', and hence was a 'declamatory mosaic,' Weber's approach to dramatic composition was by no means symphonic or developmental but instead focused primarily on the invention of 'characteristic' themes and musical effects. In fact, a number of the pieces and movements in *Euryanthe* eschew any strong sense of large-scale repetition and instead string together a number of differing ideas conditioned by the succession of conceits, images, actions and psychological states in the text, an approach that justifiably could be called a 'mosaic'. Three examples of such through-composed forms will suffice to demonstrate this mosaic approach in varying degrees.

3.1. *The Scene und Chor No. 4.*

Arguably the most extreme instances of the 'musical prose' and 'declamatory mosaic' that Weber's critics condemned are the 'kinetic' movements in three of the major ensembles—the introductory movement of No. 4, the D-flat major Allegro movement of the Act II Finale singled out by Wendt for its lack of musical coherence, and most of the Act III Finale—wherein the pursuit of dramatic truth and characterization produces a nearly through-composed patchwork of musical conceits. Because of its relative brevity, let us consider the first 119 measures of the Scene und Chor No. 4, a dramatically active movement that readily lends itself to interpretation as a 'declamatory mosaic' assembled from successive musical ideas and periods, which individually supply ingenious and effective metaphors for character and situation but collectively have little to do with one another:

　　1. *Lysiart accepts Adolar's wager and pledges his possessions as collateral* (mm. 1–8): The slow tempo (Maestoso assai) and declamatory setting of Lysiart's words bring this opening period into stylistic proximity with recitative, thereby underscoring the ceremonial nature of Lysiart's pronouncement and at the same time effecting a seamless transition from the style of the preceding recitative to that of the following Allegro. Harmonically the first two measures also smooth over the connection with the preceding recitative, for the unharmonized pitch-class $E^\flat$ at the downbeat of m. 1, the tonic for the number, may also be heard at that instant as the third degree of a C-minor triad expected to resolve the cadence at the end of the prior recitative, a perception that is strengthened by continued suggestion of C minor in measure 2. With respect to the tonal symbolism of the opera, the pull toward C minor at the outset of Lysiart's speech is of course entirely appropriate for conveying his sinister intentions. The entrance of the trombones at the downbeat

of m. 1 marks their first appearance since the Ouverture and reinforces the ceremonial solemnity of the moment.

2. *Adolar accepts Lysiart's terms and the knights react with astonishment* (mm. 9–18): two measures of arpeggiated triplet fanfares in the first violins at the beginning of the Allegro (mm. 9–10) may be heard in relationship to the gesture at the beginning of the Ouverture and perhaps function as surrogate trumpet calls signifying Adolar's resolve.[6] As noted in the preceding chapter, the loosely imitative treatment of the chorus stands in contrast to the chordal style normally employed and was interpreted by Amadeus Wendt as a symbol for the knight's shock at the turn of events. Their growing concern can perhaps also be read in the shift from E^b major at the start of their first phrase (mm. 11–14) to E^b minor in their second phrase (mm. 15–18).

3. *Adolar stakes his possessions on the outcome of the wager; Lysiart mocks him by portraying his future itinerant life as an unpropertied troubadour* (mm. 19–36): this section comprises a succession of melodic ideas that may be resolved into three periods of irregular facture (3 + 2, 4 + 2, 2 + 4[+ 1]). In the first period (mm. 19–23), Adolar sustains the B-flat harmony heard as a half-cadence at the end of the preceding period, perhaps because his rapidly declaimed words at this point are posed as an incredulous question to Lysiart. The shift to a more sustained style of singing and the cadence to E^b minor in the second period (mm. 24–9) coincide with his portrayal of the dire consequences should Euryanthe prove faithless. Lysiart's taunting in the third period (mm. 30–6) frustrates the cadential goal of Adolar's second phrase, B^b minor, by sustaining its dominant for the entire period, effectively destroying any strong sense of B^b by the end of the period. The grace notes in Lysiart's leaping fifths perhaps emulate the 'Zither' with which Adolar will be forced to earn his livelihood after losing his estates.

4. *Adolar is outraged by Lysiart's temerity and vows to summon him to trial by combat should Lysiart lose the wager; Lysiart acknowledges the challenge* (mm. 37–53): tremolando accompaniment throughout this section signifies the agitation of Adolar and the onlookers. A certain harmonic extravagance also serves to heighten the depiction of Adolar's nearly uncontrolled anger, as he first explodes into an unprepared distant key, D^b major, and then progresses to a furious *fff* climax in C^b major on the word 'Gottgericht' (m. 45), which is underscored by the addition of the bass trombone to the instrumentation.

5. *The knights react again with astonishment and plead with the antagonists*

---

[6] This fanfare figure does not appear in the draft of the movement, and in such cases it is impossible to know whether the idea was present in Weber's mind from the start or whether it was added as an afterthought to strengthen the sense that No. 4 in some way marks a return of the Ouverture.

to abandon their dangerous wager; Adolar and Lysiart are adamant (mm. 54–83): the knights once again express their dismay, quoting their earlier words and pseudo-contrapuntal music in E♭ minor ('Vermessenes Beginnen!') and then continue with a more chordal phrase, a symbol for the unanimity of their desire to halt the wager, that blossoms into a lovely, conciliatory melody with 4 + 4 phrase structure in G♭ major (mm. 62–9). Repeated with the addition of soloists, this tune is extended at measure 76 by a rising stepwise chromatic progression in the bass from e♭ to a♮ as the chorus continues to reiterate its plea for sanity ('O geht zurück'); as in other instances, the sequential repetition over a rising bass seems to connote rising levels of anxiety.

6. *Adolar implores the King to accept the wager; Adolar and Lysiart give their rings to the King as pledge* (mm. 84–99): The rising bass motion of the previous period culminates with a cadence in the courtly key of B♭ major at measure 84 for Adolar's affirmation of knightly duty to serve womankind. His chivalric impulses are also portrayed in the orchestra, where trumpets, horns, and timpani enter at precisely this moment with a dotted rhythm of the sort associated throughout the opera with knighthood.

7. *Lysiart prepares to depart, vowing to return with a sign of Euryanthe's favour; the knights express the hope that he will fail* (mm. 100–19): once again, the exchanges between Lysiart, the King, and the knights elicit a succession of unrelated declamatory phrases. The King's reminder that Lysiart must return with proof of conquest (mm. 103–4) provokes a sudden detour out of B♭ major towards C♭ major. Lysiart's pledge to bring back a token of Euryanthe's favour (mm. 106–11) subtly adumbrates Emma's music (which after all is the 'proof' that Lysiart eventually uses) through tonality (the enharmonic equivalent of B major), pianissimo dynamic and chromatic side-slipping. The quiet tremolos in the violas that punctuate the choral commentary are conventional topoi for suspense used at many places throughout the opera.

To search for the organic metaphor in such music is essentially futile. Unlike most kinetic movements in the operas of Mozart and Rossini, there is no persistent or recurring orchestral motive that undergirds the vocal declamation, nor it there a scaffold of harmonic stability and predictability that holds the music together.[7] The only instance of musical reprise within the movement, the partial restatement of the chorus's pseudo-fugato in Period 5, was not prescribed by Weber's *Textvorlage* for this number (*Web.* Cl. II A g 6) and therefore perhaps represents

---

[7] On the presence of a 'harmonic scaffold' as a secure anchor for the rhythmically and motivically unpredictable foreground gestures in Mozart's music see Thrasybulos Georgiades, 'Aus der Musiksprache des Mozart-Theaters', *Mozart-Jahrbuch 1950* (Salzburg, 1951), pp. 76–98.

a compositional decision to introduce some element of unity in what otherwise is a completely through-composed piece; yet this tune in no way acts as a 'main theme' for the movement, and to interpret the movement as a ternary form with an introduction and extended coda does not do justice to its spirit. Rather, what counts most is the succession of momentary effects and the listener's ability to concentrate on and comprehend an ever-changing mosaic of musical signifiers; hence the comment by several early critics that this opera was too taxing for the average listener seems entirely justified in a movement like this.

3.2. *The Scena No. 16*

While extended arioso movements in the major ensembles offer the most extreme instances of mosaic-like construction, two of the self-contained set pieces, Eglantine's Aria No. 6 and Euryanthe's Scena No. 16, also avoid significant reprise and instead present essentially through-composed portraits of changing psychology and situation; perhaps because of their unique structures, Weber seems originally to have been at a loss to know how to designate these pieces, since neither is given a title in the autograph score. Let us consider one of the most memorable pieces in the entire opera, Euryanthe's Scena No. 16, wherein she vividly describes the fierce struggle between Adolar and the giant snake.

As we saw in Chapter V, the poem for this piece was originally conceived as three matching strophes, but in the final version, the third stanza is structurally differentiated from the first two, thereby facilitating a more dynamic musical realization than would be possible with a purely strophic poem. The piece is essentially through-composed—Amadeus Wendt considered it a 'Rhapsodie' that 'completely transcends the usual forms of recitative and aria'[8]—with three sharply contrasted musical sections that delineate the major shifts in Euryanthe's response to the battle: (A) her prayer for angelic assistance and description of the snake, encompassing the first two stanzas of the poem (mm. 1–26); (B) her description of the battle and Adolar's evident defeat, set to the first three verses of the third stanza (mm. 27–33); and (C) her joyful reaction to Adolar's victory (mm. 34–63). Since the first section is itself divided into two approximately matching subsections (A_1: mm. 1–14, and A_2: mm. 14–26), the structure can be heard as a variety of *Barform* (A_1A_2BC), although the two *Stollen* in this case are tonally and harmonically differentiated.

Each of the three main sections can readily be interpreted as a response to a particular conceit or image in the text. The first section, combining a declamatory vocal line with a highly syncopated rising bass motive

---

[8] *BamZ* 3 (1826): 45.

and tremolando accompaniment, was interpreted by Wendt as an expression of 'both exertion and danger',[9] and the contrary motion that largely shapes the relationship between bass line and Euryanthe's part perhaps suggests a spiritual opposition of Euryanthe and the approaching monster. The fact that the first stanza of the poem is a heroic prayer also seems to have shaped the musical conception of the opening section, as its tempo, texture, and vocal style betray an ancestry in prayers of heroines in the operas of Gluck (*Iphigénie en Tauride*) and Spontini (*Fernand Cortez* and *Olympie*). Contrasts between the two parts of the opening section also demonstrate the role of harmony in the presentation of dramatic 'truth', since Euryanthe's melody in the first stanza (mm. 1–14), the prayer proper, is in the major mode and largely diatonic, whereas the second stanza (mm. 14–26), which is dominated by her description of the snake, begins in the parallel minor and entails a much higher degree of tonal instability.

For the second and third sections Weber turns to rather conventional topoi to convey, respectively, the battle and the victory. Thus the musical elements in Euryanthe's description of the battle include a winding bass pattern to depict the coiling of the snake, contrary motion in the accompaniment perhaps suggesting the opposition of the snake and Adolar, and unstable harmony, primarily a sequential progression of diminished-seventh chords, as a metaphor for the uncertainty of the battle's outcome. For the complete reversal of mood occasioned by Adolar's victory the music of the third section turns to a new set of ideas strongly stamped by traditional affective connotations for heroism: diatonic major mode; simple harmonic progressions oscillating between tonic and dominant; triadic melody; dotted rhythms; and the addition of trumpets to the orchestration. Moreover, the shift to a purely homophonic texture at this point removes one important element of struggle—contrary motion—that had characterized the first two sections of the piece.

3.3. *The Cavatina No. 5*

At first glance, Euryanthe's quiet, melancholy Cavatina No. 5 seems immune to charges of 'inorganicism' and 'musical prose'. Wendt had, after all, included this piece among the small group of numbers primarily concerned with musical cohesion, and with good reason. The 'flow' of the music is guaranteed by an almost unbroken succession of four-measure phrases. The piece entails no abrupt modulations and has only one truly surprising harmony, an E♭-major triad that suddenly appears on the second beat of measure 70. A high degree of musical coherence accrues from the presence of two persistent motives: (*x*) a dactylic rhythm

[9] Ibid.

Ex. 10. Orchestral figure in Euryanthe's Cavatina No. 5.

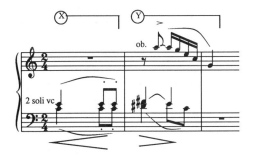

frequently heard in both the voice and orchestra; and (*y*) a descending
arpeggiated figure, given primarily to the orchestra, that is heard over
a neighbour-chord resolution (Ex. 10). Formal closure is suggested by
the return at measure 60 of music heard at measure 39. In addition,
Euryanthe's melody gradually unfolds a rising stepwise progression of
melodic peaks from e^2 (m. 31) to f^2 (m. 51–2) to g^2 (m. 66) to a^2 (m.
71), thereby effecting a subtle sense of long-range line. Thus the final
result *is* musically more 'organic' than the more obviously mosaic-like
examples in the opera like the opening movement of No. 4 and No.
16. Nevertheless, the piece is wedded to a specific text and succession
of poetic images, and a closer consideration of the factors for coherence
reveal them, in effect, to be the direct by-product of a close attention
to the poem at hand.

The 'truth' of the musical setting may be seen to lie in a number
of factors. The basic dactylic rhythm, far from being an abstract musical
element, is obviously derived from the scansion of the poem: 'Glöcklein
im Thále, | Ríeseln im Bách, | Säuseln in Lüften, | Schmélzendes Ách.'
The obbligato orchestral instruments that give the piece its characteristic
sonority easily lend themselves to a poetic, or perhaps even onomatopoe-
tic, interpretation, as they suggest the various elements of the environment—the voices of nature, as it were—to which Euryanthe attends
throughout the aria. Harmonic details may be seen to point out details
in the text. Thus the brief flirtation with G minor at measures 44–5
coincides with the first lines that address Euryanthe's own melancholy
state of being ('Ach und die Seele der Sehnsucht Raub'), and the diminished-seventh harmony at measures 54–5 is an unabashedly conventional
colouring of the text 'bangst wohl nach mir'. The fact that Euryanthe's
line occasionally introduces dissonances (m. 32, m. 34, m. 36, m. 42)
that are resolved only in the orchestral part can perhaps be understood
as a musical translation of unfulfilled yearning for contact with Adolar.

Formally, the cavatina responds more to the succession of poetic conceits than to conventional guidelines for musical form, although an element of poetic reprise does justify the brief hint of musical return at measure 60. The first stanza of the admittedly obscure poem, Euryanthe's contemplation of her surroundings, is set as a sixteen-measure period modulating from the tonic to the dominant (mm. 31–46). With the start of the second stanza at m. 52 Euryanthe's thoughts turn directly to an unnamed distant beloved ('Weilst du so ferne?'). This change of perspective effects a modulation to the subdominant and a new approach in the accompaniment (m. 52–59), as the obbligato instruments of the first section disappear in favor of a sixteenth-note string pattern.[10] With the fifth line of the second stanza at measure 60, however, Euryanthe again describes her surroundings ('Alle so golden, selig und klar'), and the solo instruments return along with one of the basic motives from the setting of the first stanza (cf. m. 39), thereby briefly suggesting a reprise despite the fact that the local tonic is still the subdominant, F major. The last line of the poem finally discloses the object of Euryanthe's *Sehnsucht* to be none other than Adolar, and this revelation coincides with a tonal clarification, the return to C major at m. 66. The mention of Adolar also triggers a stream of melodic and rhythmic figures from measure 68 to the final vocal cadence at measure 77 that have little to do with the prior motives but instead may be heard referentially as topoi for chivalry and heroism, specifically dotted rhythms, timpani-like oscillations between tonic and dominant and rising triadic contours in emulation of trumpet calls. Even the one abrupt harmonic gesture of the entire piece, the sudden plunge into an E♭-major triad at measure 70, can perhaps be heard as an allusion to the prior association of Adolar with E♭ in the Con fuoco movement of No. 4.

4. CONCLUSIONS

Although Weber clearly saw his task as a German opera composer in the continuation of the work begun by Mozart,[11] nowhere is his actual distance from classical opera more evident than in his approach to operatic form. In the operas of Mozart and Beethoven—particularly in action ensembles like the trio No. 7 in *Le nozze di Figaro* and the grave-digging duet in *Fidelio*—coherent, extended musical structures, often related to

---

[10] In the autograph score Weber entered in pencil a motive for the horn in measures 57–60 at the line 'Bringen die Sterne Grüße von dir?' thereby returning to the musical symbolism of the first section that equates wind instruments with the 'voices of nature' that potentially bring news of the distant beloved; this added motive is printed in small noteheads in Rudorff's edition of the full score.

[11] *Sämtliche Schriften*, pp. 309–10.

the forms of independent instrumental music, provide a subtle commentary on dramatic action through a variety of means, for example, by underscoring parallelisms in dramatic action through musical reprise or by suggesting greater urgency through foreshortening of phrase structure.[12] In *Euryanthe*, Weber seems not to have viewed the musical form of an individual piece as an independent agent of dramatic expression and instead to have considered large-scale form either as a way of extending and enhancing a single mood—the ternary archetype—or as a mosaic of more or less unrelated phrases and effects that attempts to follow every nuance in a developing situation with little regard for overall musical coherence or compositional-technical ingenuity. It is this latter facet of Weber's style in particular to which Edward J. Dent objected most vehemently in his rather negative assessment of the composer: 'Weber has hardly any sense of musical form. He can invent the most fascinating initial phrases, but he cannot balance them; his music tails off in interest just at the very moment where it ought to become more interesting... He is quite incapable of planning the form of a number and holding a climax in reserve...'[13] Of course, the *Euryanthe* libretto afforded Weber few opportunities for the structural sophistications of a Mozart–Da Ponte opera, but it must also be remembered that he was primarily responsible for formal aspects in the final libretto and in fact seems to have encouraged emotionally static poetic structures susceptible for treatment as terse ternary forms. In sum, ingenuity of musical form simply was not a major priority in Weber's agenda for opera.

[12] For relevant discussions of the uses of form in classical opera see Joseph Kerman, *Opera as Drama* (New York, 1956), pp. 73–98; Charles Rosen, *The Classical Style* (New York, 1971), pp. 288–302; Tim Carter, *W. A. Mozart. 'Le nozze di Figaro'* (Cambridge, 1987), pp. 88–104; and James Webster, 'To Understand Verdi and Wagner We Must Understand Mozart', *19th-Century Music* II (1987): 175–93.

[13] Edward J. Dent, *The Rise of Romantic Opera*, ed. by Winton Dean (Cambridge, 1976), p. 159.

X. Three Case Studies in the Compositional Process

Up to this point we have observed that Weber's drafts, in so far as they reveal anything about the rationale behind compositional decisions, tend to illuminate specific, localized problems that, without reference to certain fundamental aesthetic premisses, would be difficult to interpret. For three pieces, however, the surviving evidence allows us to reach inside the compositional process a little more deeply and follow the genesis of the individual piece more completely from beginning to end. We thus close our discussion of the compositional process with three case studies that seek to co-ordinate the aesthetic, critical, and compositional-technical issues broached thus far through discussions of entire pieces.

I. THE C-MAJOR ALLEGRO OF THE ACT II FINALE

The fact that the birth pangs of the C-major movement (Allegro ma non troppo) of the Act II Finale are exceptionally well documented is perhaps indicative that Weber viewed this piece as an especially difficult challenge, for it is a large ensemble that seeks to combine the sentiments of Adolar's vassals, who express their desire to follow their dispossessed lord into exile, with the conflicting personal reactions of four soloists. Like so many other movements, the piece falls into a ternary form with enhanced reprise. Following a brief introductory passage for Adolar and Euryanthe (mm. 390–9), the opening section (mm. 400–21) is principally for the chorus of knights, whose expression of loyalty to Adolar determines the basic *Affekt* of the movement. Thus the choice of a purely diatonic C-major for the choral melody, in part dictated by the desire to prepare the F-minor tonality of the following Schlußchor, also possesses a certain symbolic value, since this key is shared with other pieces that express varying degrees of devotion to Adolar (No. 5, No. 13, No. 20). The texture of the opening section also represents a certain dramatic 'truth' since the closely-spaced, synchronous four-voice choral writing, a style used in numerous situations in this opera where the chorus reacts with one will, can be seen to reflect the self-professed unanimity of sentiment ('Wir *alle* wollen mit dir gehn ...'). In contradistinction to the consoling strains of the opening section, the predominant *Affekt* of the G-minor middle section (mm. 422–42), sung only by the soloists, seems to be determined by Euryanthe's grief, and as in No. 17, this key can be heard as a symbol for abandonment. The reprise (mm. 443–65) is intensified, most obviously by the addition of a line for Euryanthe as an upper counterpoint to the main choral theme but also by certain harmonic turns not found in the first section.

A complete draft of the movement, notated in a combination of ink and pencil, was written on pages 72 and 61; in the present organization of the manuscript these two pages are of course widely separated, but at the time of composition they doubtless faced one another as the opposing pages of an opening in a gathering of two bifolios. A number of pencil sketches for the movement were written on page 65, and a pencil draft for the middle section was made on page 75; at the time of composition, both pages 65 and 75 were probably outer pages of their respective bifolios. Some time after completing the full, continuous draft of the ensemble, Weber erased the annotations on both of these pages and eventually reused them for other pieces.[1] The relative chronology of all of the entries pertaining to the ensemble is not altogether clear, a problem that is compounded by the fact that even with the aid of photographic enhancement it is not possible to transcribe pages 65 and 75 with complete confidence. Nevertheless, since these drafts afford a rare opportunity to reconstruct the composer's train of thought prior to the notation of a complete draft, it is imperative to attempt to understand what they have to tell us.

Of the preserved entries, those on page 65 obviously represent the most direct reflection of Weber's initial impulses, and for this reason it is presented in diplomatic transcription in Ex. 11; for the sake of clarity and future reference, each of the items on this page is identified by a number. The earliest notation for the ensemble must have been the twelve-measure idea for the main theme written on staves 2, 3, and 4 at the top of page 65 (Item 1), consisting in three four-measure phrases treated as a miniature ternary form: (*a*) a phrase for chorus ending on the dominant; (*b*) a four-measure outburst for Adolar; and (*a'*) another four-measure phrase for chorus that cadences in the tonic. Typically, this earliest sketch provides no glimpse into how the main theme came into being, but we have already suggested how one might interpret the idea as a 'truthful' response to a given text and set of emotions. Despite its four-measure phrasing, one can also understand how such a period could be construed as 'musical prose', since Adolar's impassioned

---

[1] Page 65 was used for the draft of the Duetto No. 13 discussed in the preceding chapter, and p. 75 for the start of Act III.

Ex. 11. Worksheet for the Act II Finale, No. 14 (C-major section), p. 65.

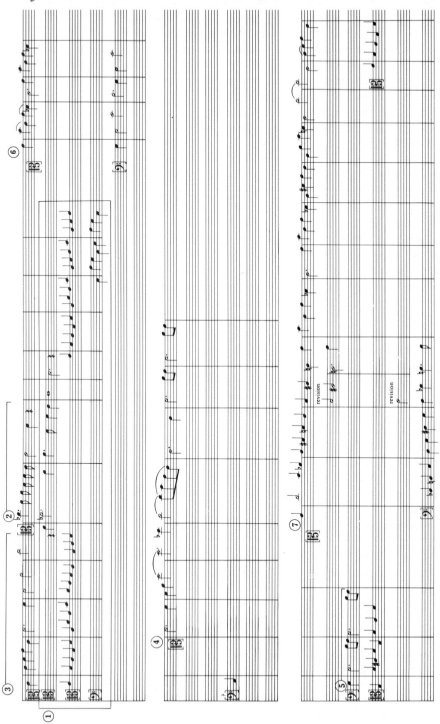

lament stands in no direct relationship to the choral melody that it interrupts; instead, it is one of many examples of the falling diminished-
seventh topos associated with grief throughout the opera, and its distance
from the main theme is a truthful metaphor for Adolar's desire for isolation ('O laßt! kein' Auge soll mich sehn'). The effect of separation
is then enhanced by a revision of Adolar's outburst that converts it
into a two-measure phrase by a simple process of rhythmic diminution
(Item 2).

What came next in the sequence of events is unclear. Although it
is possible that Weber at this point transferred the idea, with the compressed version of Adolar's exclamation, to the continuous draft on page
72, it is more likely that he next considered the reprise of the movement,
which, according to the ternary archetype, would have to be enhanced
in some way. Thus he experimented with ways of intensifying the reprise
by adding a countermelody for Euryanthe to the theme that he had
already laid out. The four-measure notation on the first stave of page
65 (Item 3) was a first attempt at projecting Euryanthe's line, 'Es wallt
dein Kind in deiner Hut', as a counterpoint against the main theme
of the movement. There is of course no way to prove that this line
was conceived from the outset for the reprise and *not* for the first section,
but the hindsight afforded by the final version suggests this, as well
as the fact that on line 7 immediately below the draft of the main theme
Weber sketched a revised continuation of Euryanthe's counter-melody
(Item 4) that was in fact eventually incorporated into the reprise of
the final version of the movement.[2] Whereas the first version of this
counterpoint had arpeggiated up to g^2, the new version pushes Euryanthe's line up to a^2 and at the same time necessitates a new harmonic
continuation towards D minor in mm. 445–6, thus providing the reprise
with both a melodic peak and new harmonic interest.

With the main theme and some idea of the reprise in mind, Weber
began to write out a continuous draft for the movement on page 72,
where his initial task was to compose the introductory material that
precedes the first statement of the main theme, Adolar's summons to
Euryanthe ('Komm 'Euryanth'!') and her response ('Willkommenes
Gebot! | Ich folge dir im Noth und Tod!'). This prefatory material
evidently had not been worked out beforehand, since the first eleven

[2] The meaning of the single, uncleffed pitch at the begining of line 10, the fourth
stave of the second system, is unclear; the only hint as to function is its placement
as a pickup to an unspecified following measure. The notation may have been a brief
short-hand indication for the start of the reprise, since, if read in bass clef, the resulting
c would in fact be the proper pitch in the bass choral part on the fourth quarter-note
of measure 442. A tenor-clef reading of g could indicate the start of the brief fugato
on the last beat of measure 411, for which a sketch exists immediately below on the
third system (lines 13–18).

measures of the draft exhibit numerous signs of tentativeness, especially in the treatment of Euryanthe's reply, for which two very different versions are sketched in pencil (Ex. 12a). The first, a six-measure phrase, answers Adolar's stepwise rising demand with an arpeggiated falling figure that continues with two measures of syncopated rhythm and reaches up to a melodic peak, a^2, on the word 'Noth'. At some later point Weber lowered this peak to g^2, perhaps in order to reserve the a^2 for the climactic moment in the reprise. The second version adopts a completely different tack in which Euryanthe takes up Adolar's rising line and extends it to the third scale degree. The rate of declamation throughout this second attempt is much faster, perhaps to convey Euryanthe's professed alacrity to follow Adolar's command, and the cadence in the new version is a free diminution of the cadence worked out in the first version. The final version (Ex. 12b), not documented in the draft, combines the first half of version 2 with the revised second half of version 1.

Immediately after copying the main theme into the continuous draft on p. 72, Weber's next problem was the transition from the main theme to the G-minor middle section (mm. 412–21), which begins imitatively. Weber began to draft the transition in ink, but as the draft unfolded progressively fewer voices were notated, with only the tenors notated in the last three measures of the first attempt (Ex. 13). At some point during this draft, Weber returned to the last system on page 65 to emend the voice leading between the King and the first tenors in measures 413–4 (Item 5), since the original version on page 72 created a parallel unison between these two voice parts; this corrected version was subsequently transferred to page 72. Weber then crossed out the last nine measures of the transition and drafted a second version of the passage, of equal length and essentially identical melodic and harmonic content as the first version. The most obvious and important revision in this second version is that Adolar and the first tenors have exchanged roles in the contrapuntal scaffold; the first tenors take over the even quarter-notes originally given to Adolar, while he now supplies the answer to the King's subject. The rationale for this switch lies, I believe, in the interplay between 'dramatic truth' and musical values in Weber's compositional choices. The first version, in which the King and the vassals share common thematic material while Adolar presents a contrasting melodic line, makes good sense from the point of view of character inasmuch as the King and the chorus are united in their common dismay at Adolar's imminent departure, whereas Adolar's sentiments are quite different. The revision sacrifices some of this dramatic logic in order to facilitate a musically more satisfactory version; by giving the answer to Adolar, the imitation is passed from one soloist to another and not

Ex. 12. Start of the C-major section of the Art II Finale.
  (a) Early versions in the continuity draft.
  (b) Final version.

(a)

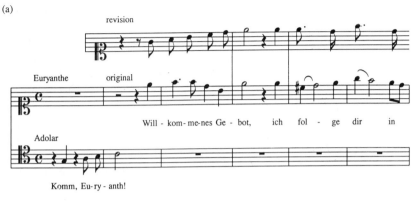

(b)

from soloist to chorus, and by taking over the constant quarter-notes, the chorus continues the steady pulses that had characterized it from the start of the movement.

Whereas the main theme and reprise were initially drafted on page 65, the middle section (mm. 422–42) was first drafted in pencil on page 75 before it was transferred to the continuous draft on pages 72 and 61. As is so often the case, this draft reveals no significant divergences from the final version of the section. But it is noteworthy that while drafting the music on p. 75, Weber returned twice to his worksheet, page 65, to write down two sketches for the last measures of the middle section. First, on the free space at the extreme right of system 1 he notated Euryanthe's and Lysiart's parts for measures 436–8 (Item 6). Then, in the middle of the third system, he incorporated the top voice of this fragment into a longer draft for the second half of the middle section, measures 432–43; for measures 432–5 in this draft Weber again included Lysiart as a counterpoint to Euryanthe's line (Item 7). While these two worksheet annotations for the middle section again do not reveal significant alternatives to the final version—the only discrepancy lies in the rhythm of measures 434–5, which originally were compressed into one measure—the fact that they both isolate the Euryanthe–Lysiart duet as the contrapuntal skeleton for the middle section once again suggests that Weber's initial compositional impulses were shaped primarily by a dramatic conception, in this case the opposition of the suffering victim Euryanthe and the gloating villain Lysiart; the same phenomenon is documented in the draft of the A-major Larghetto of the Act II Finale, and we have already observed a similar phenomenon in the chronology of large-scale composition. Further, it can be no coincidence that the dramatic opposition is mirrored, as it were, by the consistent use of contrary motion for these two characters, not only in the excerpts sketched on page 65 but throughout the entire middle section.

Since the most important new features of the reprise were already worked out on p. 65, it comes as no surprise that the continuous ink draft proceeds unproblematically until Euryanthe's cadence at measure 455, at which point material for the coda is drafted in pencil, a sign that Weber is once again faced with the task of new invention.

2. THE DUETTO NO. 15

Whereas the drafts for the C-major Allegro movement are primarily interesting for what they reveal about the micro-chronology of composition, the extant materials for the Duetto No. 15 for Euryanthe and Adolar cast more light on issues of invention and self-criticism. Here an idea-sketch as well as several significant revisions in the continuous

Ex. 13. Act II Finale. First version of mm. 412–21.

draft offer a number of toeholds for observations about Weber's compositional procedures and priorities. The Duetto falls into two large sections of contrasting tempo, determined by the basic two-part division of the poem. The first section of the text (Moderato, A major), a series of exchanges between Adolar and Euryanthe, is the more poetically active and irregular of the two. In a succession of mixed rhyme schemes in four- and five-foot verses, Adolar begins by recalling how much he had loved Euryanthe in the past. Euryanthe tries to reassure him of her innocence and continuing devotion, but Adolar will hear none of this and, accusing her of infidelity, he announces his intention to silence her forever. Convinced of his unshakeable resolve, Euryanthe accepts this sentence with characteristic devotion to her would-be executioner. The second movement of the duet (Agitato, A minor), is based on a closed poetic structure, in which the characters sum up their respective assessments of the heart-breaking situation in quatrains of iambic tetrameter with matching rhyme schemes.

If I have stressed some obvious points about the text, it is because the two differing modes of expression—the active first section and the more reflective second section—strongly coloured the way that Weber approached the very act of composition. Far from being principally lyrical, the slower first section is an example of a 'declamatory mosaic' guided by the succession of differing moods, and the problems of composition primarily concern invention and character portrayal. Because the fast section is based on a static poetic conception, however, the composer allows himself in this case a higher degree of musical repetition and at the same time is forced to confront a number of essentially musical issues.

As in other two-movement pieces (No. 12, No. 8), Weber began the Duetto with the concluding movement. The starting point for composition seems to have been an eight-measure idea-sketch for the main theme of the Agitato movement ('Du klagst mich an!') notated at the right edge of staves 5, 7, and 8 of page 54, a page otherwise given over to the Eglantine–Lysiart recitative from Act II, scene ii (Ex. 14). This item can perhaps be related to a specific entry in the Diary, since on 22 March 1823 Weber recorded that he had conceived the idea for an Adolar–Euryanthe duet ('*Idee Duett Adol. Eury.*'). Unfortunately, the Diary does not specify whether the duet in question was No. 15 or No. 13, a piece that conceivably could have been composed around the same time as well.[3] The proximity of the idea-sketch to the recita-

---

[3] The only evidence for the date of the Duetto No. 13 is that it must have been composed after the completion of the Act II Finale in late February 1823, since it is written over the erased pencil sketches on page 65 for the C-major Allegro movement of that piece.

Ex. 14. Idea sketch for the Duetto No. 15 (Agitato), p. 54.

tive draft casts a provocative light on the creative process and Weber's concept of organic connections within the opera. That is, the basic situation-motive in the recitative, in which Eglantine speaks of estranging Adolar from Euryanthe through the discovery of Emma's ring—an idea that comes to full fruition in the Duetto—hovers largely around A minor and emphasizes the raised fourth and seventh scale degrees (Ex. 15); moreover, it shares obvious rhythmic affinities with the idea-sketch as well as a two-voice texture in which rhythmic activity is similarly staggered between the voices. The presence of the idea sketch on the same page as the recitative draft thus draws attention to a subtle but dramatically appropriate melodic relationship between different parts of the opera that otherwise might have gone unnoticed in an analysis restricted only to the final score. What cannot be known is whether Weber conceived the Duetto idea at approximately the same time as the recitative—a distinct possibility since the recitative was composed some time after Lysiart's Scena ed aria No. 10, which is known to have been finished on 12 March 1823—or whether he was drawn back to page 54 at some later time in searching through the drafts for an appropriate idea for the Duetto.

The idea-sketch on page 54 presents the main theme of the Duetto in a form quite close, but not identical, to the final version. Significantly, it is from the outset a two-voice conception, with Adolar and Euryanthe

Ex. 15. Orchestral motive in Act II, scene ii.

declaiming the different texts that had been established in the *Textvorlage*, the Chezy autograph libretto *Web*. Cl. II A g 4. At first glance, this conception would seem to violate Weber's aesthetic of musical truth, since it is practically impossible for a listener to comprehend different texts presented at the same time. However, if one thinks of the piece in relationship to the Duetto No. 13, one sees that the main idea for the Duetto No. 15 is a 'negation' of the metaphors that had been used to depict the bliss of lovers united in No. 13—the key of C major, simultaneous singing of one text—in order now to portray lovers on the verge of eternal separation through Euryanthe's imminent execution at Adolar's hands. Thus although both characters are affected by the same tragic situation in No. 15, each responds differently, and for this reason it is 'truthful' that they be shown at cross purposes through the independence of their respective melodic lines. Weber obviously was aware of the problem of simultaneous declamation of different texts and seems to have attempted to mitigate it somewhat by staggering the enunciation of the two texts as much as possible, but what counted most in his conception of this piece was not the intelligibility of two specific texts, but rather a musical realization of a dramatic idea.

How much time elapsed between the notation of this idea-sketch and the composition of the continuous draft for the movement is unknown; according to the Diary the entire Duetto, presumably including the Moderato and the ritornello and recitative at the start of the third act, was completed on 6 June 1823. The draft of the Agitato on pages 74 and 75 is one of the more tortured specimens in the *Euryanthe* portfolio, since it documents a number of significant changes of mind. Because Weber typically enters revisions directly over the original versions, the 'layers' of drafting and the actual sequence in which the revisions were made are not always clear. However, the fact that some of the revisions in this particular draft were entered in red ink greatly facilitates the sorting out of the layers.

The most important revisions in the draft concern the main theme. Ex. 16 is an attempt to reconstruct the first ten measures as Weber

Ex. 16. First draft of the Duetto No. 15 (Agitato, mm. 45–54).

originally put them down on paper. Except for the first two measures, Adolar's part seems not to have been entered until after all the details of Euryanthe's part had been settled, and no text was entered until after the draft had been completed. For the sake of reference, I have included in brackets the text-setting that Weber presumbly had in mind as he wrote out the draft. As one can see, Weber began the draft with a variant of the original idea from page 54 that introduces a new syncopated pattern in measures 47–8 and 51–2. Typically, there is little evidence for the reasoning behind this revision, but the fact that the new rhythm continues into the ninth and tenth measures where it is set to the third line of text ('So bitt'rer Tod war nie gefunden') leads me to think that the syncopation first arose as a response to the third verse and was retroactively worked into the setting of the second line, as a way to achieve some sense of musical unity for the first ten measures. The fact that the tenth measure originally contained six beats rather than four, however, indicates that Weber by this point in the draft was no longer satisified with the preceding solution; perhaps the fact that the strongest poetic accents were falling in the middle of the measure offended his sense of truthful declamation.

Rather than solve the problem immediately, Weber seems for the time being to have left the extra beats in measure 54 and to have plunged

Ex. 17. First draft of the Duetto No. 15 (Agitato, mm. 69–72).

onward with the first episode of an eventual rondo structure. When he reached the first, abbreviated reprise of the main theme (m. 69*a*) he made an initial attempt to correct the deficiency that he had earlier sensed, for he shifted the entire theme by two beats, so that all of the strong poetic accents ('an', 'Pein', 'Gláuben', 'verschwúnden') now fall on the downbeat of each measure (Ex. 17). This new version seems to have entailed a harmonic revision as well, for the first three pitches in Euryanthe's part are apparently set over a dominant chord that resolves to the tonic at the start of measure 70*a*. Although earlier versions of the theme had not been explicitly harmonized, the original conception had presumably placed the start of the melody over the tonic triad.

The final revision of the main theme, entered in red ink in measures 45–54 probably after he had completed the full draft, actually restores many features of the original idea-sketch (Ex. 18). It retains the original conception of starting the piece in the first rather than the second half of the measure, so that the accents on 'an' and 'Pein' fall in the middle of measures 45 and 46. It also abandons the syncopated declamation of measures 47–8 and 51–2 in favour of the even eighth-note declamation of the original idea, thereby allowing the strong poetic accents at the end of the second verse to come out on the downbeat. As a criticism of the intermediate versions, this final version is a tacit admission that the idea sketch had been, after all, essentially truthful in its setting of the first two lines of text. The second version had, however, attempted to impose a musical sophistication—a transition within the second phrase to link the different rhythms of the refrain—that ultimately had falsified the natural declamation of the second line. In the final version, efforts

Ex. 18. Final version of the Duetto No. 15 (Agitato, mm. 45–54).

at such accommodation are abandoned, with benefit accruing to declamation at the same time that the melodic construction becomes more
'mosaic-like'. Weber then applied this final solution to the reprise at
measures 69–71 as he elaborated the draft with the addition of Adolar's
line.

One other revision within the Agitato offers a glimpse into Weber's
compositional approach and priorities. The original version of the first,
E-major episode and the retransition back to A minor (mm. 55–68)
was revised at several points, although when and in what order is not
at all clear (Ex. 19). The most important of the alterations concern measures 55–8, where Euryanthe's part was made more angular through
the substitution of lower appoggiaturas for the accented passing notes
of the original version. To interpret this revision, one could say that
the E-major melody was originally conceived as a matrix of elements—
major mode, diatonic melody, conjunct motion, rhythm initiated from
a strong downbeat—that present a sharp contrast with the main theme,
perhaps to highlight the change of mood in Euryanthe's fourth line
of text, a wistful reminiscence of lost happy days ('Mein Leben war
in dir allein').[4] The revision, of course, brings the episode into contact

----

[4] The same impulse may also be observed in the second episode (mm. 73–82), also
based on Euryanthe's nostalgic fourth verse, which once again presents a musical idea
whose choice of key (C major), narrow melodic ambitus, and orientation to the downbeat are 'characteristic' contrasts with the main theme.

Ex. 19. The Duetto No. 15 (Agitato, mm. 55–8).
   (*a*)   First verion.
   (*b*)   Final version.

(a)

(b)

with the semitone motion of the main theme. Thus the revision follows a paradigm that we have observed in several other instances in the *Euryanthe* drafts in which an original impulse guided by 'character' or dramatic effect is afterwards modified by considerations of a more purely musical sort, in this case, the desire to strengthen the sense of coherence.

The draft for the Moderato, begun on page 76 and continued at the top of page 73, also evinces a number of compositional decisions, but these are much less concerned with abstract musical problems. Rather, the approach here is dictated by a continuously unfolding situation, and the result is a succession of characteristic musical ideas with little sense of unity. For example, the key signature for the movement is A major, in this opera an appropriate tonal symbol for the former happiness to which Adolar refers at the outset of the number; after measure 12, however, A major is suppressed in favour of predominantly minor keys, as the poetic perspective shifts to Adolar's belief in Euryanthe's infidelity ('Der höchsten Liebe sprachst du Hohn'). With respect to form, the section must count as 'musical prose' in that there is no

Ex. 20. The start of the Duetto No. 15 (Moderato, mm. 1–7).

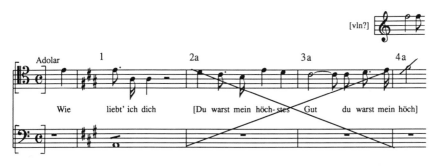

clear scheme of melodic repetition. The opening period in no way functions as a 'main theme' since it never returns, and the only thread of melodic coherence is provided by an orchestral motive, apparently associated with Adolar's threat to execute Euryanthe, that appears at measures 13, 15, 25, and 39.[5] It therefore comes as no surprise that the revisions in the Moderato address principally local effects that bear little relationship to the movement as a whole, as the composer concerns himself primarily with the invention of adequate musical symbols for the successive textual details. The first revision occurs at the very outset of the movement, where Weber began the draft with the first four measures presented in Ex. 20; however, he immediately cancelled the second, third, and fourth measures of this phrase and continued with an alternative that is the final version of the first phrase. Apart from the fact that this is a very rare instance of a substantive musical revision in an initial melodic idea, this revision brings two issues into focus.

First, the two versions cast a certain light on Weber's goals in text

---

[5] The figure also recurs in the orchestral postlude of the Agitato (mm. 91–4) prior to Euryanthe's sighting of the giant snake.

setting. As Weber emphasized in his letter to Müllner, truth of declamation is not merely a translation of strong and weak syllables into relatively long and short durational values; rather a 'truthful' musical setting has at its disposal other means, such as relative pitch and repetition, for conveying the essential meaning of the poem. The similarities between these two conceptions may be seen as the result of an impulse to portray the 'truth' of a single verse, Adolar's line 'Wie liebt' ich dich!—*Du* warst mein höchstes Gut!' Obviously, they share the same motive for the setting of Adolar's first words. The second measures in both versions set the words 'Du warst mein höchstes Gut' to the same durational values, and in both versions of measure 2 the words 'Du' and 'höchstes' are the ones that are emphasized, the former by its placement on the downbeat, the latter by its realization as a melodic peak on the third beat. In both versions the third measure repeats the words 'Du warst mein höchstes Gut' and again emphasizes the word 'höchstes' by placing it on the highest pitch heard thus far in the phrase, perhaps to emphasize exactly how much Euryanthe meant to Adolar.

Second, the differences between the two versions demonstrate once again that even in a situation where Weber does consider alternatives, the evidence is still insufficient to suggest conclusively why one version is preferred over another. In this case, the fact that the initial idea breaks off in the middle of a phrase makes it impossible to compare it to the whole shape of the final version. Speculatively, one could point to certain things that Weber may have felt wrong with the original idea. Thus he may have viewed the rhythmic reinterpretation of the words 'Du warst mein höchstes Gut' upon their repetition in measures 3*a* and 4*a* of the original version as an unnecessary variation that contradicted the 'truthful' declamation worked out in measures 2*a*–3*a*; in the final version the same truth is told by both the initial statement and its rhythmically parallel repetition. At the same time, the later version is musically more coherent because measures 4 and 5 can be heard as a natural response to measures 2 and 3, thereby effecting a more balanced phrase structure; the first version had instead presented three different melodic-rhythmic fragments in the space of four measures. The harmonic implications of the first version may also have seemed wrong, since the presumed progression beneath the first version (I–IV–V?–I–IV) somewhat redundantly moves twice to the subdominant; the final version effects a more directed progression from I to IV to V^7. Moreover, the implied shift to IV at measure 2*a* in the original version forces the falling-fifth gesture at measure 1 to do double duty, as both a cadence for the end of the preceding progression and a stable point from which to begin the Duetto; in the final version, the tonic support for measure 2 allows us to hear that measure as the true beginning of a new phrase, and when at measures

6–7 the rhythm of measure 1 is repeated, we hear its cadential function confirmed. I believe all of these factors make the final version better than the original idea, but which, if any, correspond to Weber's perception of the revision simply cannot be known.

Concern for truthful portrayal of character is apparently reflected in another significant revision in the composition of the Moderato. Two versions of measures 26–7 exist, the original version in the draft (Ex. 21*a*) and the version in the autograph score and all subsequent transmissions (Ex. 21*b*). The major musical difference between these two versions is the elongation of a single measure in the draft into two measures in the final version. Possibly this change was motivated by a desire to balance the two measures of Adolar's command ('Verstumm' auf ewig') with two measures of Euryanthe's response, but I think it more likely that the change was effected for purposes of characterization. In and of itself, the first version is a 'correct' setting of the text that was carried in *Web*. Cl. II A g 4 (and presumably also in Weber's *Textvorlage* at the time of composition, the lost fascicle of *Web*. Cl. II A g 5), 'Kann dich nichts bewegen', which underscores Euryanthe's recognition of Adolar's determination by placing the word 'nichts' on the locally highest pitch. Perhaps Weber sensed, however, that the rapidity of this eighth–note setting conveys an element of anxiety that contradicts the image of courage and acceptance portrayed in her very next words, 'So tödte mich! Mein letzter Hauch ist Segen | für dich ...' In the second version, therefore, he rearranged the word order to reconcile a primary accent on 'nichts' with a more forceful rhythm that would convey Euryanthe's strength of character in the time of crisis.

The fact that the composition of the Duetto No. 15 should have caused Weber such a large amount of effort is not without some irony. Whereas many of the best pieces in the opera have left behind practically no trace of their genesis (the Jaegerchor No. 18 is just such an example), the heavily reworked Duetto is in the opinion of the present writer one of the least successful and least memorable pieces in the entire opera. The Moderato contains little of real lyrical interest, a consequence of the essentially 'prosaic' text that it sets. Despite the logic with which it realizes the 'truth' of the situation, the main theme of the Agitato is, for this listener, an inadequate vehicle for expressing the grief and poignancy of the moment, although the situation is admittedly unnatural and one is hard pressed to identify with Adolar's murderous intentions. Weber himself seems tacitly to have acknowledged the piece's weaknesses when, pressed by Count Brühl to make additional cuts for the Berlin production of the opera, he drastically abbreviated both sections of the Duetto, the only set piece apart from the introductory Scena of No. 17 to be so affected, as if to allow the piece to finish as quickly

Ex. 21. The Duetto No. 15 (Moderato, mm. 25–8).
(a) First version.
(b) Second version.

(a)

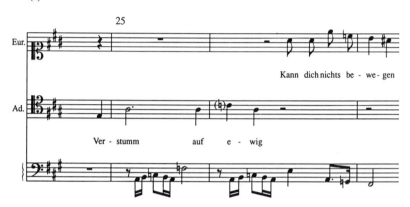

(b)

as possible. At the root of the problem seems to lie Weber's fundamental inability, acknowledged in the letter to Kannegießer cited earlier, to conceive completely different alternatives to that which his first impulses deem 'truthful' and 'characteristic'. In the large majority of cases this approach works and little or no revision is necessary. Forced to deal with a specific text, situation, and emotions in No. 15 to which he perhaps could not warm, however, Weber 'thought out' a basic solution and clung doggedly to it, and no amount of revision and fine tuning was able to rescue the piece. What was needed in this piece was a completely different approach.

3. THE OUVERTURE

3.1. *The problem of the ouverture*

Of all the pieces in the opera, the Ouverture has left behind the broadest trail of evidence for Weber's compositional decisions, as the preliminary materials consist of a worksheet for the development section that diverges significantly from the final version and a complete composition draft with four points of substantial revision. The fact that the drafts for the Ouverture should document such an atypically high incidence of compositional revision suggests at first glance that, without the blueprint afforded by a text, Weber the instrumental composer necessarily could and did explore more options. This is not to imply, however, that in the realm of instrumental music the composer was no longer under the constraint of his 'truth' ideal, nor that his compositional choices were conditioned solely by the criteria of autonomous music. In fact, certain facets of the compositional process hint that in instrumental music as in vocal music, Weber was still guided in large measure by poetic impulses and the quest for character.

Of course, by the time of *Euryanthe*, the overture was one instrumental genre that was expected to have a more or less well-defined poetic content, since it was assumed, especially by German opera composers and critics, that an overture should in some way prepare the audience for the following stage work.[6] There can be no doubt that Weber himself conceived his mature overtures as musical commentaries on the poetic content of the following drama. Even if we exclude as authentic for the time being his alleged comment to Lobe that the overture to *Der Freischütz* contained the 'entire drama *in nuce*',[7] Weber nevertheless did offer quite a detailed explanation of the *Preciosa* overture.[8] Just as clearly, however, he also recognized the central aesthetic dilemma of the genre: how to convey a poetic image in the overture without requiring prior knowledge of the opera on the part of the audience. Introducing Spohr's *Faust* to Prague audiences in 1816, he reproduced Spohr's programmatic description of its overture—a portrait of the title character torn between hedonism and more noble impulses and of his eventual demise—but noted that a listener could grasp this meaning entirely only *after* he has heard the opera.[9] Yet Weber himself abhorred

---

[6] The eighteenth-century antecedents for this view are discussed by Constantin Floros, 'Das "Programm" in Mozarts Meisterouvertüren', in his *Mozart-Studien I* (Wiesbaden, 1979), pp. 21–75, especially pp. 21–3. That Mozart subscribed to this view in his mature overtures is also persuasively argued by Daniel Heartz in 'Mozart's Overture to *Titus* as Dramatic Argument', *MQ* 64 (1978): 29–49.

[7] Lobe, 'Gespräche mit Weber', op. cit. ch. 2 n. 6 above, p. 32.

[8] *Sämtliche Schriften*, p. 218.

[9] *Sämtliche Schriften*, p. 275.

public explications of the poetic content of instrumental music—the comments about the overture to *Preciosa* were communicated privately to the play's author, P. A. Wolff—evidently feeling that any musical work should stand or fall on its own merits.[10] Weber thus seems to have conceived the overture as an exceptionally difficult challenge, an independent piece of music that should also convey more or less intelligibly some poetic conception to an audience without recourse to an explanatory programme or prior knowledge of the opera. Put another way, the problem for the overture composer was to devise musical ideas and coherent musical processes that would satisfy as music and at the same time provide graspable symbols for certain poetic ideas appropriate to the following drama.

Writing in 1841, the classically orientated aesthetician Ferdinand Hand took Weber to task precisely because he felt that the *Euryanthe* Ouverture was poetically intelligible only through the hindsight afforded by knowledge of the entire opera.[11] However, let us attempt to approach the Ouverture with innocent ears, for the time being ignorant of the sources of the quoted themes and the specific details of the plot, in order to understand that its poetic message need not reside solely in audience prescience of quoted materials with specific textual associations. Weber selected quotations from the opera not because he expected them to function as signposts to specific characters and situations that have not yet been introduced, but because they were generally intelligible as metaphors within the new, purely instrumental context of the overture. In fact, if one relies just on the listener's knowledge that *Euryanthe* is a medieval *Ritterroman*, a reasonable assumption of educated audiences of 1823 if not of modern audiences, his sense of basic expressive musical conventions like those discussed in Chapter VIII, and his ability to follow certain musical processes, one can see that the overture follows a four-part poetic paradigm paralleling the central thrust of the opera: (1) Exposition/ Idyll; (2) Largo/Threat; (3) Development/Struggle; (4) Recapitulation/ Idyll Regained and Strengthened.

As a whole, the exposition presents an essentially untroubled, major-mode world, with expressive conventions perhaps suggesting heroism and love, the twin poles of chivalry. The energetic triplet arpeggiation at measure I connotes a heroic ideal much as it does in No. 4 (mm.

---

[10] See also Weber's letter to Friedrich Rochlitz of 14 Mar. 1815, cited in Jähns, op. cit. ch. 1 n. 4 above, p. 338, concerning his reluctance to divulge the poetic inspiration for a planned piano concerto in F-minor to a public not already familiar with his artistic intentions. This piece eventually became the *Concertstück* in F minor, and, significantly, in its published form any and all poetic elements are concealed from open display.

[11] Ferdinand Hand, *Aesthetik der Tonkunst*, Part II (Jena, 1841), pp. 340–1.

9–10). The music from measures 9–25 need not be associated with a specific text for a listener to comprehend the chivalric connotations of its march-like dotted rhythms and wind-band scoring. The timpani roll at measures 53–6, which confirms B♭ major as the new tonic, easily functions as a symbol for courtly pageantry and ceremony, much in the same way that a similar figure is used for the entrance of the guests at the start of the Act II Finale. The lyrical second theme may be taken as a symbol for the more *sensible* side of courtly culture, especially through Weber's addition of conventional 'sighing' figures to the borrowed melody at measure 67.[12] The Largo also needs not be interpreted solely with respect to Emma, but rather as a puzzle, threat, or obstacle that casts an unexplained shadow over the major-mode equanimity of the exposition. The transitional measures that precede it (mm. 105–28) introduce minor-mode inflections, unstable harmonies and shifts in dynamic level that gradually cloud over the buoyant close of the exposition, and the extremely chromatic and nearly athematic Largo thus appears as the final and most complete stage in this process of breakdown.[13]

As Amadeus Wendt observed, the fugato that ensues is a struggle to overcome the mysterious cloud and return to life.[14] In the first part of the fugato (mm. 144–169), the contrapuntal development is interrupted at three points (mm. 156, 162, 168) by a quiet triplet figure over chromatically rising bass; Wendt's interpretation of these triplets as 'fearful trembling' opposing the gathering strength of the fugato is perhaps also supported by tonal phenomena, as each appearance of the hesitant triplets causes the subject to sink one degree lower, from B minor (m. 144) to A minor (m. 158) to G minor (m. 164). Apart from these temporary setbacks, most of the musical devices in the development may be interpreted as metaphors for the attempt to return to the previous, untroubled state, much in the same way as the fugal artifices in the finale of Beethoven's Op. 110 seek to overcome the depression of the Arioso dolente. These include: (1) long-range crescendo and stringendo;[15] (2) systematic compression of the fugato subject from four measures (m. 144) to two measures (m. 170) to one measure (m. 181); (3) contrary motion as a

---

[12] About the second theme Amadeus Wendt noted that 'mancher Seufzer scheint sich einzudrängen...' *BamZ* 3 (1826): 12.

[13] Here, as in Eglantine's delirium in the third act, the Largo begins with a B-minor triad rather than the B-major triad that initiates the Act I *Vision*. The use of B minor rather than B major is best understood as another element of musical contrast that distances the Largo from the major-mode Allegro that it interrupts.

[14] *BamZ* 3 (1826): 12.

[15] Through an oversight on Weber's part the instruction for a stringendo was omitted in early sources for the score and had to be explained verbally. See Weber's letter of 1 Mar. 1824 to Franz Danzi (*MMW* ii. 549) and his list of metronome settings for *Kapellmeister* Aloys Präger (*Sämtliche Schriften*, p. 220).

symbol for opposition (mm. 170–6, 181–4); (4) rising sequences in local progressions (the top voice in measures 170–4 and 181–4) and a long-range tonal ascent from B minor (m. 144) to C minor (m. 170) to Db major (m. 181) to Eb major (m. 199); (5) a shift from minor keys to major keys; and (6) progressively clearer anticipations of 'victory', as the opening triplet figure is hinted at measures 179–80 and then briefly quoted as a 'false reprise' in C major (mm. 189–92) before the definitive return at measure 199. The recapitulation is more than just a restoration of the world of the exposition, for the enhanced dynamics, enriched accompaniment and temporal and registral extension of the final cadence in the second theme (mm. 226–49) signify that the great struggle of the development has produced a stronger and more durable state than that which existed at the outset.

Many twentieth-century readers will doubtless find such a reading of the Ouverture far too allegorical for their taste, a throw-back to the nineteenth-century hermeneutics that we have sought to overcome through objectively quantifiable analysis. In fact, the *Euryanthe* Ouverture does lend itself very well to an analysis of a more traditional type, as has been demonstrated by a recent study that treats the piece solely as an autonomous musical structure, demonstrating quite extensive thematic work and a depth of musical integrity to which one could appropriately apply the organic metaphor.[16] Such 'symphonic' pretensions seem thoroughly consonant with the aspirations of this particular work to the status of 'grand opera', and in the following discussions of the composition drafts we shall point to a number of these organic features. The fact that the Ouverture remains a staple in the concert repertory at a time when most audiences know little or nothing of Adolar, Euryanthe, and Emma also testifies strongly to the success of the piece as an example of 'absolute music'. But to view the Ouverture solely as an autonomous structure apart from its poetic basis diminishes our appreciation of the artistic problem that confronted Weber and of his solution to that problem. In the Ouverture, as in Weber's vocal compositions, it is unnecessary and misleading to separate the poetic, characterizing impulses from the musical thought.

3.2. *A preliminary draft for the development*

The earliest of the extant Ouverture sketch materials are the preliminary studies for the development on page 11, a leaf from the old parts to Heigel's funeral music (J. 116, comp. 1811). Quite possibly these were

---

[16] See Matthias S. Viertel, *Die Instrumentalmusik Carl Maria von Webers* (Frankfurt am Main, etc., 1986), pp. 182–96. See also Christopher Hatch, 'Weber's Themes as Agents of "a Perfect Unity"', *Music Review* 48 (1988): 32–3.

the earliest written annotations of any kind for the Ouverture, since the relatively high incidence of significant revision in the draft of the exposition (pp. 3–4), which on textual grounds must have postdated the sketches on page II, suggests that it was the first and only draft ever written down for that section of the piece.

The preliminary materials on page II consist of three items, each of which is fraught with analytic and interpretive implications:

1. A two-measure sketch in two voices for the fugato.[17] The heavy revision in the first measure of this sketch makes transcription difficult, but three layers seem to be present. The first version (Ex. 22a) combines a bass derived from the Con fuoco of No. 4—note the falling third in the first measure and the dotted rhythms of the second—with a triplet figure in the upper voice that may ultimately be related to the very start of the Ouverture; presumably at the time that the sketch was written Weber had already planned to make these three components—falling third, dotted rhythm, and triplets—the basic building blocks in the exposition of the Ouverture. In the second version (Ex. 22b), the melodic contours of both voices are inverted in the first measure; the falling third of the bass becomes an ascending third, and the triplet figure, written in a higher register because of the heavy cancellation of the earlier version, is revised to avoid parallel octaves with the new bass. Why the start of the subject is inverted is not clear, although the final version is melodically smoother than the original idea; there may also be some strategic significance attached to the inversion of the key interval of Adolar's melody, namely, a desire to allow the original falling third to grow more gradually out of the struggle of the fugato as the triumph of the recapitulation comes within sight. The third version (Ex. 22c) converts the dotted rhythm on the second beat of the upper voice into a triplet. Of course, the most intriguing aspect of this sketch is its tonality. No key signature is present, but the accidentals imply that the fugato is conceived in a B♭ tonality. Although the absence of any accidental for the third scale degree makes it impossible to say with certainty whether the draft implies the minor mode as in the final version or a major mode chromatically tinged by the G-flat in measure 2, the sketch is decidedly not in B minor, a point to which we shall return.

2. A twenty-five-measure draft whose beginning corresponds to measure 170 of the final version, where the fugato subject in the bass is

---

[17] Whether the fugato sketch on the first two staves of page II was originally longer is impossible to say, since the remainder of the first staff after the bar line at the end of the second measure has been cut away, along with three additional staves at the top of the page, presumably some time after the sketch was made; the fact that the bass, the structural voice in this passage, does not continue after measure 2, however, strongly suggests that the sketch in fact was only two measures long.

Ex. 22. Sketch for the start of the development of the Ouverture.
(*a*) First version.
(*b*) Second version.
(*c*) Third version.

(a)

(b)

(c)

opposed by contrary motion in the soprano, which suggests more strongly
the original shape of Adolar's motto (Ex. 23). As originally sketched,
the first fifteen measures of this draft closely correspond to measures
170–84 of the final version, with the only deviation at measures 176–8,
which imply two measures of D-flat harmony (mm. 177–8), followed
by two measures of a dominant-seventh chord on A♭. A revision in

Ex. 23. Preliminary draft for the development of the Ouverture (mm. 170 ff.)

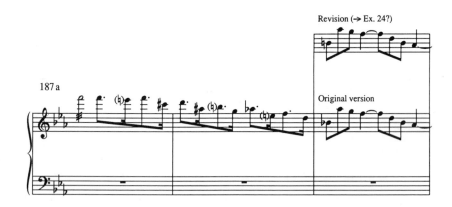

the draft, which brings it into agreement with the final version, supports
mm. 177–8 with A♭ harmony, and the arrival on D♭ is delayed until
measure 181, where the subject is compressed into one measure. The
last ten measures of the draft (mm. 185a–94a), however, bear only a
loose connection to the final version. A repetition of measures 177–80,
now supported by an implied progression from the dominant of C minor
to the dominant of E♭, leads to a cadence in E♭ minor at m. 191a,
whereupon a rising chromatic sequence in the bass is pitted against a
reiterated triplet figure derived from the last half of measure 190a. The
draft breaks off inconclusively at measure 194a as the sequence attains
D minor.

3. Immediately following is a six-measure sketch, based on the main
theme of the Duetto No. 13, that corresponds to no passage in the
final version of the Ouverture (Ex. 24). The flag at the start of the
sketch, which begins on the diminished-seventh of C minor, possibly
referred Weber to another leaf, but I now think it more likely that
the sketch was intended as an alternative for measures 191a–4a of the
prior draft, since on the one hand the B♭ at measure 189a was changed
into a B♮, thereby suggesting harmonic continuity with the new sketch,
and on the other hand the bass line in the latter also continues the
triplets that emerged in measures 189a–90a. In addition, the rising
chromatic bass of the sketch also suggests that it may have been conceived
as a replacement for the chromatic ascent in measure 191a–4a.

Ex. 24. Preliminary draft for the development of the Ouverture alluding to the Duetto No. 13.

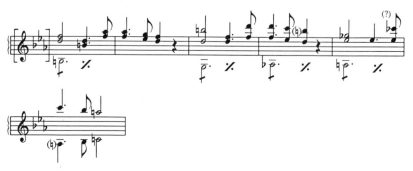

The preliminary work on page 11 provides a fascinating glimpse into Weber's conception of the development section. At this early stage of composition, the first item on the page seems to be enough of an indication to remind the composer that the first section of the development is to be a fugato that will be worked out later. That this fugato evidently was originally planned to begin in B♭ rather than the B-minor of the final version is extremely important, for it suggests that at the outset of written work on the Ouverture in early September 1823 Weber in fact had decided to proceed from the close of the exposition (B♭ major) to the fugato of the development (B♭ minor?) without the intervening Largo. Around 1860 Weber's student Julius Benedict recalled that the composer had originally written the Ouverture as a single-movement Allegro without the B-minor section based on Emma's *Vision* and that he later added the Largo in Vienna after rehearsals had begun.[18] Although Max Maria von Weber transmitted Benedict's recollection as fact and embellished it by claiming that Weber's concern for the clarity of Emma's function in the opera led him to add the Largo during the Vienna rehearsals in order to revive the earlier plan for a pantomime during the Ouverture,[19] Jähns questioned the accuracy of Benedict's assertion, because he knew that the lone continuity draft of the Ouverture contained Emma's music and the transition that leads up to it. When Jähns expressed his doubts to Benedict, the latter conceded that he might have confused certain details, but he still maintained that Weber at one time conceived the Ouverture as a single Allegro movement.[20]

Despite numerous factual errors in Benedict's memoir, the preliminary

---

[18] A copy of Benedict's memoir is preserved in *Web*. Cl. V. 5B, No. 65a.B.

[19] *MMW* ii. 460, p. 513.

[20] Jähns, op. cit. ch. 1 n. 4 above, p. 366.

sketch on page 11 now suggests that he may after all have been accurate on this one point. Putting the evidence of the sketch together with that of the extant preliminary librettos, we may attempt to summarize Weber's changing thoughts about the use of Emma's music in the Ouverture: (1) According to the libretto approved by the Viennese censor in February 1822 (*Web.* Cl. II A g 3), Weber early in the genesis of the opera envisioned a *Pantomimische Prolog Szene* during the Ouverture that depicts Euryanthe praying at Emma's crypt. As suggested in Chapter V, this addition was one of a number of libretto revisions that sought to give the supernatural a more prominent role in the drama. (2) By the spring or summer of 1823, however, the pantomime had been excised from the libretto (*Web.* Cl. II A g 5), along with any other appearance of Emma's shadow on stage. The single-tempo conception of the Ouverture suggested by the preliminary draft for the development may perhaps be seen as a consequence of this stage in the history of the libretto. (3) At the time that Weber wrote out the full composition draft of the Ouverture in the autumn of 1823 (in fact, this did take place after he and Benedict had gone to Vienna), he reverted to the earlier conception of working Emma's music into the Ouverture in some fashion. There is no evidence to support Max Maria von Weber's claim that the decision to include the Largo was prompted by a renewed interest in the possibility of staging a pantomime during the Ouverture. Rather, to understand the motivation for the eventual inclusion of Emma's music we shall first have to push ahead with the rest of the Ouverture drafts.

That the second item of the preliminary draft for the development begins with measure 170 is significant in that it suggests that Weber understood the arrival at C minor as an important point of articulation within the development, and for an obvious reason, since it reintroduces the falling third of Adolar's motto in the upper voice as a contrary-motion counterpoint to the fugato subject. Moreover, it marks the second stage in a tonal scheme that Weber seems to have envisioned from the outset as one of the guiding principles of the development, namely, a long-range ascent from Bb at the start of the fugato (and the end of the exposition) to C minor at measure 170 to Db at measure 177 or 181 and eventually to Eb minor at measure 191a. Along with this tonal intensification, the preliminary draft also shares with the final version certain basic features that we earlier interpreted as symbols for struggle. For example, it documents even more obviously than the final version the rhythmic compression that lies at the heart of the development, as the two-measure patterns at measures 170–5 give way to one-measure units at measures 181–4 and half-measure patterns at measures 191a–4a. It also documents the interruption of this process through two outbursts (mm. 177–80 and 187a–90a), perhaps to hint that the triumphant outcome of the struggle is in sight. Moreover, the preliminary draft suggests that the music at measures 191*a*–4*a*, which in the final version of the Ouverture initially appears as interruptions within the first half of the development (mm. 156–7, 162–3, and 168–9), originated as the culmination of a systematic musical development, as the half-measure patterns, rising chromatic motion in the bass, contrary motion between the outer voices, and falling third in the upper voice may be heard as the end result of processes of compression that began at measure 170.

Yet having reached this extreme point of compression, Weber seems to have been at a loss to know how to end the development, perhaps because he had not yet completely determined the content of the exposition. The last item on the page, the sketch alluding to the Duetto No. 13, suggests that the composer suddenly entertained the idea of using this theme at or near the end of the development, perhaps as a way of hinting that victory was in sight at the end of such struggles; presumably this quotation would have been prepared by an appearance of the theme in the exposition as well.

The hypothesis advanced here, that Weber began the written composition of the Ouverture with the preliminary development draft on page 11, casts a provocative light on his understanding of the compositional task and the role of the development within the Ouverture. First, the fact that the fugato is the most extended passage of new composition in the Ouverture—in contradistinction to the exposition, which relies heavily on borrowed materials—leads one to suspect that Weber first tackled what obviously would be the most difficult compositional task. Second, although Weber doubtless had already made certain fundamental decisions about the thematic content of the Ouverture—especially the prominent role to be played by triplets and the melody from No. 4— before he proceeded to sketch out page 11, the preliminary draft of the development may be seen to harbour certain ideas that retroactively were planted in the exposition of the piece: contrapuntal textures, especially contrary motion; a commitment to thematic work; and rising chromatic lines. Thus, viewed from the perspective of genesis, the development section functions more as a generator for musical thought than as a section purely dependent upon actions of the exposition; of course in the real-time experience of the piece, the Ouverture in fact is heard as a consequence of the foregoing music. Third, and closely related to the second point, the fact that Weber started with the fugato points up the special poetic function of the development in the *Euryanthe* overture. Unlike the overtures to *Freischütz* and *Preciosa*, whose central dramatic metaphors are expressed through stylistic oppositions within their introductions and expositions, the fugato of the *Euryanthe* overture is arguably the primary locus for the central dramatic idea of this opera, a struggle through adversity to reattain a lost paradise. Thus Weber seems to have begun with the part of the composition that is most crucial to the poetic image of the entire movement.

3.3. *The continuity draft*

The continuity draft of the Ouverture, notated on pages 4–5, 7, and 9, like those for the vocal pieces, presents a relatively clean short score of the entire piece, including the B-minor Largo, that was directly antecedent to the autograph score; however, it documents a number of significant revisions at key moments that make it unlikely that the draft was preceded by any written materials other than the preliminary draft for the development. At four points in particular the draft casts a certain light on the special problems confronting Weber in this piece.

(a) *The bridge*

In the draft the first problematic passage is the transition from the first group to the second group (mm. 29–52). As Matthias S. Viertel has shown, the final version of this transition is conspicuously 'symphonic', as the triplets and dotted rhythms that characterize the two parts of the first group (mm. 1–8, 9–28) are developed in a number of ingenious ways.[21] The draft for this section of the exposition reveals that the final 'organic' effect of this segment was the product of careful revision rather than spontaneous invention. As originally drafted the transition consisted of a large number of elements (see Ex. 25):[22]: (*a*) four measures in E♭ major (mm. 29–32) that combine the triplets of the opening theme with the dotted rhythms of measures 9–25. These measures were taken over into the final version. One will of course recall that the basic shape of measures 29–30 had already appeared in the preliminary draft of the development section; (*b*) a four-measure phrase (mm. 33*a*–36*a*) that suddenly disrupts the E♭ tonality that has been a constant presence up to this point. At measure 33*a* a descending triplet scale passing from the soprano to the bass briefly suggests C minor (*b*), and a three-measure sequence of dotted rhythms (*b*$_2$) then destabilizes any sense of tonal centre through its consistent chromatic ascent in the bass and its placement of resolutions on the last sixteenth of each odd-numbered beat; (*c*) a descending four-measure sequence leading from E-flat major to G minor (mm. 37*a*–40*a*) that combines triplet scales in the bass (the inversion of measure 33*a*) with a dotted-rhythm pattern in the upper voice; (*a'*) a six-measure phrase moving sequentially from the dominant

---

[21] Viertel, n. 16 above, pp. 186–187.
[22] A facsimile of the first page of the Ouverture continuity draft is published in *MGG* xiv (Kassel and Basle, 1966), Plate 18, Illus. 2.

Ex. 25. Continuity draft for the bridge in the exposition of the Ouverture.

of F major to the dominant of B-flat major (mm. 41a–6a). This passage is essentially an extended version of the music heard at measures 29–32; (*d*) two measures in G♭ major (mm. 47a–8a), abruptly established through a deceptive cadence, that are based on a dotted-rhythm turning figure derived from the measure 17; (*e*) two measures of a new syncopated pattern (mm. 49a–50a) that again eradicate any sense of tonality through down-sliding chromatic motion; (*f*) two measures in E-flat minor (mm. 51a–2a) derived from the dotted rhythms of measures 34a–6a; (*g*) a sudden restatement of the opening motive in C major (V of F minor) (mm. 53a–4a); and (*h*) a two-measure unit based on the ubiquitous dotted rhythm that begins to ascend sequentially from F major.

Having reached this point in the draft Weber immediately began the revised version of the transition,[23] and it is not too difficult to guess why he felt that his first attempt had gone astray. The first version of the bridge is essentially an improvisatory concatenation of figures derived from the dotted rhythms and triplets of the opening theme, which, filled with extravagant tonal surprises (the diminished seventh at m. 33a, the plunge into G♭ at m. 47a, and the C-major fanfare at m. 53a), betrays little sense of harmonic direction and even shows some difficulty in escaping the tonic (note the renewal of E-flat as tonic at m. 37a and m. 51a). Weber's skilful selection and rearrangement of motives in the final version at least creates the impression of a more organically effected transition. The successive juxtaposition of triplets and dotted rhythms in measures 29–32 leads smoothly to a simultaneous combination of these two elements at measures 33–6, from which emerge

---

[23] Jähns's statement (op. cit., p. 357) that 24 measures were rejected between measures 32 and 33, could be taken to imply that measure 54a continues into the next measure of the draft (m. 33), leading Viertel (op. cit., p. 185) to assume mistakenly that the original version of the exposition was 24 measures longer than the final version. This is emphatically not the case.

only the dotted rhythms of measures 37–40. The consistent contrary motion of measures 33–6 adumbrates the importance attached to that device in the further course of the piece. And tonally the final version effects a more clearly directed and purposeful modulation in three stages: (1) mm. 29–38, in which E♭ is still heard as the clear, unchallenged tonic; (2) mm. 39–42, in which the chromatic sequence effectively wipes out any sense of tonic key; and (3) mm. 43–52, in which the key of the second group, B-flat major, is swiftly brought into focus by means of a falling fifth progression from V of F major to V of B♭ major.

(b) The second theme

While it is easy to understand why the rather developmental bridge should have necessitated a certain amount of reworking to achieve its final form, the fact that the lyrical theme of the second group (mm. 61–86) was also subjected to substantial revision in the continuity draft may, at first glance, come as a surprise, since this theme is quoted from Adolar's Aria No. 12; closer inspection, however, reveals the version of the theme in the Ouverture not to be a literal quotation but rather a subtle reshaping that adapts the theme to its new context. Thus even if Weber had from the outset planned to use this melody as the second theme—whether for its symbolism, its obvious contrast of mood with the more ebullient first-theme group, the prominent fall from $\hat{5}$ to $\hat{3}$ that it shares with the melody borrowed from No. 4, or because of all of these factors—in writing it out in the continuity draft he finally had to confront issues of adaptation, and some of these have left their trace in the draft.

For the sake of comparision Ex. 26 and 27 present the theme in three stages: (1) as it appears in Adolar's No. 12, transposed to B♭ major for ease of comparison (Ex. 26); (2) as notated in the first layer of the Ouverture draft (Ex. 27); and (3) the revised, final version of the theme, where this departs from the original draft. As in many other instances, it is by no means clear whether Weber entered the revisions before or after he had drafted the entire theme. Apart from the revision on the last quarter of measure 62, perhaps simply a correction of a copying error, the problems in drafting the second theme begin at the point where the Ouverture version begins to diverge from the aria (mm. 65–9). Whereas the aria version of the theme consists of a single through-composed period whose structure is guided by a text, the version in the Ouverture is made more appropriate for purely instrumental composition by reshaping it as a double period with clear antecedent-consequent phrase structure. Thus the first version of measures 65–9 fashions a half-cadence at the end of the antecedent phrase with a descending scale from a^2 to a^1 that may be heard in reference to both scalar descents

Ex. 26. The main theme in Adolar's Aria No. 12 (transposed to B♭).

Original key: A-flat

Ex. 27. Continuity draft for the second theme in the Ouverture.

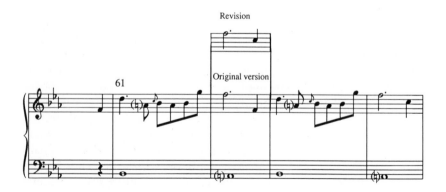

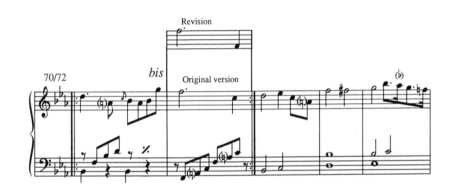

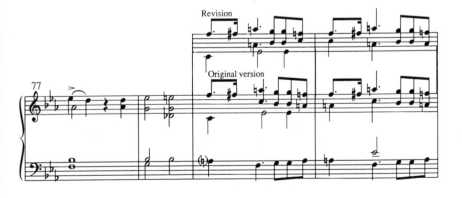

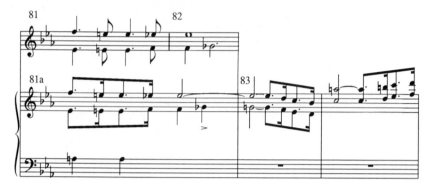

in the first theme group (e.g. m. 15 and m. 22)[24] and traditional 'sighing' figures that perhaps provide a clue to the expressive content of this passage. The revisions to which these measures are subjected improve the melodic momentum of the line in measures 65 and 66 and also enhance the expressive quality of the sighing figures by converting the weak beat passing notes into anticipations that retard the rate of descent.

The second half of the theme, which from measure 70 to measure 77 follows more closely the aria version, gradually incorporates dotted rhythms, a compositional device that brings the theme into contact with the first group, prepares the heroic closing group and perhaps also signifies a stronger mood than the *empfindsamer* antecedent phrase. These dotted rhythms cause the only trouble in the draft of this phrase, for the appearance of the figure at measure 81*a* in chromatic contrary motion hurries the end of the phrase unnecessarily; in the final version this measure is stretched out to two full measures through simple augmentation to effect a notated ritardando, and the return to the original durational values at measure 82 thus gives a new impetus for the close of the period.

[24] Viertel, op. cit., p. 188.

(c) The development

The revisions to which the preliminary draft of the development was submitted in the final version, doubtless informed now by the presence of a continuity draft for the exposition, speak to musical as well as poetic concerns. Consider, for example, the most obvious difference between the preliminary draft and the final version of the development, the addition of the B-minor Largo. Without the Largo as a cloud between the jubilant close of the exposition and the start of the fugato, the exertions of the fugato in the original version seem unmotivated, as the listener may well ask to what purpose such vigorous means are employed. The inclusion of Emma's music in a highly chromatic B tonality presents an extreme crisis that must be overcome through an extraordinary act of will. In addition, the incorporation of the *Vision* in its original key effects a chromaticization of tonal structure from the end of the exposition to measure 181 (B♭–B–C–D♭) that in a sense magnifies to a level of structural significance the local chromatic progressions that come to the fore elsewhere in the Ouverture.

Since page 11 had given only the first two measures of the fugato, it is impossible to know in what ways Weber's original plan for this section of the development differed from the final version. One may speculate that he did not originally plan to use the disruptive triplet figures at measures 156, 162, and 168 in the first half of the fugato, since the preliminary draft suggests that they arose through the various processes of *Steigerung* in the second half of the development. That the subject in the final version comprises four measures rather than two is significant, for in this way it is also brought into the plan for systematic diminution worked out in the preliminary draft for measures 170 ff.; the four-measure subject thus enhances the effect of measure 170 by allowing it to be heard not only as a contrapuntal intensification (the subject placed against itself in contrary motion), but also as a diminution of the original subject as well. The continuity draft does shed some light on the conversion of the two-measure subject on page 11 into the four-measure subject of the final version, for on the fifth system of the draft on page 5 Weber began the fugato with a four-measure subject (Ex. 28) that prefaces the two-measure idea worked out on page 11 (*y*) with a two-measure inversion of the idea (*x*). Perhaps because this version of the subject starts with a clear reference to the falling third of No. 4, thereby spoiling the effect of its return in the soprano at measure 170, Weber switched the two halves of this subject so that the fugato would begin, as in the revised sketch on page 11, with the rising third; the definitive four-measure subject and its counterpoints were then worked out in a four-measure sketch at the bottom of page 5 (Ex. 29), which served as the basis for the complete draft of the fugato on page 7.

Ex. 28. Sketch for the start of the development in the Ouverture (continuity draft).

The final version of measures 170–99 also demonstrates a number
of marked improvements over the preliminary draft. For one thing,
the tonicization of E♭ minor at measure 191*a* in the earlier version is
eliminated, perhaps because Weber felt that a return to the tonic at
this point would be premature; in the final version no key is strongly
established between D♭ major at measure 181 and E♭ major at the beginning of the recapitulation, which thus marks the culmination of the
long-range tonal ascent that started with the beginning of the development. The triplets that occur at measures 185–8 in the final version
are no longer heard as the end product of thematic processes in measures
170–84, but rather as a fortissimo transformation of the quiet triplets
from the first half of the development; metaphorically, the 'trembling'
interruptions in the first half of the fugato have become much more
sinister in order to oppose the greater energy that has accumulated
between measures 170 and 184. Lastly, the second half of the development
in the final version better prepares the return of the main theme at
the start of the recapitulation. The function of measures 187*a*–90*a* in
the preliminary draft, a somewhat redundant restatement of measures
177–80, is taken over by the 'false reprise' of the main theme over
a second-inversion C-major triad at measures 189–92, a gesture borrowed
from the aborted first version of the bridge in the exposition. Whether
the final version is to be heard solely in musical terms as an increasingly
clear anticipation of the first theme—the syncopated triplet rhythm of

Ex. 29. Contrapuntal sketch for the development in the Ouverture.

measures 179–80 leads to the stronger hint of the main theme at measure 189, which leads to the definitive restatement—or as a poetic metaphor for ever more secure anticipations of victory during the course of the struggle (the affective connotation of the C-major outburst at measure 189 should not be overlooked) depends upon the listener, but for Weber these two modes of thought were doubtless inseparable.

(d) The recapitulation apotheosis

In each of the overtures to his last three operas, Weber subjected the second half of the recapitulation to some degree of character transformation, typically inflating some element originally heard quietly—the melodies of Agathe's, Adolar's, and Reiza's arias, respectively—into a heroic gesture through variations in dynamics, accompaniment, melodic contour, phrase structure, or even tempo. Such transformations are usually interpreted as symbols for the *lieto fine* of the drama as a whole, and for such a symbolic procedure Weber would have had the brilliant codas of the so-called second and third *Leonore* overtures of Beethoven as models. Because this approach necessarily entailed some degree of compositional variation, it is not surprising that the draft of the *Euryanthe* Ouverture exhibits a certain amount of revision at this area of the recapitulation as the composer seeks the best way to conclude the Ouverture with a sense of catharsis.

Weber apparently had no trouble devising two of the chief means by which the second theme is made more heroic in the recapitulation: the striding eighth-note accompaniment of measures 235–43 and the upward extension of the melody to f^3 are both drafted with little sign of revision. However, finding an effective conclusion for the period was rather more problematic. Having attained the melodic peak of mm. 241–2, Weber's first inclination was to bring the second theme to an immediate close with a cadence earlier used at measure 102 (Ex. 30*a*), but he seems at once to have sensed the wrongness of this conclusion, which terminates the majestic period in a rather abrupt and perfunctory manner. A second attempt at closure (Ex. 30*b*) extends the cadence through an additional measure and allows the motivically important dotted rhythms to re-enter over a dominant pedal point, thus preparing the boisterous closing group, which up to m. 261*a* was originally treated as a literal transposition of measures 87–102. Following this point, a new four-measure extension (labelled *x* in the example), presumably over dominant harmony, was added as a way to intensify the sense of release at the end of this period.

Weber broke off the draft at this point, perhaps recognizing the affinity between the syncopated motive with which he had just extended the closing-group and the cadence of the second theme (m. 245). Thus in the final draft he shifted measures 262*a*–5*a* to the end of the second theme, thereby postponing its cadence through six measures of dominant harmony (mm. 244–9) to effect a more powerful sense of release at measure 250. At the same time, this revision seems to have stimulated Weber to find a new way to bring the Ouverture to a brilliant close. Shifting the four measures of triplet arpeggiations originally heard at the start of the closing group (mm. 246*a*–9*a*) toward the end of the period (mm. 262–5), he composed a new conclusion that, despite tonal stasis, continues to build in excitement to the very last measure through processes of rhythmic foreshortening. Four measures in which tonic and dominant harmonies alternate at the rate of one chord change per measure (mm. 262–5) are followed by two measures in which the same

Ex. 30. Continuity draft for the close of the recapitulation (mm. 241 ff.)

(*a*) First version.
(*b*) Second version.

(a)

(b)

chord change is made every half-measure (mm. 266–7). The effect of acceleration continues through the tonic pedal point of the last ten measures as constant quarter-notes (mm. 268–71) lead to an eighth-note figure perhaps drawn from the Schlußchor of the Act III Finale (mm. 272–3); the triplets and dotted rhythms of the last four measures cap off the rhythmic *Steigerung* of the coda and at the same time round out the Ouverture by recalling the two basic rhythms that had originally set the piece in motion .

4. CONCLUSIONS

The three examples discussed here lend themselves to few sweeping generalizations about Weber's creativity. In all cases the preserved materials shed more light on the psychology of creation than on an analytical approach. But if we are to understand works of art as history, we must be able to understand the particular problems that the artist set out to solve, and in this matter the genetic histories discussed here help clarify the ways that Weber viewed the tasks at hand. Each piece presented the composer with different problems that influenced the manner of composition, and one could in fact argue that special problems in each case were the principal reasons why precisely these pieces have left behind a relatively broad trail of genetic evidence. The task of co-ordinating the conflicting emotions of soloists and chorus in the large C-major ensemble of the Act II Finale seems to have led him to take the unusual step of working out certain decisions about melodic content and form on a preliminary worksheet, which thus provides a rare glimpse into the kinds of decisions that Weber made before he proceeded to draft out a complete movement. The problems of imposing musical unity on ideas originally conceived as 'characteristic' settings of specific conceits have left their mark on the composition draft of the Duetto No. 15, especially in the main theme of the Agitato movement, where the attempt to effect a musical link between two ideas that apparently arose independently created problems in declamation and phrase rhythm that ultimately proved insoluble. On the other hand, the special problem of the Ouverture, the portrayal of a poetic image through coherent musical procedures, led the composer to work out first an 'organic' musical process that could serve as the central dramatic metaphor, the renewal of strength during the struggle of the development.

The picture that emerges from the sketches and drafts for No. 15 and the C-major Allegro of the Act II Finale tends to confirm the more fragmentary evidence scattered throughout the drafts for the other vocal pieces. Simply put, Weber's approach to dramatic vocal composition was not in the first instance guided by purely musical criteria for invention, elaboration, and interrelation, but rather by a close attention to a given text and dramatic situation. Composition entailed the finding of appropriate musical equivalents for dramatic conceits and the assembly of such ideas into a larger structure. Structural decisions were facilitated in certain cases by archetypal moulds and in others by through-composed forms that followed the emotional swings in more dynamic poems. Questions of musical coherence and compatibility seem to be addressed principally in the process of revision. In contrast, the compositional history of the Ouverture amply demonstrates that where developmental musical processes were central to the poetic vision, Weber could and did adopt a more 'organic' approach, and succeeded brilliantly.

Weber's approach to composition will perhaps seem superficial and intellectually unstimulating to an analyst in search of the organic metaphor. Yet, it is important to remember that even Weber's severest contemporary detractors felt the problem of his music to reside not in its lack of intellectual challenge, but rather in the domination of intellection over a more spontaneous flow of music. To a certain extent, the evidence of Weber's compositional procedures supports this view, but it also challenges us to understand that the premisses that guided him were often different from those that guided Mozart, Beethoven, or Schubert. Approaching *Euryanthe* with sympathy and an ear for the 'truth' of its music, one can see that Weber's music follows its own premisses with an integrity that deserves understanding and admiration.

Conclusion

If one approaches the history of Western music in search of great, perfect works that seem to speak across the generations without benefit of explication, then one will have little use for *Euryanthe* or the foregoing study. By any standards *Euryanthe* is a flawed work that, even in its own day, rarely exerted an immediate attraction on audiences. From such a perspective, *Euryanthe* is at best an historically interesting experiment to be valued less for its own sake than for its undoubted influence on the future course of opera. But for one who looks to the history of music as an inexhaustible resource for understanding the cultures antecedent to our own, a work like *Euryanthe*, warts and all, is potentially as illuminating as the works that we accept without reservation as the 'great works' of the Western tradition, perhaps even more so, precisely because the distance that separates it from the modern listener-spectator challenges us to find ways to understand it or at the very least to understand why, in the final analysis, we are not powerfully drawn to the work. In so doing we come to understand better the culture and the specific minds that produced it and our own minds and assumptions as well.

From this perspective, the foregoing study of the genesis of *Euryanthe* particularly sensitizes us to the problems that Weber attempted to solve in this ambitious work, which was to have been the crowning glory of his career. The tortured genesis of the libretto provides an extreme example of a general problem that confronted German opera composers in the first half of the nineteenth century, the lack of competent, professional librettists upon whose knowledge of theatrical effect and operatic convention a composer could rely; in this matter the fact that both Lortzing and Wagner came to write their own librettos seems particularly telling. In the case of the *Euryanthe* libretto, this institutional problem was compounded by the fact that Weber envisioned a new type of opera with few direct models, a 'grand romantic opera' that would redefine the premises of a genre that had grown stagnant and become irrelevant to his own age. The fact that he was forced to put so much of himself into the libretto in order to solve these problems allows us to grasp certain features of his operatic dramaturgy, but by no means was his involvement entirely beneficial for the eventual success of the opera. Nevertheless, that the solution found by Weber and

Chezy—the 'romantic' subject matter, the mixture of genres, and the abrupt swings in mood—was remarkably close to the successful formula for 'grand opera' adopted by Scribe and the composers at the Paris Opera within the following decade speaks to the soundness of Weber's instincts and his sense for the spirit of the times.

The evidence of the compositional process, slim though it may be, also serves to encourage us to rethink our own analytical positions. Despite his chronological and geographical proximity to Beethoven and their shared artistic idealism, with respect to compositional technique Weber is separated from the Viennese classics by a gulf nearly as great as that which separates him from Rossini, and the analytical techniques that prove so revealing for the music of the Viennese masters afford little meaningful insight into the music of *Euryanthe*. Unless one is willing a priori to condemn music that fails to fit a Procrustean analytical bed by which it was not intended to be measured, it seems more fruitful to develop new strategies for dealing with such music. And though Weber's composition drafts by no means provide a magical 'key' to unlock these new approaches, the fact that they give little evidence that the organic metaphor mattered to him, at least at the level of the individual piece, should provoke us to ascertain the criteria that in fact were important to him. The picture that emerges is of a composer for whom dramatic composition was but a means to realize an aesthetic agenda predicated on 'truth' and 'character', and the only way to make any sense out of his music is to attempt to put analytical flesh on his principles. Admittedly, the resulting discussions will not be rigorous, traditional analysis as understood by most twentieth-century practitioners, but they do allow us to approach the spirit in which the work was written and reveal that the composer very nearly accomplished what he set out to do.

This is not to say that even on his own terms Weber was entirely successful in *Euryanthe*. At times the 'truth' in the musical setting, for example the main theme of the Agitato of No. 15, seems more contrived than deeply felt, and Weber could profitably have spent more effort in the compositional process on the reconciliation of characterization with musical values. His trust in 'truth' as the absolute arbiter of last resort for dramatic music seems to have led him to overestimate the ability of his audiences to comprehend the truth of his music and their willingness to sacrifice self-contained beauty to that end; their documented delight in the concluding movement of the Act I Finale, arguably the least truthful piece in the opera, suggests the realities of the public's priorities. Many of Weber's metaphors for 'character'—for example, the symbolic uses of tonality for key choices of entire pieces and tonal goals within recitatives—speak more readily to the eye of the analyst than to the ear of the spectator-listener. And even if one is closely attuned to the particular metaphors of Weber's musical language, the shifts in imagery and situation that occur within relatively short spans of time make it impossible to absorb all of the details of the composition; hence the comment of a sympathetic contemporary like Amadeus Wendt that one could easily be fatigued by this opera. Naturally the music of the Viennese classics cannot be comprehended in a single hearing either, but the compelling surface of their works attracts the listener who is not interested in the details and actually invites him to repeated listenings that subsequently reveal more of the details. Of course, for audiences and critics who were unwilling to grant absolute sovereignty to truth and character in the aesthetic experience of opera, Weber's music was nothing more than a patchwork mosaic or musical prose with little compelling musical content. More than any other factor this perceived 'lack of melody' seems to have accounted for the initial wave of indifference toward the opera.

But ultimately, the failure of *Euryanthe* must again come back to the text, which, despite Weber's responsibility, was severely mismatched to his own gifts and aesthetics. On the one hand, the libretto afforded him few opportunities for the kind of nature painting for which he had demonstrated a considerable talent in *Freischütz* and that would again come to the fore in *Oberon*; instead, his desire to write a 'grand opera' seems to have led him and his librettist to concentrate in *Euryanthe* on the conflict of human passions that, however, are ill-defined and understood in the libretto. By design the opera excluded the folk-like elements, especially the catchy diatonic melodies, that had made the *Freischütz* a popular work from the start; such simple music would not have been 'truthful' in the courtly milieu of *Euryanthe*, and the two pieces that are outwardly close to the popularity of the *Freischütz*, the Jaegerchor No. 18 and the May Song, betray their distance from their rustic counterparts in the *Freischütz* through their considerable rhythmic and harmonic artifice.

Most fatal of all to the aesthetic success of the opera, Weber's compositional approach was precisely the wrong one for the *Euryanthe* libretto, a point first made by Wagner in *Oper und Drama* and recently reiterated by Carl Dahlhaus.[1] Rather than make us overlook, forget, or forgive the logical inconsistencies and improbable treatments of character in the libretto, Weber's music, through its close attention to details of situation and emotion, constantly draws our attention to and actually magnifies the very weaknesses of a text that decidedly does not bear

---

[1] *GSD* iii. 292, and Carl Dahlhaus, *Die Musik des 19. Jahrhunderts* (Wiesbaden, 1980), pp. 59–60.

up under close scrutiny. Here Weber's strong influence over the text was probably most detrimental, since in his zeal to effect an indivisible fusion of all available means into a so-called '*Totaleffekt*' he shaped the libretto more with an eye to its musical realization and large-scale architecture than with considerations of logic and clarity of plot and action. The finished opera thus lacks a centre of gravity since it offers the spectator-listener neither a compelling story nor self-sufficient music *per se*. Precisely because of this close interdependence, however, any and all attempts to 'salvage' the music of the opera through the provision of a new or improved libretto are essentially misguided, and the fact that all such experiments have failed is a final witness to the integrity of Weber's idealistic, but flawed vision.

Appendix I

Diary Extracts Pertaining to the Composition of Euryanthe

1822

17 May	[Hosterwitz] Arie Adolar As dur entworfen.
20 May	Arie in As Adagio notiert, und somit die Arie vollendet entworfen.
24 May	gearbeitet. *Duett. H dur.*
26 May	Duett Eglantine Lysiart. H dur ganz entworfen.
14 June	gearbeitet. *Introd. Recit: und Ensemble in Es dur entworfen.*
19 June	gearbeitet. *Introduction.*
21 June	No. 1–6 vollendet entworfen.
26 June	gearbeitet. Vision. Rezita. H dur.
27 July	gearbeitet. Duett A dur entworfen
5 Aug.	Redigirt. Idee zu der Arie der Euryanthe im 3 Akt *Zu ihm!* gefaßt ...
24 Oct.	[Dresden] gearbeitet. Arie E♯ der Eglantine entworfen.
26 Oct.	Cav: C dur Glöklein im Thale. Eury. entworfen
28 Oct.	*Euryanthe angefangen in Partitur zu sezzen*

1823

1 Feb.	gearbeitet. Finale 2: Akt
3 Feb.	Abends Finale
5 Feb.	... Finale ...
7 Feb	gearbeitet Finale
25 Feb.	Schluß des Finales F moll geschrieben
7 Mar.	gearbeitet. Arie Lysiart
12 Mar.	Abends gearbeitet. Anfang des 2: Akts pp
20 Mar.	den 3: Akt der Euryanthe redigirt .... Idee zu dem Jagd Chor
22 Mar.	Idee Duett Adol. Eury
28 Mar.	*Charfreytag. Maylied* in Euryanthe gemacht
1 Apr.	Mittag mit Rochliz bei Gutschmidt dann zu Förster wegen Euryanthe bis 4 Uhr. die Chezy kam unerwartet an. *Erste Seite zu Euryanthe instrumentiert*
9 Apr.	gearbeitet. Ensemble D♯ *Trozze nicht.*
3 May	*Ersten Akt der Euryanthe vollendet entworfen.*
11 May	[Hosterwitz] 2 Seiten instrum:

12 May	13 Seiten instr:
13 May	8 Seiten instr:
14 May	*12 Seit: inst:*
15 May	2 Seit. Euryanthe Introd. bis zur Cavat. in C: vollendet.
17 May	*13 Seit instr.* Cavat. C dur vollendet.
19 May	9 Seiten inst:
20 May	2 Seiten instr:
21 May	14 Seit: inst:
22 May	6 Seit instr:
24 May	14 Seit inst:
25 May	Sonntag. um 10 Uhr in die Kirche. Frau von Chezy nebst Jungen Mittag da. troz dem *11 Seiten instr.* und somit den **Ersten Act der Euryanthe** vollendet. id est in 12 Tage instrumentiert. o Hosterwitz! o Ruhe. Feuerwerk!!!
26 May	Corrigiert. unwohl
28 May	Ideen. *Schirmende Engel Schaar*
9 June	früh kam Roth. *1: Akt der Euryanthe aufgeführt.*
18 June	Unwohl. gearbeitet . . . 2: Akt 10 Seiten instr.
19 June	Unwohl. 12 Seite. inst . . .
21 June	2 Seit instr:
23 June	10 Seit inst . . .
24 June	7 Seit inst.
25 June	0 Seit instr
27 June	3 Seit inst.
28 June	11 Seit instr:
29 June	6 Seit instr:
30 June	4 Seit instr.
1 July	14 Seiten instr:
2 July	4 Seiten
6 July	gearbeitet . . . Duett a moll ganz entworfen.
7 July	früh kam Roth. Lina zu Spizzen geschenkt. *Nachtische 2: Akt aufge-führt*
14 July	gearbeitet . . . 7 Seiten 2: Akt instr.
16 July	gearbeitet. 8 Seiten inst. 2: Akt
17 July	gearbeitet. **2 Akt gänzlich beendigt**
18 July	2: Akt corrigiert
27 July	zu Roth. 3: Akt durchgegangen
8 Aug.	*Finale des 3: Aktes beendiget, und somit die ganze* **Oper entworfen excl. Ouv:** Soli Deo Gloria.
12 Aug.	gearbeitet . . . 4 Seite. instrum.
14 Aug.	6 Seiten instr:
16 Aug.	gearbeitet . . . 2 Seiten instr.
17 Aug.	6 Seit: instr. corrigiert.
18 Aug.	2 Seit: instr:
19 Aug.	5 Seit: instr . . . an Kupelwieser geschrieben und Buch der Euryanthe nebst alten censierten geschikt.
20 Aug.	8 Seit: instr.

21 Aug.	6 Seit. instr: Roth kam später.
22 Aug.	11 Seit: Vormittags inst . . .
23 Aug.	6 Seit inst:
25 Aug.	noch 2 Seit: instr:
26 Aug.	1 Seit: instr:
27 Aug.	9 Seit: instr:
28 Aug.	10 Seit. instr:
29 Aug.	*8 Seit: inst*: und somit Abends 6 Uhr ***die Oper Euryanthe beendiget.*** exclusive der Ouverture. Gott gebe seinen Seegen, denn alles kommt ja doch nur von ihm!!!!
1 Sept.	gearbeitet. Ouverture. Klavier Auszug . . .
5 Sept.	. . . gearbeitet. Klavierauszug.
6 Sept.	. . . gearbeitet. Klavierauszug.
8 Sept.	. . . Klavierauszug 1: Akt vollendet.
9 Sept.	an Steiner geschrieben und ihm Klavierauszug des 1: Aktes der Euryanthe geschickt . . .
1 Oct.	[Vienna] gearbeitet Klavier Ausz: . . .
4 Oct.	Kl. gearbeitet. *12 Uhr erste Probe der Euryanthe. Wo ich sie vorlas. bis nach 3 Uhr ohne daß es Jemand bemerkte* . . .
6 Oct.	. . . gearbeitet. *um 10 Uhr bis 2 Uhr 2: Probe der Euryanthe* . . . Abends zu Hause, gearbeitet. Ouverture . . .
7 Oct.	gearbeitet. 2: Akt des Kl. Aus: vollendet. *10–2. 3: Probe der Euryanthe* . . . mit der Sonntag gesungen 4–6 . . .
13 Oct.	. . . gearbeitet . . . *10–2 7: Pr. mit Chor Euryanthe.* großer Enthusiasmus nach dem Trozze nicht. Abends gearbeitet. Ouverture.
15 Oct.	. . . gearbeitet. *Ouverture beendigt im Entwurf* . . .
16 Oct.	um 9 Uhr mit Mosel die Ouverture durchgegangen. 10–2. 10: Probe. Quartett 2. Mittag Ludlam . . . *4 Seiten Ouv: instrumentiert bis 11 Uhr* . . . *Klavier Auszug vollendet.*
17 Oct.	*früh 2 Seiten instr* . . .
18 Oct.	. . . nach Hause gearbeitet. Ouv:
19 Oct.	. . . gearbeitet. *Ouverture beendiget.* Soli deo Gloria . . .
23 Oct.	Klavier Ausz. der Ouverture beendigt und somit alles zu Euryanthe.
26 Oct.	. . . Einiges gekürzt in der Euryanthe . . .
20 Nov.	[Dresden] . . . *Traum Gesicht in der Euryanthe umgearbeitet* . . .

Appendix II

Weber's Draft for the Denouement (Web. Cl. II A g 7)

5. / :*Prachtvoller Hochzeit Zug. voran Spielleute
alles im alten Styl, dann Lysiart & Eglantine
in fürstlich reich—Brautschmuck; Todtblaß,
von ihren Frauen unterstüzt. Der Zug be-
wegt sich über die Terraßen und Zugbrücke
der Burg Nevres herab nach dem Proscenium, wo die Landleute sich an die Seite
zurückgezogen haben.*:/

Landleute. O Frevlerpaar, weh diesem schnöden
       Bunde!

Adolar. O klopfend Herz—sei stark zu
        dieser Stunde.
Eglantine./ :*mit Geberden des Schmerzes und der
Verwirrung gelangt bis auf das Proscenium
wo sie den Zug unterbricht, indem sie
mit Entsezzen das in Wahnsinn über-
geht, stehen bleibt.*:/
   Ich kann nicht weiter! Todesschauer
   Durchrieseln mein Gebein!
   Mich drückt die Luft—
   Sieh! Emma steigt aus dunkler Gruft
   Sie winket mir mit starrer Hand—
   Was forderst du zurük der Rache Pfand
   Ich gab es hin die Unschuld zu ermorden!
   Hinweg! hier bin ich Herrscherin geworden!
   Auf ewig, Lysiart, bin ich dein!
   Geschmiedet ist der Trauring, fest und eigen
   Mit Meineid, Blut und Thränen—kannst
        du schweigen?

/ :*Lysiart betrachtet sie, mit seinem Ingrimm kämpfend:*/   —— Sei ruhig! Nacht hüllt unsre Thaten ein!
Chor. Welch Entsezzen welch Gericht
    Die Vergeltung schlummert nicht.

Lysiart. Hört! daß Wahnsinn aus ihr
                                spricht!
Adolar. Ha! mir tagt ein schreklich Licht.
/ :*vortretend*:/ Erzittre ruchlos Paar gerechter Rache!
Der Himmel führt bedrückter Unschuld Sache!
Lysiart. Was zischest aus dem Staub du, nicht'ger
                                Wurm?
Vasallen, werft den Fremdling in den Thurm.
/ :*die Knechte drängen auf Adolar ein*:/
Adolar/ :*schlägt den Helmstürz auf*:/
Mich wollt ihr fahen! Mich in diesen
                                Hallen?
Chor. Er ists! Heil dir in deiner Väter Hallen,
Geliebter Herr, sieh uns zu Füßen fallen.
/ :*Alles drängt sich knieend und liebkosend*
um Adolar: Lysiart steht verlaßen.
Eglantine/ : *fährt entsetzt bei seinem Anblick*
       auf und stürzt dann von ihm sich ab-
       wendend in die Arme ihrer Frauen:
Er ists, in seiner Glorie, seiner Schöne!
                                Weh mir pp
Lysiart. Fluch und Verderben euch Verräthern
                                allen.
Verwegene Knechte, büßend sollt ihr fallen!
                 / :*tödtend werd ich fallen*:/
/ :*Alle springen auf und* [deleted: *stellen sich*] *groupiren*
sich dräuend ihm entgegen.
Trozze nicht, Vermeßner
Strafe naht, Verräther!
Fürcht des Himmels Gericht pp

                                              [f. IV]

NB *Adolar.* Zum Kampf, zum Gottgerichte
            Verruchter Frevler du!
Lysiart. Daß ich dich Feind vernichte,
            Jauchzt mir der Abgrund zu!
Adolar. Dein schwarzes Herz durchwühle
            Mein sieggewohnter Stahl
Lysiart. Dein strömend Herzblut kühle
            der Seele Folterqual!
Chor. Schande nur, und Verderben
            ist ewig dir geweiht.
Lysiart. Will nicht um Mittleid werben
            Heran ich bin bereit.

Scene.
/ :*Der König mit Gefolge tritt ernst*
zwischen sie:/
　　Laßt ruhn die Schwerdte, wo der Richter
　　　　　　　　　　　naht
　　Der Rächer jeder Missethat!
/ :*Alles beugt sich ehrerbietig, Lysiart senkt*
das Schwerdt zieht sich aber kampffertig
an ein Baum zurück. Adolar stürzt zu
des Königs Füßen:/
　　O Herr, rein wie des Himmels Licht war
　　Euryanthe, Strafe, Rette, ich ver-
　　zweifle, wo ist Sie, ich bin ihr
　　Mörder pp
König. Faß dich als Mann, das
　　　schwerste zu ertragen, Euryanthe
　　　erblich vor meinen Augen!
Eglantine/ :*in wahnsinniger Lust auf-*
fahrend:/ Triumpf! Gerochen
　　Ist mein Pein, der Feindin Herz gebrochen
　　Es stürmt der Tod durch deine Brust
　　Betrogner! war dir meine Gluth bewußt
　　Wie legtest sorglos und vermeßen
　　Die Schlange du and der Geliebten Herz,
　　So hattest du mein Flehn vergeßen,
　　Vergeßen meinen Todesschmerz!
Adolar. Abscheuliche! *Eglantine.* Grausamer
　　　　　　　　　　Adolar
Verzweifle daß sie schuldlos war
[*deleted*: Ein Bubenstück hat dich bethört]
Ich war's von deren Hand den Ring
Der Hochverräther dort empfing
Ich wars, die ihn der Gruft entwandte
Rein, wie das Licht, war Euryanthe!
Alle. O höllischer Verrath!
Lysiart. Wahnsinn'ge.
Eglantine. Schnödes Werkzeug meiner Rache
　　Du! den ich mit mir elend mache,
　　[*deleted*: Verstumme nun. Kehr]
　　　　　　　　　in dein Nichts zurük.
Dich schleudr' ich in
Lysiart.　　Was hält mich, dass ich dich zermalme
Meineidige [*deleted*: Verworfene]
　　　　　　　Verrätherin! : *Er erstickt sie:*
[*deleted*: *Eglantine.* In ewge Nacht verzweifelnd
　　　　　　　　　　sink ich hin!

Vergeßen deines Kaltsinns
Hohn
Vergeßen meines Zornes
Drohn!

Gerecht ist Gott, der Unschuld winkt die
Palme.]
/ :*Allgemeines Entsezzen:*/ ruchloser Mörder! pp
König. Greift ihn zum Tode!
Adolar. Nein, gebt ihn frey, er vollende
sein Werk, auch diese Brust durchbohre

[f. 2r]

der Mörder, doch was sag ich
ich selbst bin der verdammenswürdigste
Mörder. Unselige Verblendung du
tödtest die Treueste. pp
/ :*Er versinkt in Schmerz, der Chor
steht mitleidig zu ihm geneigt:*]
Pause der tiefsten Rührung:]
Auf einmahl Jubelruf hinter der
Szene, [*deleted: alles*]/ : wohl der Jäger die sie
fortbrachten.—
gespannte Erwartung und Ueberraschung
fliegt in
Aller. Euryanthe [*deleted: stürzt*] Adolars
Arme, mit dem Duett.
Hin nimm die Seele mein,
Dazwischen kurze Ausrufungen des
Chors, O Seligkeit, sie sind
vereint, pp
Am Ende des Duetts wann sie sich
fest umschlungen halten, schwebt
Emma mit Udo vorüber

Ein großartiger [*added: aber nicht langer*] Jubel Chor
beschließt das Ganze.
Schön wär es wenn wieder zu bringen
wäre, Vertrau auf Gott und deine
Euryanth pp

Appendix III

The Composition Draft for Euryanthe

29.   No. 11: 'H Dur. Duetto', mm. 4–59 (continuation referred to p. 55).
30.   No. 6, mm. 1–68; Act I, scene iii, Recit., mm. 70–90.
31.   Act I, scene iii, Recit., mm. 90–135 (incl. *Vision*); No. 7 'Duetto', mm. 1–6.
32.   No. 7, mm. 7–67 (mm. 33–67 are discarded).
33.   No. 7, mm. 33–70 (final version).
34.   Autograph of 'Marcia vivace für das Kögl: Preuß: Leibregiment. Schwarze Husaren', J. 288: '29. July 1822'; No. 7, mm. 81–9 (line 7).
35.   No. 7, mm. 71–80 (cont. from p. 33).
36.   Horn part for Heigel Trauermusik, J. 116.
37.   Blank.
38/39   Finale I, mm. 1–8, 49–170.
40.   Blank.
41.   Autograph of Cantata J. 283, No. 8, Finale. 'Zum Schluß des 1. Aktes der | Euryanthe benuzt 1823. | CMvWeber.'
42.   J. 283 (cont.).
43.   J. 283 (cont.).
44.   J. 283 (cont.).
45.   J. 283 (cont.).
46.   J. 283 (conclusion) 'Dresden d. 16. September 1821. CMvWeber.'
47.   J. 283: preliminary draft.
48.   J. 283: preliminary draft (cont.); unidentified single-line draft (J. Anh. I, No. 4).
49.   J. 283: preliminary draft (cont.); unidentified sketch (C major, 3/4); sketch for start of Mermaid's song in *Oberon*.
50.   Blank.
51.   '*Zweiter Act.*' No. 10, mm. 1–61.
52.   No. 10, mm. 62–171.
53.   No. 10, mm. 172–278; Recit., Act II, scene ii, mm. 279–98.
54.   Recit., II, ii, mm. 299–344; '*Duett*' No. 11, mm. 1–3; No. 15: sketch for main theme of Agitato (lines 5, 7–8)
55.   No. 11, mm. 60–114.
56.   No. 11, mm. 115–57; No. 12, mm. 1–33.
57.   No. 12, mm. 89–139; '4½M.'
58.   No. 1: mm. 101–16, 136–44 (preliminary draft, cont. from p. 59, bottom).
59.   No. 1, mm. 67–100 (preliminary draft).
60.   No. 12, mm. 34–88.
61.   Finale II, mm. 423–63 (cont. from p. 72).
62.   Finale II, mm. 464–88.
63.   Finale II: 'f moll', mm. 489–529 (NB: 2 extra measures at start).
64.   Finale II, mm. 530–56; lines 15–17: contrapuntal sketch for accompaniment of mm. 530–3.
65.   No. 12 (postlude), mm. 140–150; No. 13 'Duetto', mm. 1–86.
66.   Finale II, mm. 1–71; '3 M:'

67.   Finale II, mm. 72–165; '15 Minuten'.

68.   Finale II, mm. 166–271.

69.   Finale II, mm. 272–343.

70.   Finale II, mm. 344–51 (continuation referred to p. 2/95).

71.   Blank.

72.   Finale II, mm. 390–422 (continuation on p. 61).

73.   Act III, scene i (cont. from p. 76); No. 15, mm. 2–44.

74/75.   No. 15, mm. 45–95; '8 Mi:'; mm. 95–123; No. 16, mm. 1–95.

76.   'Dritter Act', III, i, mm. 1–96; No. 15, m. 1, discarded version of mm. 2–3.

77.   '2: Scena. *Euryanthe allein.*' No. 17, mm. 1–8; Allegro marcato, mm. 1–6.

78.   Allegro marcato, mm. 7–17; No. 18, mm. 1–28; Recit., mm. 29–39; No. 19, mm. 1–2 (cont. on p. 26).

79.   Draft for chorus for lost cantata 'Deorosa, Gottes Rose' (J. Anh I, 3); No. 23, mm. 1–46 (first draft).

80.   Lines 1–4: sketch for revision of Bassoon Concerto (J. 127), first movement; lines 5–6: sketch for revision of Bassoon Concerto, third movement; lines 7–16: No. 20, mm. 1–44.

81.   No. 20, mm. 45–104.

82.   No. 8, mm. 60–131 (preceding and following measures on p. 28).

83.   '4: *Scena*' No. 21, mm. 1–125.

84.   No. 21, mm. 126–30; No. 22, mm. 1–39; No. 23, mm. 1–32 (second draft).

85.   No. 23, mm. 33–101.

86.   No. 23, mm. 102–25; No. 24, mm. 1–3.

87.   Blank.

88.   No. 24, mm. 4–34.

89.   No. 24 , mm. 35–74.

90.   No. 24 , mm. 75–82; Finale III, mm. 1–47, 221–2, 295–303.

91.   Finale III, mm. 48–96.

92.   Finale III, mm. 97–165.

93.   Finale III, mm. 166–220 (continued on p. 90).

94.   Finale III, mm. 224–94 (continued on p. 90).

Index